CONTEMPORARY BUSINESS

Second Canadian Edition

BOONE • KURTZ • KHAN • CANZER

Casey G. Cegielski • Cristóbal Sánchez-Rodríguez
Ingrid Splettstoesser Hogeterp • R. Kelly Rainer

**Business Environment
BUSI 1015**

Nova Scotia Community College

— Wiley Custom Learning Solutions —

Copyright © 2016 by John Wiley & Sons, Inc.

All rights reserved.

Cover Images © Nova Scotia Community College

Printing identification and country of origin will either be included on this page and/or the end of the book. In addition, if the ISBN on this page and the back cover do not match, the ISBN on the back cover should be considered the correct ISBN.

This custom textbook may include materials submitted by the Author for publication by John Wiley & Sons, Inc. This material has not been edited by Wiley, and the Author is solely responsible for its content.

No part of this publication may be reproduced, stored in a retrieval system or transmitted in any form or by any means, electronic, mechanical, photocopying, recording, scanning or otherwise, except as permitted under Sections 107 or 108 of the 1976 United States Copyright Act, without either the prior written permission of the Publisher, or authorization through payment of the appropriate per-copy fee to the Copyright Clearance Center, Inc., 222 Rosewood Drive, Danvers, MA 01923, website www.copyright.com. Requests to the Publisher for permission should be addressed to the Permissions Department, John Wiley & Sons, Inc., 111 River Street, Hoboken, NJ 07030-5774, (201)748-6011, fax (201)748-6008, website http://www.wiley.com/go/permissions.

To order books or for customer service, please call 1(800)-CALL-WILEY (225-5945).

Printed in the United States of America.

ISBN 978-1-119-31421-9
Printed and bound by Sheridan Books.

10 9 8 7 6 5 4 3 2

List of Titles

Contemporary Business, 2nd edition
    by Louis E. Boone, David L. Kurtz, Michael H. Khan, and Brahm M. Canzer
    Copyright © 2016, ISBN: 978-1-119-19433-0

Introduction to Information Systems: Supporting and Transforming Business, Third Canadian Edition, Update
    by R. Kelly Rainer, Casey G. Cegielski, Ingrid Splettstoesser Hogeterp, and Cristóbal Sánchez-Rodríguez
    Copyright © 2016, ISBN: 978-1-119-13385-8

Table of Contents

Chapter 1. The Changing Face of Business — 6
Originally Chapter 1 of *Contemporary Business, 2nd edition*

Chapter 2. Business Ethics and Social Responsibility — 32
Originally Chapter 2 of *Contemporary Business, 2nd edition*

Chapter 3. Competing in World Markets — 62
Originally Chapter 4 of *Contemporary Business, 2nd edition*

Chapter 4. Forms of Business Ownership and Organization — 96
Originally Chapter 5 of *Contemporary Business, 2nd edition*

Chapter 5. Starting Your Own Business: The Entrepreneurship Alternative — 126
Originally Chapter 6 of *Contemporary Business, 2nd edition*

Chapter 6. E-Business and E-Commerce — 152
Originally Chapter 5 of *Introduction to Information Systems: Supporting and Transforming Business, Third Canadian Edition, Update*

Appendix E: Developing a Business Plan — 185
Originally from *Contemporary Business, 2nd edition*

Appendix G: Careers in Contemporary Business — 193
Originally from *Contemporary Business, 2nd edition*

Glossary — 211
Originally from *Contemporary Business, 2nd edition*

Notes — 221
Originally from *Contemporary Business, 2nd edition*

Name Index — 245
Originally from *Contemporary Business, 2nd edition*

Subject Index — 251
Originally from *Contemporary Business, 2nd edition*

1 | THE CHANGING FACE OF BUSINESS

LEARNING OBJECTIVES

LO 1.1 Distinguish between business and not-for-profit organizations.

LO 1.2 Identify and describe the factors of production.

LO 1.3 Describe the private enterprise system.

LO 1.4 Identify the seven eras in the history of business.

LO 1.5 Explain how today's business workforce and the nature of work itself are changing.

LO 1.6 Identify the skills and attributes needed to lead businesses in the twenty-first century.

LO 1.7 Outline the characteristics that make a company admired.

INSIDE BUSINESS
Canadian Entertainers Are Cultivating Global Audiences Online

Since its commercial debut in the mid-1990s, the Internet has evolved into an integral communications tool for the entertainment industry. Artists and audiences can easily experience two-way communication through software tools designed to create a sense of familiarity and relationship. Besides websites where samples of music can be tested out with audiences, artists can ask for feedback and create a dialogue through YouTube, Facebook, Twitter, and other social media. The Internet has democratized the industry by allowing any artist to develop a relationship with audiences online. Bypassing the traditional barriers to entry has meant many artists have been discovered who perhaps might have followed a different path to success if the Internet were not available to them.

Aubrey Drake Graham is better known to his fans by his stage name—Drake. The Toronto native was a child actor on the television series *Degrassi: The Next Generation,* but he always loved music. He released a mixtape that eventually found its way into rap-star Lil Wayne's hands, who became Drake's mentor. Drake signed with Lil Wayne's record label, Young Money Entertainment, in 2009, but it was his 2004 YouTube postings that provided him with a tool to develop his music career. By the age of 25 he had made over $25 million as a rapper—far more than the $40,000 annual salary he earned starring on *Degrassi*! Like many in his industry, Drake regularly uses social media to connect with fans and keep them up to date on his career.

Similarly, Justin Bieber, whose public image some might think of as "good boy turned bad boy turning good boy again," has made good use of the Internet as a means to interact with his fans. Love him or hate him, no one can deny that his rise to fame was meteoric. In 2007 he had a modest fan base who watched him on YouTube. Eventually these "Mom-produced" videos came to the attention of talent agent Scooter Braun, who became Bieber's agent and introduced him to the many industry insiders who would make his dream of a music career a reality.

It is an understatement to say that YouTube and social media led to Bieber's discovery and career development. Social media have made it easier for talented young artists such as Bieber and Drake to get recognized and have their chance at stardom. Agents like Scooter Braun use the Internet regularly to search for new talent. Online popularity and an online fan base can be early signs of likely success.

The Internet also plays a major role in linking the various players in the music industry. A close connection with fans is made easier by posting personal comments, articles, interviews, television shows, music videos, and other content. Such posts help to build "buzz," which is critical to drawing the attention of agents like Scooter Braun.

The Internet has become a showplace for musical entertainment and a disruptor of the old ways of doing business. As a result, the Internet has dramatically drawn advertising dollars away from traditional media such as radio, television, and magazines. These traditional media depend on large audiences to justify their high advertising costs. Social media sites succeed by providing content to much smaller niche markets. For example, when viewers want to see Drake or Justin Bieber perform, they can log on to their dedicated YouTube channels, which are also available on mobile devices. And, unlike television or radio, YouTube allows customers to not only listen to songs but also purchase the songs through sites such as Apple's iTunes store or subscribe to Apple Music.

Today, the Internet delivers samples of an artist's work to fans. It also delivers related content to help develop a relationship with fans and provides a direct channel for customers to purchase products. The Internet's promotional power speaks to the new world of music and entertainment today.[1]

CHAPTER 1 OVERVIEW

Business is the nation's engine for growth. A growing economy is an economy that produces more goods and services but uses fewer resources over time. Growing economies are important because they yield more income for business owners, their employees, and shareholders. A country depends on the wealth its businesses generate, from large enterprises like BlackBerry to startups like Justin Bieber, and from venerable firms like Bell Canada Enterprises to powerhouses like the Royal Bank of Canada. These companies and many others share a creative approach to meeting society's needs and wants while generating the wealth we enjoy.

Businesses solve our transportation problems by marketing cars, tires, gasoline, and airline tickets. They bring food to our tables by growing, harvesting, processing, packaging, and shipping everything from spring water to cake mix and frozen shrimp. Restaurants buy, prepare, and serve food, and some even deliver. Construction companies build our schools, homes, and hospitals, while real estate firms bring property buyers and sellers together. Clothing manufacturers design, create, import, and deliver our jeans, sports shoes, work uniforms, and party wear. Hundreds of firms work at entertaining us during our leisure hours. They create, produce, and distribute films, television shows, video games, books, and music downloads.

To succeed, business firms must know what their customers want, and they must supply it quickly and efficiently. The products that firms produce often reflect changes in consumer tastes, such as the growing preference for sports drinks and vitamin-fortified water. But firms can also *lead* by promoting technology and other changes. Firms have the resources, the know-how, and the financial incentive to bring about real innovations, such as smartphones, new cancer treatments, and alternative energy sources like wind power. Thus, when businesses succeed, everybody wins.

You'll see throughout this book that businesses require physical inputs such as auto parts, chemicals, sugar, thread, and electricity. They also need the accumulated knowledge and experience of their managers and employees. Businesses also rely heavily on their own ability to change with the times and with the marketplace. Flexibility is a key to long-term success—and to growth.

Business is a leading force in our economy—and *Contemporary Business* is right there with it. This book explores the strategies that allow companies to grow and compete in today's interactive marketplace. This book also explores the skills you will need to turn ideas into action for your own success in business. This chapter sets the stage for the entire text by defining what business is and describing its role in society. The chapter's discussion illustrates how the private enterprise system encourages competition and innovation while preserving business ethics.

LO 1.1 Distinguish between business and not-for-profit organizations.

WHAT IS BUSINESS?

What do you think of when you hear the word *business*? Do you think of big corporations like Rogers Communications or TD Bank? Or do you think about your local bakery or shoe store? Maybe you recall your first summer job. *Business* is a broad, all-inclusive term that can be applied to many kinds of enterprises. Businesses provide most of our employment opportunities and most of the products that we enjoy every day.

Business consists of all profit-seeking activities and enterprises that provide goods and services necessary to an economic system. Some businesses produce tangible goods, such as automobiles, breakfast cereals, and digital music players; others provide services, such as insurance, hair styling, and entertainment, ranging from theme parks and sports events to concerts.

Business drives the economic pulse of a nation. It provides the means for improving a nation's standard of living. At the heart of every business is an exchange between a buyer and a seller. A buyer has a need for a good or service and trades money with a seller to receive that product or service. The seller hopes to gain a profit—a main indicator of business success and what continuously improves society's standard of living.

Profits are rewards for businesspeople who take the risks involved in blending people, technology, and information to create and market want-satisfying goods and services. In contrast,

---

business all profit-seeking activities and enterprises that provide goods and services necessary to an economic system.

profits rewards for businesspeople who take the risks involved in offering goods and services to customers.

accountants only think of profits as the difference between a firm's revenues and the expenses it incurs in generating these revenues. More generally, however, profits serve as incentives for people to start companies, expand them, and provide consistently high-quality competitive goods and services. Profits are also a primary source of funds needed to expand operations.

The quest for profits is a central focus of business: without profits, a company could not survive or grow. But businesspeople also recognize their social and ethical responsibilities. To succeed in the long run, companies must deal responsibly with employees, customers, suppliers, competitors, government, and the general public.

Not-for-Profit Organizations

A business survives because of the exchange between buyer and seller. In this hair salon, the exchange occurs between the customer and the stylist.

What is a common feature of Simon Fraser University's athletic department, the Canadian Society for the Prevention of Cruelty to Animals, the Canadian Red Cross, and your local library? They are all **not-for-profit organizations**, business-like establishments that have primary goals other than returning profits to their owners. These organizations play important roles in society by placing public service above profits. It is important to understand that these organizations need to raise money to operate and to achieve their social goals. Not-for-profit organizations operate in both the private and public sectors. Private sector not-for-profits include museums, libraries, trade associations, and charitable and religious organizations. Government agencies, political parties, and labour unions are not-for-profit organizations that are part of the public sector.

not-for-profit organizations organizations whose primary aims are public service, not returning a profit to their owners.

Not-for-profit organizations form a large part of the Canadian economy. The not-for-profit field is an industry just like any other industry: Revenues are raised and employees earn incomes by providing services. Canada has more than 160,000 registered not-for-profit organizations in categories ranging from arts and culture to science and technology. Most are local organizations that provide sports and recreational activities. Not-for-profits receive funding from both government sources and private sources, including donations. These organizations are commonly exempt from federal, provincial, and local taxes. Not-for-profits raise more than $112 billion in revenues each year and employ more than 2 million people. Approximately one-third of these jobs are in hospitals, universities, and colleges. About half of all revenue comes from government grants, mostly provincial. These organizations also receive more than $8 billion in donations from individuals and require more than 2 billion volunteer hours, the equivalent of more than 1 million full-time jobs.[2]

Managers of not-for-profit organizations focus on goals other than making profits, but they face many of the same challenges as executives of for-profit businesses. Without funding, organizations cannot do research, obtain raw materials, or provide services. Toronto's Hospital for Sick Children (SickKids) is one of the world's top healthcare institutions for children. It is Canada's leading centre dedicated to children's health and succeeds by uniting patient care, research, and education. SickKids was founded in 1875 and is affiliated with the University of Toronto. It is one of Canada's most research-intensive hospitals: Its more than 600 staff researchers operate within a $140 million budget.[3]

Other not-for-profits organize their resources to respond to emergencies. For example, the Red Cross and Doctors Without Borders (also known as Médecins Sans Frontières, or MSF) acted quickly when the earthquake in Nepal in 2015 left hundreds of thousands of people homeless. Relief agencies around the world worked hard to supply enough tents and tarpaulins for immediate shelter. These agencies then turned their attention to constructing more permanent living spaces.[4]

Some not-for-profits sell merchandise or set up profit-making side businesses to sell goods and services that people are willing and able to pay for. For example, college bookstores sell products with the school logo—everything from sweatshirts to coffee mugs. SickKids supports learning for families and healthcare providers by selling parenting books, many of which are Canadian

The Red Cross organizes its efforts to respond to natural disasters around the world, such as setting up medical clinics in the aftermath of the earthquake in Nepal.

ASSESSMENT CHECK

1.1.1 What activity lies at the heart of every business endeavour?

1.1.2 What are the primary objectives of a not-for-profit organization?

bestsellers.[5] The Livestrong Foundation, formerly the Lance Armstrong Foundation, has sold more than 40 million yellow Livestrong wristbands. It also sells sports gear and accessories for men, women, and children. All funds raised through these sales are used to fight cancer and support patients and their families.[6]

Merchandising programs and fundraising campaigns need managers who have effective business skills and experience. As a result, many of the concepts discussed in this book apply both to not-for-profit organizations and to for-profit firms.

LO 1.2 Identify and describe the factors of production.

factors of production four basic inputs for effective economic operation: natural resources, capital, human resources, and entrepreneurship.

natural resources all production inputs that are useful in their natural states, including agricultural land, building sites, forests, and mineral deposits.

FACTORS OF PRODUCTION

An economic system requires certain inputs for successful operation. Economists use the term **factors of production** to refer to the four basic inputs: natural resources, capital, human resources, and entrepreneurship. Table 1.1 identifies each of these inputs and gives examples of the types of payment received by firms and individuals who supply them.

Natural resources include all production inputs that are useful in their natural states. Examples are agricultural land, building sites, forests, water, and mineral deposits. Calgary-based Encana Corporation is a leading Canadian developer of natural gas supply in North America. Toronto-based Barrick Gold Corporation is the global gold industry leader. Its 25 operating mines

Table 1.1 Factors of Production and Their Factor Payments

FACTOR OF PRODUCTION	CORRESPONDING FACTOR PAYMENT
Natural resources	Rent for land leased for operations
Capital	Interest for money used to acquire capital items
Human resources	Wages for employees
Entrepreneurship	Profit for starting and managing operations

and projects are located on five continents and include African Barrick Gold. Mining companies generally pay landowners for the right to extract minerals. Farmers expand their operations by paying rent for the right to grow more crops on a neighbour's land. Natural resources are the basic inputs required in any economic system and are the genesis of wealth creation. Places in the world with valuable natural resources have an economic advantage in developing more wealth, whereas those without natural resources will have to acquire them.

Capital, another key resource, includes technology, tools, information, and physical facilities. *Technology* refers to such machinery and equipment as computers and software, telecommunications, and inventions designed to improve production. Information, which is frequently improved by technological innovations, is another critical factor. Both managers and employees require accurate, timely information to effectively perform their assigned tasks. Technology plays an important role in the success of many businesses. Technology can lead to a new product, such as hybrid cars that run on a combination of gasoline and electricity. In recent years, most major car companies have introduced hybrid versions of their bestselling models.

Technology often helps a company improve its own products. Netflix, once famous for its subscription-based DVD-by-mail service, now offers on-demand Internet streaming media and original content streaming over their TV service. Netflix has exclusive rights to streaming movies and original TV shows like *Orange Is the New Black* and pays for the rights to distribute content produced by others to its subscribers. Like YouTube, Netflix is a company disrupting the old business method of distributing digital entertainment.[7]

Technology can also help a company operate more smoothly by tracking deliveries, providing more efficient communication, analyzing data, or training employees. Canada Post cut costs by expanding the electronic side of its business. Customers can now track their own registered mail online.

To remain competitive, a firm needs to continually acquire, maintain, and upgrade its capital. All these activities need money. A company's funds may come from the owner's investments, profits that are turned back into the business, or loans from others. Money is used to build factories; purchase raw materials and component parts; and to hire, train, and pay employees. People and firms that supply (lend) capital receive factor payments in the form of interest.

Human resources represent another important input in every economic system. Human resources include anyone who works, from the chief executive officer (CEO) of a huge corporation to a self-employed editor. Their input includes both physical labour and intellectual effort. Companies rely on their employees' ideas, innovation, and physical effort. Some companies ask for employee ideas through traditional means, such as through staff meetings and by setting up an online "suggestion box." Others encourage creative thinking during company-sponsored events, such as hiking or rafting trips, or during social gatherings. Effective, well-trained human resources can provide firms with a significant competitive edge. Competitors cannot easily match another company's talented, motivated employees in the same way they can buy the same computer system or purchase the same grade of natural resources.

Hiring and keeping the right people matters. Competent, effective human resources can be a company's best asset. Providing perks to those employees to keep them is often in a company's best interest.

Entrepreneurship is the willingness to take risks to create and operate a business. An entrepreneur is someone who sees an opportunity to make a profit and creates a plan to earn those profits and achieve success. Montreal-based Beyond the Rack is a private online shopping club for women and men. Authentic designer merchandise is offered at deeply discounted sale prices to members through limited-time events. Each event starts at a specific time and typically lasts only 48 hours. After each event ends, the merchandise is no longer available. Members are notified by email in advance of each event that matches their preferences. Beyond the Rack's customer base has grown to more than 2.5 million members, and it is recognized as an industry leader in the emerging field of online marketing.[8]

Canadian businesses operate within an economic system called the *private enterprise system*. The next section looks at the private enterprise system, including competition, private property, and the entrepreneurship alternative.

capital production inputs consisting of technology, tools, information, and physical facilities.

human resources production inputs consisting of anyone who works, including both the physical labour and the intellectual inputs contributed by workers.

entrepreneurship the willingness to take risks to create and operate a business.

✓ ASSESSMENT CHECK

1.2.1 Identify the four basic inputs to an economic system.

1.2.2 List four types of capital.

LO 1.3 Describe the private enterprise system.

THE PRIVATE ENTERPRISE SYSTEM

No business operates completely freely and on its own. All businesses operate within a larger economic system of rules and constraints that directs how goods and services are produced, distributed, and consumed. The type of economic system used in a society also affects the patterns of resource use. Some economic systems enforce strict controls on business ownership, profits, and resources whereas others, like Canada's, offer more freedoms to individuals.

In Canada, businesses function within the **private enterprise system**, an economic system that rewards firms for their ability to identify and serve the needs and demands of customers. The private enterprise system minimizes government interference in business activity. Businesses that are skillful at satisfying customers are able to gain access to the necessary factors of production and earn profits. Success primarily depends on the businesspeople involved.

Another name for the private enterprise system is **capitalism**. Adam Smith, often called the father of capitalism, first described the concept of capitalism in his book *The Wealth of Nations*, published in 1776. Smith believed that an economy is best regulated by the "invisible hand" of **competition**, which is the battle among businesses for consumer acceptance. Smith thought that competition among firms would lead to consumers receiving the best possible products and prices because less efficient producers would gradually be driven from the marketplace.

The idea of the "invisible hand" is a basic principle of the private enterprise system. In Canada, competition shapes much of economic life. To compete successfully, each firm must find a basis for its **competitive differentiation**, the unique combination of organizational abilities, products, and approaches that sets one company apart from its competitors in the minds of customers. Businesses in a private enterprise system must keep up with changing marketplace conditions. Firms that fail to adjust to shifts in consumer preferences and firms that ignore their competitors risk failure. Live Nation Entertainment connects millions of concert-goers with their favourite artists at venues worldwide; see the "Hit & Miss" feature for keys to the company's success.

Our discussion in this book focuses on the tools and methods that twenty-first-century businesses apply to compete and differentiate their goods and services. We also discuss many of the ways that market changes will affect business and the private enterprise system in the future.

private enterprise system an economic system that rewards firms for their ability to identify and serve the needs and demands of customers.

capitalism an economic system that rewards firms for their ability to perceive and serve the needs and demands of consumers; also called the private enterprise system.

competition the battle among businesses for consumer acceptance.

competitive differentiation the unique combination of organizational abilities, products, and approaches that sets one company apart from its competitors in the minds of customers.

Basic Rights in the Private Enterprise System

For capitalism to operate effectively, the citizens of a private enterprise economy must have certain rights. As shown in **Figure 1.1**, these include the rights to private property, profits, freedom of choice, and competition.

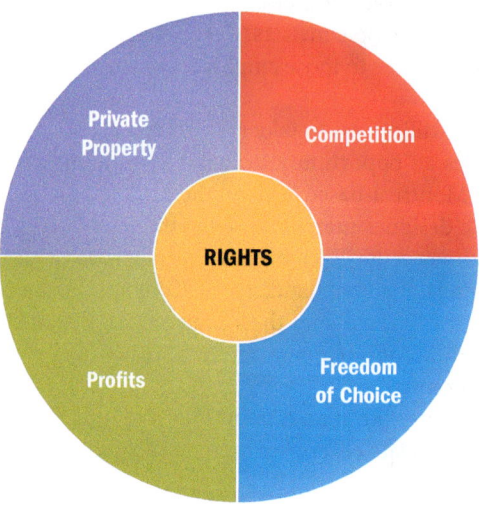

FIGURE 1.1 Basic Rights within a Private Enterprise System

HIT & MISS

Live Nation Connects Superstar Artists and Fans

Chances are, the last concert you attended may have been produced by Live Nation Entertainment of Beverly Hills, California. Michael Rapino, a Canadian-born music mogul, has guided the firm since he became CEO and president in 2005 and is credited with its rapid growth and diversification of services. The largest producer of live music concerts worldwide, Live Nation sells millions of tickets each year for events that range from folk to electronic dance music and that feature entertainers from new artists to music legends. A few years ago, Live Nation merged with ticket-selling giant Ticketmaster Entertainment to create Live Nation Entertainment.

Over 250 million fans access various entertainment platforms each year, attending more than 180,000 events in 47 countries. While more than 65 percent of the company's revenues come from its concert segment, other distinct business units include venue operations, ticketing services, and artist management and services. In an interview, Michael Rapino talked about the 2015 deal Live Nation made with Vice to "launch a full 24-hour, live, choice music channel with original programming and ongoing concerts. We think it's going to find a sweet spot with consumers who are looking for some high-quality, editorial original program and access to that magical live moment."

If you've ever thought about a career as a concert promoter, consider the "accidental trajectory" of then–college student Jodi Goodman. After urging a failing jazz club owner in Boston to allow her to book a few rock music events, Goodman not only turned the club around, but word soon got out about her knack for managing both artists and fans. It was not long before other venues sought her talent, and her career took her to San Francisco. Jodi Goodman is now president of Live Nation Entertainment for Northern California. With skill and market expertise, Goodman continues to bring artists and fans together in one of the top music markets in the country.

Concert revenues continue to rise and the future looks bright. Some of this success can be attributed to the Boston college kid who read the local music market by bringing some good old rock 'n' roll to a jazz club on the brink of closure, and creative thinkers like Michael Rapino.

Questions for Critical Thinking

1. Ticketmaster, now part of Live Nation Entertainment, responded to the threat of the secondary ticket resale market (by firms like Craigslist and StubHub) by launching its own ticket marketplace. How will Ticketmaster's marketplace impact secondary market competitors?

2. Live Nation anticipates double-digit growth in the number of concert-goers worldwide over the next several years. What factors could contribute to such a healthy increase in attendance?

Sources: Katie Richards, "Live Nation CEO Michael Rapino Discusses Why Rock Stars Are the Greatest Marketers in the World," *Adweek*, March 18, 2015, accessed March 20, 2015, www.adweek.com/news/advertising-branding/live-nation-ceo-michael-rapino-discusses-why-rock-stars-are-best-marketers-world-163430; Tim Adams, "Shane Smith: 'I Want to Build the Next CNN with Vice—It's within My Grasp," *The Guardian*, March 24, 2013, accessed Marc 20, 2015, www.theguardian.com/media/2013/mar/23/shane-smith-vice-interview;; Live Nation, 2013 *Annual Report*, accessed January 9, 2014, http://livenation.com; "Live Nation's New Groove: Electronic Dance Music and Scalped Tickets," *Bloomberg Businessweek*, August 9, 2013, accessed January 9, 2014, www.bloomberg.com/bw/articles/2013-08-09/live-nation-jumps-on-electronic-dance-music-scalped-tickets; Glenn Peoples, "Live Nation Revenue Hits a Record $2.26 Billion in Third Quarter," *Billboard Biz*, November 5, 2013, accessed January 9, 2014, www.billboard.com/biz/articles/news/touring/5778225/live-nation-revenue-hits-a-record-226-billion-in-third-quarter; Christine Ryan, "Hot 20: The Music Woman, Jodi Goodman," *7x7 Magazine*, October 14, 2013, accessed January 9, 2014, www.7x7.com/music-nightlife/hot-20-music-woman-jodi-goodman; Ina Fried, "Live Nation Aims to Unify Ticketmaster, Ticket Resale Businesses," *All Things Digital*, February 12, 2013, accessed January 9, 2014, http://allthingsd.com/20130212/live-nation-aims-to-unify-ticketmaster-ticket-resale-businesses.

The right to **private property** is the most basic freedom in the private enterprise system. Every participant has the right to own, use, buy, sell, and hand down most forms of property, including land, buildings, machinery, equipment, patents on inventions, individual possessions, and intangible properties.

The private enterprise system also guarantees business owners the right to all after-tax profits they earn through their activities. Although a business is not assured of earning a profit, its owner is legally and ethically entitled to any income it makes that is greater than its costs.

Freedom of choice means that a private enterprise system relies on citizens to choose their own employment, purchases, and investments. They can change jobs, discuss and agree on wages, join labour unions, and choose among many different brands of goods and services. People living in the capitalist nations of North America, Europe, and other parts of the world are so conditioned to having this freedom of choice that they sometimes forget how important it is. A private enterprise economy maximizes individual wealth by providing options. Other economic systems

private property the most basic freedom under the private enterprise system; the right to own, use, buy, sell, and hand down land, buildings, machinery, equipment, patents, individual possessions, and various intangible kinds of property.

sometimes limit the freedom of choice to accomplish government goals, such as by increasing industrial production of certain items or by military strength.

The private enterprise system also allows fair competition by allowing the public to set the rules for competitive activity. For this reason, the Canadian government has passed laws to prohibit excessively aggressive competitive practices designed to remove the competition. The Canadian government has established ground rules that make the following illegal: price discrimination, fraud in financial markets, and deceptive advertising and packaging. For example, in recent years, the Canadian Radio-television and Telecommunications Commission (CRTC) issued a decision that increased the costs charged to small Internet service providers (ISPs) that buy access to the larger ISP networks of Bell and Bell Aliant, mainly in Ontario and Quebec. The CRTC allowed the larger ISPs to control network traffic, especially high-volume traffic, to the smaller ISPs. The CRTC also began charging "usage-based billing." The smaller ISPs, who sold popular unlimited packages before, were forced to introduce limits, charge more for bandwidth, and change their infrastructure strategy. These changes ended their competitive advantage over the bigger ISPs, which typically charge more for high-volume users. After much complaining from the smaller ISP customers, a compromise pricing model was introduced. The new pricing model limits usage but still allows the smaller ISPs to offer unlimited usage packages to those customers that demanded them.[9]

The Entrepreneurship Alternative

entrepreneur a person who seeks a profitable opportunity and takes the necessary risks to set up and operate a business.

The entrepreneurial spirit beats at the heart of private enterprise. An **entrepreneur** is a risk taker in the private enterprise system. You hear about entrepreneurs all the time—two college students starting a software business in their dorm room, or a mom who invents a better baby carrier. Many times their success is modest, but once in a while the risk pays off in huge profits, as it did for Justin Bieber. People who can see marketplace opportunities are able to use their capital, time, and talents to pursue those opportunities for profit. The willingness of people to start new ventures leads to economic growth and keeps pressure on existing companies to continue to satisfy customers. If no one were willing to take economic risks, the private enterprise system wouldn't exist.

The entrepreneurial spirit leads to growth in the Canadian economy. Of all new businesses created in Canada, 99 percent are small businesses. Thousands of new businesses start each year. The Canadian economy depends on small businesses for their growth and strength. Statistics Canada data suggest that 5 percent of all businesses employ fewer than five employees, and 95 percent employ fewer than 50. The small-business sector creates 80 percent of all new jobs and generates 45 percent of Canada's economic output. Thus, Canada's small businesses are the majority of all Canadian businesses.[10]

So where are the jobs in Canada? **Figure 1.2** shows that the most employment is in the retail trade, followed by accommodation and food services. Notice that small businesses are major employers in these and other segments.[11]

Entrepreneurship creates jobs and sells products. Entrepreneurship also leads to innovation. In contrast to more established firms, startup companies tend to innovate in fields of technology that are new and have few competitors. Because small companies are more flexible than large companies, they can change their products and processes more quickly than larger corporations. Entrepreneurs often find new ways to use natural resources, technology, and other factors of production. Often they find these new ways because they have to—they may not have enough money to build an expensive prototype or launch a nationwide ad campaign. Sometimes, an entrepreneur may innovate by simply tweaking an existing idea or technology. For example, Quebec-based ExoPC introduced the Ciara Vibe tablet to the North American market after selling earlier versions in Europe and Asia. Software engineer Jean-Baptiste Martinoli adapted Microsoft's Windows 7 operating system to make it able to function with a touch screen and perform like a PC or tablet. By making the screen larger and adding some additional features, he created another competitor for Apple's iPad. By collaborating with Microsoft, this small business created a niche for itself in a global marketplace.[12]

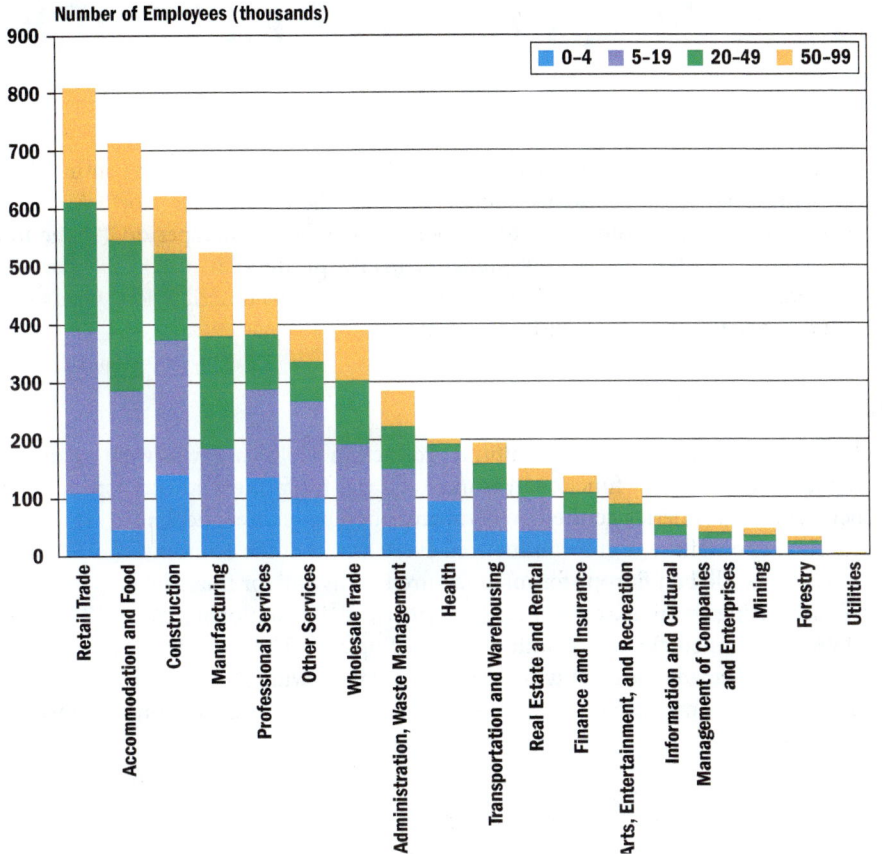

FIGURE 1.2 Number of Private Sector Employees by Industry and Size of Business Enterprise, 2011

Source: From Industry Canada, "Key Small Business Statistics, July 2012," Figure 7, p. 20. Statistics Canada, *Survey of Employment, Payrolls and Hours* (SEPH), April 2012, and calculations by Industry Canada. Industry data are classified in accordance with the North American Industry Classification System (NAICS). Reprinted with the permission of the Minister of Industry, 2015.

✓ **ASSESSMENT CHECK**

1.3.1 What is an alternative term for the private enterprise system?

1.3.2 What is the most basic freedom under the private enterprise system?

1.3.3 What is an entrepreneur?

Entrepreneurship is also important to existing companies. More and more, large firms are realizing the value of entrepreneurial thinking among their employees. These companies hope to benefit from enhanced flexibility, improved innovation, and new market opportunities. Apple also reaches out to its customers by inviting entrepreneurs of all kinds to develop applications for the iPhone. If the new apps are successful, then Apple profits from those efforts. Already, the iPhone has more than a million different applications, including some developed by Apple. Together, all the apps have been downloaded billions of times.[13] Introduction of the Apple Watch and other wearable technologies is expected to generate a new wave of opportunities for app developers.

As the next section explains, entrepreneurs have played a vital role in the history of Canadian business. They have helped create new industries, developed successful new business methods, and improved Canadian standing in global competition.

Apple invites entrepreneurs of all kinds to develop applications for the iPhone. If the new apps are successful, then Apple profits from those efforts.

© NetPhotos/Alamy

LO 1.4 Identify the seven eras in the history of business.

SEVEN ERAS IN THE HISTORY OF BUSINESS

In the 400 or so years since the first Europeans settled on the North American continent, amazing changes have occurred in the size, focus, and goals of Canadian businesses. North American business history is divided into seven distinct time periods: (1) the colonial period, (2) the Industrial Revolution, (3) the age of industrial entrepreneurs, (4) the production era, (5) the marketing era, (6) the relationship era, and (7) the social era. The next sections describe how events in each of these time periods have influenced business practices.

The Colonial Period

Colonial society featured rural and agricultural production. Colonial towns were small compared with European cities, and they functioned as marketplaces for farmers and craftspeople. The economic focus of North America centred on rural areas because success depended on the output of farms. The success or failure of crops influenced every aspect of the economy.

Colonists depended on Europe for manufactured items and for financial help for their infant industries. Surprising to some, even after the American Revolutionary War (1775–1783), the United States maintained close economic ties with England. The Canadian experience is more understandable. In Canada, British investors continued to provide much of the money needed for developing the North American business system. This financial influence continued well into the nineteenth century.

The Industrial Revolution

The Industrial Revolution began in England around 1750. It changed how businesses operated. Instead of a focus on independent, skilled workers who specialized in building products one by one, businesses moved to a factory system that mass produced items by using numerous semi-skilled workers. The factories made profit from the savings created by large-scale production and by increasing their use of machines. As businesses grew, they could often purchase raw materials more cheaply in larger lots. Production was also improved by specialization of labour, such as by limiting each worker to a few specific tasks in the production process.

Because of these events in England, Canadian businesses also began a time of rapid industrialization. Agriculture became mechanized, and factories set up in cities. During the mid-1800s, the pace of the revolution increased as newly built railroad systems provided fast, economical transportation. The railroads opened up the West and transported people and the agricultural products they grew, the timber they felled, and the furs they trapped to markets back east and on to Europe.

The Age of Industrial Entrepreneurs

The Industrial Revolution created opportunities, and those opportunities increased entrepreneurship in Canada.

Inventors created new production methods and a virtually endless number of commercially useful products. Many of these products are famous today:

- Alexander Graham Bell, his father, Melville, and friend Reverend Thomas Henderson started basic short-distance telephone service between office buildings and warehouses in 1877. The company later became Bell Canada Inc.
- In the United States, Eli Whitney introduced the idea of interchangeable parts, which later led the way to mass production on a previously impossible scale.

The entrepreneurial spirit of this golden age in business advanced the Canadian business system and increased the overall standard of living for Canadians. That market transformation, in turn, created new demand for manufactured goods.

The Production Era

Demand for manufactured goods continued to increase in the 1920s. Businesses focused even more attention on the activities needed to produce those goods. Work became more specialized, and huge, labour-intensive factories were common in North America. Henry Ford started using assembly lines, which later became commonplace in major industries. Business owners turned over their responsibilities to a new group of managers who had been trained in operating companies. These new managers were able to produce even more goods by using quicker methods.

During the production era, business focused their attention on internal processes instead of external influences. Marketing was rare and was used only to distribute a business's products. Little attention was paid to what the consumer wanted or needed. Instead, businesses decided what products were available to purchase. If you wanted to buy a Ford Model T automobile, your colour choice was black—the only colour the company made.

The Marketing Era

The Great Depression of the early 1930s changed Canadian businesses yet again. When most people's incomes dropped, businesses could no longer count on selling everything they produced. Managers began to pay more attention to the markets for their goods and services, and sales and advertising became important activities. During this period, selling often meant the same as marketing.

After World War II, demand increased for all kinds of consumer goods. After nearly five years without new automobiles, appliances, and other items, consumers were buying again. At the same time, competition was also increasing. Businesses soon began to think of marketing as more than just selling; managers thought about a process of deciding what consumers wanted and needed first, and then designing products to meet those needs. In short, they developed a **consumer orientation**.

Alexander Graham Bell opening a long distance phone line from New York to Chicago in 1892. In 1877, Alexander Graham Bell assigned 75 percent of the Canadian telephone patents rights to his father, Melville Bell. He and his friend Reverend Thomas Henderson then began leasing out pairs of wooden hand telephones for use on private lines. These lines were constructed by their clients between close locations, such as between a store and warehouse.

Businesses began to analyze consumer desires before beginning any production. Consumer choices skyrocketed. Automobiles were sold in a wide variety of colours and styles, and car buyers could choose their favourite colour. Companies also learned how important it was for their goods and services to stand out from those of competitors. **Branding** is the process of creating in consumer's minds an identity for a good, service, or company. Branding is an important marketing tool in contemporary business. A **brand** can be a name, term, sign, symbol, design, or some combination that identifies the products of one firm and shows how they differ from competitors' offerings.

The Home Depot, the world's largest home improvement specialty retailer, operates more than 2,200 retail stores in the United States, Canada, Mexico, and China. It also exports products around the world. Its carefully guarded brand name stands for excellent customer service, an entrepreneurial spirit, and the desire to give back to the communities where it operates. The company sells thousands of products, including RIDGID tools, Behr paint, LG appliances, and Toro lawn equipment, as well as many of its own sub-brands.[14]

consumer orientation a business philosophy that focuses first on consumers' unmet wants and needs, and then designs products to meet those needs.

branding the process of creating in consumers' minds an identity for a good, service, or company; a major marketing tool in contemporary business.

brand a name, term, sign, symbol, design, or some combination that identifies the products of one firm and shows how they differ from competitors' offerings.

The marketing era has had a huge impact on the way business is conducted today. Even the smallest business owners recognize the importance of understanding what customers want and the reasons they buy.

The Relationship Era

In the twenty-first century, a major change is taking place in the ways companies relate with their customers. Since the Industrial Revolution, most businesses have concentrated on building and promoting products in the hope that enough customers will buy the products to cover costs and earn acceptable profits. This approach is called **transaction management**.

In contrast, in the **relationship era** businesses are taking a different, longer-term approach to how they relate with customers. Firms now look for ways to actively promote customer loyalty by carefully managing every interaction. These firms earn huge paybacks for their efforts. A company that keeps its customers over the long term reduces its advertising and sales costs. Because customer spending tends to increase over time, the firm's revenues also grow. Companies with long-term customers often find they no longer need to offer price discounts to attract new business. Instead, they find that many new customers are referred by their loyal customers.

Business owners gain several advantages when they develop ongoing relationships with customers. Serving existing customers is less costly than trying to attract new customers. Thus, businesses that develop long-term customer relationships can reduce their overall costs. Long-term relationships with customers mean that businesses can improve their understanding of what customers want and prefer from the company. As a result, these businesses increase their chances of holding on to real advantages through competitive differentiation.

The relationship era is an age of connections—between businesses and customers, employers and employees, technology and manufacturing, and even between separate companies. More and more, the world economy is interconnected as businesses expand beyond their national boundaries. In this new environment, techniques for managing networks of people, businesses, information, and technology are critically important to contemporary business success. As you begin your

transaction management building and promoting products in the hope that enough customers will buy them to cover costs and earn profits.

relationship era the business era where firms seek to actively promote customer loyalty by carefully managing every interaction.

CAREER KICKSTART

Social Networking

Most young people hear a lot of career advice. One reliably good tip is to build a network of personal contacts in your chosen field. Online social networks make this task especially easy—but the Internet's informality can make it tricky to network in a professional way. Here are suggestions for presenting yourself in a positive light on sites like Facebook, LinkedIn, Twitter, and others.

1. Know the purpose of the networking site you choose. Most people consider Facebook more social, while LinkedIn purposely maintains a more professional look and feel.

2. Remember that potential employers, mentors, and other professionals will check your Facebook page to learn about you, despite the site's mostly fun-oriented profile. Look objectively at what they'll see there.

3. Review and edit your posted photos to make sure they present the image of yourself you want others to see.

4. Resist the impulse to share. Keep your posts brief and neither overly detailed nor overly personal. People you hope to tap for potential job leads don't need to know what you ate for breakfast. Limit the information about your family, too.

5. To network with someone you haven't met, first find someone you have in common and ask that person to make an online introduction.

6. Contribute to the community. "Help the people around you and you help yourself," advises one author. Posting interesting information about your area of professional expertise is one way to both help the community and build relationships.

7. Avoid posting any information or opinions about your current or past employers.

8. Always remember that everything you post is as public as the newspaper's front page. Edit yourself, and check your privacy settings.

Sources: Lauren Simonds, "Business, Etiquette and Social Media," *Time*, August 13, 2013, accessed January 9, 2014, http://business.time.com/2013/08/13/business-etiquette-and-social-media; C. G. Lynch, "Facebook Etiquette: Five Dos and Don'ts," *PC World*, November 22, 2008, accessed January 9, 2014, www.pcworld.com/article/154374/facebook_etiquette.html; Susan M. Heathfield, "10 Reasons Social Media Should Rock Your World," About.com, accessed January 9, 2014, http://humanresources.about.com.

own career, you will soon see the importance of relationships, including your online presence. See the "Career Kickstart" feature for suggestions on presenting yourself in a positive way through social networking.

The Social Era

The **social era** of business can be described as a new approach to the way businesses and individuals interact, connect, communicate, share, and exchange information with each other in virtual communities and networks around the world.

The social era, based on the premise that organizations create value through connections with groups or networks of people with similar goals and interests, offers businesses immense opportunities, particularly through the use of technology and **relationship management**—the collection of activities that build and maintain ongoing, mutually beneficial ties with customers and other parties.

Social media tools and technologies come in various shapes and sizes. They include blogs, podcasts, and microblogs (such as Twitter); social and professional networks (such as Facebook and LinkedIn); picture-sharing platforms (such as Instagram and Tumblr); and content communities (such as YouTube), to name a few.[15]

As consumers continue to log fewer hours on computers and more time on mobile devices, companies have implemented mobile strategies using real-time data and location-based technology. Businesses use mobile social media applications to engage in marketing research, communications, sales promotions, loyalty programs, and other processes. In the social era, businesses tailor specific promotions to specific users in specific locations at specific times to build customer loyalty and long-term relationships. For example, Facebook offers free Wi-Fi to users in exchange for checking in at selected retailers, hotels, and restaurants.[16]

Businesses are also finding that they must form partnerships with other organizations to take full advantage of opportunities—often using social media tools and technologies for communications. One form of partnership between organizations is a **strategic alliance**, which creates a competitive advantage for the businesses involved.

Ebusiness has created a new type of strategic alliance. A firm whose entire business is conducted online, such as Amazon or Overstock.com, may team up with traditional retailers who have expertise in distribution and in buying the right amount of the right merchandise. Overstock.com is an online-only retailer for bargain hunters looking for discount prices on brand-name consumer goods, including clothing, appliances, electronics, and sporting goods. Overstock.com partners with manufacturers and distributors that gain a new outlet for reducing their inventory; in return, Overstock.com sells more than 2 million different products on its website. Overstock.com earned revenues of more than $800 million in one recent year and received several top customer service awards.[17]

Another way to build relationships is to have your business address some of the issues that your customers care about using social media. For example, environmental concerns now influence consumers' choices on everything from yogurt to clothing to cars and light bulbs; many observers say the question about "going green" is no longer whether a company should, but how. The need to develop environmentally friendly products and processes is a major new force in business today. Companies in every industry are researching how to save energy, cut emissions and pollution, reduce waste, and of course save money and increase profits. Endura Energy is an Ontario-based developer of large-scale rooftop solar energy systems. This company works with building owners to capture value from unused roof space and to promote green energy. Using the Ontario government's Feed-in Tariff Program, Endura Energy is building a 100-kilowatt rooftop solar power system in Richmond Hill, just north of Toronto. This system will generate approximately 110,000 kilowatt hours of clean energy each year, equivalent to reducing approximately 85 tonnes of carbon emissions annually. The owners of the building do not need to contribute financially, which will make it easier to develop more rooftop systems that will contribute to the electric grid. Endura uses Facebook and other social media tools to reach out to businesses and consumers interested in building greener solutions.[18]

Energy is among the biggest costs for most firms. Traditional carbon-based fuels like coal are responsible for most of the additional carbon dioxide in the atmosphere. Ford Motor Company is upgrading lighting fixtures in its manufacturing facilities. The old, inefficient equipment will be replaced with fluorescent lighting that saves energy and money. The new lighting will include

social era the business era in which firms seek ways to connect and interact with customers using technology.

relationship management the collection of activities that build and maintain ongoing, mutually beneficial ties with customers and other parties.

strategic alliance a partnership formed to create a competitive advantage for the businesses involved; in international business, the business strategy of one company partnering with another company in the country where it wants to do business.

HIT & MISS

Twitter's Dorsey: 140 Characters at a Time

At age 13, Jack Dorsey was fascinated with dispatch routing. While a student in college, he began to create software related to dispatch logistics, which is still used by taxi companies today.

Dorsey has always been interested in business. In San Francisco, he started Odeo, a podcasting company that quickly became extinct when iTunes surfaced. This setback didn't stop Dorsey from trying again, though. Twitter began as an interoffice microblogging platform created by Odeo programmers. When a small earthquake shook San Francisco, word of the quake spread quickly via Twitter—and a new company was born.

Square, Dorsey's most recent business venture, allows credit card payments to be made to individuals and businesses by attaching a small device to a smartphone or tablet.

Dorsey is guided by three principles—simplicity, constraint, and craftsmanship—which are still very much part of Twitter's culture today. Dorsey serves as Twitter's executive chair, Square's CEO, and recently joined Disney's board of directors.

Questions for Critical Thinking

1. How can businesses apply Dorsey's three guiding principles to create a strategic vision?
2. What lessons can be learned from Jack Dorsey about perseverance, technology, and starting a business?

Sources: Anthony Ha, "Dorsey Joins Disney's Board of Directors," *TechCrunch*, December 23, 2013, accessed January 12, 2014, http://techcrunch.com/2013/12/23/jack-dorsey-joins-disney; Kit Eaton, "The Twitter IPO Player's Club," *Fast Company*, accessed January 12, 2014, www.fastcompany.com/tag/ipo-players-club; Nicholas Carlson, "The Real History of Twitter," *Business Insider*, April 13, 2011, accessed January 12, 2014, www.businessinsider.com/how-twitter-was-founded-2011-4; Brandon Griggs, "Twitter's Jack Dorsey Eyes New York Mayor's Job," CNN.com, March 18, 2013, accessed January 12, 2014, www.cnn.com/2013/03/18/tech/social-media/dorsey-twitter-nyc; Noah Robischon, "Square Brings Credit Card Swiping to Mobile Masses," *Fast Company*, accessed January 12, 2014, www.fastcompany.com/1643271/square-brings-credit-card-swiping-mobile-masses-starting-today; Mitch Wagner, "Twitter CEO Jack Dorsey Talks About Its Business Model," *InformationWeek*, June 4, 2008, accessed January 12, 2014, www.informationweek.com/desktop/twitter-ceo-jack-dorsey-talks-about-its-business-model/d/d-id/1068539.

---

motion detectors to reduce energy use during periods of low activity.[19] Clean solar energy is becoming more common and may soon be easier to set up and more widely available. Endura Energy is currently developing more than 5 megawatts of projects covering more than 93,000 square metres of roof space across 20 separate sites. The Ontario government's Feed-in Tariff Program guarantees the purchase of electricity produced at set rates. Thus, we will likely see more projects built on available rooftops.[20]

Companies in every industry are researching how to save energy, cut emissions, reduce waste, and save company money. Clean solar energy is one option that is becoming more common and may soon be easier to set up and more widely available.

Going Green

INTERNET BILLIONAIRE'S GOAL: HELP CHINA BREATHE EASIER

Less than two decades ago, Jack Ma founded Alibaba Group in his Hangzhou apartment. Alibaba Group includes an online payment system, Alipay, and two ecommerce sites, Tmall and Taobao. The company has been described as the Chinese version of eBay, Amazon, and PayPal combined. Its most recent sales exceed the combined sales of eBay and Amazon.

The *Financial Times* recently named Ma its Person of the Year, referring to him as the "godfather of China's scrappy entrepreneurial spirit." Ma, in his late forties, commands a cult-like following among the younger Chinese generation and is the face of China's new age of entrepreneurs.

At a speech given upon his retirement as Alibaba's CEO, Ma reminded the audience that business cannot prosper when it continues to be ruined by overdevelopment, which includes China's hazardous levels of pollution.

Alluding to China's increased economic prosperity and rising middle class, Ma points out that the dreams of the Chinese people may fade away if they cannot see the sun. He has committed 0.3 percent of Alibaba's annual profits to help preserve the environment. As a self-made Internet billionaire, Ma's next business plan involves making China's air a little easier to breathe.

Questions for Critical Thinking

1. How can Ma enlist other business owners to get involved in his environmental causes?

2. What are some of the issues that can arise in a country experiencing substantial economic prosperity among segments of its population?

Sources: Jamil Anderlini, "Person of the Year: Jack Ma," *Financial Times*, December 12, 2013, accessed January 9, 2014, www.ft.com/cms/s/2/308e46a8-6189-11e3-916e-00144feabdc0.html#axzz3ZYLESUcn; Steven Millward, "'Godfather of China's Scrappy Entrepreneurial Spirit': Alibaba's Jack Ma Is FT's Person of the Year," *Techinasia*, December 13, 2013, accessed January 9, 2014, www.techinasia.com/alibaba-founder-jack-ma-ft-person-of-year-2013; Bryan Walsh, "From Gold to Green," *Time*, June 10, 2013, accessed January 9, 2014, http://content.time.com/time/magazine/article/0,9171,2144568,00.html; William Brent, "With Jack Ma Out, Who Is the Next Global Chinese CEO?" *Forbes*, May 6, 2013, accessed January 9, 2014, www.forbes.com/sites/williambrent/2013/05/06/with-jack-ma-out-who-is-the-next-global-chinese-ceo.

Some "green" initiatives can be costly for firms. General Electric, though, has found a hit in its Ecomagination line of environmentally friendly products. For General Electric, thinking "green" satisfies not only consumers' environmental concerns but also shareholders' concerns about saving money and earning profits. "We've sold out in eco-certified products for [a year in advance]," says Bob Corcoran, the company's vice-president for corporate citizenship. The company's energy-saving wind turbines are backordered for two years. GE believes it is doing what its shareholders expect it to do. "No good business can call itself a good corporate citizen if it fritters away shareholder money," Corcoran says.[21] The "Going Green" feature provides an example of how entrepreneurial success can translate into a better environment.

In each new era in business history, managers have had to re-examine their tools and techniques. Tomorrow's managers will need creativity and vision to stay on top of rapidly changing technology and to manage complex relationships in the global business world of the fast-paced twenty-first century. As green operations become more cost effective, and as consumers and shareholders demand more responsive management, few firms will want to be left behind.

> ✓ **ASSESSMENT CHECK**
>
> 1.4.1 What was the Industrial Revolution?
>
> 1.4.2 During which era was the idea of branding developed?
>
> 1.4.2 What is the difference between transaction management and relationship management?

TODAY'S BUSINESS WORKFORCE

LO 1.5 Explain how today's business workforce and the nature of work itself are changing.

A skilled and knowledgeable workforce is an essential resource for keeping pace with the rapid rate of change in today's business world. Employers need reliable workers who are dedicated to promoting strong ties with customers and partners. Employers need to build workforces that are capable of efficient, high-quality production, which is needed to compete in global markets. Smart business leaders also realize that the brainpower of employees plays a vital role in a firm staying on top of new technologies and innovations. In short, a first-class workforce can be the foundation of a firm's competitive differentiation, providing important advantages over competing businesses.

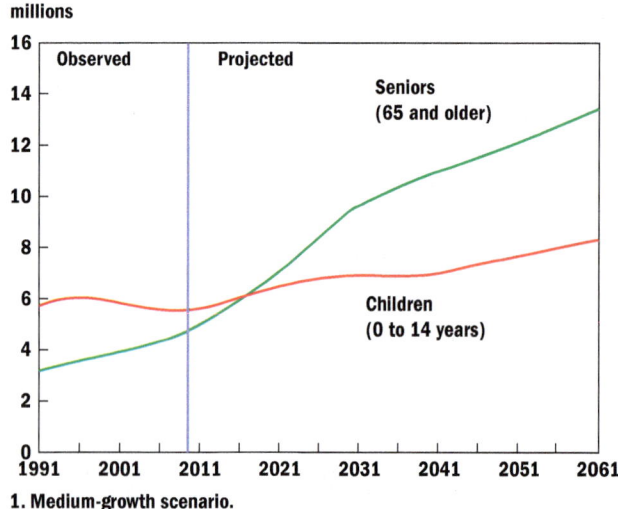

FIGURE 1.3 Population Projections, Children and Seniors

Source: Statistics Canada, CANSIM tables 051-001 and 052-005.

Changes in the Workforce

Companies face several trends that challenge their skills for managing and developing human resources. These challenges include the aging population and a shrinking labour pool, the growing diversity of the workforce, the changing nature of work, the need for flexibility and mobility, and the need to work with others to innovate.

The Aging Population and a Shrinking Labour Pool

As people retire from the workforce, they take their experience and expertise with them. As **Figure 1.3** shows, the Canadian population as a whole is aging. Today, though, many of those from the baby boom generation, the huge number of people born between 1946 and 1964, are still hitting the peaks of their careers. At the same time, members of so-called Generation X (born from 1965 to 1981) and Generation Y (born from 1982 to 2005) are building their careers. As a result, employers are finding more people from different generations together in the workforce than ever before. This broad age diversity brings management challenges, such as the need to accept a variety of work–life styles, the changing expectations of work, and varying levels of technological expertise. Still, despite the wide range of ages in the workforce today, some economists predict the Canadian labour pool could soon fall short as the baby boomers retire.

Technology has intensified the hiring challenge by requiring workers to have ever-more advanced skills. Although the number of college-educated workers has increased, the demand for these workers is still greater than the supply. Because of these changes, companies are increasingly seeking—and finding—talent at the extreme ends of the working-age spectrum. Teenagers are entering the workforce sooner, and some seniors are working longer—or seeking new careers after retiring from their primary careers. Many older workers work part time or flexible hours. Meanwhile, for those older employees who do retire, employers must look after a variety of retirement planning and disability programs, retraining, and insurance benefits.

Increasingly Diverse Workforce

The Canadian workforce is growing more diverse, in age and in other ways, too. Two-thirds of Canada's population growth is due to international immigration, particularly from Asia. As illustrated in **Figure 1.4**, Chinese immigration is closely followed by immigration from India and other Asian countries.

Diversity is the blending of individuals of different genders, ethnic backgrounds, cultures, religions, ages, and physical and mental abilities. Having a diverse workplace can enhance a firm's chances of success. Some firms that recently made the top 10 in a list of "Top 50 Companies for Diversity" were also leaders and innovators in their industries, including Johnson & Johnson (number one on the list), AT&T, the accounting firm Ernst & Young, Marriott International, The Coca-Cola Company, and IBM.[22] Several studies have shown that diverse employee teams and workforces tend to perform tasks more effectively. They also develop better solutions to business problems than homogeneous employee groups. This result is due in part to the varied perspectives and experiences that promote innovation and creativity in multicultural teams.

FIGURE 1.4 Top 10 Birthplaces of Immigrants Who Landed in Canada from 2001 to 2006

Source: Statistics Canada, 2006 Census of Population.

diversity the blending of individuals of different genders, ethnic backgrounds, cultures, religions, ages, and physical and mental abilities to enhance a firm's chances of success.

Practical managers also know that attention to diversity issues can help them avoid damaging legal battles. Losing a discrimination lawsuit can be very costly; yet, in a recent survey, a majority of executives from racial and cultural minorities said they had seen discrimination in work assignments.[23]

Outsourcing and the Changing Nature of Work

The Canadian workforce is changing, but so is the nature of work. Manufacturing once accounted for most of Canada's annual output, but most Canadian employment has now shifted to services, such as financial management and communications. Because of this change, firms must now rely on well-trained service workers who have knowledge, technical skills, the ability to communicate and deal with people, and a talent for creative thinking. The Internet offers another business tool for increasing employment flexibility. **Outsourcing** is the use of outside vendors to produce goods or fulfill services and functions that were previously handled in-house or in-country. In the best situation, outsourcing can reduce costs and allow a firm to concentrate on what it does best, while also accessing expertise it may not have. But outsourcing also creates its own challenges, such as differences in language or culture.

Offshoring is the relocation of business processes to lower-cost locations overseas. Offshoring can involve both production and services. In recent years, China has emerged as a prime location for production offshoring, whereas India has become the key player in offshoring services. Some companies are now structured so that entire divisions or functions are developed and staffed overseas—the jobs were never in Canada to start with. Another trend in some industries is **nearshoring**, outsourcing production or services to nations near a firm's home base.

outsourcing using outside vendors to produce goods or fulfill services and functions that were previously handled in-house or in-country.

offshoring the relocation of business processes to lower-cost locations overseas.

nearshoring the outsourcing of production or services to locations near a firm's home base.

Flexibility and Mobility

Younger workers are looking for an experience different from the "work comes first" lifestyle of the baby boom generation. Workers of all ages are exploring different work arrangements, such as telecommuting from remote locations and sharing jobs among two or more employees. Employers are also hiring more temporary and part-time employees, some of whom are less interested in climbing the corporate ladder and more interested in using and developing their skills. The cubicle-filled office will likely never disappear, but technology has made certain tasks easier. For example, employees can take part in productive networking and virtual teams because technology allows people to work from where they choose yet easily share knowledge, a sense of purpose or mission, and a free flow of ideas across any geographical distance or time zone.

Managers of such spread-out workforces need to work hard to build and earn the trust of their staff. Managers aim to retain valued employees and ensure that all members are acting ethically and contributing their share without the day-to-day supervision of a conventional workplace. These managers and their employees need to be flexible and sensitive to change, while work, technology, and the relationships between them continue to evolve.

Innovation through Collaboration

Some observers also see a trend toward more collaborative work in the future, as opposed to individuals working alone. Businesses that use teamwork hope to build a creative setting where all members contribute their knowledge and skills to solve problems or seize opportunities.

The old relationship between employers and employees was simple: Workers arrived at a certain hour, worked at their jobs, and went home every day at the same time. Companies rarely laid off workers, and employees rarely left for a job at another firm. But all that—and more—has changed. Employees are no longer likely to remain with a single company throughout their entire careers. Employees do not expect lifetime loyalty from the companies they work for, and they do not expect to give that loyalty to any company either. Instead, today's employees build their own careers however and wherever they can. These changes mean that many firms now recognize the value of partnering with employees to encourage creative thinking and problem solving and to reward risk taking and innovation.

ASSESSMENT CHECK

1.5.1 Define *outsourcing*, *offshoring*, and *nearshoring*.

1.5.2 Describe the importance of collaboration and employee partnership.

LO 1.6 Identify the skills and attributes needed to lead businesses in the twenty-first century.

THE TWENTY-FIRST-CENTURY MANAGER

Today's companies look for managers who are intelligent, highly motivated people who can create and sustain a vision of how an organization can succeed. The twenty-first-century manager must apply critical thinking skills and creativity to business challenges and lead change.

Importance of Vision

vision the ability to perceive marketplace needs and what an organization must do to satisfy them.

To thrive in the twenty-first century, businesspeople need **vision**, the ability to perceive marketplace needs and what an organization must do to satisfy them. Canadian James Cameron is the Oscar-winning writer and director of such blockbuster sci-fi films as *The Terminator*, *Aliens*, *The Abyss*, and the most successful film of all time, *Avatar*. Cameron has an uncanny ability to know what audiences want and how to produce it. After he exceeded the budget for *Titanic*, Cameron persuaded his financial backers to continue funding the project. To show his confidence that *Titanic* would succeed, he offered to give up his fees for writing the screenplay and directing in exchange for receiving a percentage of box office sales. His financial backers recognized his motivation to complete the film, and their funding of the film proved to be a good decision. *Titanic* earned more than $25 million the first weekend of its release and went on to replace George Lucas's *Star Wars* as the biggest money-making film in history. Cameron's futuristic 3D creation *Avatar* broke through that milestone and won 11 Oscars.[24]

Film director, writer, and inventor James Cameron knows how to entertain audiences.

The Importance of Critical Thinking and Creativity

Critical thinking and creativity are essential characteristics of workers in the twenty-first century. Today's businesspeople need to look at a wide variety of situations, draw connections between dissimilar information, and develop future-oriented solutions. This need applies to top executives, mid-level managers, and entry-level workers.

critical thinking the ability to analyze and assess information to pinpoint problems or opportunities.

Critical thinking is the ability to analyze and assess information to pinpoint problems or opportunities. The critical thinking process includes activities such as determining the authenticity, accuracy, and worth of information, knowledge, and arguments. It involves looking beneath

- In a group, brainstorm by listing ideas as they come to mind. Don't criticize other people's ideas, but build on them. Wait until later to evaluate and organize the ideas.
- Think about how to make familiar concepts unfamiliar. A glue that doesn't stick very well? That's the basis for 3M's popular Post-it® notes.
- Plan ways to rearrange your thinking by asking simple questions, such as "What features can we leave out?" or by imagining what it feels like to be the customer.
- Cultivate curiosity, openness, risk, and energy as you meet people and encounter new situations. View these encounters as opportunities to learn.
- Treat failures as additional opportunities to learn.
- Get regular physical exercise. When you work out, your brain releases endorphins, and these chemicals stimulate creative thinking.
- Pay attention to your dreams and daydreams. You might find that you already know the answer to a problem.

Figure 1.5 Exercises and Guidelines to Promote Creative Thinking

the surface for deeper meaning and connections that can help identify critical issues and solutions. Without critical thinking, a firm may encounter serious problems.

Creativity is the capacity to develop novel solutions to perceived organizational problems. Most people think of creativity in terms of writers, artists, musicians, and inventors, but that definition is very limited. In business, creativity refers to being able to see better and different ways of doing business. A computer engineer who solves a glitch in a software program is performing a creative act, as is a shipping clerk who finds a way to speed up the delivery of the company's overnight packages. Sometimes a crisis calls for creative leadership. For example, Captain Chesley Sullenberger famously guided US Airways Flight 1549 to a safe landing in New York's Hudson River. In doing so, he had already made immediate and critical decisions when both his plane's engines quit after hitting birds upon takeoff. Sullenberger's quick thinking and years of training saved the lives of his passengers and crew members and the people on the ground. "Losing thrust on both engines, at low speed, at a low altitude, over one of the most densely populated areas on the planet. Yes, I knew it was a very challenging situation," he said. As the plane lost altitude, Sullenberger ruled out returning to LaGuardia Airport or attempting to land at a nearby New Jersey airport. Instead, he opted to splash down in the river, close to a ferry terminal. "I needed to touch down with the wings exactly level . . . the nose slightly up . . . [and] just above our minimum flying speed, but not below it." He accomplished those seemingly impossible feats and saved all 155 people on board.[25]

creativity the capacity to develop novel solutions to perceived organizational problems.

Some practice and mental exercise can cultivate your own ability to think creatively. See **Figure 1.5** for some exercises and guidelines to improve your creativity.

Creativity and critical thinking must do more than generate new ideas. They must lead to action. In addition to creating an environment in which employees can nurture ideas, managers must give employees opportunities to take risks and try new solutions.

Ability to Lead Change

Today's business leaders must guide their employees and organizations through the changes brought about by technology, marketplace demands, and global competition. Managers must be skilled at recognizing employee strengths and motivating people to move toward common goals as members of a team. Throughout this book, real-world examples show how companies have initiated major change initiatives. Most, if not all of these companies, have been led by managers who are comfortable with making the tough decisions that are needed in today's fluctuating conditions.

Factors that require organizational change can come from both external and internal sources; successful managers must be aware of both types of factors. External forces might include feedback from customers, developments in the international marketplace, economic trends, and new technologies. Internal factors might arise from new company goals, emerging employee needs, labour union demands, or production problems.

ASSESSMENT CHECK

1.6.1 Why is vision an important managerial quality?

1.6.2 What is the difference between creativity and critical thinking?

LO 1.7 Outline the characteristics that make a company admired.

WHAT MAKES A COMPANY ADMIRED?

Who is your hero? Is it someone who has achieved great feats in sports, government, entertainment, or business? Why do you admire this person? Does he or she run a company, earn a lot of money, or give back to the community and society? Every year, business magazines and organizations publish lists of companies that they consider to be "most admired." Companies, like individuals, may be admired for many reasons. Some of these reasons might include solid profits,

---

SOLVING AN **ETHICAL** CONTROVERSY

Securities Oversight?

In Canada and the United States, the laws surrounding buying and selling securities, such as stocks and bonds, require full disclosure of information to discourage fraud. Enforcement is typically by authorities and the businesspeople who earn their living persuading investors to undertake risks with their money. This arrangement has worked well enough that extreme cases of abuse of trust are very rare. However, when they do happen they can be extreme.

A whopping $65 billion securities fraud came to light during the economic downturn that began in 2008. The investment company run by Bernard Madoff turned out to be the biggest Ponzi scheme of all time. Madoff used new investors' funds to pay off the older investors. The investment profits that Madoff claimed were only an illusion. Independent investigator Harry Markopolos told U.S. Congress he had been warning the Securities and Exchange Commission (SEC) about Madoff's activities for years. "I gift-wrapped and delivered the largest Ponzi scheme in history to them and somehow they couldn't be bothered to conduct a thorough and proper investigation because they were too busy on matters of higher priority," Markopolos testified. Thousands of individual and institutional investors faced financial ruin as Madoff's scheme evaporated.

If the SEC was not doing its job, does it bear part of the blame for investors' losses?

PRO

1. A $65 billion fraud could flourish only under a flawed regulatory system. "Our current fragmented regulatory system can allow bad actors to engage in misconduct outside the view and reach of some regulators," said an officer of the securities industry's watchdog organization. "It is undeniable that . . . the system failed to protect investors."
2. "The SEC is . . . captive to the industry it regulates, and it is afraid of bringing big cases against the largest, most powerful firms," said Markopolos. "Clearly the SEC was afraid of Mr. Madoff."

CON

1. The SEC's director of enforcement told a Senate committee, "We don't turn a blind eye to fraud. If we see it and we suspect it, we pursue it. We don't want fraudsters out there."
2. The director also said the SEC doesn't have enough resources to pursue all the tipoffs of potential fraud that come before it: "If we had more resources, we could clearly do more." Other regulators blamed lack of coordination among government agencies for the lapses in oversight that allowed Madoff to operate.

Summary

Madoff pled guilty to charges of felony securities fraud and was sentenced to 150 years in prison. The SEC is conducting an internal investigation to learn why it failed to act on the information that Markopolos and others had provided over the years.

Sources: Jenny Anderson and Zachery Kouwe, "SEC Enforcers Focus on Avoiding Madoff Repeat," *New York Times*, February 8, 2010, www.nytimes.com/2010/02/09/business/09sec.html; U.S. Securities and Exchange Commission, "The Investor's Advocate: How the SEC Protects Investors, Maintains Market Integrity, and Facilitates Capital Formation," accessed February 13, 2009, www.sec.gov/about/whatwedo.shtml; Linda Sandler, "Madoff Said Only Brother Could Do Audit, Witness Tells Congress," *Bloomberg News*, February 5, 2009, www.bloomberg.com/apps/news?pid=newsarchive&sid=aLCQkCIE6JHl; Allan Chernoff, "Madoff Whistleblower Blasts SEC," CNNMoney, February 4, 2009, http://money.cnn.com/2009/02/04/news/newsmakers/madoff_whistleblower; Diana B. Henriques, "Witness on Madoff Tells of Fear for Safety," *New York Times*, February 3, 2009, www.nytimes.com/2009/02/04/business/04madoff.html; Julian Cummings, "Madoff: SEC Defends Its Role," *CNNMoney*, January 28, 2009, http://money.cnn.com/2009/01/27/news/economy/madoff_senate/?postversion=2009012809; Liz Moyer, "How Regulators Missed Madoff," *Forbes*, January 27, 2009, www.forbes.com/2009/01/27/bernard-madoff-sec-business-wall-street_0127_regulators.html.

stable growth, a safe and challenging work environment, high-quality goods and services, and business ethics and social responsibility. *Business ethics* refers to the standards of conduct and moral values involved in decisions made in the work environment. *Social responsibility* is a management philosophy that includes contributing resources to the community, preserving the natural environment, and developing or participating in not-for-profit programs designed to promote the well-being of the general public. We explore these topics more deeply in Chapter 2. You'll also find business ethics and social responsibility examples throughout this book. For businesses to behave ethically and responsibly, their employees need strong moral guidance. The "Solving an Ethical Controversy" feature debates the responsibility of watchdogs—the people and organizations that monitor companies—when they fail to perform their duties.

As you read this text, you'll be able to make up your mind about why companies should—or should not—be admired. *Fortune* publishes two lists of most-admired companies each year, one for U.S.-based firms and one for the world. The list is compiled from surveys and other research conducted by the Hay Group, a global human resources and organizational consulting firm. Criteria for making the list include innovation, people management, use of corporate assets, social responsibility, quality of management, and quality of products and services.[26] *Fortune* ranked Apple as the number-one most-admired company in 2014. Their complete "Top Ten" list can be found online.

✓ **ASSESSMENT CHECK**

1.7.1 Define *business ethics* and *social responsibility*.

1.7.2 Identify three criteria used to judge whether a company might be considered admirable.

WHAT'S AHEAD

As business speeds along in the twenty-first century, new technologies, population shifts, and shrinking global barriers will alter the world at a frantic pace. Businesspeople trigger many of these changes by creating new opportunities for individuals who are prepared to take action. Studying contemporary business will help you prepare for the future.

Throughout this book, you'll be exposed to the real-life stories of many businesspeople. You'll learn about a range of business careers and the daily decisions, tasks, and challenges that businesspeople face. By the end of the course, you'll understand how marketing, production, accounting, finance, and management work together to provide competitive advantages for firms. This knowledge can help you become a more capable employee and enhance your career potential.

Now that this chapter has introduced some basic terms and issues in the business world of the twenty-first century, Chapter 2 takes a detailed look at the ethical and social responsibility issues facing contemporary business. Chapter 3 deals with economic challenges, and Chapter 4 focuses on the difficulties and opportunities faced by firms competing in world markets.

RETURN TO INSIDE BUSINESS

Canadian Entertainers Are Cultivating Global Audiences Online

The Internet has changed the way many artists like Drake and Justin Bieber communicate and develop their relationships with their fan base using social media. Drake and Justin Bieber use a variety of tools such as blogs, tweets, and videos to develop and maintain their relationship with fans.

QUESTIONS FOR CRITICAL THINKING

1. How would you improve Drake's or Justin Bieber's web presence?
2. What is another type of business that could use the Internet to improve communications between participants?

SUMMARY OF LEARNING OBJECTIVES

LO 1.1 Distinguish between business and not-for-profit organizations.

Business consists of all profit-seeking activities that provide goods and services necessary to an economic system. Not-for-profit organizations are business-like establishments whose primary objectives involve social, political, governmental, educational, or similar functions instead of profits.

 ASSESSMENT CHECK ANSWERS

1.1.1 What activity lies at the heart of every business endeavour? At the heart of every business endeavour is an exchange between a buyer and a seller.

1.1.2 What are the primary objectives of a not-for-profit organization? Not-for-profit organizations place public service above profits, although they need to raise money to operate and achieve their social goals.

LO 1.2 Identify and describe the factors of production.

The factors of production have four basic inputs: natural resources, capital, human resources, and entrepreneurship. Natural resources include all productive inputs that are useful in their natural states. Capital includes technology, tools, information, and physical facilities. Human resources include anyone who works for the firm. Entrepreneurship is the willingness to take risks to create and operate a business.

 ASSESSMENT CHECK ANSWERS

1.2.1 Identify the four basic inputs to an economic system. The four basic inputs are natural resources, capital, human resources, and entrepreneurship.

1.2.2 List four types of capital. Four types of capital are technology, tools, information, and physical facilities.

LO 1.3 Describe the private enterprise system.

The private enterprise system is an economic system that rewards firms for being able to perceive and serve the needs and demands of consumers. Competition in the private enterprise system means success for firms that satisfy consumer demands. Citizens in a private enterprise economy enjoy rights to private property, profits, freedom of choice, and competition. Entrepreneurship drives economic growth.

 ASSESSMENT CHECK ANSWERS

1.3.1 What is an alternative term for the private enterprise system? *Capitalism* is an alternative term for private enterprise system.

1.3.2 What is the most basic freedom under the private enterprise system? The most basic freedom is the right to private property.

1.3.3 What is an entrepreneur? An entrepreneur is a risk taker who is willing to start, own, and operate a business.

LO 1.4 Identify the seven eras in the history of business.

The seven historical eras are the colonial period, the Industrial Revolution, the age of industrial entrepreneurs, the production era, the marketing era, the relationship era, and the social era. In the colonial period, businesses were small and rural, emphasizing agricultural production. The Industrial Revolution brought factories and mass production to business. The age of industrial entrepreneurs built on the Industrial Revolution through an expansion in the number and size of firms. The production era focused on the growth of factory operations through assembly lines and other efficient internal processes. During and following the Great Depression, businesses concentrated on finding markets for their products through advertising and selling, giving rise to the marketing era. In the relationship era, businesspeople focus on developing and sustaining long-term relationships with customers and other businesses. The social era of business can be described as a new approach to the way businesses and individuals interact, connect, communicate, share, and exchange information with each other in virtual communities and networks around the world. Technology promotes innovation and communication, while alliances create a competitive advantage through partnerships. Concern for the environment also helps build strong relationships with customers.

 ASSESSMENT CHECK ANSWERS

1.4.1 What was the Industrial Revolution? The Industrial Revolution began around 1750 in England. It moved business operations from an emphasis on independent, skilled workers to a factory system that mass-produced items.

1.4.2 During which era was the idea of branding developed? The idea of branding began in the marketing era.

1.4.3 What is the difference between transaction management and relationship management? Transaction management focuses on building, promoting, and selling enough products to cover costs and earn profits. Relationship management is the collection of activities that build and maintain ongoing ties with customers and other parties.

LO 1.5 Explain how today's business workforce and the nature of work itself are changing.

The workforce is changing in several significant ways: (1) It is aging and the labour pool is shrinking and (2) it is becoming increasingly diverse. The nature of work has shifted toward services and a focus on information. More firms now rely on outsourcing, offshoring, and nearshoring to produce goods or to fulfill services and functions that were previously handled in-house or in-country. Today's workplaces are also becoming increasingly flexible, allowing employees to work from different locations and through different relationships. Companies promote innovation through teamwork and collaboration.

✓ ASSESSMENT CHECK ANSWERS

1.5.1 Define *outsourcing*, *offshoring*, and *nearshoring*. Outsourcing involves using outside vendors to produce goods or to fulfill services and functions that were once handled in-house. Offshoring is the relocation of business processes to lower-cost locations overseas. Nearshoring is the outsourcing of production or services to nations near a firm's home base.

1.5.2 Describe the importance of collaboration and employee partnership. Businesses are increasingly focusing on collaboration, rather than on individuals working alone. No longer do employees just put in their time at a job they hold their entire career. The new employer–employee partnership encourages teamwork, creative thinking, problem solving, and innovation. Managers are trained to listen to and respect employees.

LO 1.6 Identify the skills and attributes needed to lead businesses in the twenty-first century.

Today's managers need vision, which is the ability to perceive both marketplace needs and the way their firm can satisfy those needs. Critical thinking skills and creativity allow managers to pinpoint problems and opportunities and plan novel solutions. Finally, managers are dealing with rapid change, and they need skills to help lead their organizations through shifts in external and internal conditions.

✓ ASSESSMENT CHECK ANSWERS

1.6.1 Why is vision an important managerial quality? Managerial vision allows a firm to innovate and adapt to meet changes in the marketplace.

1.6.2 What is the difference between creativity and critical thinking? Critical thinking is the ability to analyze and assess information to pinpoint problems or opportunities. Creativity is the capacity to develop novel solutions to perceived organizational problems.

LO 1.7 Outline the characteristics that make a company admired.

A company is usually admired for its solid profits, stable growth, a safe and challenging work environment, high-quality goods and services, and business ethics and social responsibility.

✓ ASSESSMENT CHECK ANSWERS

1.7.1 Define *business ethics* and *social responsibility*. Business ethics refers to the standards of conduct and moral values involved in decisions made in the work environment. Social responsibility is a management philosophy that includes contributing resources to the community, preserving the natural environment, and developing or participating in not-for-profit programs designed to promote the well-being of the general public.

1.7.2 Identify three criteria used to judge whether a company might be considered admirable. Criteria in judging whether companies are admirable include the following: solid profits, stable growth, a safe and challenging work environment, high-quality goods and services, and business ethics and social responsibility.

BUSINESS TERMS YOU NEED TO KNOW

brand 13	creativity 21	nearshoring 19	relationship management 15
branding 13	critical thinking 20	not-for-profit organizations 5	social era 15
business 4	diversity 18	offshoring 19	strategic alliance 15
capital 7	entrepreneur 10	outsourcing 19	transaction management 14
capitalism 8	entrepreneurship 7	private enterprise system 8	vision 20
competition 8	factors of production 6	private property 9	
competitive differentiation 8	human resources 7	profits 4	
consumer orientation 13	natural resources 6	relationship era 14	

REVIEW QUESTIONS

1. Why is business so important to a country's economy?
2. In what ways are not-for-profit organizations a substantial part of the Canadian economy? What challenges do not-for-profits face?
3. Identify and describe the four basic inputs that make up the factors of production. Give an example of each factor of production that an auto manufacturer might use.
4. What is a private enterprise system? What four rights are critical to the operation of capitalism? Why would capitalism function poorly in a society that does not ensure these rights for its citizens?
5. In what ways is entrepreneurship vital to the private enterprise system?
6. Identify the seven eras of business in North America. How were businesses changed during each era?
7. Describe the focus of the most recent era of business. How is this era different from previous eras?
8. Define *partnership* and *strategic alliance*. How might a motorcycle dealer and a local radio station benefit from an alliance?
9. Identify the major changes in the workforce that will affect the way managers build a world-class workforce in the twenty-first century. Why is brainpower so important?
10. Identify four qualities required by the "new" managers of the twenty-first century. Why are these qualities important in a competitive business environment?

PROJECTS AND TEAMWORK APPLICATIONS

1. The entrepreneurial spirit fuels growth in the Canadian economy. Choose a company that interests you—one you have worked for or dealt with as a customer—and read about the company in the library or visit its website. Learn what you can about the company's early history: Who founded it and why? Is the founder still with the organization? Do you think the founder's original vision is still embraced by the company? If not, how has the vision changed?

2. Brands distinguish one company's goods or services from its competitors. Each company you purchase from hopes that you will become loyal to its brand. Some well-known brands are Tim Hortons, Burger King, Coca-Cola, Hilton, and Old Navy. Choose a type of good or service you use regularly and identify the major brands associated with it. Are you loyal to a particular brand? Why or why not?

3. More and more businesses are forming strategic alliances to become more competitive. Sometimes, businesses pair up with not-for-profit organizations in a relationship that is beneficial to both. Choose a company whose goods or services interest you, such as Lululemon Athletica, Timberland, FedEx, General Mills, or Canadian Tire. On your own or with a classmate, research the firm on the Internet to learn about its alliances with not-for-profit organizations. Describe one of the alliances, including the goals and benefits to both parties. Create a presentation for your class.

4. This chapter describes how the nature of the workforce is changing: the population is aging, the labour pool is shrinking, the workforce is becoming more diverse, the nature of work is changing, the workplace is becoming more flexible and mobile, and employers are promoting innovation and collaboration among their employees. Form teams of two to three students. Select a company and research how that company is responding to changes in the workforce. When you have completed your research, be prepared to present it to your class. Choose one of the following companies or select your own: BCE, TELUS, 3M, Marriott, or Dell.

5. Many successful companies today use technology to help them improve their relationship management. Suppose a major grocery store chain's management team has asked you to assess its use of technology for this purpose. On your own or with a classmate, visit one or two local grocery stores and explore their corporate websites. Note the ways in which firms in this industry already use technology to connect with their customers. List at least three new ways these firms can use technology to connect with their customers, or list three improvements to their existing methods. Present your findings to the class as if you were presenting to the management team.

WEB ASSIGNMENTS

1. **Using search engines.** Gathering information is one of the most popular applications of the Internet. Using two of the major search engines, such as Google and Bing, search the Internet for information pertaining to brand and relationship management. Sort through your results—you're likely to gets thousands of "hits"—and identify the three most useful. What did you learn from this experience regarding the use of a search engine?

    www.google.ca

    www.bing.com

2. **Companies and not-for-profits.** In addition to companies, virtually all not-for-profit organizations have websites. Four websites are listed below, two for companies (Alcoa and Sony) and two for not-for-profits (the Humane Society of Canada and the National Audubon Society). What is the purpose of each website? What type of information is available? How are the sites similar? How are they different?

    www.alcoa.com

    www.sony.com

    www.humanesociety.com

    www.audubon.org

3. **Characteristics of the Canadian workforce.** Visit the website listed below. It is the home page for the *Canada Year Book*. Published annually by Statistics Canada, the *Canada Year Book* is a good source of basic demographic and economic data. Use the relevant data tables to prepare a brief profile of the Canadian workforce (gender, age, educational level, etc.). How is this profile expected to change over the next 10 to 20 years?

    www.statcan.gc.ca/pub/11-402-x/index-eng.htm

Note: Internet Web addresses change frequently. If you don't find the exact sites listed, you may need to access the organization's home page and search from there or use a search engine such as Bing or Google.

© loops7/iStockphoto

2 | BUSINESS ETHICS AND SOCIAL RESPONSIBILITY

LEARNING OBJECTIVES

LO 2.1 Explain the concepts of business ethics and social responsibility.

LO 2.2 Describe the factors that influence business ethics.

LO 2.3 Discuss how organizations shape ethical behaviour.

LO 2.4 Describe how businesses can act responsibly to satisfy society.

LO 2.5 Explain the ethical responsibilities of businesses to investors and the financial community.

INSIDE BUSINESS

Cirque du Soleil: A Class Act in Social Responsibility

Have you ever attended a Cirque du Soleil (Cirque) performance? If you have, you've seen creativity, ingenuity, and perseverance throughout the show from beginning to end. Maybe you saw "O" at the Bellagio, where performers dive into and out of a 5.7-million-litre pool. Or perhaps "Michael Jackson, the Immortal World Tour." Cirque puts on a great show and is a hard act for its imitators to follow.

How creative can a company like Cirque be, in terms of social responsibility? Cirque prides itself on impressing audiences. But what can it do to impress the wider community?

Cirque's founder, Guy Laliberté, has an idea. He is convinced that the company can become a leader in promoting social responsibility. Then, a trickle-down effect will inspire other companies to follow suit. Cirque has decided to publicize its efforts. It hopes to encourage other companies to be more socially responsible. Cirque also wants to keep its stakeholders aware of its plans.

Cirque's work on global citizenship affects the community, the environment, the workplace, its business partners, and its suppliers.

Cirque du Monde (one of Cirque's social action programs) can be found in nearly 80 communities in 20 countries. The company spends, on average, 1 percent of its earnings on cultural and social action programs. Laliberté set up the One Drop Foundation, which works with Oxfam and others to provide sanitation and access to water in countries where there is a need. Project Haiti began after an earthquake devastated the country in 2010 and continued until 2013. It involved 135,000 participants and had a $2.8-million budget. Cirque du Monde also helps at-risk youth regain their self-confidence. These youth are invited to attend personal development programs presented by circus instructors and social workers.

Cirque has also been a major innovator in the area of environmental responsibility. The rate of global warming has been increasing, especially over the past two decades, which were the hottest in more than 400 years. Cirque has started many projects to reduce its carbon footprint and protect the environment. Yannick Spierkel, Cirque's tour general manager, believes Cirque can "influence the lives and buying habits of employees and even set up awareness campaigns with clients." At home, Cirque chose to build its Montreal headquarters on a recovered landfill. Recently, Cirque was able to reduce its headquarters' water consumption by 20 percent, or 8.4 million litres (equivalent to the water in 168 swimming pools). Cirque reduced water use by installing rainwater collection basins in the parking lot and on the building's seventh floor and by replacing plumbing fixtures with low-flow models. When Cirque goes on tour, Green Committees look at how the group can continue to operate in an environmentally responsible manner in the cities it visits. For example, in Las Vegas, the staff of "Mystère" has been given the task of going completely paperless by rethinking all of their work habits.

Cirque is well aware that its responsibility to the community begins with its own staff right at its international headquarters. Marie Trottier, director of property services, says, "Working for a company that promotes and facilitates environmental initiatives and provides the means to make a difference has certainly influenced me personally." For example, Cirque takes pride in ensuring its staff is well taken care of. Cirque has no dress code, so staff can come to work wearing whatever feels comfortable. This physical comfort suits the workplace's sense of creativity. Staff can watch the performers practise and thus see the result of their efforts behind the scenes. "Wherever you go, you can feel creativity, you can smell it, you can touch it, because that is what we are about," says Murielle Cantin, senior vice-president of creative content. Staff can relax on couches or have lunch from a low-cost cafeteria that serves vegetables grown in in-house gardens.

Companies can indirectly have a large impact on their community and the environment through their suppliers. Cirque takes an extra step to ensure that its relationships with business partners also include an attitude of social responsibility. Cirque is part of Business for Social Responsibility (BSR). This global network of more than 250 companies seeks to develop and maintain sustainable business strategies and solutions. As a result, Cirque has reduced its deliveries to tour destinations by approximately 40 percent. It also groups its inbound shipments to warehouses to reduce transportation-related emissions. A tool has also been developed to help buyers select more environmentally friendly materials. Formal training sessions ensure that buyers are trained on how to purchase supplies in an environmentally responsible manner.

Cirque is trying to create a ripple effect with its business partners by making social responsibility a requirement when selecting future business partners. It has also built a social responsibility clause into all of its partnership agreements. This clause applies to employee relations, working conditions, ethical sourcing, environmental protection, and social and cultural actions in the community. Éric Choquette, Cirque's merchandising director, explains: "The objective is to keep the bottom line in mind while making increasingly responsible choices."[1]

CHAPTER 2 OVERVIEW

Cirque du Soleil's efforts to create sustainable operations are not unique in the world of business. Many companies are concerned about the environment and the societies in which they do business. This concern may lead to action, such as growing more slowly than they might have or reducing short-term profits for longer, sustainable benefits. Cirque du Soleil changed its own operations to help the environment while still maintaining a reasonable profit.

Most organizations strive to combine ethical behaviour with profitable operation. Some have had difficulties overcoming major ethical errors in recent years. Ethical failures in many large and well-known firms have led to lawsuits, indictments, and judgments against firms. We have all seen news reports of executives receiving millions of dollars in pay while their companies struggle to operate. This kind of news has damaged the image of the chief executive officer (CEO)—and of business in general.

Sometimes, though, bad news leads to good news. As a result of such bad news stories, both the government and companies have made changes. Businesses have renewed their efforts to behave in an ethical manner to show their responsibility to society, to consumers, and to the environment. In 2010, Industry Canada began a new voluntary standard on social responsibility known as ISO 26000. It focuses on seven principles: accountability, transparency, ethical behaviour, stakeholder interests, rule of law, international norms of behaviour, and human rights. This new standard has led to more firms paying attention to creating clearer standards and procedures for ethical behaviour. Companies now understand the enormous impact of setting a good example instead of a bad one. Today, you are likely to hear about the goodwill produced by such companies as CIBC, TELUS, and Tim Hortons. These companies create goodwill when they give back to their communities by funding youth camping programs and recycling or energy-conservation programs, or by paying fair prices to suppliers.[2]

As we discussed in Chapter 1, the basic aim of business is to serve customers at a profit. Most companies try to do more than that. Most companies want to give back to customers, society, and the environment. Sometimes, though, they face difficult questions. When does a company's self-interest work against society's and customers' well-being? Does the goal of seeking profits always work against having high principles of what is right and wrong? Many businesses of all sizes answer no.

CONCERN FOR ETHICAL AND SOCIETAL ISSUES

LO 2.1 Explain the concepts of business ethics and social responsibility.

business ethics standards of conduct and moral values regarding right and wrong actions in the business environment.

An organization that wants to do well over the long term should consider its **business ethics**. Business ethics refers to the standards of conduct and moral values that lead to our actions and decisions in the business environment. Businesses also must consider a wide range of social issues, including how a decision will affect the environment, employees, and customers. These issues are at the heart of *corporate social responsibility (CSR)*. CSR's primary objective is to enhance society's well-being through philosophies, policies, procedures, and actions. In other words, businesses must find a balance between doing what is right and doing what is profitable.

Maclean's has partnered with Sustainalytics to create a list showcasing the top 50 Canadian companies demonstrating exceptional corporate social responsibility. Tim Hortons, for example, requires its Canadian millwork suppliers to use only wood certified by the Forest Stewardship Council in its Canadian restaurants. Through the expansion of their recycling and waste-diversion programs, the company is also currently diverting 80 percent of its waste from landfills. Bank of Montreal (BMO), who also made the list, enacted a board diversity policy that requires at least one-third of the bank's independent board of directors to be women. Furthermore BMO provides funds for a financial literacy program with the goal of educating 45,000 students in personal finance.[3]

In business, as in life, deciding what is right or wrong is not always an easy choice. Firms have many responsibilities—to customers, to employees, to investors, and to society as a whole. Trying to serve the different needs of these groups can lead to conflicts. The ethical values of executives and individual employees at all levels can influence a business's decisions and actions. In your own career, you will encounter many situations where you will need to weigh right and wrong before making a decision or taking action. We begin our discussion of business ethics by focusing on individual ethics.

The concept of right and wrong can be complex. It is certainly not "black and white." Business ethics are also shaped by the ethical climate within an organization or even within a country. For example, an acceptable age to start working may be 16 in a developed country but could be 10 in a developing country. Ethics also goes beyond what is legal and what is not legal. Codes of conduct and ethical standards play important roles in businesses that support and applaud doing the right thing. This chapter shows how a firm can create a framework to encourage—and even demand—high standards of ethical behaviour and social responsibility from its employees. The chapter also considers the complex questions of what business owes to society and how society's forces shape the actions of businesses. Finally, this chapter examines the influence of business ethics and social responsibility on global businesses.

This boy from Bangladesh is working to help earn money for his family. Is this ethical?

✓ ASSESSMENT CHECK

2.1.1 To whom do businesses have responsibilities?

2.1.2 If a firm is meeting all its responsibilities to others, why do ethical conflicts arise?

THE CONTEMPORARY ETHICAL ENVIRONMENT

LO 2.2 Describe the factors that influence business ethics.

Business ethics is in the spotlight now as never before. Companies realize that they need to work harder to earn the public's trust. Many companies have taken on the challenge as if their survival depends on it. This movement toward corporate social responsibility should benefit everyone—consumers, the environment, and the companies themselves.

Most business owners and managers have built and maintained successful companies without breaking the rules. One example of a firm with a long-term commitment to ethical practice is Johnson & Johnson, the giant multinational manufacturer of healthcare products. It is the most admired pharmaceutical maker and the nineteenth most-admired company in the world, according to *Fortune*. Johnson & Johnson has worked with the same basic code of ethics, its well-known credo, for more than 50 years (see **Figure 2.1**).[4]

Many business schools include programs on ethics and social responsibility in their course curriculum. MBA students from the University of Ottawa's Telfer School of Management are now required to swear an ethics-related oath upon graduation (see **Figure 2.2**).

Many companies are aware of how ethical standards can translate into concern for the environment and society at large. According to Shelley Broader, president and CEO of Walmart Canada, the company has grouped its social responsibility priorities into four broad categories:

1. Environmental sustainability
2. People
3. Ethical sourcing
4. Community giving and investment

FIGURE 2.1 Johnson & Johnson Credo

Our Credo

We believe our first responsibility is to the doctors, nurses and patients, to mothers and fathers and all others who use our products and services. In meeting their needs everything we do must be of high quality. We must constantly strive to reduce our costs in order to maintain reasonable prices. Customers' orders must be serviced promptly and accurately. Our suppliers and distributors must have an opportunity to make a fair profit.

We are responsible to our employees, the men and women who work with us throughout the world. Everyone must be considered as an individual. We must respect their dignity and recognize their merit. They must have a sense of security in their jobs. Compensation must be fair and adequate, and working conditions clean, orderly and safe. We must be mindful of ways to help our employees fulfill their family responsibilities. Employees must feel free to make suggestions and complaints. There must be equal opportunity for employment, development and advancement for those qualified. We must provide competent management, and their actions must be just and ethical.

We are responsible to the communities in which we live and work and to the world community as well. We must be good citizens—support good works and charities and bear our fair share of taxes. We must encourage civic improvements and better health and education. We must maintain in good order the property we are privileged to use, protecting the environment and natural resources.

Our final responsibility is to our stockholders. Business must make a sound profit. We must experiment with new ideas. Research must be carried on, innovative programs developed and mistakes paid for. New equipment must be purchased, new facilities provided and new products launched. Reserves must be created to provide for adverse times. When we operate according to these principles, the stockholders should realize a fair return.

Source: Johnson & Johnson, "Our Company: Our Credo," accessed August 11, 2014, http://www.jnj.com. © Johnson & Johnson.

FIGURE 2.2 Telfer School of Management MBA Oath

As a manager my actions will affect the wellbeing of all stakeholders; accordingly, I will strive to create and sustain value over the long term while maintaining a commitment to social, ethical and global values.

I will be responsible to all stakeholders, and this will include employees, shareholders, customers, the community in which I operate, and all those that may be affected by my actions.

I will act with integrity and respect in all my dealings, making transparency paramount and demanding the same in return.

Source: Excerpted from Telfer School of Management, "Taking the Oath," http://sites.telfer.uottawa.ca/mbaoath/taking-the-oath/.

Walmart Canada has started selling fresh produce. The company has developed an efficient, cost-effective, and more sustainable process by sourcing produce locally, where possible. Local sourcing means lower transportation costs and reduced transportation-related emissions. Local sourcing also supports local suppliers, addressing many concerns raised that shopping at Walmart leads to lost Canadian jobs.[5]

Walmart also surveyed its suppliers about their sustainability practices. This survey was a first step in developing a "sustainability index" to help its customers measure the impact of Walmart products on the environment and on society. In 2013 Walmart topped the list of companies using solar energy. CSR is important for Walmart because of the ongoing controversy about some of its business practices.[6]

Not all companies set and meet high ethical standards, but the ethical climate is improving despite the recent recession. A recent study found that 41 percent of employees surveyed "witnessed misconduct on the job" in 2013, down from a record high of 55 percent in 2007. However, fewer employees said they reported misconduct when they saw it, down to 63 percent in 2013 from 65 percent in 2011. About 25 percent of employees said the recent recession had a negative impact on their company's ethical culture.[7]

Sarbanes-Oxley and Bill 198

In the United States, the **Sarbanes-Oxley Act of 2002** established new rules and regulations for securities trading and accounting practices. Companies are now required to publish their code of ethics, if they have one, and inform the public of any changes made to it. The law may actually motivate even more firms to develop written codes and guidelines for ethical business behaviour. The provisions of this act apply to Canadian companies who trade on any American stock exchange. Similar legislation has been enacted in Canada, known as Bill 198 of 2003, which has come to be referred to as "C-SOX," or the Canadian version of Sarbanes-Oxley.

Today's ethical environment for business also includes new corporate officers who are appointed to deter wrongdoing and ensure that ethical standards are met. Ethics compliance officers are responsible for conducting employee training programs that help spot potential fraud and abuse, investigating sexual harassment and discrimination charges, and monitoring potential conflicts of interest. Practising corporate social responsibility is more than just monitoring behaviour. Many companies now adopt a three-pronged approach to ethics and social responsibility:

1. Engaging in traditional corporate philanthropy, such as giving to worthy causes
2. Anticipating and managing risks
3. Identifying opportunities to create value by doing the right thing[8]

Walmart Canada has started sourcing produce locally, such as these Quebec-grown radishes on sale in its Laval store, to increase efficiency, lower costs, and reduce greenhouse gas emissions.

Sarbanes-Oxley Act of 2002 U.S. federal legislation designed to deter and punish corporate and accounting fraud and corruption. It is also designed to protect the interests of workers and shareholders by requiring enhanced financial disclosures, criminal penalties for CEOs and CFOs who defraud investors, and safeguards for whistle-blowers. The act also established a new regulatory body for public accounting firms.

Individuals Make a Difference

In today's business environment, individuals can make the difference in ethical expectations and behaviour. Executives, managers, and employees show their personal ethical principles—or lack of ethical principles. In turn, their behaviour can affect the expectations and actions of those who work for them and with them.

What is the current state of individual business ethics in Canada? Ethical behaviour can be difficult to track or define in all situations. The evidence suggests that some individuals act unethically or illegally on the job. Their behaviour includes putting their own interests ahead of the organization, lying to employees, misreporting hours worked, Internet abuse, and safety violations.[9]

Technology may have expanded the range and impact of unethical behaviour. For example, anyone who has computer access to data may be able to steal or manipulate the data or shut down the system, even from a remote location. Recently, Target alerted customers that a data breach compromised 40 million credit card numbers. This data breach led to both the CIO and CEO losing their jobs. The cost of dealing with a data breach can be up to $5.4 million per incident.[10] Although some people might not be concerned about these breaches, they can affect how investors, customers, and the general public view a firm. It can be difficult to rebuild trust. The company may also lose some long-term customers.

Nearly every employee at every level faces ethical questions at some time. Some people explain questionable behaviour by saying, "Everybody's doing it." Others act unethically because they feel pressured in their jobs or because they need to meet performance goals. Yet others avoid unethical acts because these acts don't fit with their personal values and morals. We all use different methods to make our ethical choices. The next section focuses on how we develop our personal ethics and morals.

Development of Individual Ethics

An individual's moral and ethical development is the result of many factors. Experiences shape our responses to different situations. Our family, educational, cultural, and religious backgrounds also play a role, as does the environment within the firm. We also have different styles of deciding ethical dilemmas, no matter what our stage of moral development.

This textbook can help you understand and prepare for the ethical dilemmas you may face in your career. Let's take a closer look at the factors that can help you solve ethical questions on the job.

CAREER KICKSTART

How to Avoid Ethical Issues at Work

Creating a Good Ethical Foundation

You might be surprised to discover how easy it is to make an ethical slip at work. If you've mastered the fundamentals of business etiquette, however, you'll have a good ethical foundation for making good decisions in tough situations. Here are some guidelines:

- Stay focused on your business purpose. If you develop a close personal relationship with a client or supplier, you may risk a conflict of interest.

- Don't abuse privileges. It's tempting to use sick days or personal days for mini-vacations, but if your company distinguishes between these breaks, you should too.

- Live your values. Few people are brought up to be untrustworthy. Even if no one knows about it, an unethical choice that betrays your personal values weakens your self-respect and reduces your contribution to the workplace.

- Don't depend on excuses. If you're constantly making excuses for your behaviour, what does that say about your behaviour?

- Monitor your digital reputation. Never post anything online you wouldn't want to see on the news tomorrow.

- Don't steal. Using your work computer for personal tasks like shopping and social networking is just as much theft of company resources as is taking home office supplies.

- Treat others as you would be treated. This rule never fails to point the way to ethical behaviour and decisions you can be proud of.

Sources: Pamela Eyring, "Modern Etiquette: Minding Your Manners in the Workplace," Reuters, accessed January 17, 2014, www.reuters.com; Susan M. Healthfield, "Did You Bring Your Ethics to Work Today?" About.com, accessed January 17, 2014, http://humanresources.about.com; Lydia Ramsey, "The Top Twelve Business Etiquette Tips for Social Media," Business Know How, accessed January 17, 2014, www.businessknowhow.com.

On-the-Job Ethical Dilemmas

In the fast-paced world of business, you will sometimes be asked to consider the ethics of your decisions. These decisions can affect not just your own future but also the futures of your co-workers, your company, and its customers. As we already mentioned, deciding what is right and wrong can be difficult in many business situations. The decision is especially tricky when the needs and concerns of two or more parties conflict. In the recent past, some CEOs (or their companies) who were accused of wrongdoing simply claimed that they had no idea crimes were being committed. Today's top executives make a greater effort to be aware of all activities taking place in their firms.

For example, many clothing retailers donate unworn, unsold garments to charities such as clothing banks. A graduate student discovered that the H&M store on New York's 34th Street was destroying unsold clothing. She tried to speak to store officials and then tried to speak to someone at the company's headquarters in Sweden. Her requests for information and her offer to put H&M in contact with aid organizations went unanswered. She then contacted the *New York Times*. The newspaper published a story about how H&M—among other retailers—was damaging unsold garments before discarding them. The damage was intended to make the clothing unsalable by street vendors or other black-market sellers. The New York City Clothing Bank, founded by the city's mayor during the 1980s, accepts unsold garments and slightly defaces them—not to destroy them, but to protect retailers by negating the garments' street value. When the story was published, H&M promised to stop destroying unsold clothing and instead donate the garments to charity. A company spokesperson in New York declared, "It will not happen again. We are committed 100 percent to make sure this practice is not happening anywhere else, as it is not our standard practice."[11]

On a global level, businesses sometimes refuse to purchase goods or services from a particular country because of civil rights abuses by that country's government. Some of the world's largest and most prestigious jewellers, including Cartier and Tiffany & Co., announced they would not purchase rubies and other gems from Myanmar (formerly Burma). Their boycott is the result of that government's civil rights violations and the severe measures it has taken against protests by students and monks. The United States and the European Union have also agreed to ban the import of gems from Myanmar.[12]

Solving ethical dilemmas is not easy. Often, each possible decision can lead to both good and bad outcomes that must be considered. The ethical issues that face manufacturers who have unsold merchandise are one example of many different types of ethical situations in the workplace. **Figure 2.3** identifies four of the most common ethical challenges that businesspeople face: conflict of interest, honesty and integrity, loyalty versus truth, and whistle-blowing.

FIGURE 2.3 Common Business Ethical Challenges

Conflict of Interest

A **conflict of interest** occurs when a businessperson is faced with a situation where an action that benefits one person or group has the potential to harm another. Conflicts of interest may pose ethical challenges when they involve the businessperson's own interests and the interests of a person or party to whom the businessperson has a duty. For example, lawyers, business consultants, and advertising agencies face a conflict of interest if they represent two competing companies: A strategy that might benefit one client might harm the other client. Similarly, a real estate agent would face an ethical conflict by representing both the buyer and seller in a transaction. Handling the situation responsibly is possible, but is also difficult. A conflict may also exist between someone's personal interests and the interests of an organization or its customers. An offer of gifts or bribes for special treatment can lead to a situation where the buyer may benefit personally, but the company may not.

A conflict of interest may also occur when one person holds two or more similar jobs in two different workplaces. Conflicts of interest can be handled ethically by (1) avoiding them and (2) disclosing them. Some companies have policies against taking on clients who are competitors of existing clients. Most businesses and government agencies have written policies that either prevent employees from accepting gifts or specify a maximum gift value. A member of a board of directors or a committee member might abstain from voting when he or she has a personal interest in the decision. In other situations, people state their potential conflict of interest so that others can decide whether to use another source instead.

conflict of interest a situation in which an employee must choose between a business's welfare and personal gain.

Honesty and Integrity

Employers highly value honesty and integrity. An employee who is honest can be relied on to tell the truth. An employee with **integrity** goes beyond truthfulness. Having integrity means behaving according to one's deeply felt ethical principles in business situations. It includes doing what you say you will do and accepting responsibility for your mistakes. Behaving with honesty and integrity inspires trust. As a result, integrity can help to build long-term relationships with customers, employers, suppliers, and the public. Employees, in turn, want their managers and the company as a whole to treat them honestly and with integrity.

Unfortunately, violations of honesty and integrity are common. Some people misrepresent their academic standing and previous work experience on their résumés or job applications. An ADP survey revealed that one in five Canadians has lied on his or her résumé. Although it may be tempting to

integrity behaving according to one's deeply felt ethical principles in business situations.

Employers and employees value honesty and integrity, but what should happen when employees misuse their Internet privileges for personal purposes?

lie on a résumé in a competitive job market, it shows a lack of honesty and integrity—and eventually the lies will catch up with you. Recently, it was learned that an Osgoode Hall law student, Quami Frederick, had purchased a fake undergraduate degree to gain admission to law school. She also submitted an Osgoode Hall transcript with inflated grades to obtain an articling position at the Bay Street law firm Wildeboer Dellelce, LLP. Frederick now faces a disciplinary hearing that will likely result in her expulsion from Osgoode Hall. The law firm has withdrawn its offer.[13]

Some employees steal from their employers by taking home supplies or products without permission or by carrying out personal business when they are being paid to work. For example, Internet misuse during the workday is increasing. Employees use the Internet during work hours for personal email, shopping, gaming, and visiting bulletin boards and blogs or social networking sites such as Facebook and YouTube. The use of laptops, cellphones, and other wireless devices makes this misconduct easier to hide.[14] The frequency of such activity varies widely. Employers may feel more strongly about taking strong measures on some activities than on others. Most people will agree that Internet misuse is a problem. Some employers have resorted to electronic monitoring and surveillance. These employers have another reason to monitor their employees: complying with the laws regarding the privacy and security of client information.

Loyalty versus Truth

Businesspeople expect their employees to be loyal and to act in the best interests of the company. But when the truth about a company is not favourable, an ethical conflict can arise. Individual employees may need to decide between loyalty to the company and truthfulness in business relationships. People resolve such dilemmas in various ways. Some place the highest value on loyalty, even at the expense of truth. Others avoid volunteering negative information but answer truthfully when asked a direct question. People may emphasize truthfulness and actively disclose negative information, especially when the cost of silence is high, such as when operating a malfunctioning aircraft or selling tainted food.

Whistle-Blowing

When an employee encounters unethical or illegal actions at work, that employee must decide what action to take. This person may conclude that the only solution is to "blow the whistle." **Whistle-blowing** is usually an employee's disclosure to company officials, government authorities, or the media of illegal, immoral, or unethical practices.

Whistle-blowing disclosure to company officials, government authorities, or the media of illegal, immoral, or unethical practices committed by an organization.

For example, in May 2014, Robert Buckingham, a University of Saskatchewan dean, was fired and escorted by police from university grounds after alerting the public to planned university budget cuts (in an initiative known as TransformUS) and expressing his opposition to the cuts. Buckingham indicated that the former university president Ilene Busch-Vishniac "expected her senior leaders to not 'publicly disagree with the process or findings of TransformUS'; she added that if we did our 'tenure would be short.'" In a matter of days the University of Saskatchewan reconsidered its decision to fire Mr. Buckingham and strip him of his tenure. His tenure was reinstated, but he was not allowed to return to his former role of dean. Hundreds of angry students, staff, and alumni staged a protest demanding that the school's administration be held accountable. Brett Fairbairn resigned from his position as provost, and Ilene Busch-Vishniac was fired from her position as president.[15]

Although no specific law protects whistle-blowers in Canada, many Canadian companies, such as Air Canada, have policies to protect whistle-blowers. In 2004, Bill C-25, the Public Servants Disclosure Protection Act, was introduced. This bill was intended to protect people who expose problems in the government's bureaucracy. The government said this act will help ensure "transparency, accountability, financial responsibility and ethical conduct."[16]

Despite these protections, whistle-blowing has its risks. Zues Yaghi from Edmonton blew the whistle on casino video slot machines. He said the machines could be made to pay on demand. Yaghi claimed that the computer program had a "back door" that would allow players to collect jackpots after making a few clicks. Yaghi was sued by the company for $10 million, and a warrant was issued to search Yaghi's home. A few days later, a gag order was issued to prevent him from saying how a player could make the slots pay out. The company offered him $50,000 to remain quiet about the issue, but Yaghi asked for more money.[17]

Obviously, whistle-blowing and other ethical issues are rare in firms that have strong organizational climates of ethical behaviour. The next section examines how a business can develop an environment that discourages unethical behaviour among individuals.

✓ ASSESSMENT CHECK

2.2.1 What is the role of a firm's ethics compliance officer?

2.2.2 What factors influence the ethical environment of a business?

HOW ORGANIZATIONS SHAPE ETHICAL CONDUCT

LO 2.3 Discuss how organizations shape ethical behaviour.

No individual makes decisions in a vacuum. Most organizations have established standards of conduct that strongly influence the choices employees make. Most ethical lapses in business reflect the values in the firms' corporate cultures.

As shown in **Figure 2.4**, a corporate culture that supports business ethics develops on four levels:

1. Ethical awareness
2. Ethical education
3. Ethical action
4. Ethical leadership

If any of these four factors is missing, the ethical climate in an organization will weaken.

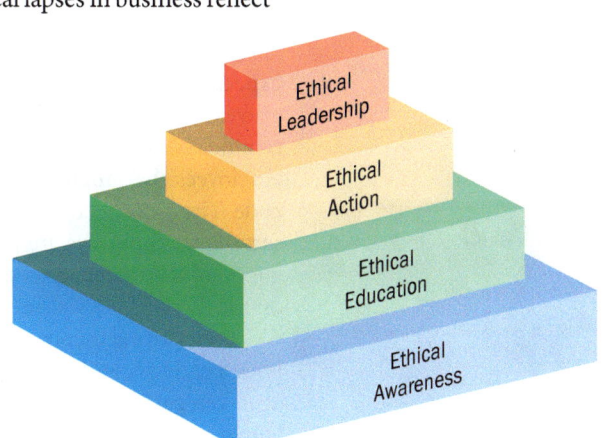

FIGURE 2.4 Structure of an Ethical Environment

Ethical Awareness

The foundation of an ethical climate is ethical awareness. As we have already seen, ethical dilemmas occur frequently in the workplace. Employees need help in identifying ethical problems when they occur. They also need guidance about how the firm expects them to respond.

One way for a firm to provide this support is to develop a **code of conduct**. This formal statement defines how the organization expects its employees to resolve ethical questions. Johnson & Johnson's credo, presented in **Figure 2.1**, is such a code. At the most basic level, a code of conduct may simply be the ground rules for acceptable behaviour, such as the laws and regulations that employees must obey. Other companies use their codes of conduct to identify key corporate values and provide frameworks that guide employees as they resolve moral and ethical dilemmas.

Air Canada is headquartered in Montreal, Quebec, and has offices around the world. Its code of conduct defines the company's values and helps employees to put these values into practice. The code of conduct emphasizes "honesty and integrity" and treating employees with fairness, dignity, and respect. The code applies to "all directors, officers and employees." Portions of the policy even include retirees who have travel pass privileges. All employees at every level are

code of conduct a formal statement that defines how an organization expects its employees to resolve ethical issues.

Air Canada requires all of its directors, officers, and employees, and even some of its retirees, to sign a code of conduct to promote ethical behaviour.

expected to treat fellow employees, suppliers, and customers with dignity and respect. They are also expected to comply with environmental, health, and safety regulations. The code of conduct reminds leaders that their language and behaviour must not even seem to put pressure on their employees that might suggest they should perform a task differently from the standards in the code. The code of conduct also outlines how to report violations to a supervisor or the corporate secretary. Employees are promised confidentiality and non-retaliation for problems reported in good faith. Air Canada requires all employees to sign this code of conduct, which is also posted on the Air Canada website.[18]

Other firms incorporate similar codes in their policy manuals or mission statements; some issue a code of conduct or statement of values in the form of a small card that employees and managers can carry with them. For example, Harley-Davidson has developed a brief code of ethics that employees can apply both at work and in their personal lives. It reads: "Tell the truth, keep your promises, be fair, respect the individual and encourage intellectual curiosity."

Ethical Education

A code of conduct can provide an overall framework, but it does not have a solution for every ethical situation. Some ethical questions have black-and-white answers, but others do not. Businesses must provide the tools employees need to evaluate the options and arrive at suitable decisions.

Many firms have started their own ethics training programs. Other firms have hired organizations such as The Skald Group, based in Hamilton, Ontario, which provides outsourced ethics programs to businesses.[19] Other organizations, such as SAI Global, host employee-reporting services that offer an anonymous hotline and an ethics case management system. SAI Global also helps companies to develop ethics codes and customizes ethics training to each company's needs, including specialized online, interactive training systems.[20]

Many have debated whether ethics can be taught. Ethics training is helpful, though, because employees can practise applying ethical values to sample situations before they face real-world situations. Similar strategies are used in many business schools, where case studies and practical scenarios work best. Walter Pavlo is a convicted white-collar criminal and a former employee at the telecommunications firm MCI. Pavlo once worked with other MCI staff to hide $6 million in offshore accounts. He now speaks at colleges and universities about his experiences, both in the firm and in prison, to warn students of the consequences of cheating.

Ethical Action

Codes of conduct and ethics training help employees recognize and reason through ethical problems. In addition, firms must provide structures and approaches that allow decisions to be turned into ethical actions. Texas Instruments gives its employees a reference card to help them make ethical decisions on the job. The card is the size of a standard business card and lists the following guidelines:

- Is the action legal?
- Does it comply with our values?
- If you do it, will you feel bad?
- How will it look in the newspaper?
- If you know it's wrong, don't do it!
- If you're not sure, ask.
- Keep asking until you get an answer.

Businesses often set goals for the whole business and for individual departments and employees. These goals can affect ethical behaviour. For example, a firm's managers may set unrealistic goals for employee performance. These goals may lead to an increase in cheating, lying, and other misdeeds as employees attempt to protect themselves. In today's Internet economy, a high value is often placed on speed. But valuing speed can lead to a climate where ethical behaviour is challenged. Ethical decisions often require careful and quiet thought, which can be a challenging task in today's fast-paced business world.

Some companies encourage ethical action. These companies provide support for employees facing dilemmas. One common tool is an employee hotline, which is a telephone number that employees can call anonymously for advice or to report unethical behaviour they have seen. As already mentioned, some firms have ethics compliance officers who guide employees through difficult ethical issues.

Ethical Leadership

Executives must not just talk about ethical behaviour—they also need to show it in their actions. Employees need to be personally committed to the company's core values, and they must be willing to base their actions on those values. The recent recession exposed executive-level misdeeds that damaged or even destroyed entire organizations; some people lost their life savings. After hearing of these misdeeds, two students at the Harvard Business School interviewed corporate leaders they regarded as being highly moral. The students concluded that these "ethical mavericks" follow a moral code with three simple characteristics:

1. Use clear, explicit language rather than euphemisms for corrupt behaviour.
2. Encourage behaviour that generates and fosters ethical values.
3. Practise moral absolutism, insisting on doing right even if it proves financially costly.[21]

However, ethical leadership should also go one step further. Each employee at every level should be charged with the responsibility to be an ethical leader. Everyone should be aware of problems and be willing to defend the organization's standards.

Unfortunately, not all organizations can build a solid framework of business ethics. Because the damage from ethical misconduct can powerfully affect a firm's **stakeholders**—customers,

stakeholders customers, investors, employees, and the public who are affected by or have an interest in a company.

ASSESSMENT CHECK

2.3.1 For an employee, when does loyalty conflict with truth?

2.3.2 How does ethical leadership contribute to ethical standards throughout a company?

investors, employees, and the public—businesses are pressured to act in acceptable ways. But when businesses fail, the law must step in to enforce good business practices. Many of the laws that affect specific industries or individuals are described in other chapters in this book. For example, legislation affecting international business operations is discussed in Chapter 4; laws designed to assist small businesses are examined in Chapter 5; laws related to labour unions are described in Chapter 8; legislation related to banking and the securities markets is discussed in Chapters 16 and 17; and finally, for an examination of the legal and governmental forces designed to safeguard society's interests when businesses fail at self-regulation, see Appendix B, "Business Law."

LO 2.4 Describe how businesses can act responsibly to satisfy society.

ACTING RESPONSIBLY TO SATISFY SOCIETY

social responsibility a business's consideration of society's well-being and consumer satisfaction in addition to profits.

A second major issue affecting business is the question of social responsibility. In a general sense, **social responsibility** is management's acceptance of its obligation, when evaluating firm performance, to consider profit to be of equal value to other qualitative indicators, such as employee satisfaction, consumer satisfaction, and societal well-being. Businesses may exercise social responsibility for many reasons: because such behaviour is required by law, because it enhances the company's image, or because management believes it is the ethical course of action. The "Going Green" feature discusses Starbucks's efforts to introduce environmentally sound practices.

Going Green: STARBUCKS INTRODUCES A NEW STORE-DESIGN STRATEGY

In June 2009, the coffee-selling giant Starbucks announced that the company will design new stores and renovate existing stores worldwide with two goals in mind: to reflect the character of the neighbourhood and to reduce the company's environmental impact.

The project is part of Starbucks's efforts to reposition itself. Arthur Rubinfeld, chief creative officer for Starbucks and president of Global Innovation and Evolution Fresh Retail, said, "We recognize the importance of continuously evolving with our customers' interests, lifestyles and values in order to stay relevant over the long term."

The company will make each store unique by employing local artisans and local materials, including recycled and reclaimed items. It has also committed to conserving water and energy, recycling where possible, and using "green" construction methods. Among its goals are the following:

- To use renewable resources for 50 percent of the energy used in its stores
- To make its stores 25 percent more energy efficient to reduce greenhouse gas emissions
- To meet U.S. Green Building Code LEED (Leadership in Energy and Environmental Design) certification standards for all its new stores
- To implement a 100 percent reusable or recyclable cup supply
- To have recycling in stores where it controls waste collection

The company has already met some of these goals. For instance, it reduces its prices by 10 cents for customers who bring in their own travel cup. This reduced the amount of paper the company sends to landfills by 1.4 million pounds in 2013. The company is also replacing incandescent light bulbs with LED bulbs to save energy and expense. Signage will be installed in new and renovated stores to explain their "green" and sustainable features and construction methods.

This new strategy is shaping Starbucks stores in more than 40 countries, including Hong Kong, Saudi Arabia, Spain, and Argentina.

Questions for Critical Thinking

1. How do Starbucks's new plans for its stores reflect its sense of social responsibility?
2. How has Starbucks involved its customers in these efforts?

Sources: Starbucks, "Starbucks Reinvents the Store Experience to Speak to the Heart and Soul of Local Communities," June 25, 2009, accessed January 31, 2012, http://news.starbucks.com; "Make a Difference," Starbucks, accessed January 31, 2012, www.starbucks.com/thebigpicture; Brian Clark Howard, "5 Major Companies Innovate by Going Green," *Daily Green*, November 18, 2009, accessed August 11, 2014, www.thedailygreen.com; Sharon van Schagen, "Starbucks Brews Global Green-Building Plan, Renovates Seattle Shop," *Grist*, June 30, 2009, accessed August 11, 2014, www.thedailygreen.com.

A business is often judged by its interactions with the community. To demonstrate their social responsibility, many corporations highlight their charitable contributions and community service in their annual reports and on their websites. PricewaterhouseCoopers Canada (PwC) has a "Team Volunteering" program that regularly sets up teams to work with charities throughout Canada in day-long projects. Upon request, PwC will send up to 50 PwC employees to volunteer for a day for registered Canadian charities. All PwC employees are also given a paid day off to volunteer for a local charity.[22]

Tim Hortons Camp Day highlights the company's commitment to the community and social responsibility.

The Tim Horton Children's Foundation was established in 1974. It provides camp environments for children from disadvantaged homes. Each year, one day is set aside as Camp Day, when every Tim Hortons store in Canada and the United States donates the value of all that day's coffee sales to the Tim Horton Children's Foundation. In 2013, Camp Day raised more than $11.8 million to fund community outreach programs.[23]

Some firms measure social performance by conducting **social audits**, which are formal procedures that identify and evaluate all company activities related to social issues, such as conservation, employment practices, environmental protection, and philanthropy. The social audit tells management how well the company is performing in these areas. After seeing this information, management may decide to revise its current programs or develop new ones.

social audits formal procedures that identify and evaluate all company activities related to social issues, such as conservation, employment practices, environmental protection, and philanthropy.

Outside groups may do their own evaluations of businesses. Various environmental, religious, and public-interest groups have created standards of corporate performance. Reports on many of these evaluations are available to the general public. The Canadian Business for Social Responsibility (CBSR) organization offers CSR assessments that examine the internal activities of a company and compares them to industry CSR best practices. The CBSR also offers advisory services to assist firms in creating a companywide CSR strategy.

As **Figure 2.5** shows, businesses' social responsibilities can be segmented by their relationships to the general public, customers, employees, investors, and other members of the financial community. Many of these relationships extend beyond national borders.

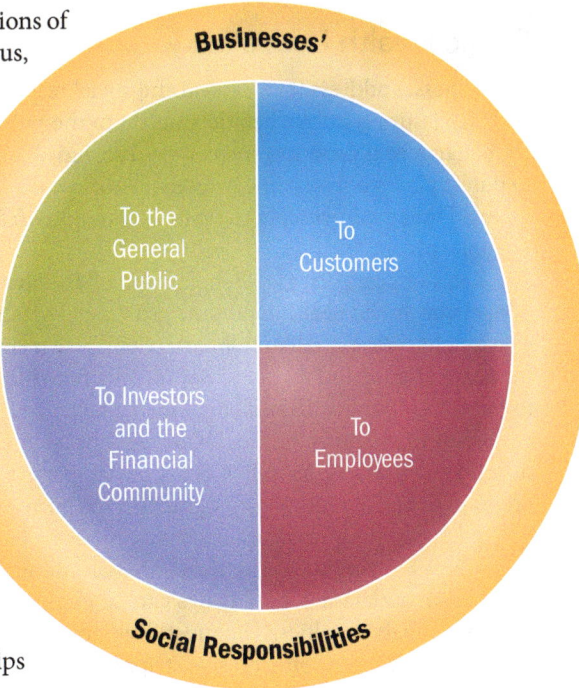

FIGURE 2.5 Businesses' Social Responsibilities

To do its part to aid the general public, Coca-Cola supports programs such as the Boys & Girls Clubs of America's Triple Play program, a healthy lifestyles program whose goal is to promote health and wellness among youth and their families.

Responsibilities to the General Public

The responsibilities of business to the general public include dealing with public health issues, protecting the environment, and developing the quality of the workforce. Many argue that businesses also have responsibilities to support charitable and social causes and organizations that work toward the greater public good. In other words, businesses should give back to the communities in which they earn profits. Such efforts are called *corporate philanthropy*.

Public Health Issues

As businesses address their ethical and social responsibilities to the general public, one of the most complex issues is public health. Central to the public health debate is what businesses should do about dangerous products such as tobacco and alcohol. Many cities have banned smoking not only in public places but also in commercial businesses such as restaurants. A 10-year study in Toronto revealed that cardiovascular hospital admissions dropped by 39 percent after smoking was banned in public places.[24]

Rates of heart disease, diabetes, and obesity have been increasing. These three conditions are now major public health issues. Approximately 1.6 million Canadian children (or 26 percent) are overweight or obese.[25] Three-quarters of obese teenagers will become obese adults who are at risk for heart disease and diabetes. Soft drink companies have been highly criticized for contributing to this and other health related issues. In response, the Coca-Cola Foundation provided a $3 million grant to establish the Coca-Cola Troops for Fitness, a fitness program with classes instructed by military veterans. As well, Coca-Cola supports the Boys & Girls Clubs of America's Triple Play program, a healthy lifestyles program geared to youth and their families.[26]

Substance abuse is another serious public health problem worldwide. Many of the drugs used by athletes are similar to chemicals that are naturally present in the body. As a result, knowing whether an athlete has used drugs can be extremely difficult. Professional players who fail drug tests face tough penalties. The most disappointing drug use scandal involving a Canadian athlete was likely when Ben Johnson was stripped of his gold medal for the 100-metre sprint at the 1988 Olympics for having used the anabolic steroid stanozolol.[27]

SOLVING AN **ETHICAL** CONTROVERSY

To What Extent Should a CEO Be Held Responsible?

In September 2015, Volkswagen was accused of installing software in its vehicles that would "trick" emissions tests. This software would recognize that an emissions test was being performed and put the vehicle in a mode to temporarily reduce the emissions for the duration of the test. After the test was completed, the emissions would return to as high as 40 times the legal limit. Engineers later admitted to installing this software for as far back as seven years in as many as 11 million cars. The scandal led to Volkswagen shares dropping by 40 percent and expected costs of over 39 billion euros in fines and recalls. CEO Martin Winterkorn resigned shortly after the scandal started.

Should CEOs be replaced for scandals such as the one at Volkswagen in 2015?

PRO

1. Holding the CEO responsible demonstrates to the public that the head of the company is willing to accept responsibility for the actions of all of the company's employees.
2. Current and prospective customers may renew their trust in the company if they feel that someone at a high level is held accountable and that significant measures have been taken to "repair" the problem.

CON

1. Holding the CEO responsible punishes the CEO for something he or she may not have been aware of, as the problem may not have made its way all the way up the corporate ladder.
2. Replacing the CEO creates a clear admission of guilt, which could cause irreparable damage to the company and its brand.

Summary

While in this case the CEO voluntarily stepped down from his position, a company forcing the replacement of a CEO would draw further attention to the situation and portray an admission of guilt. In the case of Volkswagen, several jobs were put at risk since one in seven jobs in Germany are linked to the auto sector, as is 14 percent of the country's GDP. On the other hand, not holding the CEO responsible could have been perceived as the company as a whole not taking responsibility for the impact of its employees' actions.

Sources: *CBC News*, "Volkswagen Flouting Emissions Rules for 7 Years: Report," October 5, 2015, www.cbc.ca/news/business/volkswagen-flouting-emissions-rules-for-7-years-report-1.3257254; *CTV News*, "Costs from Emissions Scandal Piling up for Volkswagen," October 6, 2015, www.ctvnews.ca/autos/costs-from-emissions-scandal-piling-up-for-volkswagen-1.2596840; Kritika Sethi, "Volkswagen Diesel Scandal: Engineers Reportedly Admit to Installing Software," *Car and Bike*, October 5, 2015, http://auto.ndtv.com/news/volkswagen-diesel-scandal-engineers-reportedly-admit-to-installing-software-1226257; Thomson Reuters, "Volkswagen CEO Matthias Mueller Warns of 'Massive' Cost Cutting," *CBC News*, October 6, 2015, www.cbc.ca/news/business/volkswagen-ceo-matthias-mueller-warns-of-massive-cost-cutting-1.3258438; Bronte Lord, "3 Things You Need to Know about the Volkswagen Scandal," *CNN Money*, http://money.cnn.com/video/news/2015/09/22/volkswagen-emissions-cheating-scandal-explained.cnnmoney?iid=EL; Kalyeena Makortoff, "What You Need to Know about the Volkswagen Scandal," *CNBC*, September 22, 2015, www.cnbc.com/2015/09/22/what-you-need-to-know-about-the-volkswagen-scandal.html; "Volkswagen Hit by Cheating Allegations," *CNN Money*, http://money.cnn.com/video/news/2015/09/21/volkswagen-cheating-allegations.cnnmoney.

Protecting the Environment

Businesses consume huge amounts of energy, which increases the use of fossil fuels such as coal and oil for energy production. This activity introduces carbon dioxide and sulphur into Earth's atmosphere. Meanwhile, the sulphur from fossil fuels combines with water vapour in the air to form sulphuric acid. The acid rain that results can travel across continents, killing fish and trees and polluting groundwater. Although acid rain has been tracked for many decades, companies are still being identified and punished for their violations. Mount Polley Mining Corporation currently faces fines of up to $1 million for mistakes leading to the breach of a dam in British Columbia that resulted in the release of 4.5 million cubic metres of metals-laden fine sand that contaminated several lakes, creeks, and rivers in the Cariboo region. This dumping took place on the same day that Ottawa promised to improve environmental monitoring of the Canadian oil sands.[28] In another example of environmental violation, automaker Volkswagen admitted to installing software that would "trick" emissions tests in some of its diesel vehicles. While the company faces potentially billions of dollars in fines and lawsuits, the more immediate fallout from the scandal was the suspension of senior managers and the resignation of its CEO (see "Solving an Ethical Controversy").

Other production and manufacturing methods leave behind large quantities of waste materials. These materials can further pollute the environment and fill already bulging landfills. Some products are difficult to reuse or recycle, particularly electronics that contain toxins such as lead and mercury. Few manufacturers are equipped to deal with recycled materials; some refurbish products and sell them abroad—where they are less likely to be recycled. Hewlett-Packard, however, is making its scanners with a combination of new and recycled plastics. Lead, mercury, and cadmium will soon be banned from new equipment manufactured in Europe. As stricter laws on electronics recycling are passed, many manufacturers and retailers are offering take-back, mail-in, and trade-in programs for discarded electronic equipment. For example, many Best Buy stores now accept televisions, DVD players, computer monitors, cellphones, and other electronic devices. The stores charge a small fee for televisions 81 centimetres and under, CRTs (cathode ray tubes, which are now obsolete), monitors, and laptops, but will give customers a gift card in an equal amount.[29]

Recycling can help companies do their part to protect the environment. Best Buy stores will take your old TVs, DVD players, computers, cellphones, and other electronic devices to avoid having them end up in landfills.

For many managers, minimizing pollution and other environmental damage caused by their products or their operating processes is an important economic, legal, and social issue. When General Motors unveiled the Chevrolet Volt, the new car instantly became more popular than conventional hybrids that use a combination of electricity and gasoline. The Volt is entirely electric. After its battery runs down, a gasoline engine powers an onboard generator that recharges the battery. In 2014, Elon Musk, CEO of Tesla Motors, announced that "Tesla will not initiate patent lawsuits against anyone who, in good faith, wants to use our technology." Tesla Motors wants to accelerate the advent of sustainable technology. By sharing their technology with the world in an open-source fashion, the economy can move toward more environmentally friendly modes of transportation that use renewable energy sources. BMW has also entered the mix of electric car manufacturers. The BMW i3 was created as an emissions-free car for city driving that is designed in an environmentally sustainable manner.[31]

Canadian Tire demonstrates its commitment to preserving the environment through its "Take Back the Light" program. Consumers can take their old CFLs and fluorescent tube light bulbs to Canadian Tire for safe disposal.[30]

Despite difficulties, companies find they can be environmentally friendly and profitable too. Another solution to the problems of pollutants is **recycling**—reprocessing used materials for reuse. Recycling can sometimes provide much of the raw material that manufacturers need, thereby conserving the world's natural resources and reducing the amount of waste sent to landfills.

According to Statistics Canada, the diversion of discarded electronic items away from landfill sites has increased by 115 percent in two years.[32] Manufacturers and federal agencies are struggling to devise a workable system to further manage the problem of electronic waste. In some provinces, consumers pay a surcharge on certain electronics purchases, such as computers, monitors, fax machines, and televisions. In Ontario, this surcharge is part of the Waste Electrical and Electronic Equipment (WEEE) Program.[33] In the meantime, Best Buy, Staples, and other retailers accept all

recycling reprocessing used materials for reuse.

HIT & MISS

Pacific Biodiesel Recycles Oil from French Fries to Fuel

In 1980, Robert King founded King Diesel on the island of Maui in Hawaii. The company used conventional diesel fuel to run the generators at the Central Maui Landfill. In 1995, King became concerned about the large amounts of used cooking oil being dumped. He contacted Daryl Reece at the University of Idaho. Reece helped develop a process that successfully converted used restaurant oils into biodiesel fuel. Together, King and Reece founded Pacific Biodiesel. This company uses biodiesel to run the generators at the landfill in one of America's first commercially viable, community-based biodiesel plants. Today, Pacific Biodiesel and its associated companies produce and sell biodiesel fuel. They also design, build, and support biodiesel plants throughout the United States.

Biodiesel fuel is biodegradable and nontoxic and can be used in any diesel engine. This fuel is produced from renewable resources such as used cooking oil and soybean oil. If not converted to fuel, these oils would be dumped in landfills or down drains. Biodiesel significantly reduces many pollutants and reduces dependence on foreign oil.

On Maui, restaurants pay haulers to take their used cooking oil to the landfill. The haulers pay the county of Oahu for the right to dump garbage at waste facilities. Pacific Biodiesel's facility at the landfill is rent free. The haulers' fees cover most of the county's payment to Pacific Biodiesel for processing the waste. Shipping this waste off the island would be much more expensive, while recycling the oil prolongs the useful life of the landfills and guarantees a local source of energy. On Maui alone, Pacific Biodiesel recycles about 757,000 litres of oil and grease each year.

King says, "We definitely took a leap of faith, but . . . we wanted to do more . . . something to contribute to society . . . [I]t is important to do . . . something that brings you happiness—because the feeling you get by 'doing the right thing' never disappears."

Canadian Pacific and Natural Resources Canada have recently partnered in a pilot project to test the effectiveness of biodiesel in Canada's cold weather regions. So far, these tests have indicated that biodiesel could work effectively despite Canada's colder climate.

Questions for Critical Thinking

1. How might Pacific Biodiesel spread the message that recycling is not only good for the environment, but also good business? How might it reach out to other industries?

2. How does Pacific Biodiesel fulfill its responsibilities to the general public?

3. Would Canadian Pacific likely be as successful as Pacific Biodiesel in making a public impact, given that a U.S. competitor has already established the technology?

Sources: Pacific Biodiesel, accessed February 2010, http://biodiesel.com/; U.S. Environmental Protection Agency, "Food to Fuel: Pacific Biodiesel, Inc.," accessed February 2010, http://www.epa.gov/; Deidre Tegarden, "Pacific Biodiesel," Maui Weekly, November 26, 2009; Canadian Pacific, "Cold Weather Biofuel Testing," accessed March 2, 2012, http://www.cpr.ca/en/in-your-community/environment/Pages/cold-weather-biodiesel-testing.aspx.

---

gadgets for recycling, no matter where they were purchased. Manufacturers Hewlett-Packard and Dell have agreed not to send waste materials overseas. The "Hit & Miss" feature describes a company that puts a creative twist on recycling: Pacific Biodiesel turns used restaurant oil and grease into clean, biodegradable biodiesel fuel.

Many consumers like to support environmentally conscious businesses. To target these customers, companies often use **green marketing**, a marketing strategy that promotes environmentally safe products and production methods. But a business cannot simply claim that its goods or services are environmentally friendly. The Competition Bureau has guidelines for environmental claims. For example, a firm must be able to prove that any environmental claim can be supported by reliable scientific evidence. In addition, as shown in **Table 2.1**, the Competition Bureau states how various environmental terms can be used in advertising and marketing.[34]

Many firms focus on other environmental issues, such as finding renewable sources of clean energy and developing **sustainable** agriculture. Vinod Khosla, founder of Sun Microsystems, is working with a group of high-powered entrepreneurs and investors in the Silicon Valley. They hope to develop a new generation of energy.[35] They're not alone. Many entrepreneurs, large energy firms, and small engineering companies are developing solar energy, geothermal energy, biodiesel, and wind power. As we saw in the "Hit & Miss" feature, Pacific Biodiesel started with one plant and now has branches across the United States. Canadian Pacific is likely to match Pacific Biodiesel's growth in Canada, especially with the support of the Canadian government which has spent nearly $5 billion on the ecoENERGY Innovation Initiative that encourages Canadians and Canadian companies to use and develop cleaner technologies.[36]

green marketing a marketing strategy that promotes environmentally safe products and production methods.

sustainable the capacity to endure in ecology.

Table 2.1 Competition Bureau's Guidelines for Environmental Claims in Green Marketing

IF A COMPANY SAYS A PRODUCT IS...	THE PRODUCT OR PACKAGE MUST...
Degradable	be photodegradable or biodegradable within a given period of time under normal disposal conditions for that type of product or package.
Compostable	biodegrade, generating a relatively homogeneous and stable humus-like substance.
Recyclable	be able to be processed and returned to use in the form of raw materials or products.
Refillable	to be refillable with the same or similar product.

Source: Competition Bureau, *Environmental Claims: A Guide for Industry and Advisors,* June 2008, accessed August 12, 2014, http://www.competitionbureau.gc.ca/eic/site/cb-bc.nsf/eng/02701.html#s10_2.

As another example, the Tim Hortons Coffee Partnership works with the Hanns R. Neumann Stiftung Foundation to contribute to the sustainability of the coffee sector in Guatemala, Colombia, Brazil, Honduras, and El Salvador by working with both the private sector (primarily coffee roasters) and the public sector (donors).[37]

Developing the Quality of the Workforce

In the past, a nation's wealth was often based on its money, production equipment, and natural resources. But a country's true wealth is in its people. An educated, skilled workforce provides the know-how needed to develop new technology, improve productivity, and compete in the global marketplace. To remain competitive, Canadian businesses must take more responsibility for enhancing the quality of its workforce, including encouraging diversity of all kinds.

In developed economies like Canada, many new jobs require a university or college education. Demand is high for workers with advanced skills. That means the difference between the highest-paid and lowest-paid workers is increasing. Education plays an important role in earnings, despite success stories of those who dropped out of college or high school to start a business. Workers with education beyond an undergraduate degree earn an average of $1,200 a week, whereas those with some high school but no diploma earn about $750. Businesses must encourage students to stay in school, continue their education, and sharpen their skills. Tim Hortons provides 220 post-secondary scholarships each year to students who "believe in giving back to the community (through volunteer work)." These scholarships are valued at $1,000 each and are awarded to students in Canada and the United States.[38]

Organizations also face responsibilities for helping women, members of various cultural groups, and those who are physically challenged to contribute fully to the economy. Failure to do so is not only a waste of more than half the nation's workforce, but may be harmful to a firm's public image. Some socially responsible firms also encourage diversity in their business suppliers. COSTI Immigrant Services, based in Toronto, has set up programs to assist immigrant women move into strong roles in the workforce, helping them overcome economic challenges and cultural barriers. COSTI has been helping new immigrants for over 50 years.[39]

The Coca-Cola Company is committed to developing employee diversity. It strives to create an inclusive atmosphere, offers diversity training for employees and managers, and encourages regular dialogue among colleagues, suppliers, customers, and stakeholders. "By building an inclusive workplace environment, The Coca-Cola Company seeks to leverage its worldwide team, which is rich in diverse people, talent, and ideas" according to the company's website.[40] For any global organization to function competitively, diversity is vital.

Corporate Philanthropy

As noted in Chapter 1, not-for-profit organizations play an important role in society by serving the public good. They provide the human resources that enhance the quality of life in communities around the world. To fulfill this mission, many not-for-profit organizations rely on financial donations from the business community. Firms donate billions of dollars each year to not-for-profit organizations. This **corporate philanthropy** includes cash contributions, donations of equipment and products, and supporting the volunteer efforts of company employees. Recipients include cultural organizations, adopt-a-school programs, community development agencies, and housing and job training programs.

corporate philanthropy an organization's contribution to the communities where it earns profits.

Corporate philanthropy can have many positive benefits beyond the "feel-good" rewards of giving. Corporate philanthropy can lead to higher employee morale, enhanced company image, and improved customer relationships. Each year, CIBC and other Canadian companies sponsor the CIBC Run for the Cure, Canada's largest single-day, volunteer-led fundraising event specifically for breast cancer research, education, and awareness. This event not only raises funds for an important cause, but also increases the corporate profiles of CIBC and the other corporate sponsors.[41]

Companies often want to tie their marketing efforts to their charitable giving. For example, many firms contribute to the Olympics; they then create advertising that features the company's sponsorship. This type of advertising is known as *cause-related marketing*. In a recent survey, nearly nine out of ten young people said they believed companies had a duty to support social causes. Nearly seven in eight said they would switch brands to reward a company that supported social causes. Consumers will often pay more for a product if they know the proceeds are going to a good cause. KitchenAid Canada started a "Cook for the Cure" campaign, where it donates $75 of the $470 selling price of its pink line of stand mixers and $50 for every "Cook for the Cure" party to the Canadian Breast Cancer Foundation.[42]

CIBC has taken the lead in the CIBC Run for the Cure, which encourages many other businesses to also participate.

Another form of corporate philanthropy is volunteerism. Thousands of businesses encourage their employees to contribute their time to such projects as Habitat for Humanity, the Red Cross, and the Humane Society. These programs make tangible contributions to the well-being of other citizens while also creating public support and goodwill for the companies and their employees. Sometimes the volunteer work takes place when employees are off the job. Other times firms allow their employees to volunteer during regular working hours. Volunteers with special skills are always needed. After the earthquake in Haiti in 2010, the pilots' union at UPS volunteered to transport supplies and personnel as part of the relief effort.[43]

Responsibilities to Customers

Businesspeople share a social and ethical responsibility to treat their customers fairly and to act in a way that does not cause harm. **Consumerism** is the public demand that a business consider the wants and needs of its customers when making decisions. Consumerism has gained wide acceptance. It is based on the belief that consumers have certain rights. In 1962, U.S. President John F.

Consumerism public demand that a business consider the wants and needs of its customers when making decisions.

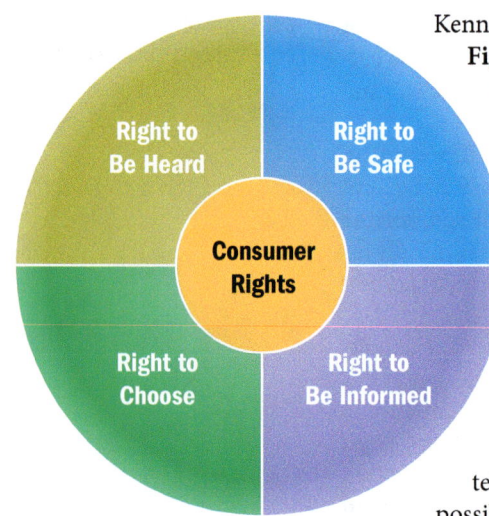

FIGURE 2.6 Commonly Referred-to Consumer Rights

product liability the responsibility of manufacturers for injuries and damages caused by their products.

Kennedy extolled four basic consumer rights, later called the Consumer Bill of Rights. **Figure 2.6** summarizes these consumer rights. The Consumers' Association of Canada (CAC) was formed in 1947. It helps educate and inform consumers on issues related to buying products and services. It also helps people solve consumer problems by working with government and industry.[44]

The Right to Be Safe

Today's businesspeople have moral and legal obligations to ensure their products are safe to use. Consumers should know that the products they purchase will not cause injuries in normal use. **Product liability** refers to the responsibility of manufacturers for injuries and damages caused by their products. Items that lead to injuries, either directly or indirectly, can have lasting consequences for their manufacturers.

Many companies test their products thoroughly to avoid safety problems. Still, testing cannot check for every possible problem. Companies must try to think of all possible problems and warn consumers of any potential dangers. When a product poses a threat to customer safety, a responsible manufacturer responds quickly. The manufacturer can either correct the problem or recall the dangerous product. We often take for granted that our food supply is safe. But contamination can leak in, causing illness or even death. Maple Leaf Foods had a listeria outbreak at one of its Toronto plants. The company recalled 220 packaged meats in August 2008. Maple Leaf had direct costs of more than $20 million, which did not include the loss of future customer goodwill. At least 42 cases of listeriosis were confirmed, and at least 15 deaths were blamed on the outbreak, resulting in a class action lawsuit settlement of between $25 million and $27 million.[45]

The Right to Be Informed

Consumers should be able to get enough education and product information to make responsible buying decisions. Companies can easily forget the consumer's right to be fully informed while they are busy promoting and selling their goods and services. The Competition Act contains provisions against false or misleading representations and deceptive marketing as well as rules and regulations that lead to advertising truthfulness. These rules keep businesses from making unproven claims about how its products perform or why its products are superior. The act also requires businesses to avoid misleading consumers. Businesses that don't follow these rules may face questions from the Competition Bureau and consumer protection organizations. Persons who are guilty can face criminal penalties of up to 14 years in prison and fines, or both. On a civil level, if a person is found to be liable the fine could be up to $1 million or $15 million for corporations. For instance, Rogers Communications Inc. aired ads that claimed its new discount text-and-talk service Chatr had fewer dropped calls than its competitors. In 2010, the Competition Bureau started an investigation against Rogers resulting in a $500,000 fine, significantly less than the $10 million the Competition Bureau was seeking. The Competition Bureau said that Rogers's claims were misleading according to the Competition Act. "We take misleading advertising very seriously," says Melanie Aitken, commissioner of competition. "Consumers deserve accurate information when making purchasing decisions and need to have confidence they are not being misled by false advertising campaigns." Rogers also aired ads that claimed it had Canada's most reliable network. Competitor TELUS took Rogers to court, and Rogers pulled the ads.[46]

Health Canada supports the Food and Drugs Act. This act defines the standards for safety and advertising to be followed by makers of drugs, cosmetics, and therapeutic devices. The act also requires that all ingredients be listed on product labels so consumers are fully informed.[47]

A business's responsibility to maintain the consumer's right to be informed goes beyond avoiding advertising that misleads. All communications with customers—from salespeople's comments to warranties and invoices—must be checked so that they clearly and accurately inform customers. The labels of most packaged goods, personal computers, and other products include toll-free customer service telephone numbers so that consumers can get answers to their questions.

The Right to Choose

Consumers should have the right to choose the goods and services they need and the goods they want to purchase. Socially responsible firms try to preserve this right, even if it means they need to reduce their own sales and profits. Brand-name drug makers have taken a defensive stand in an issue being discussed by provincial governments, insurance companies, consumer groups, unions, and major employers such as General Motors. These groups want to force down the rising price of prescription drugs. They believe that the government should ensure that consumers have the right and the opportunity to buy cheaper generic brands of drugs. In 2011, however, Ontario enacted regulations stopping pharmacies such as Shoppers Drug Mart and Rexall from selling their lower-priced generic alternatives to brand-name drugs. The reason? Experts claimed these savings were unlikely to be passed on to consumers.[48]

The Right to Be Heard

Consumers should be able to express their valid complaints to the appropriate people. Many companies expend much effort to ensure that consumers' complaints receive a full hearing. The auction website eBay assists buyers and sellers who believe they were unfairly treated in transactions that occur through the site. It uses a 200-employee team to work with eBay users and law enforcement agencies to fight against fraud. The company has strict guidelines for buyers and sellers. It also has rules about leaving feedback about a buyer or seller. For example, sellers must only sell items that are included on a list of acceptable goods for sale. They cannot offer such items as alcohol, pornography, drugs, counterfeit currency, or artifacts from cave formations or graves. The protection of copyright is also an important part of eBay's policy.[49]

Responsibilities to Employees

Companies that can attract skilled and knowledgeable employees are better able to meet the challenges of competing globally. In return, businesses have wide-ranging responsibilities to their employees, both here and abroad. These responsibilities include workplace safety, quality-of-life issues, ensuring equal opportunity on the job, avoiding age discrimination, and preventing sexual harassment and sexism.

Workplace Safety

The safety and health of workers on the job is an important business responsibility. The Canadian Centre for Occupational Health and Safety (CCOHS) promotes workplace health and safety. Workers' compensation programs are managed mostly at the provincial level by organizations such as the Workplace Safety and Insurance Board in Ontario, the Workers' Compensation Board of Nova Scotia, and the Workers' Compensation Board of Alberta. These organizations are responsible for setting workplace safety and health standards. These standards range from broad guidelines on storing hazardous materials to specific standards for worker safety in industries such as construction, manufacturing, and mining. These organizations track and investigate workplace accidents and pay claims to employees who are injured on the job.

According to a 2010 research study, 1 in every 53 employed workers each year is injured and receives workers' compensation.[50] Many people die every year in Canada as a result of work-related injuries. Most of these fatalities occur because of unsafe equipment, inadequate safety training, and dangerous work that is illegal or inappropriate for youth. Provincial workers' compensation boards, labour ministries, and the CCOHS are working to educate employers and young workers about safety, health, and a positive work environment.

Workplace safety is an important business responsibility. Workers are required to wear safety equipment, such as hard hats, goggles, and reflective wear, when in potentially dangerous areas.

Quality-of-Life Issues

Balancing work and family is becoming harder for many employees. They work long hours then go home to face childcare tasks, caring for their elderly parents, and solving other family crises. A *sandwich generation* of households has arisen. This term refers to people caring for two generations—their children and their aging parents. The population is growing older, and more and more Canadians provide some type of care to a relative or friend aged 50 or older. At the same time, most mothers spend more time working outside the home. That means they have fewer hours to spend with their family.

The employees who juggle work with life's other demands aren't just working mothers. Childless couples, single people, and men all say they are frustrated with having to balance work with family and personal needs. Some employers are trying to help their employees find a work–life balance. They do this by offering flexible work schedules so that parents can do their jobs *and* meet the needs of their children (or aging parents). Each year, the editors of *Canada's Top 100 Employers* organize a competition called Canada's Top Family-Friendly Employers. Employers who make the top 100 have made a big commitment to help their employees balance work and family commitments. Some of the employers who made this list in 2014 were the University of Toronto, Manitoba Hydro, and CIBC.[51]

Increasingly, women are starting their own businesses so they can set their own hours and goals. The "Hit & Miss" feature describes one woman who started her own business so she could provide her ailing son with the care he needed.

Some companies have come up with truly innovative ways to deal with work schedules, including paid time off for vacation or illness. At some of its locations, IBM has done away with vacation time altogether—instead, the focus is on results. Employees have an informal agreement with their supervisors about when they will be out of the office. This time away is based on their ability to complete their work on schedule. The number of days they take off is not tracked; instead,

fair trade a market-based approach of paying higher prices to producers for goods exported from developing countries to developed countries in an effort to promote sustainability and to ensure the people in developing countries receive better trading conditions.

HIT & MISS

Balancing Life and Work with a Cup of Tea

In 2000, Zhena Muzyka, a 25-year-old single mother, had an infant son who needed kidney surgery. Muzyka had no health insurance and only a few dollars in the bank. As a young girl, she had watched her Rom (gypsy) grandmother tend a huge garden and blend teas. Muzyka had always been interested in herbal medicine, so she borrowed money from her parents and her brother and started Zhena's Gypsy Tea. She started selling tea from a cart in a friend's antique store. At first, she worked with her son, Sage, in a baby carrier at her side. When her teas became popular—and Sage outgrew the carrier—she knew she had reached a turning point.

Muzyka searched for new sources and started blending her own loose-leaf teas. She added essential oils for their medicinal value. She learned that none of the teas she was buying was organic or **fair trade**. She made the change to fair trade teas after learning that infant mortality rates among tea pickers on non-fair trade farms can reach 70 percent. Fair trade tea workers have guaranteed healthcare, clean water, education, and maternity leave and childcare.

As Zhena's Gypsy Tea has grown and diversified, Muzyka has searched for new ways to put her values into practice. Her Pink Tea for Women's Health is a partner of the Breast Cancer Research Foundation. The company now uses corn silk for its teabags. It buys wind credits, even though it lowers profits. Muzyka says, "[Zhena's Gypsy Tea] is the most 'worth it' thing I've ever done. Knowing that we're sincerely making a difference for people and helping them out of poverty—while providing a delicious cup of tea for consumers here—is pretty satisfying."

And Sage? After three operations, he had a clean bill of health in 2007.

Questions for Critical Thinking

1. How did Zhena Muzyka translate her life experiences into her company's ethics culture?

2. Do you have an idea for starting your own business? If so, brainstorm some ideas for balancing your life and values with your work.

3. What key provincial or federal legislation would you need to be aware of, especially if your business was to grow and employ a significant number of staff members?

Sources: Zhena's Gypsy Tea, www.zhenas.com, accessed February 2010; Eve Gumpel, "Gypsy Tea Steeped in Health and Fun," *Women Entrepreneur.com*, January 24, 2010, www.womenentrepreneur.com; "Oh, That's So Yesterday: A California Tea Company Gets a Brand Makeover," *Inc.*, December 2009/January 2010.

vacation time is considered open ended. But the catch is, the work needs to be done. With some surprises, the firm found that employees put in just as many hours, if not more hours, under the new program. According to an IBM representative, "there is no policing, and employees are empowered to take vacation when they want."[52]

Ensuring Equal Opportunity on the Job

Businesspeople face many challenges when managing an increasingly diverse workforce in the twenty-first century. Technological advances are expanding the ways people with physical disabilities can contribute in the workplace. Businesses also need to find ways to responsibly recruit and manage older workers and workers with varying lifestyles. In 1982, Lotus Development (later Lotus Software) was the first major company to offer full benefits to its employees' partners, regardless of sexual orientation. This means that the company offers such benefits as health insurance to its employees' unmarried domestic partners if it also offers the same benefits to its employees' married spouses. Companies that now offer these gender-neutral benefits include Avon Products, Costco Wholesale, Disney, General Mills, and Mattel. Companies such as WestJet and BlackBerry advertise that their hiring practices do not discriminate in terms of sexual orientation, colour, race, religion, and so on.[53]

The Canadian Charter of Rights and Freedoms is an all-encompassing act that addresses **discrimination** in Canada. Section 15 states "Every individual is equal before and under the law and has the right to the equal protection and equal benefit of the law without discrimination and, in particular, without discrimination based on race, national or ethnic origin, colour, religion, sex, age, or mental or physical disability." **Table 2.2** describes other specific types of equal opportunity employee protections.[54]

discrimination biased treatment toward a job candidate or employee.

Table 2.2 Protections Designed to Ensure Equal Opportunity

FOCUS	LAW	KEY PROVISIONS
Equal rights	Canadian Charter of Rights and Freedoms, 1982	Every individual is equal before and under the law and has the right to the equal protection and equal benefit of the law without discrimination and, in particular, without discrimination based on race, national or ethnic origin, colour, religion, sex, age, or mental or physical disability.
Physical and mental disabilities	Canadian Human Rights Act and provincial human rights codes	Forbids age discrimination in employment—with exceptions in some cases regarding mandatory retirement and bona fide occupational requirements. Requires employers to make reasonable accommodations for employees with new or pre-existing mental or physical disabilities.
Equal pay for equal work	Provincial employment standards acts	Ensures equal pay for equal work when work is substantially the same, requires the same effort, and is performed under the same working conditions at the same establishment.
Physical and mental disabilities	Canadian Disability Vocational Rehabilitation Program and provincial vocational rehabilitation acts	Provides work and personal adjustment training and support for people with disabilities who seek gainful employment.
Pregnancy and parental leave	Provincial labour ministries	Employers cannot penalize employees for taking pregnancy or parental leave. Employees who take such leaves have the right to earn credit toward their length of service. They typically must be returned to their job after their pregnancy or parental leave is over.
Family medical leave	Provincial labour ministries	Allows an employee to take up to 8 weeks of unpaid leave in a 26-week period to care for a seriously ill family member.
Reservists	Provincial labour ministries	Employees who are reservists and deployed on an operation are to be granted unpaid leave without benefits. While on leave, their seniority and length of service will accumulate.

Employment Equity Act (EEA) an act created (1) to increase job opportunities for women and members of minority groups and (2) to help end discrimination based on race, colour, religion, disability, gender, or national origin.

The **Employment Equity Act (EEA)** was created for two reasons: to increase job opportunities for women and members of minority groups and to help end discrimination in any personnel action that is based on race, colour, religion, disability, gender, or national origin. To enforce fair-employment laws, this act is overseen by the Canadian Human Rights Commission, which investigates charges of discrimination and harassment. The EEA can also help employers set up programs to increase job opportunities for women, members of minority groups, people with disabilities, and people in other protected categories.

Age Discrimination

The average age of Canadian workers is steadily rising. In a few years, more than half the workforce will be aged 40 or older. Some employers find it less expensive to hire and retain younger workers. These younger employees generally have lower medical bills and typically receive lower salaries and benefits packages. But many older workers have training and skills that younger workers lack. The Canadian Human Rights Act (CHRA) prohibits age discrimination except in very specific cases.

In 2008, Kim Ouwroulis, aged 44, was an exotic dancer at the New Locomotion club in Mississauga, Ontario. She filed a complaint with the Ontario Human Rights Commission, claiming she was fired because of her age. These types of cases require the employer to prove that "sex appeal is the essence of the job," says Denise Reaume, a University of Toronto professor who specializes in discrimination law. "This is tricky because sexual response is as variable as human beings are."[55]

Legal issues aside, employers should consider not only the experience that older workers bring to the workplace but also their enthusiasm. "Job satisfaction is especially high among those 65 and over because most people working at that age are not forced to still work, due to financial reasons, but choose to do so because they like their jobs," says the leader of a recent study. Nearly 75 percent of people over age 65 who were interviewed said they were very happy with their jobs.[56]

In all cases, employers need to plan ahead for the aging of the workforce. Such planning includes finding ways to retain accumulated business wisdom, preparing for the demand for health services, and being ready for growth in the industries that serve older adults. The number of people aged 55 to 64 has increased by almost 30 percent in the past few years. It is expected that the retirement of the baby boomers will lead to an $11,500 per capita loss of productivity.[57] These numbers show a coming shift in the workforce and in the goods and services needed.

Employers are responsible for avoiding age discrimination in the workplace. As the average age of workers rises, employers will benefit from the older generation's knowledge.

Sexual Harassment and Sexism

Every employer has a responsibility to ensure that all workers are treated fairly and are safe from sexual harassment. **Sexual harassment** refers to unwelcome and inappropriate actions of a sexual nature. It is a form of sex discrimination that violates the CHRA, which gives both men and women the right to file lawsuits for intentional sexual harassment. Thousands of sexual harassment complaints are filed each year, and many complaints are filed by men. Thousands of other cases are either handled internally by companies or never reported.

The workplace has two types of sexual harassment. The first type occurs when an employee is pressured to go along with unwelcome advances and requests for sexual favours in return for job security, promotions, and raises. The second type results from a hostile work environment, where an employee feels hassled or degraded because of unwelcome flirting, lewd comments, or obscene jokes. The courts have ruled that allowing sexually oriented materials in the workplace can create a hostile atmosphere that interferes with an employee's ability to work. Employers are also legally responsible to protect employees from sexual harassment by customers and clients. The Canadian Human Rights Commission's website helps employers and employees by listing the criteria for identifying sexual harassment and how it should be handled in the workplace.

Firms should prevent sexual harassment for ethical and legal reasons. But did you know that sexual harassment can also be costly? The cost in settlements or fines can be huge. It makes good business sense for firms to prevent this kind of behaviour. Many firms have set up policies and employee education programs aimed at preventing such problems. An effective harassment prevention program should include the following:

- A specific policy statement prohibiting sexual harassment
- A complaint procedure for employees to follow
- A work atmosphere that encourages sexually harassed staffers to come forward
- A commitment to investigate and resolve complaints quickly and to take disciplinary action against harassers

These components need to be supported by top management; otherwise, sexual harassment is difficult to get rid of.

Sexual harassment is often part of the broader problem of **sexism**—discrimination against members of either sex, but usually against women. One important sexism issue is equal pay for equal work.

On average, a Canadian woman earns 74 percent of what a man earns.[58] The difference can't be explained by differences in education, occupation, work hours, or other factors. The only explanation seems to be being female.[59] In some extreme cases, differences in pay and advancement can lead to sex discrimination suits. These suits, like sexual harassment suits, can be costly and time consuming to settle. As in all business practices, it is better to act legally and ethically in the first place.

Sexual harassment unwelcome and inappropriate actions of a sexual nature.

sexism discrimination against members of either sex, but usually against women.

✓ ASSESSMENT CHECK

2.4.1 What is meant by social responsibility, and why do firms pay attention to it?

2.4.2 What is green marketing?

2.4.3 What are the four main consumer rights?

RESPONSIBILITIES TO INVESTORS AND THE FINANCIAL COMMUNITY

LO 2.5 Explain the ethical responsibilities of businesses to investors and the financial community.

A fundamental goal of any business is to make a profit for its shareholders. But investors and the financial community also demand that businesses behave ethically and legally. When firms fail in this responsibility, thousands of investors and consumers can suffer.

Provincial regulators such as the Ontario Securities Commission and the Alberta Securities Commission are primarily responsible for protecting investors from financial misdeeds. These provincial regulators investigate suspicions of unethical or illegal behaviour by publicly traded

ASSESSMENT CHECK

2.5.1 Why do firms need to do more than just earn a profit?

2.5.2 What is the role of the provincial securities regulators?

firms. They look into accusations that a business is using faulty accounting practices to inaccurately report its financial resources and profits to investors. Recall that legislation such as Bill 198 in Canada and the Sarbanes-Oxley Act of 2002 in the United States protect investors from unethical accounting practices. In 2009, Garth Drabinsky and Myron Gottlieb were found guilty of preparing fraudulent accounting information at Toronto-based Livent Inc. They defrauded investors of approximately $500 million. Livent was well known as the producer of *The Phantom of the Opera,* Toronto's longest-running musical.[60] Chapter 16 discusses securities trading practices further.

WHAT'S AHEAD

The decisions and actions of businesspeople are often influenced by outside forces, such as the legal environment and society's expectations about business responsibility. Firms are also affected by the economic environment where they operate. The next chapter discusses the broad economic issues that influence businesses around the world. Our discussion will focus on how certain factors—supply and demand, unemployment, inflation, and government monetary policies—pose both challenges and opportunities when firms seek to compete in the global marketplace.

RETURN TO INSIDE BUSINESS

Cirque du Soleil: A Class Act in Social Responsibility

Businesses in today's corporate environment try to operate in a socially responsible manner. Companies like the Cirque du Soleil have taken significant measures to both operate in a socially responsible manner and publicize their efforts.

QUESTIONS FOR CRITICAL THINKING

1. Do you feel that corporate social responsibility has a significant impact on Cirque du Soleil's success, or is it just a "nice to have"?

2. Does a firm need to publicize its corporate social responsibility efforts? Or does company-sponsored publicity make it appear that these efforts are undertaken solely to generate revenues through positive public relations?

SUMMARY OF LEARNING OBJECTIVES

LO 2.1 Explain the concepts of business ethics and social responsibility.

Business ethics are the standards of conduct and moral values that businesspeople rely on to guide their actions and decisions in the workplace. Businesspeople must consider a wide range of social issues when making decisions. Social responsibility is management's acceptance of the obligation to put an equal value on profit, consumer satisfaction, and societal well-being when evaluating the firm's performance.

 ASSESSMENT CHECK ANSWERS

2.1.1 To whom do businesses have responsibilities? Businesses have responsibilities to customers, employees, investors, and society.

2.1.2 If a firm is meeting all its responsibilities to others, why do ethical conflicts arise? Ethical conflicts arise because businesses must balance doing what is right and doing what is profitable.

LO 2.2 Describe the factors that influence business ethics.

Many factors shape individual ethics, including personal experience, peer pressure, and organizational culture. Individual ethics are also influenced by family, cultural, and religious standards. The culture of the workplace can also be a factor.

 ASSESSMENT CHECK ANSWERS

2.2.1 What is the role of a firm's ethics compliance officer? Ethics compliance officers must discourage wrongdoing and ensure that ethical standards are met.

2.2.2 What factors influence the ethical environment of a business? Individual ethics and technology influence the ethical environment of a business.

LO 2.3 Discuss how organizations shape ethical behaviour.

Conflicts of interest occur when an action that benefits one person may harm another person. For example, a businessperson's own interests may conflict with the interests of a customer. Honesty and integrity are valued qualities that lead to trust, but a person's immediate self-interest may lead to actions that go against these principles. Loyalty to an employer sometimes conflicts with being truthful. When misconduct occurs in the workplace, some employees may think about being whistle-blowers, but the personal costs may be high. Employees are strongly influenced by the standards of conduct already set up and supported in their workplace. Businesses can help shape ethical behaviour by using codes of conduct that define what they expect from employees. Organizations can also use this training to develop employees' ethics awareness and reasoning. Employers can promote ethical action by providing decision-making tools, supporting goals that are consistent with ethical behaviour, and by setting up advice hotlines. Executives must also provide ethical leadership by showing ethical behaviour in all their decisions and actions.

 ASSESSMENT CHECK ANSWERS

2.3.1 For an employee, when does loyalty conflict with truth? Truth conflicts with loyalty when the truth about a company or a situation is unfavourable.

2.3.2 How does ethical leadership contribute to ethical standards throughout a company? When leaders and managers behave ethically, employees are more likely to commit to the company's core values.

LO 2.4 Describe how businesses can act responsibly to satisfy society.

Today's businesses are expected to weigh two things: their qualitative impact on consumers and society and their quantitative economic contributions in terms of sales, employment levels, and profits. Social responsibility can be measured by charitable contributions and compliance with labour laws and consumer protection laws. Some businesses choose to conduct social audits. Public-interest groups also create standards for measuring companies' performance. A business's responsibilities to the general public include protecting public health and the environment and developing the quality of the workforce. Some also argue that businesses have a social responsibility to support charitable and social causes in the communities where they earn profits. Businesses must also treat customers fairly and protect consumers. Businesses do this by upholding consumers' rights to be safe, to be informed, to choose, and to be heard. Businesses have wide-ranging responsibilities to their employees. They need to ensure that the workplace is safe, address quality-of-life issues, ensure equal opportunity, and prevent sexual harassment and other forms of discrimination.

 ASSESSMENT CHECK ANSWERS

2.4.1 What is meant by social responsibility, and why do firms pay attention to it? Social responsibility is management's responsibility to consider profit, consumer satisfaction, and society's well-being as having equal value when evaluating the firm's performance. Businesses pay attention to it for many reasons: because it is required by law, because it enhances the company's image, and because it is the right thing to do.

2.4.2 What is green marketing? Green marketing is a marketing strategy that promotes environmentally safe products and production methods.

2.4.3 What are the four main consumer rights? The four main consumer rights are the rights to be safe, to be informed, to choose, and to be heard.

LO 2.5 Explain the ethical responsibilities of businesses to investors and the financial community.

Investors and the financial community demand that businesses behave ethically and legally in their handling of financial transactions. Businesses must be honest in reporting their profits and financial performance to avoid misleading investors. Provincial securities regulators investigate suspicions that publicly traded firms have engaged in unethical or illegal financial behaviour.

ASSESSMENT CHECK ANSWERS

2.5.1 Why do firms need to do more than just earn a profit?
Firms need to do more than just earn a profit for two reasons: because the law requires them to behave in a legal and ethical manner and because investors and shareholders demand such behaviour.

2.5.2 What is the role of the provincial securities regulators?
Among other functions, provincial securities regulators investigate suspicions of unethical or illegal behaviour by publicly traded firms.

BUSINESS TERMS YOU NEED TO KNOW

business ethics 30
code of conduct 37
conflict of interest 35
consumerism 47
corporate philanthropy 47
discrimination 51
Employment Equity Act (EEA) 52

fair trade 50
green marketing 45
integrity 35
product liability 48
recycling 44
Sarbanes-Oxley Act of 2002 33
sexism 53

sexual harassment 53
social audits 41
social responsibility 40
stakeholders 39
sustainable 45
whistle-blowing 36

REVIEW QUESTIONS

1. What do the terms *business ethics* and *social responsibility* mean? Why are they important components of a firm's overall philosophy in conducting business?

2. How do individuals make a difference in a firm's commitment to ethics? Describe the three stages an individual goes through when developing ethical standards.

3. Identify the ethical dilemmas in each of the following situations (a situation might involve more than one dilemma):
   a. Due to the breakup with a client, an advertising agency finds itself working with rival companies.
   b. A newly hired employee learns that the office manager plays computer games on company time.
   c. A drug manufacturer offers a doctor an expensive gift to encourage the doctor to prescribe a new brand-name drug.
   d. An employee is told to destroy documents that show a firm's role in spreading pollution.
   e. A company spokesperson agrees to a media conference that puts a positive spin on the firm's use of underpaid labour.

4. Describe how ethical leadership helps to develop each of the other ethical standards.

5. How do firms demonstrate their social responsibility?

6. What are the four major areas where businesses have responsibilities to the general public? How can meeting these responsibilities lead to a competitive advantage?

7. Describe the four basic rights that consumerism tries to protect. How has consumerism improved the contemporary business environment? What challenges has consumerism created for businesses?

8. What five major responsibilities do companies have to their employees? What changes in society are affecting these responsibilities?

9. Which equal opportunity laws or acts protect the following workers?
   a. An employee who must care for an elderly parent.
   b. A Canadian Armed Forces member who is returning from deployment overseas.
   c. A job applicant who is HIV positive.
   d. A person who is over 40 years old.
   e. A woman who has been sexually harassed on the job.
   f. A woman who has a family history of breast cancer.

10. How does a company show its responsibility to investors and to the financial community?

PROJECTS AND TEAMWORK APPLICATIONS

1. Write your own personal code of ethics. Create standards for your behaviour at school, in personal relationships, and on the job. Assess how well you meet your own standards. Revise your code of ethics, if necessary.

2. On your own or with a classmate, visit the website of one of the following firms, or choose another that interests you. Use what you can learn about the company from the website to construct a chart or figure that shows examples of the firm's ethical awareness, ethical education, ethical actions, and ethical leadership. Present your findings to the class.

   a. Tim Hortons
   b. National Hockey League (NHL), or any major professional sports league
   c. TELUS Mobility
   d. RBC Financial Group
   e. BlackBerry
   f. RONA
   g. IKEA

3. Using the company you studied for question 2 (or another company), conduct a social audit. Do your findings match the firm's culture of ethics? If not, what are the differences and why did they occur?

4. On your own or with a classmate, go online, flip through a magazine, or surf television channels to identify a firm that uses green marketing. If you see a commercial on television, go to the firm's website to learn more about the product or process advertised. Does the firm make claims that comply with the Competition Bureau's guidelines? Present your findings in class.

5. As a consumer, you expect the companies you do business with will have a certain level of responsibility toward you. Describe a situation when you felt that a company did not recognize your rights as a consumer. How did you handle the situation? How did the company handle it? What was the final outcome?

WEB ASSIGNMENTS

1. **Ethical standards.** Go to the website listed below. It summarizes the ethical standards for all TELUS employees. Read the material and write a brief report that compares TELUS's ethical standards to the discussion on corporate ethics in this chapter. In addition, consider how TELUS's ethical standards are integrated into the firm's overall efforts at global citizenship.

   http://about.telus.com/community/english/investor_relations/corporate_governance

2. **Starting a career.** Each year, *Canada's Top 100 Employers* rates the best companies to work for. Visit the *Canada's Top 100 Employers* website and review the most recent list. What criteria did *Canada's Top 100 Employers* use when building this list? What role does ethics and social responsibility play?

   www.canadastop100.com/national

3. **Social responsibility.** Footwear manufacturer La Canadienne is one of the few companies in its industry that still manufactures products in Canada. Go to the website listed below to learn more about the firm's commitment to Canadian manufacturing. Prepare a report that relates this commitment to the firm's other core values.

   www.lacanadienneshoes.com

Note: Internet addresses change frequently. If you don't find the exact sites listed, you may need to access the organization's home page and search from there or use a search engine such as Bing or Google.

4 | COMPETING IN WORLD MARKETS

LEARNING OBJECTIVES

LO 4.1 Explain the primary reasons why nations trade.

LO 4.2 Describe how trade is measured between nations.

LO 4.3 Identify the major barriers to international trade.

LO 4.4 Explain how international trade organizations and economic communities reduce barriers to international trade.

LO 4.5 Compare the different levels of involvement used by businesses when entering global markets.

LO 4.6 Distinguish between a global business strategy and a multidomestic business strategy.

INSIDE BUSINESS

PotashCorp: Genesis for Economic Development

Where does wealth come from? How did Canada become the complex economic society it is today? Why do some countries have wealth while others seem to always be living in poverty? What roles do Canadian businesses play in the challenge to generate and distribute wealth in our country and around the world? We need to understand these questions, concepts, and our framework for how business and economic development work. Let's take a closer look at just one international Canadian business.

PotashCorp of Saskatoon, Saskatchewan, is one of many businesses that generate wealth by producing commodities for Canadian and international customers. Commodities are basic products like oil, natural gas, gold, silver, forest products, and many other resources that businesses need to make the products they sell.

Sometimes a commodity is used directly in production. For example, natural gas is burned in kilns to dry fresh-cut lumber when making building materials like 2 × 4 wall studs. But commodities can also be ingredients in a recipe for producing an important product—fertilizer.

PotashCorp is the world's largest producer of fertilizer. It has about 20 percent of the entire global capacity and annual sales of about $6.5 billion. Fertilizer replaces the nutrients in the soil that are absorbed by crops. In simple terms, the key recipe ingredients of fertilizer—potash, phosphate, and nitrogen—are put back in the soil so that the soil can continue to produce higher-yield crops. Potash and phosphate are mined, and nitrogen is extracted from the air. This simple but important product has allowed PotashCorp to grow into a $50 billion giant. It has global operations and part ownership in businesses in China, Chile, Israel, and Jordan.

The demand for fertilizer is directly related to two factors: the demand for agricultural products and the ability of the growers to pay. The growing demand for agricultural products is clearly associated with population growth. For example, the populations of India and China together make up more than one-third of the world's population. As these countries grow economically richer, they are more able to afford the cost of fertilizers to better feed their growing populations.

Let's think about what happened during the global financial crises that occurred between 2008 and 2010. Around the world, demand dropped for all commodities, particularly in India and China. As a result, sales and prices of commodities, including fertilizers, also dropped. Mining of the ingredients decreased, and some mines were closed until prices and demand became profitable again.

At the same time, PotashCorp's shares dropped from $233 per share on June 20, 2008, down to $67 per share on December 5, 2008. By January 2011, demand and prices had recovered to increase the share value to $170, which meant the business could be profitable again.

China has the world's largest population, estimated to be more than 1.3 billion people. China is also the world's largest user of fertilizer, using 28 percent of all available fertilizer. China's own potash production is limited. Historically, 75 percent of potash used in China is imported. As incomes have grown in China, Chinese agribusinesses have increased their use of fertilizers to meet the growing demand for more food, and for meat products in particular. India, with an estimated 1.2 billion people, is the second-largest consumer of fertilizer. It takes up about 13 percent of the world demand for fertilizer. Brazil has an estimated population of 200 million people. It imports 90 percent of the potash it needs, and uses 7 percent of the world's fertilizer. North America has an estimated population of about 340 million people; it needs about 14 percent of the world's fertilizer. North American demand has been more stable than in these other markets. Demand for fertilizer has increased by 85 percent in China, India, Southeast Asia, and Brazil over the past 20 years. These figures closely match food production trends during that time.

Some countries are rich in highly valued commodities. These countries have an immediate source of wealth on which they can build more economic activity. The countries that are not rich in these commodities must look for other strategies or face the economic consequences. Canada has an economic advantage over other countries because of our rich natural resources. Canadians benefit from the sale of commodities to customers in other countries, wherever they may be in the world.[1]

CHAPTER 4 OVERVIEW

Take a moment and think about how many products you used today that came from outside Canada. Did you drink Brazilian coffee with your breakfast? Are your clothes manufactured in China? Did you drive to class in a German or Japanese car fuelled by gasoline refined from Venezuelan crude oil? Or did you watch a movie on a television set assembled in Mexico for a Japanese company such as Sony? A fellow student in Germany may be wearing Zara jeans, using a BlackBerry smartphone, and drinking Pepsi.

Canadian and foreign companies know the importance of international trade to their future success. Economic interdependence is increasing throughout the world as companies look for new markets for their goods and services and the most cost-effective locations to set up factories. Businesses cannot rely only on sales in their home country. Today, Canadian mining, manufacturing, agricultural, and service firms need foreign sales. Other countries are sources of new markets and profit opportunities. Foreign companies also look to Canada when they need new markets.

Thousands of products cross national borders every day. The automobiles that Canadian manufacturers sell in the United States are **exports**, domestically produced goods and services sold in markets in other countries. **Imports** are foreign-made products purchased by domestic consumers. Together, Canadian exports and imports make up about 30 percent of Canadian gross domestic product (GDP). Canada is the world's tenth-largest exporter. Canada's exports and imports are worth about $525 billion each.[2]

Sometimes goods are bought and sold across national boundaries. Companies that do business with other countries need to work with new social and cultural practices, different economic and political environments, and legal restrictions. Before entering world markets, companies must take the business plans they use in their home market and change them to work with the markets in other countries.

This chapter looks at the world of international business. We will see how large and small companies deal with globalization. First, we look at why nations trade, the importance of the global marketplace, the features of the global marketplace, and how nations measure international trade. Then we look at barriers to international trade as a result of cultural and environmental differences. To reduce these barriers, countries turn to organizations that promote global business. Finally, we look at the strategies firms use for entering foreign markets and how they create international business strategies.

exports domestically produced goods and services sold in other countries.

imports foreign goods and services purchased by domestic customers.

LO 4.1 Explain the primary reasons why nations trade.

WHY NATIONS TRADE

When their home markets mature and sales slow, companies in every industry know the importance of expanding business to other countries. TD Ameritrade is Toronto Dominion Bank's online brokerage business in the United States. It was set up when TD Bank acquired Ameritrade in 2006. Lululemon Athletica is based in Vancouver, British Columbia, but operates stores in the United States. Bombardier sells jet aircraft to companies around the world. These are only a few of the thousands of Canadian companies selling their products in other countries. These firms take advantage of large populations, healthy resources, and rising standards of living abroad that increase foreign interest in their goods and services. Likewise, the Canadian market's high purchasing power attracts thousands of foreign companies to its shores.

International trade is vital to a nation and its businesses. Trading with other countries increases economic growth in two ways: by providing a new market for products and by providing access to needed resources. Companies can expand their markets, seek growth opportunities in other nations, and make their production and distribution systems more efficient. They can also reduce their dependence on the economies of their home nations.

International Sources of Factors of Production

Business decisions to operate abroad depend on the basic factors of production in the other country: the availability, price, and quality of labour, natural resources, capital, and entrepreneurship. Indian colleges and universities produce thousands of highly qualified computer scientists and engineers each year. To take advantage of this talent, many global computer software and hardware firms have set up operations in India. Many other companies outsource their information technology and customer service jobs to Indian companies.

Trading with other countries also allows a company to spread risk, because different nations may be at different stages of the business cycle or in different phases of development. If demand falls in one country, the company may find strong demand in other nations. In India and China, sales of automobiles for personal use are just getting started. For many years, companies such as General Motors, Kellogg, and IKEA have used international sales to balance lower sales at home.

Size of the International Marketplace

We have discussed that companies choose international trade because of the benefits to human and natural resources, entrepreneurship, and capital. Companies are also attracted to international business because of the size of the global marketplace. The world's population is approximately 7.2 billion now, but only one in six people live in a well-developed country. The portion of the world's population living in less-developed countries will increase in the coming years because more-developed nations have lower birthrates. But the global birthrate is slowing overall. Today's average woman has half as many children as the average woman had 35 years ago.[3]

When firms in developing nations increase their global business, they also increase their ability to reach new groups of customers. Firms that are looking for new revenue are usually attracted to giant markets such as China and India. China has a population of about 1.3 billion, and India's population is 1.2 billion. But people alone do not create a market. Consumer demand also needs purchasing power. **Table 4.1** shows that population size does not guarantee economic prosperity. Of the 10 countries with the highest population, only one country also has a GDP on the top 10 list—the United States. Note also that countries with smaller populations can create great wealth for their citizens, as measured by GDP per capita. Where does Canada rank? With a population of 35 million people, Canada places 36th from the top of the population rankings but 12th with $51,958 per capita real GDP.

People in developing nations have lower per capita incomes than people in the highly developed economies of North America and Western Europe. Despite having lower incomes, the huge populations in developing countries represent profitable markets for some companies. The higher-income group may only be a small percentage of the entire country's population, but their numbers still represent important and growing markets.

Table 4.1 The World's Top 10 Nations

BASED ON POPULATION			BASED ON WEALTH		
Rank	COUNTRY	POPULATION (IN MILLIONS)	Rank	COUNTRY	PER CAPITA GDP (IN REAL U.S. DOLLARS)
1	China	1,349	1	Luxembourg	$110,697
2	India	1,221	2	Norway	$100,818
3	United States	317	3	Qatar	$93,714
4	Indonesia	251	4	Macau SAR, China	$91,376
5	Brazil	201	5	Switzerland	$84,815
6	Pakistan	193	6	Australia	$67,458
7	Nigeria	175	7	Sweden	$60,430
8	Bangladesh	164	8	Denmark	$59,831
9	Russia	142	9	Singapore	$55,182
10	Japan	127	10	United States	$53,042
36	Canada	38	12	Canada	$51,958

Sources: CIA, *World Factbook*, accessed January 6, 2014, www.cia.gov; World Bank, "GDP per Capita (Current US$)," accessed March 25, 2015 http://data.worldbank.org.

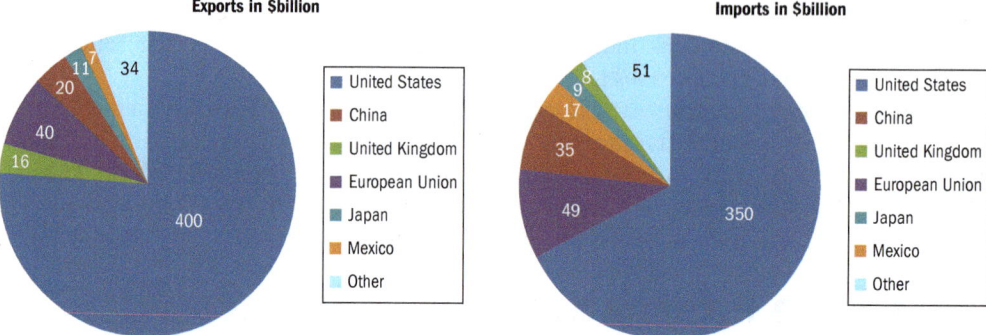

FIGURE 4.1 Canada's Top International Trade Partners

Source: Data from Statistics Canada, "Imports, Exports and Trade Balance of Goods on a Balance-of-Payments Basis, by Country or Country Grouping," accessed March 25, 2015, www.statcan.gc.ca/tables-tableaux/sum-som/l01/cst01/gblec02a-eng.htm.

Many developing countries have typically posted high growth rates in their annual GDP. Until the 2008–2010 economic slowdown, U.S. and Canadian GDP rates grew at an annual rate of about 4 percent. By contrast, GDP growth in less-developed countries was much greater—China's GDP growth rate, recently slowing, had exceeded double digits for most of the last decade, and India's averaged 7.5 percent over the last decade.[4] These countries represent opportunities for global businesses, even though their per capita incomes are lower than in more-developed countries. Many North American firms are setting up operations in these and other developing countries. They want to benefit from local sales as a result of expanding economies and rising standards of living. For example, Walmart has opened dozens of new stores in developing countries from China to Brazil. As the largest retail firm in the world, Walmart employs 2.2 million workers (called "associates") in 11,000 stores worldwide. Walmart International is currently the fastest-growing segment of Walmart's business, with more than 6,400 stores and 900,000 employees in 27 countries as far-ranging as Lesotho and Swaziland in Africa. More than 90 percent of Walmart's overseas stores operate under a local banner.[5]

Canada's trade is overwhelmingly tied to the United States, and U.S. trade is tied to Canada. Both countries are similar in their social and cultural values. That means that when a business finds a market in one country, it will most likely find buyers in the other country, too. Almost all of Canada's population is spread along the American border. The closeness of the two countries makes it easier to transport goods and to communicate, and that helps develop cross-border trade.

Figure 4.1 shows Canada's top trade partners. Notice the amount of trade Canada has with the United States. Much of our trade with the United States is resource based. The demand for Canada's energy supplies of oil, natural gas, and hydro-electricity will continue to grow as the United States continues to need safe, secure, and reliable sources of energy.

Absolute and Comparative Advantage

Few countries can produce all the goods and services they need. For centuries, trading has helped countries meet the demand for goods and services. A country can focus on producing what it does best. It can then export the extra output and buy foreign products that it doesn't have or cannot produce efficiently. The foreign sales of a product depend on whether the country has an absolute advantage or a comparative advantage.

A country has an *absolute advantage* in making a product when it has a monopoly on making that product or when it can produce the product at a lower cost than any other country. China has had an absolute advantage in silk production for centuries. Silk is woven from fibres from silkworm cocoons

Saffron is possibly the world's most expensive spice. This pricey spice is extracted from crocus flowers. The plants grow well in Spain but not in most other countries. Spain has a near absolute advantage in saffron production.

and is a prized raw material in high-quality clothing. European demand for silk led to the famous Silk Road, an 8,000-kilometre link between Rome and the ancient Chinese capital city of Xian.

Today, absolute advantages are rare. Some countries almost have absolute advantages in some products. For example, climate differences can give some nations or regions an advantage in growing certain plants, such as the plant that produces saffron. Saffron may be the world's most expensive spice, costing around $4,650 per kilogram. Saffron is the stigma of a flowering plant in the crocus family that is native to the Mediterranean, Asia Minor, and India. Today, saffron is grown mainly in Spain, where the plant thrives in the Spanish soil and climate. Attempts to grow saffron in other parts of the world have generally been unsuccessful.[6]

A nation can develop a *comparative advantage* when it can supply its products more efficiently and at a lower price than it can supply other goods, compared with the outputs of other countries. For example, China profits from its comparative advantage in producing textiles. A nation can also develop a comparative advantage in skilled human resources by ensuring that its people are well educated. India, for example, has a comparative advantage in software development because of its highly educated workforce and low wage scale. Several companies have moved part or all of their software development to India.

IBM wanted to increase its longstanding advantage in research and innovation as global competition increased. The company took the unusual step of forming six global research collaborations with companies, universities, and governments in Saudi Arabia, China, Switzerland, Ireland, Taiwan, and India. IBM hopes to sign at least four more international partnerships. Working with these countries breaks the tradition of doing research in secret. "The world is our lab now," says IBM's director of research.[7]

ASSESSMENT CHECK

4.1.1 Why do nations trade?

4.1.2 What are some measures of the size of the international marketplace?

4.1.3 How does a nation acquire a comparative advantage?

MEASURING TRADE BETWEEN NATIONS

LO 4.2 Describe how trade is measured between nations.

International trade provides competitive advantages to both the countries and the individual companies involved. But how do we measure global business activity? We need to look at two ideas: the balance of trade and the balance of payments. These two ideas can help us understand what the trade inflows and outflows mean for a country. Another important factor is the currency exchange rates for the trading countries.

A nation's **balance of trade** is the difference between its exports and imports. When a country exports more than it imports, it has a positive balance of trade, called a *trade surplus*. When a country imports more than it exports, it produces a negative balance of trade, called a *trade deficit*. Canada tends to maintain a balance between exports and imports by running a trade surplus with the United States and a trade deficit with other trading partners, particularly China.[8] The United States has run a trade deficit every year since 1976. The United States is one of the world's top exporters, but it has an even greater demand for foreign-made goods, which creates a trade deficit.

A nation's balance of trade plays a central role in shaping its **balance of payments**—the overall flow of money into or out of a country. The balance of payments is also affected by overseas loans and borrowing, international investments, profits from international investments, and foreign aid payments. To calculate a nation's balance of payments, subtract the monetary outflows from the monetary inflows. A positive balance of payments, or a *balance-of-payments surplus*, means more money has moved into a country than out of it. A negative balance of payments, or a *balance-of-payments deficit*, means more money has gone out of the country than entered it.

balance of trade the difference between a nation's exports and imports.

balance of payments the overall money flows into and out of a country.

Major Canadian Exports and Imports

The global economy has grown to more than $74 trillion of total GDP. Canada's economy represents about $1.8 trillion, and the U.S. economy represents about $16.7 trillion. Trade is an important reason why global GDP has grown and keeps growing.[9]

Table 4.2 Major Canadian Imports and Exports in 2014

	EXPORTS $ BILLIONS		IMPORTS $ BILLIONS	
	2014	RANK	2014	RANK
Totals from All Categories	529		524	
Farm, fishing, and intermediate food products	31	7	15	10
Energy products	129	1	44	7
Metal ores and nonmetallic minerals	18	11	11	11
Metal and nonmetallic mineral products	58	4	46	5
Basic and industrial chemical, plastic, and rubber products	36	6	45	6
Forestry products and building and packaging materials	37	5	23	8
Industrial machinery, equipment, and parts	29	8	51	4
Electronic and electrical equipment and parts	24	9	59	3
Motor vehicles and parts	75	2	90	2
Aircraft and other transportation equipment and parts	22	10	17	9
Consumer goods	59	3	106	1
Special transactions trade	2	12	7	13
Other balance of payments adjustments	9	13	10	12

Source: Data from Statistics Canada, "Exports of Goods on a Balance-of-Payments Basis, by Product," accessed March 26, 2015, www.statcan.gc.ca/tables-tableaux/sum-som/l01/cst01/gblec04-eng.htm; "Imports of Goods on a Balance-of-Payments Basis, by Product," accessed March 26, 2015, www.statcan.gc.ca/tables-tableaux/sum-som/l01/cst01/gblec05-eng.htm.

Table 4.2 shows the ranking of the major categories of Canadian merchandise exports and imports. Canada's top merchandise exports in 2014 were energy products ($129 billion), motor vehicles and parts ($75 billion), and consumer goods ($59 billion). Energy product exports increased 38 percent from 2010 to 2014 after doubling from 2000 to 2010. This growth reflects both increased export quantities and the dramatic increase in market prices for oil. Prices peaked in 2014 at about $150 per barrel before falling back to the $50 range in early 2015. The average price of oil in 2000 was about $27 per barrel, and it was about $71 in 2010.[10] Canadian manufacturing export sales increased as the 2008–2010 recession gave way to economic recovery and increasing exports of Canadian motor vehicle products and consumer goods.

On the import side, Canada's top imports were consumer goods ($106 billion), motor vehicles and parts ($90 billion), and electronic and electrical equipment and parts ($58 billion). These increases grew as the 2008–2010 recession gave way to economic recovery and Canadians returned to normal spending on the imported goods we enjoy.

In 2014, Canada exported over $84 billion of services and imported over $106 billion worth. Services include travel and tourism as well as consulting and business services. The service sector employs thousands of Canadian workers who are often working in conjunction with international companies.[11]

The United States leads the world in the international trade of goods and services. It has combined exports and imports of about $4.9 trillion. The goods exchanged by U.S. exporters and importers range from machinery and vehicles to crude oil and chemicals.

Although the United States imports more goods than it exports, the opposite is true for services. U.S. exporters sell more than $600 billion in services annually. Much of that money comes from travel and tourism—money spent by foreign nationals visiting the United States.[12]

U.S. annual imports are nearing $2.7 trillion, making the United States the world's leading importer. Like Canadians, Americans demand foreign-made goods for everything from clothing to consumer electronics. These preferences create huge trade deficits with the two nations that export the most consumer goods to North America—China and Japan.

Exchange Rates

An **exchange rate** is the value of one country's currency in terms of the currencies of other countries. We need to learn how foreign exchange works because we live in a global community. The value of currency is an important economic measure for every country. Each currency's exchange rate is usually stated in terms of another currency. For example, about 12 Mexican pesos are needed to purchase one Canadian dollar. A Canadian dollar can also be exchanged for approximately $0.85 in the United States at the time of writing this textbook. The euro is the currency used in most European Union (EU) member countries, and like any currency the euro has had ups and downs in value. European consumers and businesses use the euro to pay bills by cheque, credit card, or bank transfer. Euro coins and notes are also used in many EU member countries.

Many factors can affect foreign exchange rates: economic and political conditions, actions by the central bank, balance-of-payments position, and speculation over future currency values. Currency values fluctuate, or "float," depending on the supply and demand for each currency in the world market. In this system of *floating exchange rates*, currency traders create a market for the world's currencies based on each country's trade and the likelihood of investments. The idea is that exchange rates can go up and down freely as supply and demand change. But exchange rates do not float in total freedom. National governments often step in to change their exchange rates.

Nations can affect exchange rates in other ways. They may form currency blocs by linking their exchange rates to each other. Many governments practise protectionist policies that try to protect their economies against trade imbalances. For example, nations sometimes take actions to devalue their currencies as a way to increase exports and encourage foreign investment. **Devaluation** is a reduction in a currency's value in terms of other currencies or in terms of a fixed standard. Brazil recently devalued its currency, making investing in Brazil less costly than investing in other countries. After the devaluation, foreign investment in Brazil increased. Pillsbury bought Brazil's Brisco, a company that makes *pao de queijo*, a cheese bread formed into rolls and served with morning coffee. Other foreign companies invested in Brazil's construction, tourism, banking, communications, and other industries.

For an individual business, the impact of currency devaluation depends on where the business buys its materials and where it sells its products. Usually, business transactions use the currency of the country where the transactions take place. When business takes place in Japan, the transactions will likely be in yen. In the United Kingdom, transactions are in pounds. Many EU countries now use the euro, so fewer currencies are used in Europe. Today, the EU member countries that use the euro include Austria, Belgium, Cyprus, Estonia, Finland, France, Germany, Greece, Ireland, Italy, Latvia, Luxembourg, Malta, the Netherlands, Portugal, Slovakia, Slovenia, and Spain. Other currencies include the British pound, the Australian dollar, the Indian rupee, the Brazilian real, the Mexican peso, the Taiwanese dollar, and the South African rand.

Exchange rate changes can quickly create—or destroy—a competitive advantage. They are important factors when investors decide whether to invest in other countries. In Europe, a declining Canadian or American dollar means that the price of euros go up, so European companies are pressured to lower their prices to keep foreign customers who generally pay for goods in U.S. dollars. When the value of the Canadian dollar falls, European vacations are more costly for Canadian tourists because their dollars are worth less in terms of the euro.

Currencies that easily convert into other currencies are called *hard currencies*. Examples of hard currencies are the euro, the U.S. dollar, and

exchange rate the value of one country's currency in terms of the currencies of other countries.

devaluation a reduction in a currency's value in terms of other currencies or in terms of a fixed standard.

Because we live in a global community, we need to understand how currency exchange rates work. Many factors affect foreign exchange rates.

ASSESSMENT CHECK

4.2.1 Compare balance of trade and balance of payments.

4.2.2 Explain the function of an exchange rate.

4.2.3 What happens when a currency is devalued?

the Japanese yen. The Russian ruble and many central European currencies are soft currencies because they cannot be converted as easily. Exporters that trade with these countries sometimes prefer to barter, or accept payment not in cash but in goods, such as oil, timber, or other commodities. They then resell these goods in exchange for payment in hard currencies.

The foreign currency market is the largest financial market in the world. Its daily volume is more than US$5.3 trillion.[13] This amount is about 10 times the size of all the world's stock markets combined. The foreign exchange market is the most liquid and most efficient financial market in the world.

LO 4.3 Identify the major barriers to international trade.

BARRIERS TO INTERNATIONAL TRADE

All businesses face barriers, whether they sell only to local customers or trade in international markets. International companies must follow a variety of laws and deal with multiple exchange currencies. They may also need to change their products to suit different tastes in other countries. Kraft recently won nearly a quarter of China's $1.6 billion cookie market by making its Oreo cookies less sweet to suit local tastes. The company also launched new products such as Oreo Wafer Sticks, Wafer Rolls, Soft Cakes, and Strawberry Cremes.[14]

Companies that do international business face social and cultural differences, economic barriers, and legal and political barriers. Some of the barriers are shown in **Figure 4.2**. Some of these barriers are easy to deal with, but other barriers require a company to make major changes in its business strategy. To be successful in global markets, companies and their managers need to understand not only how these barriers affect international trade but also how to overcome these barriers.

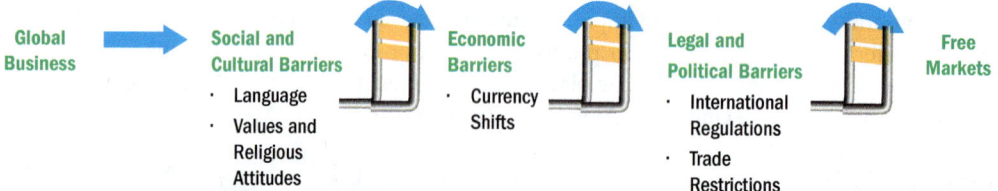

FIGURE 4.2 Barriers to International Trade

Social and Cultural Differences

The social and cultural differences among nations range from language and customs to educational background and religious holidays. Understanding and respecting these differences are important for international business success. Businesspeople who understand the host country's cultures, languages, social values, and religious attitudes and practices are prepared for the marketplace and the negotiating table. Businesspeople can win customers and meet their business goals by being sensitive to local views, to how people like to be addressed, and to suitable ways of dressing, using body language, and being on time.

English is the second most-widely spoken language in the world, followed by Hindustani, Spanish, Russian, and Arabic. Only Mandarin Chinese is more common than English. In other countries, some students whose first language is not English take eight years of English language classes in elementary and high school. Understanding a business colleague's primary language can make the difference between closing an international business transaction and losing the sale. Company workers in foreign markets not only must choose the correct and suitable words, but also need to translate words correctly so they say what they want to say. Some firms rename their products or rewrite slogans for foreign markets.

Some communication barriers involve more than just bad translations. Companies may make mistakes by presenting messages using unsuitable media, overlooking local customs and regulations, or ignoring differences in taste. One executive recently lost a deal in China because he gave the prospective client a set of four antique clocks wrapped in white paper. But the number four and the Chinese word for *clock* sound like the word *death*. And white is the traditional colour for funerals.[15]

Cultural sensitivity is especially important in cyberspace. Website developers need to remember that website visitors come from anywhere in the world. Some icons that seem friendly to Canadian Internet users may shock people from other countries. For example, a person making a high-five hand signal would be insulting people in Greece, and making a circle with the thumb and index finger in Brazil is not appropriate, nor is using a thumbs-up sign in Egypt or showing a two-fingered peace sign with the back of the hand facing out in Great Britain.

Gift-giving traditions use the language of symbolism. For example, in Latin America knives and scissors are not suitable gifts because they represent the severing of friendship. Flowers are generally acceptable, but Mexicans use yellow flowers in their Day of the Dead activities, so yellow flowers are linked to death.

Values and Religious Attitudes

Today's world is shrinking in many ways, but people in different countries do not always share the same values or religious feelings. Major differences can exist between people—even those living in the same country.

North American society places a higher value on business efficiency and lower unemployment than European society. But in Europe, employee benefits are more valued. In Canada, vacation time is decided on by each provincial government. For example, in Ontario the Employment Standards Act states that employees earn two weeks' vacation after working for a 12-month vacation entitlement period. In contrast, the EU gives employees a minimum paid vacation of four weeks per year, but most Europeans get five or six weeks. When a Canadian company opens a factory in an EU country, it can hire local employees only if it offers vacation time as set by that nation's business practices.

North American culture values national unity and accepts regional differences. Canada and the United States are seen as separate national markets that have independent economies. European countries that are part of the 27-member EU are trying to create a similar marketplace, but many people don't like the idea of being European citizens first and British, Danish, or Dutch citizens second. British consumers differ from Italian consumers in important ways. Canadian companies that don't understand these differences and that don't change their activities to suit the other country will face problems with being accepted.

Religion plays an important role in every society. Businesspeople must also learn to be sensitive to the major religions in countries where they operate. International businesspeople need to understand religious cycles and the timing of major holidays. Their knowledge can help prevent embarrassing moments when booking meetings, trade shows, conferences, and events such as the opening of a new factory. People who do business in Saudi Arabia need to remember Islam's month-long observance of Ramadan, when work ends at noon. Friday is the Muslim Sabbath, so the Saudi workweek runs from Saturday through Thursday. Also, Muslims don't drink alcohol and think of pork as being unclean. That means gifts of pigskin or liquor would not be welcomed.

Economic Differences

North American businesses usually do well in densely populated countries such as China and India. There, the local consumers eagerly buy Western products. Although selling products there is tempting for Canadian firms, managers must think about the economic factors of doing business in China or India: the country's size, its per capita income, and its stage of economic development. These economic factors are important to think about when deciding whether a country is right for an international business venture. For example, Tata Motors, the largest automobile company in India, is thinking about selling cars to Western auto buyers, even as it works on selling its low-cost Nano car in its home market. The "Hit & Miss" feature discusses the Nano's evolution.

HIT & MISS

The Tiny Nano—A Potential Hit for Tata Motors

The Tata Nano is a tiny car that sells for $2,500 in India. When the Tata Nano arrived in North America it wasn't on the road—it was on display at the Cooper–Hewitt Smithsonian Design Museum in New York as "the world's most affordable car [and] a design achievement," said a museum director.

The Nano is a safe and sturdy vehicle, but more importantly it is a major step in changing transportation for millions of Indian families that can't afford the high price of most cars. Tata built "the people's car" by using existing parts and a simple design to keep costs down.

"My particular fascination about the Nano is what I refer to as the 'Nano effect' on the rest of the world's vehicle industry," said one research director. He thinks that people everywhere will ask, "If Indians can buy a four-door car for $2,500, why can't I?"

Maybe they soon can. Tata is a $63-billion Indian company. It backed the Nano during legal issues over the land needed for a factory, which delayed production for two years. The recent recession also meant Tata had its first financial losses in seven years, occurring about the same time as the company faced heavy debts after having bought the money-losing Jaguar and Land Rover brands from Ford.

Tata's strategic plan is still to achieve international standing by solving the transportation problems of low-income car markets in the developing world. Tata will sell the Nano in Nigeria next, and it has already passed Europe's crash-safety test. In just a few years, you may see slightly higher-priced Nanos on the streets of Europe and even in North America.

Questions for Critical Thinking

1. Do you think Tata's goal of making transportation affordable in developing countries is realistic? Why or why not?

2. Can you think of any disadvantages for low-income markets if thousands of cars suddenly show up on the road?

Sources: Phil Patton, "A Tata Nano Takes Manhattan," *New York Times*, February 11, 2010, accessed May 28, 2015, www.nytimes.com/2010/02/14/automobiles/14NANO.html; April K, Gupta and Haiyan Wang, "Tata Nano: Not Just a Car but also a Platform," *Businessweek*, January 20, 2010, accessed May 28, 2015, www.bloomberg.com/bw/stories/2010-01-29/tata-nano-not-just-a-car-but-also-a-platformbusinessweek-business-news-stock-market-and-financial-advice; Madhur Singh, "India's Top Automaker, Tata Motors, Hits a Rough Patch," *Time*, February 24, 2009, accessed May 28, 2015, http://content.time.com/time/world/article/0,8599,1881404,00.html.

Infrastructure

infrastructure the basic systems of a country's communication, transportation, and energy facilities.

Businesses that compete in world markets need to think about the host country's economic measures, including its **infrastructure**. Infrastructure refers to the basic systems of communication (telecommunications, television, radio, and print media), transportation (roads and highways, railroads, and airports), and energy facilities (power plants and gas and electric utilities). The Internet and technology use can also be considered part of infrastructure.

India's industrialization is growing. A recent forecast estimates that India will soon have 30 million air passengers each year. India's civil aviation minister says that means India will soon need at least 400 new airports. The Indian aviation industry is growing at nearly 20 percent a year, so 3,000 new planes will also be needed. It will take about one year to complete the bidding process for contractors to work on building a new airport in the capital city of Mumbai. "Our job is not over by creating infrastructure for aviation industry to grow," said the minister. "We need safe and secure aviation. Indian aviation will not grow at the cost of safety and security." Part of India's new air travel security is a CT scanner that inspects luggage at India's biggest new airport in New Delhi, which was built in only three years.[16]

Financial systems provide a type of infrastructure for businesses. In Canada, buyers have widespread access to cheques, credit cards, debit cards, and the electronic systems needed to process these payments. In many African countries, like Ethiopia, local businesses do not accept credit cards. Visitors to Ethiopia's capital city, Addis Ababa, are warned to bring plenty of cash and traveller's cheques with them.

Currency Conversion and Shifts

Countries share many similarities in their infrastructure. But businesses that cross national borders face a basic economic difference: national currencies. Foreign currency fluctuations, or ups and downs, may mean more problems for global businesses. As explained earlier in the chapter, the values of the world's major currencies rise and fall in relation to each other. Rapid and unexpected currency shifts can make it difficult to price items in the local currency. Shifts in exchange rates can also affect business decisions. A devalued currency may make a nation less desirable as a country to export to because of reduced demand in that country. But devaluation can also make the nation desirable as an investment opportunity. Investments there will be a bargain in terms of the buying power of the investor's currency.

Political and Legal Differences

We have discussed how social, cultural, and economic differences can build barriers to international trade. Legal and political differences can also act as barriers. To compete in today's world marketplace, managers in international businesses need to be familiar with the legislation that affects their industries. Some countries have general trade restrictions. Others have detailed rules that state how foreign companies can operate.

Political Climate

In any international business investment, an important factor is the stability of the political situation. The political structures of many nations promote stability similar to the political stability in Canada. Other nations have very different political structures that change frequently. This is the situation in Indonesia, the Congo, and Thailand. Nations often pass laws to protect their own interests, sometimes at the expense of foreign businesses. See the "Solving an Ethical Controversy" feature for a look at the environmental issues involved in energy trade between Canada and the United States.

SOLVING AN **ETHICAL** CONTROVERSY

Delivering Alberta Oil through the Keystone XL Pipeline versus by Rail

The Keystone XL Pipeline proposal from Calgary-based TransCanada Corporation would connect Alberta oil production fields with the American pipeline grid that transports oil south to refineries on the Gulf of Mexico. There are two areas of debate that have surrounded the proposal to build the pipeline: There is the positive economic value of the project, but there is also the negative environmental impact.

PRO

1. The pipeline would provide thousands of jobs as it is built and would be a safer and cheaper way to transport oil to refineries.
2. Producing more oil would result in lower fuel prices and lower inflation in general.
3. North American consumers would reduce dependency on Middle Eastern sources of oil.

CON

1. Increased Alberta oil production would be environmentally damaging to Alberta as well as cause more pollution by users burning more fossil fuels.
2. Making more oil products available at lower prices would delay development of alternative, more ecologically friendly energy technologies.
3. Potential spills from the pipeline would be devastating to local ecosystems and may even threaten sources of drinking water.

Summary

Higher-priced oil may speed up the adoption of more ecofriendly alternative energy sources, but it will impede economic development, especially for those countries that can least afford it. Energy is a requisite for economic development. Without it, little happens in the way of manufacturing and transportation of goods and people.

Further complicating this debate is the use of rail to transport oil because pipeline is unavailable. Rail is considered more dangerous and risky than pipeline, and recent events like the tragic derailment in Lac-Mégantic, Quebec, in 2013 have driven public debate over rail safety.

Approximately 90 billion barrels of oil are consumed each day. About 4.5 billion barrels of Middle East oil enter through the Gulf coast every day. Alberta oil is an alternative supply that would keep revenues within North America.

Sources: Geoffrey Morgan, "A 'Pure Fabrication': TransCanada CEO Fuels War of Words over Obama's Keystone Comments," *Financial Post*, November 19, 2014, accessed March 29, 2015, http://business.financialpost.com; Mark Silva, "Obama's Keystone Options Shrink as State Downplays Impact," January 21, 2014, Bloomberg, accessed March 29, 2015, www.bloomberg.com/news; CNNMoney, "Goldman Sachs CEO on the Benefits of Low Oil," March 2, 2015, accessed March 29, 2015, http://money.cnn.com/video/investing/2015/02/24/lloyd-blankfein-goldman-sachs-oil.cnnmoney; "Are Low Oil Prices Good or Bad for the Economy?" *Fortune*, January 19, 2015, accessed March 29, 2015, http://for.tn/1BcnAhx; Nathan Vanderrklippe, "With Pipelines under Attack, Railways Lead Race to Move Oil," *The Globe and Mail*, January 12, 2013, accessed March 29, 2015, www.theglobeandmail.com.

The political structures have had huge impacts in Russia, Turkey, the former Yugoslavia, Hong Kong, and several central European countries, including the Czech Republic and Poland. Such political changes almost always bring changes in the legal environment. Hong Kong is considered to be part of China. Thus, political developments have led to changes in Hong Kong's legal and cultural environments. Since the collapse of the Soviet Union, Russia has struggled to develop a new market structure and political processes.

Legal Environment

When doing business internationally, managers must be familiar with three dimensions of the legal environment: Canadian law, international regulations, and the laws of the countries in which they plan to trade. Some laws protect the rights of foreign companies to compete in Canada. Others spell out the actions allowed for Canadian companies doing business in foreign countries.

Canada's Corruption of Foreign Public Officials Act (CFPOA) and the U.S. Foreign Corrupt Practices Act (FCPA) make it illegal for companies to bribe foreign officials, political candidates, or government representatives. These acts set out the fines and jail time for managers who are aware of illegal payoffs.

The Russian national flag flies atop Bank Rossii, Russia's central bank, in Moscow, Russia. Since the collapse of the Soviet Union, the political and economic structures in Russia have undergone huge changes and the country has struggled to develop a new market structure.

Until recently, many countries, including France and Germany, accepted the practice of bribing foreign officials in countries where such practices were customary—and even allowed tax deductions for these expenses. Canada, the United States, the United Kingdom, France, Germany, and 35 other countries have signed the Organisation for Economic Co-operation and Development's Anti-Bribery Convention. Many police forces do not actively enforce this law, but this agreement makes offering or paying bribes a criminal offence. It also ends the tax deduction for bribes.[17] Regardless of global business strategies, companies need to be aware of cultural and business customs in the countries in which they do business and of whether certain behaviours are accepted or possibly illegal.

Corruption continues to be an international problem from which no country is immune, as illustrated by the European-based FIFA soccer bribery scandal which emerged in 2015. The commonness of bribing and the international rules against bribery create difficulties for Canadian businesspeople who want to do business in foreign countries: Chinese pay *huilu*, and Russians rely on *vzyatka*, while in the Middle East palms are greased with *baksheesh*. **Figure 4.3** compares 179 countries on measures of supposed corruption. This Corruption Perceptions Index is computed by Transparency International, a Berlin-based organization that rates the degree of corruption observed by businesspeople and the general public.

The growth of online business has introduced new elements to the legal situation of international businesses. Patents, brand names, trademarks, copyrights, and other intellectual property are difficult to keep watch over, given the availability of information on the Internet. Some countries have laws to protect information obtained by electronic contacts. Malaysia has stiff fines and long jail terms for people convicted of illegally accessing computers and using the information that passes through them.

International Regulations

To make international commerce more standard, Canada and many other countries have treaties and signed agreements that describe the expected conduct of international business and protect some of its activities. Canada has entered into many *friendship, commerce, and navigation treaties*

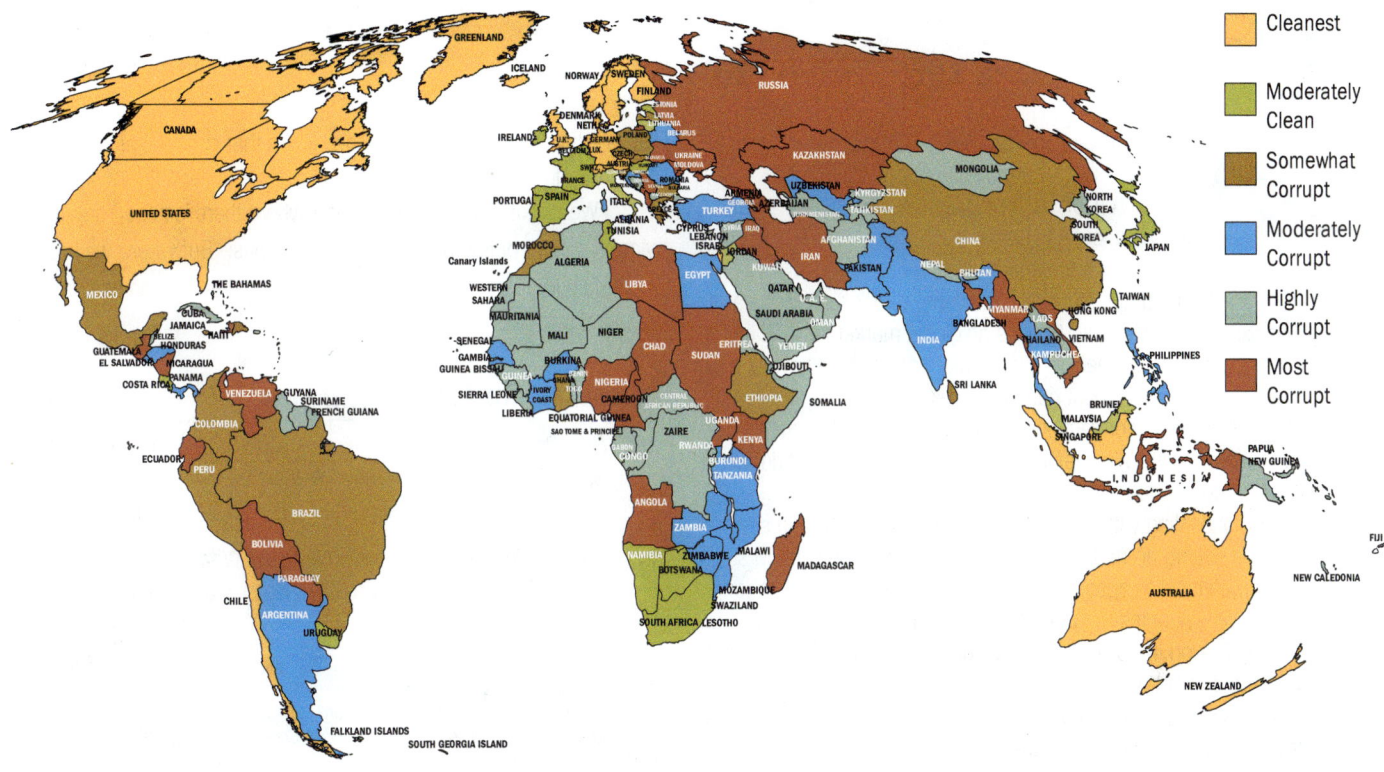

Source: Data from Transparency International, "Annual Corruption Perceptions Index," accessed January 6, 2014, www.transparency.org.

FIGURE 4.3 Corruption in Business and Government

with other nations. These treaties describe many aspects of international business relations, including the right to conduct business in the treaty partner's home market. Other international business agreements involve product standards, patents, trademarks, tax policies, export controls, international air travel, and international communications. One area has no international regulations—the use and protection of water supplies. IBM is stepping in to help provide the international community with water management methods and tools, as we see in the "Going Green" feature.

After China was granted full trade relations with the United States, China agreed to lower its trade barriers, including subsidies that hold down the prices of food exports, restrictions on where foreign law firms can open offices, and taxes charged on imported goods. In exchange for China's promise to halve these taxes, called *tariffs*, the United States granted Chinese businesses access to U.S. markets equal to the access enjoyed by most other countries.

Many rules affect the actions of managers that do business in international markets. Worldwide producers and marketers must keep required minimum levels of quality in all countries where they operate. They must also comply with numerous local regulations. In Britain, advertisers cannot encourage children to engage in unhealthy behaviour such as overeating or skipping regular meals and having candy and snack foods instead. Malaysia's Censorship Board outlaws nudity and swearing on TV. Germany and France let publishers set the prices that retailers charge for books.

Italian clothing manufacturers have long enjoyed high status for their fabrics and workmanship. However, they believed they were being victimized by a lax labelling system when international clothing designers bought less-expensive fabric in China or Bulgaria, had the garments cut in countries with lower labour costs, then sent them to Italy for final sewing. There, they tacked on the prestigious "Made in Italy" label and charged a high price for the goods. The Italian manufacturers pushed for a law requiring that two of the four stages of clothing production must take place in Italy to earn the "Made in Italy" label.[18]

GOING GREEN

IBM HELPS KEEP WATER FLOWING

Did you know it takes 42 litres of water to make one slice of bread, and 133 litres to make a single cup of coffee? Water is one of our greatest resources, but it is under much stress. One in five people worldwide lack access to safe drinking water.

IBM is taking major steps to protect the world's supply of water. Water exists worldwide, but there is no global market for it. There is also very little international or national information about how to conserve water. "Water is about quantity, quality, space, and time," says IBM's Global Innovation Outlook report on the world's water management problems. "Whether you have a big problem or not depends entirely on where you live."

IBM is dealing with the future of water management in several ways. It is setting up meters and sensors that use special IBM software to monitor the capacity and quality of water systems that serve nations, communities, organizations, and individual homes. The company is working to ensure that treated drinking water doesn't come into contact with waste from thousands of kilometres of old underground pipes. IBM's acoustic technology helps to find the worst leaks so they can be repaired right away. IBM is also collecting information on pollution, marine life, and waves for commercial fishers. It is also working to improve filters that can take arsenic and salt from drinking water at a low cost in developing countries.

"We're not going to create water where there is none," says the vice-president of IBM's Big Green Innovations. "But where we know water is under stress, we need to monitor what's going on and better manage it."

Questions for Critical Thinking

1. *Fast Company* magazine recently voted IBM eighteenth in the world in innovation because of IBM's water management efforts. What makes IBM particularly suitable for this award?

2. IBM is an information services company. What can other socially responsible firms learn from IBM's water management efforts?

Sources: IBM, "Advanced Water Management," accessed March 23, 2010, www-304.ibm.com/easyaccess/fileserve?contentid=182044; IBM "Smarter Water Management," accessed March 23, 2010, www.ibm.com/smarterplanet/ca/en/water_management/ideas; Chuck Salter, "#18. IBM," *Fast Company*, February 17, 2010, www.fastcompany.com; Mary Tripsas, "Everybody in the Pool of Green Innovation," *New York Times*, October 31, 2009, accessed March 23, 2010, www.nytimes.com/2009/11/01/business/01proto.html.

Types of Trade Restrictions

Trade restrictions such as taxes on imports and complicated administrative procedures create additional barriers to international business. They may limit the products and services available to consumers and can increase the costs of foreign-made products. Trade restrictions are also used to protect citizens' security, health, and jobs. A government may limit exports of strategic goods to unfriendly countries and ban imports of farm products that have been contaminated by insecticide to protect people's health. Imports are also restricted to protect domestic jobs in the importing country.

Other restrictions are used to promote trade with certain countries. Still other restrictions protect countries from unfair competition. Trade restrictions may be used for different political reasons, but most are in the form of tariffs. Governments also impose some nontariff barriers, also called *administrative barriers*. These barriers include quotas, embargoes, and exchange controls.

Tariffs

tariffs taxes imposed on imported goods.

Taxes, surcharges, and duties on foreign products are referred to as **tariffs**. Governments assess two types of tariffs—revenue tariffs and protective tariffs. Both tariffs make imports more expensive for domestic buyers. Revenue tariffs generate income for the government. For example, Canadian leisure travellers who have been outside Canada for 24 to 48 hours can bring back only up to $200 worth of goods free of duty and tax, and after 48 hours or more, $800 worth of goods. Any amounts greater are charged revenue tariffs.[19]

A protective tariff has one purpose: to raise the retail price of imported products to match or top the prices of similar products made in the home country. In other words, protective tariffs try to limit imports and give local competitors an equal chance to succeed.

Tariffs are a disadvantage to companies that want to export to the countries that have the tariffs. Governments do not always agree on the reasons behind protective tariffs. As a result, tariffs do not always have the desired effect. Canada, like most countries, has a tariff on foreign competitors selling products in Canada at prices lower than Canadian manufacturers charge.

Nontariff Barriers

Nontariff trade barriers are also called administrative trade barriers. These barriers restrict imports without using the strict rules that tariffs use. Nontariff trade barriers may be in the form of quotas on imports, restrictive standards for imports, and export subsidies. Many countries have recently reduced their tariffs or removed them entirely. These countries can use nontariff barriers to control the flow of imported products.

Quotas limit the amounts of particular products that countries can import during specified time periods. Limits may be set as quantities, such as the number of cars or bushels of wheat. Limits can also be set as values, such as dollars' worth of cigarettes.

Quotas help prevent **dumping**. In one form of dumping, a company sells products in other countries at prices below the cost of production. In another form of dumping, a company exports a large quantity of a product at a lower price than the same product in the home market. This action drives down the price of the domestic product. Dumping benefits domestic consumers in the importing market, but it hurts domestic producers. Dumping is also a way for companies to gain quick entry to foreign markets.

An **embargo** is more severe than a quota. An embargo is a total ban on importing a specified product. It can also be a complete stop to trading with a particular country. Many countries, including Canada, have longstanding trade embargoes with North Korea and Iran. Embargo durations can vary depending on changes in foreign policy.

Another form of administrative trade restriction is **exchange control**. A central bank or government agency applies the exchange controls, which affect both exporters and importers. Firms that gain foreign currencies by exporting must sell those currencies to the central bank or another agency. Importers must buy foreign currencies to pay for their purchases from the same agency. The exchange control authority then assigns, expands, or restricts foreign exchange, depending on the national policy.

quota a limit set on the amounts of particular products that can be imported.

dumping selling products in other countries at prices below production costs or below typical prices in the home market to capture market share from domestic competitors.

embargo a total ban on importing specific products or a total stop to trading with a particular country.

exchange control a restriction on importing certain products or a restriction against certain companies to reduce trade and the spending of foreign currency.

✓ ASSESSMENT CHECK

4.3.1 How can values and attitudes form a barrier to trade, and how can these barriers be overcome?

4.3.2 What is a tariff? What is its purpose?

4.3.3 Why is dumping a problem for companies marketing goods internationally?

International trade restrictions include *quotas*, or limits, on the amount of a product, such as wheat, that can be imported into a country.

LO 4.4 Explain how international trade organizations and economic communities reduce barriers to international trade.

REDUCING BARRIERS TO INTERNATIONAL TRADE

Although tariffs and administrative barriers restrict trade, the world is generally moving toward free trade. Several types of organizations ease barriers to international trade, such as groups that monitor trade policies and practices and institutions that offer monetary assistance. The multinational economic community, like the European Union, is made up of multiple federations designed to ease trade barriers. This section looks at the roles these organizations play.

Organizations Promoting International Trade

The **General Agreement on Tariffs and Trade (GATT)** is an international trade accord. Since GATT began more than 60 years ago, it has sponsored a series of negotiations, called rounds, that have greatly reduced worldwide tariffs and other barriers. Major industrialized nations founded the multinational organization in 1947. GATT's aim is to work toward reducing tariffs and relaxing import quotas. The last set of completed negotiations—the Uruguay Round—cut average tariffs by one-third, or by more than $700 billion; reduced farm subsidies; and improved protection for copyright and patent holders. Also, international trading rules now apply to various service industries. Finally, the new agreement established the **World Trade Organization (WTO)** to succeed GATT. This organization includes representatives from 157 countries.

General Agreement on Tariffs and Trade (GATT) an international trade accord that has greatly reduced worldwide tariffs and other trade barriers.

World Trade Organization (WTO) a 157-member international institution that monitors GATT agreements and mediates international trade disputes.

World Trade Organization

Since 1995, the WTO has monitored GATT agreements among its member nations. It has also mediated disputes and continues GATT's aim to reduce trade barriers throughout the world. Unlike the provisions in GATT, the WTO's decisions are final and must be followed by all parties involved in disputes.

The WTO has had its fair share of controversy in recent years. Much disagreement has come from WTO decisions that affect working conditions and the environment in member nations. Many are concerned that the WTO's focus on lowering trade barriers encourages businesses to keep costs down by using methods that may increase both pollution and human rights abuses. Some find it troubling that the organization's member nations must agree on policies. The problem is that developing countries do not want to lose their low-cost advantage by agreeing to stricter labour and environmental policies. Other critics say that if wealthy firms such as fast-food chains, entertainment companies, and Internet retailers can freely enter foreign markets, they may mean the end of smaller foreign businesses that serve the unique tastes and practices of other countries' cultures.

Trade unions in developed nations complain about the WTO's support of free trade. They say free trade makes it easier to export manufacturing jobs to low-wage countries. For example, Canadian textile manufacturing has just about disappeared, and U.S. glassmaking is in a long decline that began in the 1990s, aided by increased imports and bigger profits to be made overseas.[20] In recent years, more new auto plants are being built in Mexico as Canadian and American plants are closed or reduced in size.

The most recent round of WTO talks was called the Doha Round, after the city in Qatar where it began. After several years of heated discussions and negotiations that fell apart, the eight leading industrial nations recommitted themselves to successfully concluding the talks. The discussion included ways to improve global agricultural trade and trade among developing countries. The leaders worked to reduce domestic price supports, eliminate export subsidies, and improve market access for goods. Such changes can help farmers in developing countries compete in the global marketplace.[21]

World Bank

World Bank an organization established by industrialized nations to lend money to less-developed countries.

Soon after the end of World War II, industrialized nations formed an organization to lend money to less-developed and developing countries. The **World Bank** primarily funds projects that build or expand nations' infrastructure. These projects include transportation, education, and medical systems and facilities. The World Bank and other development banks provide the largest source of advice and assistance to developing nations. In exchange for granting loans, the World Bank often sets requirements that are meant to help build the economies of borrower nations.

Some say the World Bank makes loans with conditions that ultimately hurt the borrower nations. When developing nations need to balance government budgets, they are sometimes forced to cut vital social programs. Critics also say that the World Bank should consider the impact of its loans on the environment and working conditions.

International Monetary Fund

The **International Monetary Fund (IMF)** was established a year after the World Bank. It was created to promote trade through financial cooperation and, in the process, eliminate barriers. The IMF makes short-term loans to member nations that cannot meet their expenses. It operates as a lender of last resort for troubled nations. In exchange for these emergency loans, IMF lenders frequently require the borrowing nations to address the problems that led to the crises. These steps may include limiting imports or devaluing currencies. Since it began, the IMF has worked to prevent financial crises by warning the international business community when countries face difficulty meeting their financial obligations. Often, the IMF lends to countries to keep them from defaulting on prior debts. These loans also help to prevent an economic crisis in one country from spreading to other countries.

Some countries owe more money than they can ever hope to repay. The debt payments make it impossible for their governments to deliver desperately needed services to their citizens. After a devastating earthquake in Haiti, the G7 countries (the world's most industrialized nations, including the United States, Canada, and France) promised to cancel any remaining debt owed to them by Haiti. The World Bank not only decided to financially support Haiti but also chose to drop the payments on Haiti's debt for five years. It was also looking for a way to cancel the remaining debt.[22]

International Monetary Fund (IMF) an organization created to promote trade, eliminate barriers, and make short-term loans to member nations that are unable to meet their budgets.

International Economic Communities

International economic communities reduce trade barriers and promote working together to create regions that share economic benefits. In the simplest approach, countries may establish a *free-trade area* where they trade freely among themselves without tariffs or trade restrictions. Each country maintains its own tariffs for trade outside this area. A *customs union* sets up a free-trade area and specifies a tariff structure for members' trade with nonmember nations. In a *common market*, or economic union, members go beyond a customs union and try to bring all of their trade rules into agreement.

One example of a free-trade area is the **North American Free Trade Agreement (NAFTA)** agreed to by the United States, Canada, and Mexico. In 2015, Canada, the United States, and Mexico signed on to the Trans-Pacific Partnership (TPP), a growing list of Pacific Rim countries (Japan, Malaysia, Vietnam, Australia, New Zealand, Peru, Singapore, Brunei, and Chile) working towards reducing trade restrictions. The TPP is seen by many observers as a means to counter the tremendous trading power of China in the region. Other examples of regional trading blocs include the Mercosur customs union (joining Brazil, Argentina, Paraguay, and Uruguay) and the 10-country Association of Southeast Asian Nations (ASEAN).

North American Free Trade Agreement (NAFTA) an agreement among the United States, Canada, and Mexico to break down tariffs and trade restrictions.

NAFTA

NAFTA became effective in 1994. It created the world's largest free-trade zone with the United States, Canada, and Mexico. North America has a combined population of more than 471 million and a total GDP of more than $20 trillion. North America is one of the world's most attractive markets. The United States is the single-largest market, and it controls much of North America's business. Although fewer than 1 person in 20 lives in the United States, the nation's more than $16 trillion GDP represents about one-fifth of total world output.[23]

Canada is far less densely populated but has reached a similar level of economic standing. Canada's economy has been growing at a faster rate than the U.S. economy

NAFTA permits free trade for the United States, Canada, and Mexico. The amount of goods and services traded is healthy for the economy, both in Canada and in the United States.

HIT & MISS

Ford Motor Company: Engineered and Made in Mexico

Three of Ford Motor Company's 77 worldwide factories are located in Mexico, a country once viewed by carmakers as an assembly-only manufacturing destination. Ford's Mexico unit has tripled its engineering staff and produced 40 patents in less than three years, which may be one reason why the number of engineering students enrolled in Mexican universities has doubled.

Mexico's appeal to U.S. and foreign carmakers alike has to do with its proximity to the largest auto market in the world, lower wages, and the growing demand for cars in other parts of Latin and South America. In addition, labour costs for engineers in Mexico are 40 percent of what they are for their U.S. counterparts.

As Mexico continues to transform into a world-class manufacturing destination, foreign carmakers have also taken notice and poured over $12 billion of investments into the country over the last few years. With less than a decade of experience, as Ford's engineers gain momentum, look for quality Ford cars not only to be made but also designed by engineers in Mexico.

Questions for Critical Thinking

1. Considering Mexico's history of drug violence, what challenges do you see for the auto industry in Mexico?

2. How can foreign auto companies ensure there are skilled job candidates available to work in Mexican manufacturing facilities?

Sources: Ford Motor Company, "List of Operations Worldwide," accessed January 6, 2014, http://corporate.ford.com; Brendan Case, "Mexico's Surprising Engineering Strength," *Bloomberg Businessweek*, November 27, 2013, accessed January 6, 2014, www.bloomberg.com/bw/articles/2013-11-27/mexicos-surprising-engineering-strength; "Mexico's Car Industry: Steaming Hot," *The Economist*, November 15, 2013, accessed January 6, 2014, www.economist.com/blogs/schumpeter/2013/11/mexico-s-car-industry; Andrés Martinez, "Mexico: The Stranger Next Door," *Bloomberg Businessweek*, May 1, 2013, accessed January 6, 2014, www.bloomberg.com/bw/articles/2013-05-01/mexico-the-stranger-next-door.

---

in recent years. More than two-thirds of Canada's GDP is generated in the services sector. That makes sense because three of every four Canadian workers work in service occupations. Canada's per capita GDP places it among the top nations in terms of its spending power. Canada's economy is fuelled by trade with the United States, and its home markets are strong. The United States and Canada are each other's biggest trading partners. About 75 percent of Canada's exports and about 50 percent of its imports involve the United States.[24] U.S. business is also attracted to Canada's human resources. For example, all major U.S. automakers have large production facilities in Canada.

Mexico is moving from being a developing nation to gaining industrial nation status because of NAFTA (see the "Hit & Miss" feature). Mexico's trade with the United States and Canada has tripled since the signing of NAFTA. But 15 percent of the country's 119 million people live below the poverty line, and Mexico's per capita income is about a third of the per capita income in the United States. Mexico's border with the United States is busy with a stream of traffic moving goods from Mexican factories into the United States. The United States is Mexico's largest trading partner, receiving about 78 percent of Mexico's total exports and supplying almost 50 percent of Mexico's imports.[25]

The United States, Canada, and Mexico removed all trade barriers and investment restrictions over a 15-year period. NAFTA opened more doors for free trade. The agreement also eased rules about services, such as banking, and set up standard legal requirements for protecting intellectual property. The three nations can now trade with one another without tariffs or other trade barriers. It is also easier to ship goods across the partners' borders, since standardized customs and labelling regulations create economic efficiencies. They also help to make importing and exporting easier. Trade among the partners has increased and is now more than double what it was before NAFTA took effect.

CAFTA-DR

Central America–Dominican Republic Free Trade Agreement (CAFTA-DR) an agreement among the united states, costa rica, the dominican republic, el salvador, guatemala, honduras, and nicaragua to reduce tariffs and trade restrictions.

The **Central America–Dominican Republic Free Trade Agreement (CAFTA-DR)** created a free-trade area among the United States, Costa Rica, the Dominican Republic (the DR of the title), El Salvador, Guatemala, Honduras, and Nicaragua. The agreement ends most tariffs on nearly $56 billion in products traded between the United States and its Latin American neighbours.[26] Agricultural producers such as corn, soybean, and dairy farmers stand to gain under the relaxed trade rules. U.S. sugar producers fought against CAFTA-DR's passage. They had been supported

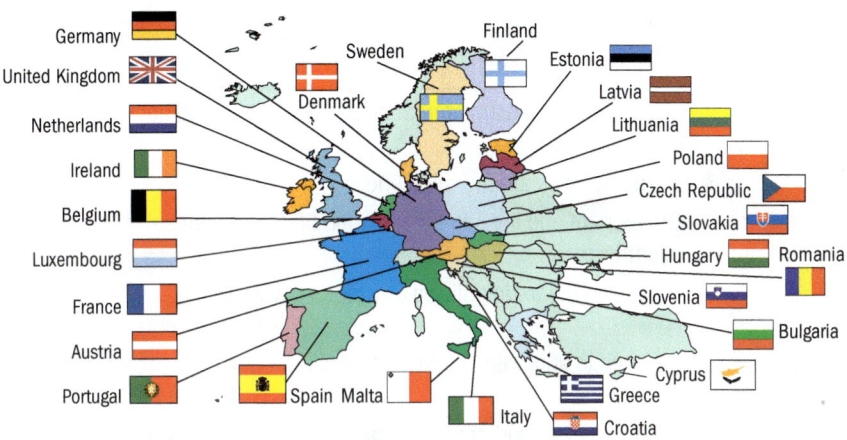

Figure 4.4 The 28 Nations of the European Union

by subsidies that kept their prices higher than in the rest of the world. Labour unions complained that the agreement would lower labour standards and export millions more jobs to lower-wage countries. Overall, CAFTA-DR's effects should be positive and have increased both exports and imports, much as NAFTA did.

European Union

The best-known example of a common market is the **European Union (EU)**. The EU combines 28 countries, nearly 506 million people, and a total GDP of roughly $16 trillion to form a huge common market representing 20 percent of the world's GDP.[27] **Figure 4.4** illustrates the 28 member states. Thirteen countries are the latest EU members—Croatia, Cyprus, Malta, Estonia, Latvia, Lithuania, Hungary, Poland, the Czech Republic, Slovakia, Slovenia, Bulgaria, and Romania. The Treaty of Lisbon took effect in 2009. Its goal is to make the union governance more efficient.

The EU's goals are to promote economic and social progress, to introduce European citizenship as a complement to national citizenship, and to give the EU a major role in international affairs. To achieve its goal of a borderless Europe, the EU is first removing barriers to free trade among its members. This highly complex process involves standardizing business regulations and requirements, standardizing import duties and taxes, and getting rid of customs checks so that companies can transport goods from England to Italy or Poland as easily as goods can be moved from St. John's to Vancouver.

Bringing standards and laws together can contribute to economic growth. But NAFTA had scared people in Canada and the United States who weren't sure about free trade with Mexico. Some people in Western Europe feel the same. They are worried that opening trade with such countries as Poland, Hungary, and the Czech Republic will cause jobs to flow to those lower-wage economies.

The EU also introduced the euro to replace currencies such as the French franc and Italian lira. For the 18 member nations that have adopted the euro, potential benefits include eliminating the economic costs of currency exchange and simplifying price comparisons. Businesses and their customers now make cheque and credit card transactions in euros and use euro notes and coins in making cash purchases.

European Union (EU) a 28-nation european economic alliance.

✓ ASSESSMENT CHECK

4.4.1 What international trade organization succeeded GATT, and what is its goal?

4.4.2 Compare and contrast the goals of the World Bank and the International Monetary Fund.

4.4.3 What are the goals of the European Union, and how do these goals promote international trade?

GOING GLOBAL

Expanding into overseas markets can increase profits and marketing opportunities. It can also make a firm's business operations more complex. Before deciding to go global, a company must make many key decisions, such as the following:

- Which foreign market(s) to enter
- The costs of entering a new market
- The best way to organize the overseas operations

LO 4.5 Compare the different levels of involvement used by businesses when entering global markets.

Table 4.3 International Trade Research Resources on the Internet

WEBSITE AND ADDRESS	GENERAL DESCRIPTION
Foreign Affairs, Trade and Development Canada www.international.gc.ca	Gateway to Canadian international trade and foreign activities involving businesses.
Bloomberg—www.bloomberg.com	Business news around the world.
Europages www.europages.com	Directory of and links to Europe's top 500,000 companies in 33 European countries.
World Trade Organization www.wto.org	Details on the trade policies of various governments.
CIA *World Factbook* www.cia.gov/library/publications/resources/the-world-factbook/index.html	Basic facts about the world's nations, from geography to economic conditions.
STAT-USA www.usa.gov/Topics/Reference-Shelf/Data.shtml	Extensive trade and economic data, information about trends, daily intelligence reports, and background data (access requires paid subscription to the service).
The Canadian Trade Commissioner Service www.tradecommissioner.gc.ca/eng/home.jsp	Valuable information that will help companies prepare an export plan and develop a market entry strategy. Canada's trade commissioners, located in more than 160 cities worldwide, can help implement strategies and provide advice on how to take advantage of international business opportunities.
Canadian Trade Data Online www.ic.gc.ca/eic/site/tdo-dcd.nsf/eng/Home	Customized reports can be generated on Canada and U.S. trade in goods with over 200 countries.
Canada's Gateways www.canadasgateways.gc.ca/index2.html	Information on Canada's *National Policy Framework for Strategic Gateways and Trade Corridors*, which supports strategies to strengthen Canada's position in international commerce. Here you will find links to Canada's three main gateway and corridor initiatives and information on foreign trade zones.

These issues have more or less importance depending on the level of involvement a company chooses. Education and employee training in the host country are much more important for an electronics manufacturer building an Asian factory than for a firm that plans to export Canadian-made products.

Before deciding which markets to enter, companies usually take time to do research. This research focuses on local demand for the firm's products, availability of needed resources, and ability of the local workforce to make world-class, quality products. Other factors are existing and potential competition, tariff rates, currency stability, and investment barriers. Government and other sources can help with this research. A good starting place is the CIA's *World Factbook*. It contains country-by-country information on geography, population, government, economy, and infrastructure.

Foreign Affairs, Trade and Development Canada and the U.S. Department of Commerce have counsellors who work at district offices. These counsellors offer a full range of international business advice, including computerized market data and names of business and government contacts in dozens of countries. As **Table 4.3** shows, the Internet provides access to many resources for international trade information.

Levels of Involvement

After a firm has completed its research and has decided to do business overseas, it can choose one or more strategies:

- Exporting or importing
- Entering into contract-based agreements such as franchising, licensing, and subcontracting deals
- Choosing direct investment in the foreign market through acquisitions, joint ventures, or by setting up an overseas division

The company's risk increases with the level of its global involvement. But its overall control of all aspects of producing and selling its goods or services also increases.

Importers and Exporters

An *importer* is a firm that brings in goods produced abroad to sell at home. *Exporters* are companies that produce or purchase goods at home and sell them in other countries. An importing or exporting strategy provides the most basic level of international involvement and the least risk and control.

Exports are often handled by export trading companies. These firms search out competitively priced local merchandise, and then resell these items abroad at prices high enough to cover expenses and earn profits. Suppose a retail chain such as Pier 1 Imports wants to purchase West African products to sell in its stores. It may contact an export trading company that deals in a country such as Ghana. The local firm monitors the quality of goods, packs the order for overseas shipment, arranges transportation, and completes customs paperwork and other steps to move the product from Ghana to Canada.

Exporting can be one of two types: indirect or direct. A company uses *indirect exporting* when it makes a product, such as an electronic component, that becomes part of another product sold in foreign markets. The second method is *direct exporting*. This type of exporting occurs when a company tries to sell its products in markets outside its own country. Direct exporting is often the first step for companies entering foreign markets. It is also the most common form of international business. Firms that succeed at direct exporting may then move on to other strategies.

Export trading companies are one way to reach foreign markets. Two other methods are to use export management companies or offset agreements. An export management company can give an exporting firm advice and expertise. These international specialists help the exporter complete paperwork, make contacts with local buyers, and comply with local laws for labelling, product safety, and performance testing. The exporting firm retains more control than it would if it used an export trading company.

An *offset agreement* matches a major international firm with a smaller business. The smaller firm basically becomes a subcontractor to the larger firm. For example, Bombardier might contract with a small American supplier of electrical cables used to manufacture aircraft made in Canada and exported to the United States. Both firms benefit from the agreement, and the smaller firm can often gain international experience.

Countertrade

International trade often involves payments made in the form of local products, not currency. This system of international bartering agreements is called **countertrade**.

A common reason for using international barter is poor access to the needed foreign currency. To complete an international sales agreement, the seller may agree to accept part or all of the purchase cost in merchandise instead of in currency. The seller may try to find a buyer for the bartered goods before the transaction is completed. To make this task easier, several international buyers and sellers sometimes join together in a single agreement.

Countertrade is sometimes a firm's only way to enter a certain market. Many developing countries simply cannot get enough credit or financial help to afford the imports that their people want. Countries that have heavy debt also use countertrade. Russian buyers sometimes find their currency is less acceptable to foreign traders than the stronger currencies of the United States, Great Britain, Japan, and EU countries. Thus, Russian buyers may trade local products, ranging from crude oil to diamonds to vodka. These products become the payments when the foreign companies selling goods do not want to receive Russian rubles. Other countries, such as China, may restrict imports. For those countries, countertrade may be the only practical way to get government approval to import needed products.

countertrade a barter agreement whereby trade between two or more nations involves payment made in the form of local products instead of currency.

Contract-Based Agreements

After a company gains some experience in international sales, it may decide to enter into contract-based agreements with local parties. These agreements can include franchising, foreign licensing, and subcontracting.

Franchising Franchising is common among Canadian and U.S. companies. Franchising can also work well for companies that want to expand into international markets. A **franchise** is a contract-based agreement in which a wholesaler or retailer (the franchisee) can sell the

franchise a contract-based agreement in which a franchisee can produce or sell the franchisor's products under that company's brand name if the franchisee agrees to the operating terms and requirements.

franchisor's products under that company's brand name if the franchisee agrees to the operating terms and requirements. The franchisor also helps the franchisee with marketing, management, and business services. Franchises are common in the leading fast-food brands, such as Tim Hortons and McDonald's. In 1995, Tim Hortons merged with Wendy's International, Inc., which helped Tim Hortons gain entry into the United States. Tim Hortons can be found in Michigan, Maine, Connecticut, Ohio, West Virginia, Kentucky, Pennsylvania, Rhode Island, Massachusetts, and New York. Tim Hortons's Canadian operation is 95 percent franchise owned and operated. In 2014, Tim Hortons agreed to be acquired by 3G Capital, the investment firm that owns Burger King. At the time of the merger Tim Hortons had more than 3,000 restaurants across Canada and more than 600 locations in the United States. Burger King had over 13,667 restaurants in over 100 countries. The combined company is the third-largest fast-food restaurant in the world, generating over $22 billion in sales.[28] Franchising is described in detail in Chapter 5.

Foreign Licensing In a **foreign licensing agreement**, one firm allows another firm to produce or sell its product or use its trademark, patent, or manufacturing processes in a specific geographical area. In return, the firm receives a royalty or other compensation.

Licensing can be good for a small manufacturer that wants to launch a well-known product overseas. The small manufacturer gets a proven product from another market, and just a little or no investment is needed to start operating. Licensing can also allow a company entry into a market that would otherwise be closed to imports because of government restrictions. Sometimes a licensing agreement can ensure product freshness by allowing manufacturing to take place in the local market. For example, Morinaga, a Japanese food manufacturer, holds licences to produce Lipton teas, Kraft cheeses, and Sunkist fruit drinks and desserts in Japan.[29]

Subcontracting The third type of contract-based agreement is **subcontracting**. This agreement involves hiring local companies to produce, distribute, or sell goods or services. Subcontracting allows a foreign firm to use the subcontractor's expertise in local culture, contacts, and regulations. Subcontracting works equally well for mail-order companies. They can hire local businesses to fill the orders and serve customers. Manufacturers use subcontracting to save money on import duties and labour costs. Businesses choose to subcontract to market products that are best sold by locals in a given country.

The key downside of subcontracting is that companies cannot always control their subcontractors' business practices. Several major companies have been embarrassed by reports that their subcontractors used child labour to manufacture clothing.

foreign licensing agreement an international agreement in which one firm allows another firm to produce or sell its product or use its trademark, patent, or manufacturing processes in a specific geographical area in return for royalties or other compensation.

subcontracting an agreement that involves hiring other companies to produce, distribute, or sell goods or services; in international subcontracting, local companies in a specific country or geographical region are hired to produce, distribute, or sell goods or services.

Offshoring

Offshoring is not generally considered to be a way of starting business internationally. *Offshoring* is the moving of business processes to a lower-cost location overseas. It has become a widespread practice. China is the preferred location for production offshoring, and India is the preferred location for services offshoring. Many business leaders support offshoring. They believe that global firms must keep their costs as low as possible to stay competitive. The apparent link between jobs sent overseas and jobs lost at home has led to much debate about offshoring.

Offshoring shows no signs of slowing down, but it is changing, mostly for manufacturers. Mexico, India, and Vietnam are now the countries with the lowest manufacturing costs. According to one consultant, during 2005–2006 there was a surge in companies moving manufacturing to China. At the time, China offered competitive advantages, such as more infrastructure, over other low-cost countries. However, by 2007–2008, with the increasing costs of transportation and materials, that began to change. If companies are setting up factories abroad to sell to foreign markets, offshoring may make some sense. But it doesn't make sense to make heavy or bulky products abroad and then ship them to North American markets. The time needed to move the goods is also a factor. Offshoring to a few low-cost locations may be an international firm's lowest-risk strategy. For example, if India's currency, the rupee, strengthens, North American manufacturers can move some production away from India and if transportation costs start to climb, they can shift more production closer to home, in Mexico.[30]

International Direct Investment

The highest level of control is investing directly in another country's production and marketing. Over time, a firm may become successful at doing business in other countries through exporting

HIT & MISS

Apple Brings Manufacturing Work Back Home

As recently as a decade ago, you could purchase an Apple product made in the USA. Apple, along with numerous other companies, took pride in their "Made in USA" status. But in recent years, Apple and other companies chose a lower-cost labour structure in overseas countries. But that strategy seems to be slowly changing, with a small but gradual boomerang back to the United States—mainly from China. It's called reshoring, and Apple is part of the trend to bring manufacturing back to the United States.

Recently, the company created 2,000 engineering, manufacturing, and construction jobs in a facility in Arizona, where components for its products will be produced. In addition, Apple is producing its redesigned Mac Pro computer in Austin, Texas. The benefits of this move back home include quicker response to production problems and increased quality control.

Significant wage increases in China over the past decade and concerns over protecting intellectual property overseas are two reasons that helped prompt the move. In addition, geographically close-knit design and production teams leave less room for error in the manufacturing process.

For Apple, bringing jobs home is certainly a positive way to help the U.S. economy. With reshoring—and reuniting design and production in one country—Apple will need to change the slogan on some of its products back to "Made in USA."

Questions for Critical Thinking

1. Are there certain types of products, companies, or industries in which reshoring makes the most sense?
2. Is your decision to purchase a product ever influenced by where it was produced? If so, explain.

Sources: Clare Goldsberry, "As 'Made in USA' Gains in Popularity, Companies Reshore Manufacturing," *Plastics Today*, January 3, 2014, accessed January 6, 2014, www.plasticstoday.com/articles/%E2%80%9Cmade-usa%E2%80%9D-gains-popularity-companies-reshore-manufacturing; Juliette Garside, "Apple Creates 2,000 Jobs Shifting Production Back to US," *The Guardian*, November 5, 2013, accessed January 6, 2014, www.theguardian.com/technology/2013/nov/05/apple-creates-us-jobs-renewable-energy; Joel Johnson, "'Made in America,' or How Re-Shoring Can Transform the Global Procurement Landscape," *Spend Matters*, October 22, 2013, accessed January 6, 2014, http://spendmatters.com/2013/10/22/made-america-re-shoring-can-transform-global-procurement-landscape.

---

and contract-based agreements. Its managers may then decide to start manufacturing in those countries, open branch offices, or buy ownership in local companies. Apple is involved in the trend of reshoring, or bringing jobs back to the United States, mainly from China. See the "Hit & Miss" feature for more.

In an *acquisition*, a company purchases another firm in the host country. An acquisition means that a mostly domestic business operation can quickly become an international company. For example, the big U.S. retailer Target paid $1.8 billion to Hudson's Bay Company to acquire Canadian retailer Zellers. Target gained a quick entry to 133 prime locations in the Canadian market. However, the planned expansion into Canada failed, and Target closed its Canadian operations in 2015, losing an estimated $6 billion.[31]

In a **joint venture**, a company shares risks, costs, profits, and management responsibilities with one or more host-country companies. By setting up an *overseas division*, a company can do much of its business overseas. This strategy differs from a multinational company's strategy. A firm with overseas divisions stays primarily a domestic organization with international operations. Matsushita established Panasonic Automotive Systems Asia Pacific to develop and sell new technology products in India, Thailand, Indonesia, Malaysia, the Philippines, and Vietnam.

From Multinational Corporation to Global Business

A **multinational corporation (MNC)** is an organization with many foreign operations. Many U.S. multinationals, including Nike and Walmart, have expanded their overseas operations. They believe that domestic markets are peaking, and foreign markets offer greater potential for sales and profit. Other MNCs are making large investments in developing countries, partly because these countries provide low-cost labour compared with the wages in North America and Western Europe. In addition, many MNCs are locating high-tech facilities in countries that have large numbers of technical school graduates.

joint venture a partnership between companies for a specific activity.

multinational corporation (MNC) a firm with many operations and marketing activities outside its home country.

 ASSESSMENT CHECK

4.5.1 Name three possible strategies for beginning overseas operations.

4.5.2 What is countertrade?

4.5.3 Compare and contrast licensing and subcontracting.

4.5.4 Describe joint ventures.

LO 4.6 Distinguish between a global business strategy and a multidomestic business strategy.

DEVELOPING A STRATEGY FOR INTERNATIONAL BUSINESS

Managers need to develop a framework from which to conduct international business. But managers must first evaluate their corporate objectives, organizational strengths and weaknesses, and strategies for product development and marketing. They can choose to combine these elements in either a global strategy or a multidomestic strategy.

Global Business Strategies

global business strategy the offering of a standardized worldwide product and the selling of it in basically the same way throughout a firm's domestic and foreign markets.

In a **global business strategy** (or a *standardization strategy*), a firm sells the same product in basically the same way all over the world. Many companies simply change their domestic business strategies by translating promotional brochures and instructions into the languages of the host nations.

A global marketing perspective can be suitable for some goods and services and for market segments that are common to many nations. The approach works for products with nearly universal appeal, for luxury items such as jewellery, and for commodities such as chemicals and metals. Alcoa, for example, is the world's largest producer of aluminum for use in aerospace and automotive building and construction, consumer electronics, packaging, and commercial transportation. In many applications, aluminum's strength and light weight mean there are no good substitutes for it. The company forecasts a long-term increase in global demand, especially in China, India, Russia, the Middle East, and Latin America. It also sees itself as committed to a global strategy that blends sustainability with profitability. That means it will "build financial success, environmental excellence, and social responsibility through partnerships in order to deliver net long-term benefits to our shareowners, employees, customers, suppliers, and the communities in which we operate."[32]

Multidomestic Business Strategies

multidomestic business strategy a plan to develop and market products to serve different needs and tastes in separate national markets.

In a **multidomestic business strategy** (or an *adaptation strategy*), the firm treats each national market in a different way. It develops products and marketing strategies that appeal to the customs, tastes, and buying habits of specific national markets. Some companies do not change their strategy

Internet users in Western Europe were slow initially to order products online, but now make online purchases for such items as railroad tickets.

for different markets. These companies don't pay attention to the global nature of the Internet, which can cause problems for potential customers. For example, European consumers were slow to order products online. But Internet use in Western Europe has had huge growth. All types of companies have seen increases in the number of website visitors and in their Internet revenues.

✓ **ASSESSMENT CHECK**

4.6.1 What is a global business strategy? What are its advantages?

4.6.2 What is a multidomestic business strategy? What are its advantages?

WHAT'S AHEAD

The examples in this chapter show that both large and small businesses rely on world trade, not just major corporations. Chapter 5 looks at the special advantages and challenges facing small-business owners. A critical decision facing any new business is choosing the most suitable form of business ownership. Chapter 5 also looks at the major ownership structures—sole proprietorship, partnership, and corporation—and measures the pros and cons of each. The chapter closes by discussing recent trends affecting business ownership, such as the growing impact of franchising and business consolidations through mergers and acquisitions.

RETURN TO INSIDE BUSINESS

PotashCorp: Genesis for Economic Development

PotashCorp is a good example of a resource business that has a comparative advantage. Canadian mines are very profitable operating at today's commodity prices. The firm can expand globally by using its expertise at other mines around the world. As mentioned earlier, potash is a commodity, which means the product is the same whether it comes from this mine or that mine. That means PotashCorp can sell potash throughout its distribution network. International mining firms sometimes merge or acquire other firms to grow the business and increase profits. PotashCorp was the object of a takeover bid by Australian mining giant BHP Billiton, which also operates in Saskatchewan. The Saskatchewan government refused the sale with the argument that it was not in the best interests of the company and people of Saskatchewan.

QUESTIONS FOR CRITICAL THINKING

1. What are the upsides and downsides to a company that sells a commodity in competitive international markets?
2. Is PotashCorp an MNC or a global business?

SUMMARY OF LEARNING OBJECTIVES

LO 4.1 Explain the primary reasons why nations trade.

The world's economies are becoming increasingly global. That means Canadian and other foreign businesses have opportunities to expand into new markets for their goods and services. Doing business globally provides new sources of materials and labour. Trading with other countries reduces a company's dependence on economic conditions in its home market. Countries that encourage international trade usually have higher levels of economic activity, employment, and wages than countries that restrict international trade.

Nations usually benefit if they specialize in producing certain goods or services. A country has an absolute advantage if it holds a monopoly or if it produces a good or service at a lower cost than other nations. It has a comparative advantage if it can supply one product more efficiently or at a lower cost than it can produce other products.

✓ **ASSESSMENT CHECK ANSWERS**

4.1.1 **Why do nations trade?** Nations trade because trading increases economic growth. Trade provides a new market for products and access to needed resources. Trading makes production and distribution systems more efficient and reduces dependence on the economy of the domestic market.

4.1.2 **What are some measures of the size of the international marketplace?** Developing countries have lower per capita incomes than the developed nations in North America and Western Europe, but developing nations have populations that are large and growing. China's population is about 1.3 billion and India's is roughly 1.2 billion.

4.1.3 **How does a nation acquire a comparative advantage?** A nation has a comparative advantage when it can supply a product more efficiently and at a lower price than it can supply other goods, compared with the outputs of other countries.

LO 4.2 Describe how trade is measured between nations.

Countries measure their level of international trade by comparing exports and imports. They then calculate whether they have a trade surplus or a trade deficit. The balance of trade is the difference between a country's exports and its imports. The term *balance of payments* refers to the overall flow of money into or out of a country. It includes overseas loans and borrowing, international investments, and profits from such investments. An exchange rate is the value of one country's currency in terms of the currency of another country. Currency values fluctuate, or "float," depending on the supply and demand for each currency in the world market. When the value of the Canadian dollar falls compared with other currencies, the cost paid by foreign businesses and households for Canadian products declines, and demand for exports may rise. An increase in the value of the dollar raises the prices of Canadian products sold abroad, but it reduces the prices of foreign products sold in Canada.

 ASSESSMENT CHECK ANSWERS

4.2.1 Compare balance of trade and balance of payments. Balance of trade is the difference between exports and imports; balance of payments is the overall flow of money into or out of a country.

4.2.2 Explain the function of an exchange rate. A nation's exchange rate is the rate at which its currency can be exchanged for the currencies of other nations. An exchange rate makes it easier for countries with different currencies to trade with each another.

4.2.3 What happens when a currency is devalued? Devaluation is a reduction in a currency's value in terms of other currencies or in terms of a fixed standard.

LO 4.3 Identify the major barriers to international trade.

Businesses face several barriers in the global marketplace. Companies that operate in other countries need to be sensitive to social and cultural differences, such as languages, values, and religions. Economic differences include standard-of-living variations and levels of infrastructure development. Legal and political barriers are difficult to judge. Each country sets its own laws for business practices. Trade restrictions such as tariffs and administrative barriers are also barriers to international business.

 ASSESSMENT CHECK ANSWERS

4.3.1 How can values and attitudes form a barrier to trade, and how can these barriers be overcome? Marked differences in values and attitudes, such as religious attitudes, can form barriers between traditionally capitalist countries and countries adopting new capitalist systems. Many of these barriers can be overcome by learning about the values and attitudes in other cultures and by respecting such differences.

4.3.2 What is a tariff? What is its purpose? A tariff is a surcharge or duty charged on foreign products. Its purpose is to protect domestic producers of those items.

4.3.3 Why is dumping a problem for companies marketing goods internationally? Dumping is selling products in other countries at prices below production costs or below typical prices in the home market. Dumping decreases the cost of products in the market where they are dumped. Thus, dumping hurts the domestic producers of those products.

LO 4.4 Explain how international trade organizations and economic communities reduce barriers to international trade.

Many international organizations try to promote international trade by reducing trade barriers among nations. Some of these organizations are the World Trade Organization, the World Bank, and the International Monetary Fund. Multinational economic communities create partnerships to remove barriers to the flow of goods, capital, and people across the borders of its member countries. Three economic agreements are the North American Free Trade Agreement, CAFTA-DR, and the European Union.

 ASSESSMENT CHECK ANSWERS

4.4.1 What international trade organization succeeded GATT, and what is its goal? The World Trade Organization (WTO) succeeded GATT. Its goals are to monitor GATT agreements, mediate disputes, and continue GATT's aim to reduce trade barriers throughout the world.

4.4.2 Compare and contrast the goals of the World Bank and the International Monetary Fund. The World Bank funds projects that build or expand nations' infrastructure. These projects include transportation, education, and medical systems and facilities. The International Monetary Fund makes short-term loans to member nations that cannot meet their expenses. The fund operates as a lender of last resort for troubled nations.

4.4.3 What are the goals of the European Union, and how do these goals promote international trade? The European Union's goals are to promote economic and social progress, to introduce European citizenship as a complement to national citizenship, and to give the EU a major role in international affairs. Bringing standards and laws together can contribute to international trade and economic growth.

LO 4.5 Compare the different levels of involvement used by businesses when entering global markets.

The first level of involvement in international business is exporting and importing. This strategy involves the lowest degree of both risk and control. Companies may use export trading companies or management companies to help distribute their products. Other options are contract-based agreements, such as franchising, foreign licensing, and subcontracting. Franchising and licensing are especially suitable for services. Companies may also use local subcontractors to produce goods for local sales. The highest level of control is investing directly in another country's production and marketing, known as international direct investment. This strategy also has the greatest risk. Firms make direct investments by acquiring foreign companies or facilities, forming joint ventures with local firms, or setting up their own overseas divisions.

ASSESSMENT CHECK ANSWERS

4.5.1 Name three possible strategies for beginning overseas operations. Three strategies are exporting or importing; using contract-based agreements such as franchising, licensing, or subcontracting; and making direct investments in foreign markets through acquisition, joint venture, or setting up an overseas division.

4.5.2 What is countertrade? Countertrade is an agreement to make payments in the form of local products, not in currency.

4.5.3 Compare and contrast licensing and subcontracting. In a foreign licensing agreement, one firm allows another firm to produce or sell its product or use its trademark, patent, or manufacturing process in a specific geographical area. In return, the firm receives royalty payments or other compensation. In international subcontracting, a firm hires local companies in other countries to produce, distribute, or sell its goods and services.

4.5.4 Describe joint ventures. In a joint venture, a company shares risks, costs, profits, and management responsibilities with one or more host-country companies.

LO 4.6 Distinguish between a global business strategy and a multidomestic business strategy.

A company that adopts a global strategy (or a standardization strategy) develops a single, standardized product and marketing strategy for worldwide sales. The firm sells the same product in basically the same way in all countries where it operates. Under a multidomestic strategy (or an adaptation strategy), the firm treats each foreign market in a different way. It develops products and marketing strategies that appeal to the customs, tastes, and buying habits of specific nations.

ASSESSMENT CHECK ANSWERS

4.6.1 What is a global business strategy? What are its advantages? A global business strategy is a standardized competitive strategy. The firm sells the same product in basically the same way all over the world. This strategy works well for goods and services that are common to many nations. The firm can market the products to many countries without making many changes.

4.6.2 What is a multidomestic business strategy? What are its advantages? In a multidomestic business strategy, the firm treats each foreign market in a different way. The firm tries to appeal to the customs, tastes, and buying habits of specific national markets. This strategy allows the firm to change its marketing appeals to suit individual cultures or areas.

BUSINESS TERMS YOU NEED TO KNOW

balance of payments 93

balance of trade 93

Central America–Dominican Republic Free Trade Agreement (CAFTA-DR) 106

countertrade 109

devaluation 95

dumping 103

embargo 103

European Union (EU) 107

exchange control 103

exchange rate 95

exports 90

foreign licensing agreement 110

franchise 109

General Agreement on Tariffs and Trade (GATT) 104

global business strategy 112

imports 90

infrastructure 98

International Monetary Fund (IMF) 105

joint venture 111

multidomestic business strategy 112

multinational corporation (MNC) 111

North American Free Trade Agreement (NAFTA) 105

quota 103

subcontracting 110

tariffs 102

World Bank 104

World Trade Organization (WTO) 104

REVIEW QUESTIONS

1. How does a business decide whether to trade with a foreign country? What are the key factors for participating in the information economy on a global basis?
2. Why are developing countries such as China and India becoming important international markets?
3. What is the difference between absolute advantage and comparative advantage? Give an example of each.
4. Can a nation have a favourable balance of trade and an unfavourable balance of payments? Why or why not?
5. Identify several potential barriers to communication when a company attempts to do business in another country. How might these be overcome?
6. Identify and describe briefly the three dimensions of the legal environment for global business.
7. What are the major nontariff restrictions affecting international business? Describe the difference between tariff and nontariff restrictions.
8. What is NAFTA? How does it work?
9. How has the EU helped trade among European businesses?
10. What are the key choices a company must make before reaching the final decision to go global?

PROJECTS AND TEAMWORK APPLICATIONS

1. In 1997, Britain transferred Hong Kong to China. China agreed to grant Hong Kong a high degree of autonomy as a capitalist economy for 50 years. Do you think this agreement is holding up? Why or why not? Consider China's economy, population, infrastructure, and other factors in your answer.
2. The huge growth of online business has introduced new legal concerns for international business. Patents, brand names, copyrights, and trademarks are difficult to monitor because the Internet has no boundaries. What steps can businesses take to protect their trademarks and brands online? Come up with at least five suggestions. Compare your list with your classmates' lists.
3. The WTO monitors GATT agreements, mediates disputes, and continues the effort to reduce trade barriers all over world. But many are concerned that the WTO's focus on lowering trade barriers encourages businesses to keep costs down by using methods that may lead to pollution and human rights abuses. Others argue that human rights should not be linked to international business. Do you think environmental and human rights issues should be linked to trade? Why or why not?
4. Describe briefly the EU and its goals. What are the pros and cons of the EU? Do you think the European alliance will hold up over the next 20 years? Why or why not?
5. Find the most recent edition of "The *Fortune* Global 500." It is usually published in *Fortune* magazine in late July or early August. You can also go to *Fortune's* online version at http://fortune.com/global500. Use the Global 500 to answer the following questions.
   a. On what is the Global 500 ranking based (e.g., profits, number of employees, revenues)?
   b. List the home countries of the world's 10 largest corporations.
   c. For the following industry classifications, identify the top-ranked company, its Global 500 ranking, and country: food and drug stores; industrial and farm equipment; petroleum refining; utilities: gas and electric; telecommunications; pharmaceuticals.

WEB ASSIGNMENTS

1. **WTO.** Visit the website of the World Trade Organization (www.wto.org). Research two current trade disputes. Which countries and products are involved? Do the two disputes have anything in common? What steps does the WTO follow to resolve trade disputes between member countries?
2. **EU.** Europa.eu is the Web portal for the European Union. Go to the http://europa.eu/index_en.htm and answer the following questions:
   a. What steps must a country take to become a member of the EU?
   b. How many EU members have adopted the euro? Which countries will be adopting the euro over the next few years?
   c. What is the combined GDP of EU members? Which EU member has the largest GDP? Which has the smallest GDP?
3. **Nestlé.** Nestlé is one of the world's largest global corporations. Visit the firm's website (www.nestle.com). Where is the company headquartered? What are some of its best-known brands? Are these brands sold in specific countries, or are they sold worldwide? List three or four issues Nestlé faces as a global corporation.

Note: Internet Web addresses change frequently. If you do not find the exact sites listed, you may need to access the organization's or company's home page and search from there or use a search engine such as Bing or Google.

PART 1: CASE STUDY Beau's All Natural Brewing Company
Building a Craft Brewery in a Competitive Canadian Industry

Meet Co-Founders Steve and Tim Beauchesne

Steve Beauchesne was familiar with the "hows and whys" of running a business. He grew up working at his father's leather finishing plant in the small farming community of Vankleek Hill, about an hour drive south of Ottawa. The plant finished leather for use in the fashion industry, which was rapidly moving offshore to places like China and India. Business was in a gradual decline. Although Steve was never particularly enamoured with the business, his time spent at the plant was a worthwhile education on how things get done. In his words, "I learned how to work with people, how people should be treated and I gained the confidence to run things." After studying business at Ryerson University in Toronto, he found himself working for a provincial government agency researching and writing business plans. At the same time he was developing a musical career in a band and promoting his record label. Life was good.

Meanwhile, back in Vankleek Hill, Tim Beauchesne had just said goodbye to his last customer. Like most small-business owners, he had planned to sell his business and cash out what would be his retirement funds when the time came. Tim had invested 20 years in the business but was still at least 10 years away from retirement. If his retirement was going to be what he had envisioned, an alternative course of action would be needed. Like many small-business owners, he had no debts and could have sold the land and building the plant stood on but was open to the idea of starting another business, if Steve was interested.

On a visit to Toronto, father and son talked about the possibilities and what course of action to take. Obviously the choice, if there was to be one, would have to resonate with Steve and be motivating enough for him to want to take over full management responsibilities one day and leave the secure government career path he was presently pursuing. The discussions eventually came around to starting a microbrewery—something Steve and Tim were equally passionate about. Steve was an amateur brewer and considered himself knowledgeable about small-batch production, but both men recognized that larger-scale production and distribution would require careful research and consideration before jumping in with Tim's current pool of retirement funds.

The Canadian Craft Brewing Industry

The craft beer industry is growing in Canada, as it is elsewhere in the world. Long-established beer giants are facing competition from much smaller craft beer producers. Also referred to as microbrewers, craft brewers are known for their unique beer products that provide something "different" for beer drinkers looking for more variety in beer tastes. The basic recipe of barley, hops, and yeast can result in very unusual and creative tastes once spices, herbs, and other flavourings like fruit were introduced to the brew.

The concept is a familiar one found in other industries where customers seek out variety, especially food and beverages. And because of new technology that allows for smaller but economical production operations, craft brewers can start up small and gradually expanded as sales grow. Many craft brewers are also built around a pub or restaurant where beer is normally sold and then look to expand sales through other restaurants, pubs, and venues such as golf courses.

Today, about 10 million Canadians drink over $5 billion worth of beer annually. Total beer consumption in Canada amounts to more than 2 billion litres, averaging 64 litres per capita. It is greatest in Newfoundland (79 litres), followed by Quebec (73 litres) and Alberta (69 litres) with the remaining provinces close to the national average. There are two large-scale brewers: Anheuser-Busch InBev, headquartered in Belgium, is the largest brewing company in the world and has a 41 percent share of the Canadian market. U.S.-based Molson Coors, the world's seventh-largest brewer, is in second place in Canada with a 33 percent share. The remainder is divided among more than 200 breweries, mostly craft brewers defined as producing less than 2 million barrels (117 litres = 1 barrel) annually and whose ownership by a large brewer is no greater than 25 percent. Together, more than 9,000 people work directly in the industry. From large cities to small towns, local entrepreneurs are considering the opportunities and risks that come with starting up a craft brewery.

Steve Reflects on His Decision

In 2004, Tim Beauchesne and his son Steve began exploring the idea of becoming craft brewers. Two years later they opened Beau's All Natural Brewing Company in the refurbished leather finishing plant with a loan and Tim's capital totalling $300,000. Upon reflection, Steve said, "I just couldn't say no to the idea of doing something I had only dreamed about. I loved everything about the idea—the product, running my own business. I knew in my gut that people would love our beer if we offered them something different than 'same old standard beer' the big breweries were pumping out." In their first year of operation Beau's produced and sold 30,000 litres of beer, and eight years later were selling 3.5 million litres—a 100-fold increase.

Questions for Critical Thinking

1. What were the specific factors of production Steve and Tim Beauchesne needed to start the brewery?
2. How has Beau's contributed to the local and national economies?
3. Given the risks and barriers to entry at the time, would you have started Beau's? Explain your reasoning.

1 LAUNCHING YOUR...

GLOBAL BUSINESS AND ECONOMICS CAREER

In Part 1, "Business in a Global Environment," you have learned about the role of contemporary business in today's society. You also learned about the major forces that shape contemporary business. The part includes four chapters that discuss the changing face of business, business ethics and social responsibility, economic challenges facing contemporary business, and competing in world markets. Business has always been an exciting career field. You can choose to start your own company, work at a local business, or take a position with a multi-national corporation. Today's business opportunities are very attractive. Businesses are expanding to compete in a global economy—and they need loyal and talented people to help them reach their goals. Professional and business service jobs are found in some of the fastest-growing industries in the North American economy. These jobs are projected to grow by more than 23 percent over a decade.[1] Now is the time to learn about several career options that can lead you to your dream job. Each part in this text includes a profile of some of the many opportunities available in business. Here are a few opportunities related to Chapters 1 through 4.

If you're good at numbers and are interested in how societies and companies work, then you may be suited to a career as an *economist*. Economists study how resources are divided up, research information by collecting and studying data, watch economic trends, and develop forecasts. Economists study the cost of energy, foreign trade and exchange between countries, the effect of taxes, and employment levels—both from a national or global viewpoint and from the viewpoint of individual businesses. Some economists work for corporations to help them run more efficiently. Others work for consulting firms to offer their special knowledge, or for government agencies to oversee economic decision making. Usually economists need advanced degrees to work in top-level positions. Economists usually earn more than $80,000 per year.[2]

Are you interested in global business? Many companies search the world for the best employees, supplies, and markets. You could work in Canada for a foreign-based firm such as Nokia or Toyota. Or you could work in Australia, Asia, Europe, or Latin America for a Canadian-based firm such as Royal Bank of Canada. You could also use computer networks to work with overseas co-workers to develop new products for a firm such as General Electric. Today's technology and telecommunications mean that distance is no longer a barrier to doing business. Global business careers can be found in all the areas you will read about in this text—business ownership, management, marketing, technology, and finance.

Global business leaders are not born, they're made. So how can you start on that career path? Businesses consider three areas when hiring employees for overseas assignments:

- *Competence*—technical knowledge, language skills, leadership ability, experience, and past performance
- *Adaptability*—interest in overseas work, communication skills and other personal skills, empathy for other cultures, and appreciation for varied management styles and work environments
- *Personal characteristics*—education, experience, and social compatibility with the host country[3]

Solid experience in your field or company is the most needed skill. Firms want employees who are skilled in their business and are loyal to the firm. Only the best are hired to represent the firm overseas. People who obtain their master's of business administration (MBA) degree are doing well financially; in a recent year, the average salary for MBA graduates a few years out of school was $126,000.[4] Companies don't usually want to send new graduates overseas immediately. Instead, they invest in training to make sure employees are suited to the new assignment.

The second-highest skill that companies look for is two-fold: knowledge of and interest in other languages and cultures. Businesspeople need to be able to work smoothly in another society, so they are selected for their abilities with other languages and cultures. China is a business hotspot, so some people have become fluent in Mandarin Chinese to increase their career prospects. Some school systems offer Chinese language classes in addition to the standard offerings of French, German, and Spanish.

Finally, employees are assessed on their personal characteristics. After all, firms want to be certain that employees will fit well in their new country. A person's talent is still the most important factor when assigning work, but executives with cross-cultural skills are in high demand.[5]

CAREER ASSESSMENT EXERCISES IN ECONOMICS AND GLOBAL BUSINESS

1. The Canadian economy has had many ups and downs. As a result, economists are often in the news. The head of the Bank of Canada, Stephen Poloz, manages the country's general financial condition. To learn about the role economists play in a federal government agency, research Poloz's background and qualifications. Assess how he is performing at the Bank of Canada. Now make a list of your own skills. Are there areas where your skills match his? What do you need to change?

2. To see the effect of the global economy in your community, visit a major retailer. List the countries that make the products on the shelves. Compare your list with your classmates' lists. See who found the most countries and what goods those countries made. Go online to research the career opportunities at the retailer's website.

3. To learn more about other countries, go online and research a country you are interested in. The following sources may be useful:

   - *The World Factbook*, published by the Central Intelligence Agency, www.cia.gov/library/publications/the-world-factbook. This publication is updated yearly. It contains much information about countries—geography and climate, population statistics, cultural and political information, transportation and communications methods, and economic data.

   - *Bloomberg Businessweek*, www.bloomberg.com/businessweek. This site provides business news from around the world and information on global companies.

   - Online news sites Yahoo! News and Google News, http://news.yahoo.com and http://news.google.com. Both of these online news sites have links to global business news.

   Write a one-page summary of the information you found. List the abilities and skills you would need to function well as a businessperson in that country. Focus on the areas of competence, adaptability, and personal characteristics. Now formulate a plan to gain those skills.

5 | FORMS OF BUSINESS OWNERSHIP AND ORGANIZATION

LEARNING OBJECTIVES

LO 5.1 Describe the characteristics of a small business.

LO 5.2 Discuss the contributions of small businesses to the economy.

LO 5.3 Discuss why small businesses fail.

LO 5.4 Describe the features of an effective business plan.

LO 5.5 Identify the assistance available to small businesses.

LO 5.6 Explain franchising.

LO 5.7 Outline the forms of private business ownership.

LO 5.8 Describe public and collective business ownership.

LO 5.9 Discuss the organizational structure of corporations.

LO 5.10 Describe mergers, acquisitions, and joint ventures.

INSIDE BUSINESS

Pi Athlete Management Inc.: Advising Athletes about Their Careers and More

Young athletes and their families face many challenges. Take a moment and imagine their complex world of information and decision making. Most successful athletes are very young when they first realize they have talent in a sport. These athletes and their families need to figure out how to encourage further athletic development and plan for higher education. The smart players know the value of education and think about what they can do if a sports career doesn't work out. Coaches and trainers remind them that injuries have ended many sports careers and will continue to do so—just ask Sidney Crosby how injuries have affected his career. At some point, aging brings all athletic careers to an end. Professional athletes often retire in their early thirties—if they can stay healthy and active. Hockey players Gordie Howe and Chris Chelios played into their forties, but their long careers are a rarity.

Some athletes want to work at a career in sports while getting a college or university education. These athletes need to look for scholarship programs, especially programs affiliated with the National Collegiate Athletic Association (NCAA) in the United States. Some amateur athletes succeed and become professional athletes. These athletes will face contract negotiations, relocation costs, and many financial, tax, and legal issues. Amateur athletes cannot be represented directly by agents. Usually their families act as the go-between, dealing with the agents and consulting firms until the athlete becomes a professional.

During their careers, athletes use their public recognition to make extra money through endorsements and speaking engagements. Some athletes develop products such as games, books, and equipment. Sports personalities often earn more money through their activities off the field than on. For example, Tiger Woods has earned more than $100 million through tournament winnings but more than $1 billion when you include his earnings from product endorsements, especially his profitable relationship with Nike.

So where do athletes find a team of consultants to help manage their careers and advise them along the way? Pi Athlete Management Inc. of Montreal offers a full set of services under one roof.

The firm has a team of consultants to advise athletes and their families when making decisions related to education, athletic training, media relations, marketing and endorsements, and financial planning. Pi Athlete Management provides services and develops trusting relationships with athletes and their families—and hopes to share in their professional success. Receiving fees for services helps to pay the bills, but the big money is earned when a sports professional starts earning big salaries, bonuses, and revenues from endorsements. Agents who manage this part of the business activity usually earn money on a commission. The average player's salary is high: in basketball, $5.15 million; in baseball, $3.3 million; in hockey, $2.4 million; and in football, $1.9 million. It is easy to understand why athletes, their families, and their agents are all attracted to the dream of a professional sports career.

For example, 22-year-old Marc Bourgeois, from Granby, Quebec, signed as a free agent with the Arizona Diamondbacks in 2011. He played for the University of Southern Mississippi, and then was drafted by the Minnesota Twins in 2009. His friend and former teammate from Granby, Michael Carbone, suffered a back injury that ended his dream of a sports career. But today, Michael Carbone is an agent (working with Pi Athlete Management), and Marc Bourgeois receives public relations help from the firm's PR expert and co-founder, Daniel Smajovits.

The formal structure of the business requires a contract with the consultants and agents that provide services on behalf of Pi Athletic Management. According to Marty Bindman, one of the founding partners of Pi Athlete Management, "every member of our team, with the exception of the founding partners, can be considered as an independent contractor. They operate under our brand as affiliates and receive our support. In exchange, they are paid a referral fee and we cover their expenses. Daniel Smajovits and I are involved in all meetings with clients and potential clients. Client contracts are entered into with Pi. Michael Carbone is affiliated with us in just such a capacity. He is heading up our baseball initiative. He recently graduated with an MBA in sports management under an NCAA baseball scholarship. His career was cut short by a back injury. Marc Bourgeois came to us through Michael. He was not happy with his previous representation and asked us to take over after signing with the Diamondbacks organization."

As more athletes and their families share their stories with others who need management services, word-of-mouth will help build the enterprise.[1]

CHAPTER 5 OVERVIEW

Do you want to work for a big company or a small one? Do you plan to start your own business? If you want to start your own company, you're not alone. Every day, more North Americans are starting a new business than those who are getting married or having a baby. Before you enter the business world—as an employee or an owner—you need to know a few things: the industry the company operates in and the size and framework of the firm. For example, Pi Athlete Management Inc. is a small company that has many associates. These associates and the founders bring to the firm their knowledge and past work experience with professional sports management.

Several factors affect how a business is organized, including how easily it can be set up, its access to financing, its tolerance of financial risk, its strengths and weaknesses, and the strengths and weaknesses of competing firms.

This chapter begins by focusing on small-business ownership, including the advantages and disadvantages of small-business ventures, the contributions of small businesses to the economy, and the reasons small businesses fail. The chapter examines the services provided by the Business Development Bank of Canada (BDC), the role of women and members of minority groups in small business, and alternatives for small businesses, such as franchising.

The chapter then discusses the forms of private business ownership—sole proprietorships, partnerships, and corporations. In addition, we discuss the features of not-for-profit organizations. Public and collective ownership are also examined. The chapter concludes with an explanation of structures and operations typical of larger companies, and a review of the major types of business alliances.

LO 5.1 Describe the characteristics of a small business.

MOST BUSINESSES ARE SMALL BUSINESSES

When we hear the term *business*, many of us think of big corporations, such as Bell Canada Enterprises, Royal Bank of Canada, or Rogers Communications. But most businesses are small businesses. In fact, more than 98 percent of all Canadian businesses, just over 1.1 million, employ fewer than 100 people. Small businesses employ people other than the owner, but Canada also has 2.7 million self-employed individuals. Setting up a self-employed business is not the same as running a business that employs other people. Interestingly, Statistics Canada reports that the numbers of self-employed people have been quite steady for the past decade.[2]

What Is a Small Business?

How can you tell a small business from a large one? The definition varies depending on the source, but Industry Canada defines a **small business** as an "independent business having fewer than 100 employees, not dominant in its market and revenues not more than $2 million."[3]

small business an independent business with fewer than 100 employees and revenues less than $2 million that is not dominant in its market.

Natura Foods Inc. is a Quebec-based manufacturer of tofu, almond, rice, and soy milk beverages. It sells products under the brand name Natur-a. The company is making products that meet North Americans's growing demand for natural and healthy foods and beverages. Today, this industry is valued at more than $4 billion in revenue, 10 times what it was 15 years ago. When the company was acquired in 1988, its revenue was only about $400,000. That made it a small business by Industry Canada's definition. Today, Natura's revenue is more than $30 million annually. The firm is both a small business and a mid-sized business. Its revenue places it above the cut-off revenue for small businesses, but its 20 employees fall within the definition for a small company. Many businesses fall into this sort of hybrid definition: When trying to classify the business, one requirement conflicts with another requirement. Whether a company is small or medium sized does not really matter unless the firm is applying for work, grants, or loans. Then, a means test is used to decide which firms qualify.[4]

Government agencies offer benefits to help small businesses compete with larger firms. Thus, small-business owners will want to know whether their companies meet the standards for being a small business. If a company qualifies, it may be able to receive government loans or take part in government programs that encourage purchasing goods and services from smaller suppliers. Some companies that receive such assistance might one day expand to other areas of the country and eventually become a larger business.

Typical Small-Business Ventures

Small businesses have always competed against each other and against some of the world's largest organizations. John Stanton created a retail concept for runners and walkers like himself in 1981, when sports retailing didn't try to meet the needs of such small markets like they do today. North America has 100 Running Room retail stores that employ more than 1,200 people. The Edmonton-based firm continues to grow, profiting from the popularity of walking and running. John Stanton uses the firm's website to build on personal relationships with loyal followers who support healthier living and giving back to the communities where they live. That formula seems to have been successful for Stanton, and The Running Room has been voted one of Canada's 50 Best Managed companies.[5]

John Stanton has built The Running Room into one of Canada's 50 Best Managed Companies.

In the past 15 years, many small businesses have closed because larger firms have bought out the small independent businesses and replaced them with larger operations. For example, we have fewer independent bookstores and hardware stores because bigger chains such as Indigo or Home Depot have increased the size and number of their stores. Some businesses are not very likely to be gobbled up by bigger firms, such as businesses that sell personalized services, rely on certain locations, and keep their overhead costs low.

Small firms have created an important space for themselves: They provide busy consumers with customized services that range from pet sitting to personal shopping. These businesses meet the needs of individual customers in a way that big firms often can't. About 25 percent of all business establishments produce goods; the remainder provide services. Small firms make up 98 percent of goods-producing businesses and 98 percent of all service-producing businesses.[6] **Table 5.1** provides a breakdown of the number of small, medium, and large employer businesses by sector. The majority of small businesses are concentrated in four industries—wholesale trade and retail; construction; professional, scientific and technical services; and other services.

Small business also plays a major role in agriculture. Canada has 68 million hectares of farmland. Most of this land is owned by large corporate farms, but most of Canada's 327,000 farms are owned by individual farmers or their families. The family farm is a classic example of a small-business operation. It is independently owned and operated, and it employs a limited number of people, including family members.[7]

Many small businesses are **home-based businesses**—firms that operate out of the business owner's residence. People often choose to operate home-based firms to have more control over both their business and their personal time. People who run home-based businesses can be morning people or night people, but they can usually choose to work when it suits them best. A home-based business is easier to run because of access to the Internet and communications devices such as smartphone technology. People who run home-based businesses don't need to worry about overhead costs such as leasing office or warehouse space. The downside is isolation and less visibility to customers—except, of course, if customers visit online. Those customers don't care where your office is located.

Many small businesses become more competitive because of the Internet. But the Internet doesn't guarantee success—there are so many websites that a small firm needs to find ways to make its online presence effective. Setting up a website is generally less expensive than opening a retail store. A website can also reach a wider range of customers.

North American business history has many stories of great inventors who started their companies in barns, garages, warehouses, and attics. For example, Steve Jobs and Steve Wozniak, who founded Apple Computer, Inc., used a family garage to transform their technical idea into a commercial reality. The impact of today's entrepreneurs, including home-based businesses, is discussed in more depth in Chapter 6.

home-based businesses firms operated from the residence of the business owner.

 **ASSESSMENT CHECK**

5.1.1 How does Industry Canada define *small business*?

5.1.2 In what industries do small businesses play a significant role?

Table 5.1 Employer Businesses by Firm Size (Number of Employees) in Industrial Sector, December 2012

INDUSTRIAL SECTOR (RANKED BY NUMBER OF EMPLOYER BUSINESSES)					EMPLOYER BUSINESSES			SMALL (1–99)			MEDIUM (100–499)	LARGE (500+)
	Total	1–4	5–9	10–19	20–49	50–99		100–199	200–499		
Wholesale Trade and Retail	208,489	81,481	57,859	37,535	20,646	6,749	204,270	3,140	1,012	4,152	67
Construction	128,021	77,811	26,013	13,336	7,588	2,094	126,842	807	286	1,093	86
Professional, Scientific and Technical Services	127,612	96,547	15,134	8,347	5,022	1,475	126,525	688	327	1,015	72
Other Services	115,655	76,052	23,577	10,297	4,273	931	115,130	345	146	491	34
Finance, Insurance, Real Estate and Leasing	97,664	59,854	15,283	9,955	9,708	1,619	96,419	620	406	1,026	219
Health Care and Social Assistance	90,078	51,008	18,125	11,443	5,967	1,988	88,531	1,056	432	1,488	59
Accommodation and Food Services	76,105	20,560	18,143	17,035	14,385	4,661	74,784	1,004	259	1,263	58
Management of Companies and Enterprises and Other Support Services*	64,814	35,192	12,525	7,452	5,155	2,143	62,467	1,255	736	1,991	356
Transportation and Warehousing	52,532	34,821	7,242	4,615	3,617	1,252	51,547	509	364	873	112
Manufacturing	51,613	17,478	10,427	8,556	8,001	3,638	48,100	2,113	1,115	3,228	285
Agriculture	39,328	28,296	6,236	2,896	1,425	328	39,181	115	28	143	4
Information, Culture and Recreation	32,493	16,057	5,894	4,423	3,742	1,284	31,400	670	285	955	138
Forestry, Fishing and Hunting	13,365	9,400	2,001	976	639	217	13,233	85	27	112	20
Mining, Quarrying, and Oil and Gas Extraction	9,771	5,621	1,312	1,165	858	418	9,374	212	127	339	58
Total	1,107,540	610,178	219,771	138,031	91,026	28,797	1,087,803	12,619	5,550	18,169	1,568

*Includes management of companies and enterprises; administrative support, waste management and remediation services.

Source: Industry Canada, "Small Business Research and Statistics: Key Small Business Statistics—August 2013, How Many Businesses Are There in Canada?" Table 3 www.ic.gc.ca/eic/site/061.nsf/eng/02804.html, accessed April 4, 2015. Reprinted with the permission of the Minister of Industry, 2015.

CONTRIBUTIONS OF SMALL BUSINESS TO THE ECONOMY

> **LO 5.2** Discuss the contributions of small businesses to the economy.

Small businesses are important to the Canadian economy. Together, they generate more than 30 percent of the nation's gross domestic product (GDP).[8] Only 10.4 percent of small and medium-sized businesses export. Nonetheless, they are responsible for $150 billion, or about 41 percent, of Canada's total value of exports.[9]

Creating New Jobs

Small businesses make significant contributions to the Canadian economy and to society as a whole. One major contribution is the number of new jobs that small businesses create each year. The number of new jobs varies from year to year, but in many years more than half of all new jobs are created by companies with fewer than 100 employees. According to Statistics Canada, small businesses created 77.7 percent of all private jobs from 2002 to 2012, which on average works out to a little over 100,000 jobs each year. Over the same 10-year period, medium-sized and large businesses created 12.5 percent and 9.8 percent, respectively, representing approximately 17,000 and 11,800 new jobs each year.[10]

Small businesses also help the economy by hiring people who have difficulty finding jobs at larger firms. Some of these employees are people returning to the workforce after a period of not working, people who receive social assistance, and workers with various challenges.

You might never want to start your own company, but you will probably work for a small business at some point in your career, especially in your first few jobs. Small firms often hire the youngest workers.

Creating New Industries

Small firms give businesspeople the opportunity and outlet for developing new ideas. Sometimes these new ideas become entirely new industries. Many of today's largest and most successful firms, such as Whole Foods, Google, and Amazon, began as small businesses. Facebook co-founders Mark Zuckerberg, Dustin Moskovitz, Chris Hughes, and Eduardo Saverin launched their new business from their college dorm room. In five years, Facebook had more than 300 million users. It had successfully positioned itself as a leader in the new industry of social networking.[11]

New industries are sometimes created when small businesses shift their focus to provide needed services to a larger corporate community. Corporate downsizing creates a demand for activities previously handled by in-house employees. These support businesses may become an industry themselves. For example, the need for wireless communication devices and services to support businesses has led to a huge number of small businesses trying to meet this demand.

New industries can be created when small businesses shift their focus to meet consumer interests and preferences. For example, many North Americans are too busy working to shop for the things they need. New businesses have been created to meet this demand by offering customized services. The Trunk Club is an online shopping service that uses Web

New industries can be created when small businesses shift their focus to meet consumer interests and preferences. One such company is Trunk Club, which combines expert advice from a personal stylist with the convenience of shopping online.

Going Green

GREEN MAMA: SMALL BUSINESS WITH A BIG MESSAGE

The Green Mama isn't a mythical figure. She's a consultant, writer, and environmentalist who believes the world can be made more sustainable, one mom at a time. Manda Aufochs Gillespie had been living and promoting an environmentally conscious lifestyle for several years when she was featured in a *Chicago Tribune* article. Suddenly, Gillespie became a guru for like-minded parents who also wanted to improve the health and lives of their families while reducing their impact on the planet. Since then she has launched a website, www.thegreen-mama.com. She also hosts a weekly playgroup/seminar for parents, the Green Mama Café; writes a blog; consults for daycare businesses and educational institutions; gives workshops; appears on television; and provides everyday advice to consumers. She's also a mom.

The website is the centre of Gillespie's green universe. "The site is for people who are trying to be green parents in any major city," she explains. "It's a tool for living." Visitors to the site can get shopping tips for the best cloth diapers, learn how to clean their floors with white vinegar (instead of commercial cleaners), become informed about buying local produce, and learn about everything from the effectiveness of hand sanitizers to the cost of organic produce. No question is too simple for Gillespie. She also suggests how to save money—and reduce waste—such as by re-gifting gently used children's clothing to another child instead of buying new clothing for a birthday gift.

How does her philosophy become a business? It's not just the $5 that each mom pays for one of Gillespie's workshops at the Green Mama Café, or her consulting fees. Marketing experts say that these moms represent some 20 million North American consumers who are now demanding green goods and services. It's not just cloth diapers and natural floor cleaners. These consumers now look carefully at every item they put in their reusable shopping bags. If they have to pay a bit more for those products, they will—because they are usually saving money somewhere else. "It turns out that what saves money also saves resources and what is better for the environment can also make parenting easier, if you have the right mindset," says one mom who goes to Gillespie's Green Mama seminars. These green moms have nearly $210 billion in purchasing power—and manufacturers, media, and service providers are paying attention.

Questions for Critical Thinking

1. Manda Gillespie owns one of many small businesses that are creating a whole new industry: green goods and services for parents. What factors will contribute to the success of these businesses? What risks do these businesses face?

2. As a consumer, do you purchase any green goods or services? Why or why not? Have these goods and services been offered by small or large companies?

Sources: Green Mama, accessed April 2, 2010, www.thegreenmama.com; Jessica Levco, "The Green Mama Speaks," *Chicago Magazine*, May 2009, www.chicagomag.com/Chicago-Magazine/May-2009/The-Green-Mama-Speaks; Robyn Monaghan, "Green Mamas Unite," *Chicago Parent*, March 20, 2009, www.chicagoparent.com/magazines/chicago-parent/2009-april/green-mamas-unite.

---

cams to meet with men who are too busy to shop for clothes. The company interviews customers to learn about their clothing needs, and then selects new clothing and sends it directly to the customer.[12]

New industries can also be created when both the business world and consumers see a need for change. For example, environmental responsibility has changed how we do things—from recycling and reusing goods to reducing the amount of energy we use. These changes have led to a new industry of green goods and services. Small companies provide many of these goods and services. The "Going Green" feature describes one small-business owner who uses her passion and talent to provide environmentally responsible services.

Innovation

Small businesses are good at innovation—developing new and improved goods and services. Innovation is often the entire reason for starting a new business. For example, 58.1 percent of small and medium-sized businesses in the manufacturing sector innovated within the three years from 2009–2011, and other industries also show high levels of innovation coming from small and medium-sized businesses: in knowledge-based industries, 50.0 percent innovated; professional, scientific, and technical services, 43.5 percent; and wholesale and retail trade, 41.1 percent.[13] In a

CAREER KICKSTART
How to Use Social Networking in Your Job Search

Online social networking is likely part of your everyday life. But you can also use this technology to look for a job. During one recent year, networking sites such as LinkedIn registered 1 million new users each month. Worried you'll get lost when so many other people are also using social networking? Use a few simple tips to stand out from the millions of others who have discovered the benefits of social networking.

- *Research a network before jumping in.* Some networks, such as Facebook, are mainly for connecting with friends. Others, such as LinkedIn, are stronger networks when looking for work. Twitter attracts both types of users. To decide what is right for you—and to make the most of a social network—learn about it before you log on to look for work.

- *Complete your online profile.* Help prospective employers by filling out your online profile, and update your bio as often as you can. Provide a link to your own blog or webpage. Don't try to be perfect—if you know your weaknesses or if you made a mistake in a previous job, describe how you've improved or learned from your mistakes.

- *Share information.* Be willing to share information about companies or career opportunities with other job seekers. You can help an online employer find the right person—even if it's not you.

- *Search for people.* First, look for companies that interest you. Next, talk to your friends, family members, classmates, alumni—anyone who might know someone at those companies. A specific job might not be available now, but a personal connection can help you when that job does open up.

- *Respect privacy.* You want to provide only certain information about yourself online, so respect the privacy of potential employers and colleagues. Read about the privacy settings of a social networking site and abide by them.

Sources: DeLynn Senna, "Recruiters Reveal Pet Peeves about Job Seekers," *Yahoo! Hot Jobs*, accessed April 2, 2010, http://hotjobs.yahoo.com; Alex Williams, "Mind Your BlackBerry or Mind Your Manners," *New York Times*, June 21, 2009; David LaGesse, "Turning Social Networking into a Job Offer," *U.S. News & World Report*, May 2009, pp. 44–45.

---

typical year, small firms develop twice as many product innovations per employee as larger firms. Small firms also produce 13 times more patents per employee than larger firms.[14]

During the twentieth century, small businesses developed several major innovations: the airplane, the personal computer, soft contact lenses, and the zipper. In the twenty-first century, small businesses are developing innovations that involve social networking, security, and green energy industries. The "Career Kickstart" feature offers tips for using online social networking successfully.

> **ASSESSMENT CHECK**
> 5.2.1 What are the three key ways that small businesses contribute to the economy?
> 5.2.2 How are new industries formed?

WHY SMALL BUSINESSES FAIL

LO 5.3 Discuss why small businesses fail.

Small businesses play a huge role in the Canadian economy. One of the reasons they are so successful is the same reason they fail—the willingness to take a risk. The most common difficulties for a small firm are management inexperience, inadequate financing, and the challenge of meeting government regulations. About 96 percent of small businesses that enter the marketplace are in business for one full year, 85 percent are in business for three years, and 70 percent are in business for five years.[15] Let's see why this happens.

Management Shortcomings

One of the most common causes of small-business failure is management inexperience. For example, managers may not have the right people skills, may not have much knowledge of finance, may not be able to track inventory or sales, may be poor at judging their competition, or may simply not have enough time to do everything that needs to be done. Large firms are often big enough that they can hire specialists in marketing and finance, but the owner of a small business often has to take on all the firm's roles at the same time.

Trying to do all the business functions can lead to bad decisions that can end in the firm's failure. Krispy Kreme was once a small business that expanded too fast because its management made poor decisions. The company's near failure had nothing to do with its doughnuts. Instead, as the company grew bigger, so did its debt. Some blamed management misconduct. At the same time, consumers began to turn their attention away from doughnuts and toward more healthful snacks and breakfast foods. Krispy Kreme is now recovering. It has new management and is operating on a smaller scale.[16]

Owners of small businesses can increase their chances of success by learning the principles of business, knowing the industry they operate in, developing good interpersonal skills, understanding their own limitations, hiring motivated employees, and asking for professional advice on finance, regulations, and other legal matters.[17]

Inadequate Financing

Money is the foundation of any business. Every business—large or small—needs some financing to operate, thrive, and grow. Another big problem of small businesses is inadequate financing. First-time business owners often assume that their firms will make enough money from their initial sales to finance continuing operations. But building a business takes time. Products need to be developed, employees need to be hired, a website needs to be constructed, distribution needs to be planned, and office or retail space may need to be rented or purchased. Most small businesses—even those with minimal startup costs—sometimes don't turn a profit for months or even years.[18]

We have all heard about people starting firms with just a few hundred dollars borrowed from a friend or with a cash advance from a credit card. But most small businesses get their startup money from commercial banks and other financial institutions. This type of financing includes credit lines and loans for nonresidential mortgages, vehicles, specialized equipment, and leases.[19]

Credit cards have high interest rates. Still, they are an important source of financing for small businesses. The heaviest users of credit cards for business financing are firms with fewer than 10 employees. Inadequate financing can make management shortcomings worse by making it more difficult for small businesses to attract and keep talented people. Typically, a big company can offer a better benefits package and a higher salary.

Successful small companies need to be creative to operate with less money to spend on employees, marketing, inventory, and other business costs. Asafumi Yamashita started his business with $500. He used the money to buy specialty vegetable seeds from Japan. In his own greenhouse, he planted Japanese spinach, radishes, and other special produce. Yamashita had become friends with the head chef at a Japanese restaurant in Paris. The chef told Yamashita that these vegetables were nearly impossible to buy locally. Within a year of planting those first seeds, Yamashita was supplying several top restaurants in Paris. Others heard about Yamashita's high-quality vegetables, and he now supplies his vegetables to only the most exclusive restaurants. Yamashita has limited

Asafumi Yamashita started his business with $500. He used the money to buy specialty vegetable seeds from Japan. Within a year, Yamashita was supplying several top restaurants in Paris. Yamashita has limited his number of customers and has no employees. This means he needs less financing and maintains control over all the vegetables he grows.

his number of customers and has no employees. This means he needs less financing and maintains control over all the vegetables that leave his garden.[20]

Government Regulation

Small-business owners say that meeting the terms of government regulations is one of their biggest challenges. Some firms close because of how difficult it is to deal with government regulations. Small businesses spend billions of dollars on paperwork each year. A large company has an easier time dealing with all the government forms and reports. Larger firms can often hire or contract specialists to deal with specific regulations, such as employment law and workplace safety requirements. But small businesses often have difficulty paying the costs of government paperwork because they have fewer staff and smaller budgets. Statistics Canada is doing research to help reduce the problem. In a recent year, small and medium-sized businesses in five sectors spent $1.17 billion filling out forms to meet 11 key government information requirements, such as filing income tax forms and paying federal and provincial sales taxes.[21]

Taxes are another big expense for a small business. All employers pay provincial and federal income taxes. They must also pay taxes for workers' compensation insurance, pension payments, and unemployment benefits. Although large companies have the same expenses, most have more resources to pay their taxes. The government has created tax incentives to help small businesses. These incentives include the Small Business Investor Tax Credit, which returns a 30 percent tax credit to an investor to a maximum $75,000 credit.[22]

✓ **ASSESSMENT CHECK**

5.3.1 What percentage of small businesses are still operating five years after starting?

5.3.2 What are the three main causes of small-business failure?

THE BUSINESS PLAN: A FOUNDATION FOR SUCCESS

LO 5.4 Describe the features of an effective business plan.

Large or small, every business needs a plan to succeed. We sometimes hear about firms that started with an idea scribbled on a restaurant napkin or sketched out on graph paper in a dorm room. But a business idea must have a solid plan to become reality. A **business plan** is a formal document that details a company's goals, the methods it will use to achieve those goals, and the standards it will use to measure its achievements. Firms often need a business plan to obtain financing. The business plan also creates a framework for the organization.

business plan a formal document that details a company's goals, methods, and standards.

Business plans give the organization a sense of purpose. They identify the firm's mission and goals. Business plans create measurable standards and outline a strategy for reaching company objectives. A typical business plan includes the following sections:

- An *executive summary* that briefly answers the who, what, where, when, why, and how questions for the business
- An *introduction* that includes a general statement of the concept, purpose, and objectives of the business
- Separate *financial* and *marketing sections* that describe the firm's target market, marketing plan, and detailed financial forecasts of the need for funds and when the firm is expected to break even—the level of sales where revenues equal costs
- *Résumés of principals*—these are especially important in plans written to obtain financing.

An effective business plan uses the five sections above, contains the company's mission, and addresses the following issues:

- *The company's mission and the vision of its founders.* Look at the home page of any firm's website and you will find its mission. At the website for TOMS Shoes, visitors learn that "TOMS Shoes was founded on a simple premise: With every pair you purchase, TOMS will give a pair of new shoes to a child in need. One for one. Using the purchasing power of individuals to benefit the greater good is what we're all about."[23] This simple statement says why the company was founded and what it intends to achieve.

Firms often need a business plan to obtain financing. Business plans identify the firm's mission and goals. They create measurable standards and outline a strategy for reaching company objectives. The business plan also creates a framework for the organization.

- *An outline of why the company is unique.* Why start a business that's just like hundreds of others? An effective business plan describes why the firm and its products differ from the rest of the pack. TOMS Shoes illustrates a unique business model with its "one-for-one" donation program.

- *The customers.* A business plan identifies who the firm's customers will be and how the firm will serve their needs.

- *The competition.* A business plan addresses its existing and potential competitors. It then suggests a strategy for creating better or unique offerings. A firm can study the competition to learn valuable information about what works and what doesn't work.

- *Financial evaluation of the industry and market conditions.* This knowledge helps develop a reasonable financial forecast and budget.

- *Assessment of the risks.* Every business undertaking involves risks. A solid business plan acknowledges these risks and outlines a strategy for dealing with them.[24]

One firm may want to change an entire industry, while another firm wants to improve the lives of children by giving them shoes. Both firms need a business plan to be a success. For more information on how to write a business plan, see Appendix E, "Developing a Business Plan," at the back of the textbook.

> **✓ ASSESSMENT CHECK**
>
> 5.4.1 What are the five main sections of a business plan?
>
> 5.4.2 Why is an effective business plan important to the success of a firm?

LO 5.5 Identify the assistance available to small businesses.

ASSISTANCE FOR SMALL BUSINESSES

Financing is an important part of setting up a small business. After writing a business plan, the business owner needs to look for loans and other types of financing. Government agencies and private investors often provide the needed funds. Many people want to start a business, which means government agencies can provide funds only to some firms. A strong business plan justifying the use of funds and growth potential can help persuade lenders.

Business Development Bank of Canada

The **Business Development Bank of Canada (BDC)** is a government agency that assists, counsels, and protects the interests of small businesses in Canada. BDC was created by an act of Parliament in 1944. It operates across Canada through offices and resource centres that provide long-term financial assistance and management counselling. The BDC also provides training, technical assistance, and education to help small businesses prepare for doing business in foreign markets. Statistics show that most small-business failures happen because of poor management. For this reason, the BDC works to improve the management skills of small-business owners and managers. The BDC offers individual counselling, courses, conferences, workshops, and a wide range of publications. BDC's management courses cover all the functions, duties, and roles of managers. Instructors may be teachers from local colleges or universities. They may also be management consultants, bankers, lawyers, and accountants. Fees for these courses are low. The most popular course is a general survey of eight to ten areas of business management. Businesspeople can then focus on one or more of these areas, depending on their strengths and weaknesses. The BDC sometimes offers one-day conferences. These conferences are aimed at keeping owner-managers up to date on new management developments, tax laws, and the other helpful information.[25]

The Small Business Administration (SBA) is the main government agency that helps small U.S. firms. The SBA is the advocate, or supporter, for small businesses within the U.S. federal government. Many small-business resources are available at the websites of both organizations.

> **Business Development Bank of Canada (BDC)** a governmental agency that assists, counsels, and protects the interests of small businesses in Canada.

Financial Assistance

Most small businesses borrow money directly from Canada's financial institutions. These banks, trust companies, and credit unions actively believe in lending money to small businesses. The Canada Small Business Financing Program (CSBFP) is typical of federal and provincial government assistance. When a bank loans money to a small business and is not paid back, the government will guarantee payment for as much as 85 percent of the loan. Some small businesses cannot borrow from traditional lending institutions because they don't have a financial history. These small businesses may be funded by the BDC or other organizations that may want to help higher-risk firms.

The CSBFP tries to increase the number of loans for establishing, expanding, modernizing, and improving small businesses. It does this by encouraging financial institutions to make their financing available to small businesses. By sharing the risks with financial institutions, the program may help businesses obtain loans of up to $500,000. The loans can cover 90 percent of the costs to purchase or improve land or property, to purchase leasehold improvements or improve leased property, or to purchase new equipment or improve used equipment. Eligible small businesses must be operating for profit in Canada and must have annual gross revenues less than $5 million.[26]

Business Incubators

Some community agencies want to encourage business development. These agencies use a concept called a **business incubator** to provide low-cost, shared business facilities to small startup companies. A typical incubator might section off space in an abandoned plant and rent it to various small firms. Tenants often share clerical staff, computers, and other business services. The goal is for new businesses to be ready to move out and operate on their own after a few months or years.

The Canadian Association of Business Incubation (CABI) is a national association of member organizations. CABI supports the growth of new and early-stage businesses. According to CABI and Statistics Canada research, Canada has at least 83 operating business incubators that generate more than $45 million in funds. Their almost 900 client firms raised more than $93 million in revenue and created full- and part-time jobs for more than 13,000 people. Incubation firms make a positive impact. After one year, 2,958 client companies had generated revenues.[27]

> **business incubator** a local program designed to provide low-cost, shared business facilities to small startup companies.

Private Investors

A small business may start with cash from a personal savings account or a loan from a family member. But small-business owners need larger sums of money to continue operating and to grow. They may want to continue receiving funds from private investors. **Venture capital** is money

> **venture capital** money invested in a business by another business or a group of individuals in return for an ownership share.

CBC's *Dragons' Den* Highlights Entrepreneurial Thinking and Investing

The CBC's popular reality show *Dragons' Den* is the Canadian version of a show that is seen around the world. The format is the same in every country. Entrepreneurs present their ideas for a new business to a panel of venture capitalists with whom they hope to make a deal. The idea is to partner with one or more panel members to improve the chances the business will be developed successfully.

The show succeeds partly because of the entertainment value: the viewers at home act as armchair-panelists. The show is also educational. Viewers watch the "dragons" review the presentations. They quickly learn about business valuation, patents, and the managerial mindset that venture capital partners like to see.

Many viewers are probably thinking about starting a business of their own. The biggest lesson that all viewers learn is the role of expertise and knowledge to move the business to the "next level." The entrepreneurs that make deals with the dragons are usually business owners who have been successful but need help to grow the business. They now need the dragons' expertise and business connections as much as they need their investment funds. Having the dragons on their side can help take their business to a higher level.

Questions for Critical Thinking

1. Why is *Dragons' Den* successful in Canada and around the world?
2. How would the show differ in other countries?

Sources: CBC, *Dragons' Den*, accessed March 18, 2012, www.cbc.ca/dragonsden; "Dragons' Den" *Financial Post*, accessed March 18, 2012, http://business.financialpost.com/tag/dragons-den; "Business Titans Jim Treliving and W. Brett Wilson Jump at FROGBOX Offering," *Marketwire*, January 27, 2011, accessed March 18, 2012, www.marketwire.com/press-release/business-titans-jim-treliving-and-w-brett-wilson-jump-at-frogbox-offering-1386326.htm; "Dragons' Den & Venture Capital," *Financial Blogger*, February 13, 2012, accessed March 18, 2012, www.thefinancialblogger.com/dragons-den-venture-capital.

Arlene Dickinson started working at Venture Communications in 1988. She took full ownership of the marketing firm 10 years later. Her success in marketing and communications led her to the panel of *Dragons' Den*, the CBC's popular business show. On the show, entrepreneurs compete for funding and partnership with the panel members. Dickinson is also in demand as an author and speaker at events that highlight her entrepreneurial ability and success.

invested in the small business by another business or a group of individuals in return for an ownership share. Venture capital (VC) can give the small business the funding it needs to succeed. Even when the economy is slow, venture capitalists are looking for companies to invest in. Canada's Venture Capital and Private Equity Association reports that Canadian VC investment in 2014 increased to $1.9 billion. The story is similar in the United States. There, the U.S. National Venture Capital Association reported that venture capitalists had invested more than $7 billion in small startup firms despite a slow economy. These investors preferred funding small-business owners who had a previous success or who were proposing new ways to commercialize products such as solar energy, low-emission cars, and new medications. These investors have high requirements for a solid business plan. They also expect small-business owners to run lean operations.[28] The "Hit & Miss" feature discusses the popular show *Dragons' Den*, which features venture capitalists, such as Arlene Dickinson,[29] listening to pitches from small-business owners.

Small-Business Opportunities for Women

The number of women-owned firms in Canada has increased over the past few decades. Today, nearly half of all small and medium-sized enterprises (SMEs) in Canada have at least one female owner. Women also hold majority ownership in 18 percent of SMEs. Women-owned firms also contribute significantly to employment. About one-third of all self-employed people in Canada are women.

Women, like men, start their own companies for many different reasons. Some have a unique business idea that they want to bring to life. Others decide to form their own company when they lose their job or become frustrated with the working conditions in large companies. Many women start their own companies in hopes of finding a better balance between family and work.

The presence of women in business ownership means more than just more jobs. Majority women-owned SMEs produce annual commercial revenues of more than $72 billion, representing approximately 8 percent of all revenues from Canada's SMEs. Women are present across all sectors of the Canadian economy, although most work in service industries. Today, 80 percent of majority women-owned SMEs operate in the services sector, compared with 59 percent of SMEs owned by men.[30]

> **ASSESSMENT CHECK**
>
> 5.5.1 What are the various ways the BDC helps small businesses?
>
> 5.5.2 What are business incubators?
>
> 5.5.3 Why are small businesses good opportunities for women?

FRANCHISING

LO 5.6 Explain franchising.

Franchising combines large and small businesses into a single entity. It is also a major factor in the growth of small businesses. **Franchising** is a contract-based business arrangement between a manufacturer or another supplier and a dealer, such as a restaurant operator or a retailer. The contract spells out how the dealer will market the supplier's product. Franchises can involve both goods and services, such as food and wait staff.

Starting a small, independent company can be risky, time-consuming work, but franchising can reduce the amount of time and effort needed to grow. The parent company has already developed and tested the concept, and the brand is often already familiar to customers.

franchising a contract-based business arrangement between a manufacturer or other supplier and a dealer, such as a restaurant operator or retailer.

The Franchising Sector

Canada has the second-largest franchise industry in the world, after the United States. Canadians are as familiar with American franchise businesses in Canada, such as McDonald's, as they are with Canadian franchises, such as Tim Hortons.

The franchise industry has more than $100 billion in sales each year. Approximately one out of five consumer dollars is spent on goods and services at a franchise business. Canada has approximately 76,000 individual franchise businesses operating under 900 different brand names. These franchises employ more than 1 million people. One out of every 14 working Canadians is employed by a franchise.

The average franchise fee is $23,000, and the average franchisee investment is $160,000. Of all the franchises opened in Canada within the last five years, 86 percent are under the same ownership and 97 percent are still in business. Ontario leads the rest of Canada in franchising: 56 percent of Canadian franchises are based in Ontario, mostly in the Greater Toronto Area, and 65 percent of all Canadian franchise outlets (that is, the number of individual locations of all franchises combined) are in Ontario. The hospitality industry is the largest franchised sector, making up almost 40 percent of all Canadian franchised brand names. The franchise industry is active in more than 30 business, service, and retail sectors.[31]

Franchised businesses are also a huge part of the U.S. economy. There, franchises account for nearly 50 percent of all retail sales. The International Franchise Association reports that franchising is responsible for about 825,000 businesses, 18 million jobs, and more than $2 trillion in sales. A new franchise is opened every eight minutes every business day.[32]

Franchising overseas is also a growing trend for businesses who aim to expand into foreign markets. You can go almost anywhere in the world and find a McDonald's burger. Other international franchises are also becoming more common. The 2014 merger between Burger King and Tim Hortons was driven by the desire to accelerate growth of Tim Hortons in the United States and globally. Restaurant Brands International Inc., the parent company of Tim Hortons and Burger King, plans to follow Burger King's strategy of opening large numbers of outlets in a specific geographic area to better compete against U.S. giant Dunkin' Donuts. In France, Burger King is accelerating franchise openings with guidance from local consultants that are more familiar

International franchises are becoming more common. Baskin-Robbins has nearly 7,300 stores in more than 50 countries, including Australia, Canada, China, Japan, Vietnam, Russia, and the United Arab Emirates.

with the best locations. To do so, large investments need to be made by 3G Capital, the Brazilian investment firm that financed the merger.[33]

Franchising Agreements

A franchising agreement is a contract between the franchisee and the franchisor. The individual or business firm that buys the franchise is called the **franchisee**. This business owner agrees to sell the franchisor's goods or services under certain terms. The **franchisor** is the firm whose products are sold by the franchisee. For example, Tim Hortons Inc. is a franchisor, while your local Tim Hortons restaurant owner is a franchisee.

Franchise agreements can be complex. They involve an initial purchase fee plus agreed-on startup costs. Because the franchisee represents the franchisor's brand, the franchisor can require the franchisee to purchase certain ingredients or equipment, use standard pricing, and market the business in a certain way. McDonald's is one of the more expensive franchises—total startup costs can be more than $1 million. In contrast, the total startup cost for a SUBWAY franchise in Canada ranges from $108,000 to $234,000 including the franchise fee of $15,000.[34] Because of the costs, businesspeople often work together to purchase a more expensive franchise.

franchisee the individual or business firm purchasing a franchise.

franchisor the firm whose products are sold to customers by the franchisee.

Benefits and Problems of Franchising

Like other businesses, franchising has its upsides and downsides. The upsides for the franchisor include being able to expand a business, which might not be possible without the franchise. A franchised business can move into new locations, including overseas, at less cost than a traditional business. In other countries, franchises employ local workers and businesspeople who know what consumers like. A good franchisor can manage a much larger and more complex business—with fewer direct employees—than a traditional business. Most franchisees pay attention to how their franchises are managed because they have a stake in the company as business owners. If the business is run efficiently, the franchisor will probably make more money on the investment than if the firm were run entirely as a company-owned chain of retail shops, restaurants, or service providers.

A successful franchisor has financial strength and can usually bargain for better deals on ingredients, supplies, and even real estate. This strength is also a benefit for the franchisees if the savings are passed on to them.[35]

Franchising can be the quickest way to become a business owner. Some people say that it's also the least risky way to own a business. Franchisees benefit from having a business name that people know, such as McDonald's, Tim Hortons, SUBWAY, Pizza Hut, or Super 8 motels. Having a familiar name usually means a loyal following of customers. The franchisor has already set up a management system, and it has already shown that it can be successful. Franchisors provide support to franchisees, including financing, assistance in obtaining a location, business training, supplies, and marketing tools.[36]

Franchisees say they like the idea of franchising because it combines the freedom of business ownership with the support of a large company. Like other small-business owners, franchisees want to make their own business decisions and decide on their own work hours. They also want to have more control over the amount of money they make, instead of taking what they might earn in a salaried job. In an economic slowdown, franchisees might be former executives who have been laid off. These highly trained and motivated businesspeople are looking for a way to restart their careers.[37] Sometimes the ideas or successes of individual franchisees can be good for the entire company. That's what happened with SUBWAY, as described in the "Hit & Miss" feature.

Franchising also has its downsides—for both franchisors and franchisees. If franchisees fail, their failure reflects on the franchisor's brand and the bottom line. The same is true for the franchisee: A firm that is mismanaged at the top level, by the franchisor, can be bad for the franchisees who are running the individual locations. When a firm decides to offer franchise opportunities, it may lose money for several years. Of course, by

Tim Hortons is one of Canada's most popular and successful franchises.

HIT & MISS

One Small Franchise Produces One Big Idea

SUBWAY has enjoyed top franchise rankings consistently for more than a decade. SUBWAY has more than 30,000 sandwich restaurants in over 100 countries, including 21,000 franchisees. The firm is set to become the single largest fast-food chain in the world. But SUBWAY is made up of many small businesses—franchises. Sometimes, a small idea by one franchisee can change the entire organization.

Stuart Frankel is a SUBWAY franchisee, and his idea was simple: On weekends, he wanted to charge a special price of $5 for a footlong SUBWAY sandwich. This special price was about $1 less per sandwich than the regular price. It took some time for Frankel and two other Florida SUBWAY franchisees to convince the corporate franchisor that the idea was a good one. The economy was slow, food costs were increasing, and SUBWAY shops were almost empty because people were eating at home to save money. Frankel's employees stood around at their stations, and sandwich sales decreased. But after some time, Frankel got the OK from corporate headquarters. From there, a chain reaction began.

"I like round numbers," said Frankel about the $5 price. SUBWAY customers liked the number, too. When the special pricing was announced, customers returned for the $5 sandwiches. Sales increased by double digits. Employees made sandwiches as fast as they could. SUBWAY's corporate marketing team pushed the $5 promotion nationwide. When the initial four-week promotion was up, marketing executives extended it to seven weeks. When that time was up, they extended it indefinitely but with a limited number of sandwich variations.

Something else happened. Demand for the $5 footlongs was so great that franchise owners began to run out of certain ingredients. They couldn't get enough bread, turkey, ham, or tuna. One franchisee recalls being in a panic. "The whole thing took on a life of its own," said Jeff Moody, CEO of SUBWAY's advertising.

With one motion, Stuart Frankel had a great idea for consumers who wanted to eat out and get a good deal at the same time. "There are only a few times when a chain has been able to scramble up the whole industry, and this is one of them," notes restaurant consultant Jeffrey T. Davis. "It's huge." Sometimes a small idea is really big.

Questions for Critical Thinking

1. Why was Stuart Frankel's idea successful with consumers? Would it have been as successful during a different economic time? Why or why not?

2. A franchise company is only as good as its franchisees. And a franchisee's success is based in part on the decisions and support of corporate leadership. If the $5 footlong promotion had failed, how would that failure have affected Frankel's franchise business? How might it have affected SUBWAY?

Sources: Subway Restaurants, "Subway FAQs," accessed April 8, 2015, www.subway.com/ContactUs/CustServFAQs.aspx; "Subway Brand Ranked Number One Provider of Healthy Options in Zagat Survey," accessed April 2, 2010, www.subway.com; "Subway Restaurants Again Named #1 Worldwide Franchise Opportunity for 2009," accessed April 2, 2010, www.subway.com; Matthew Boyle, "The Accidental Hero," *Businessweek*, November 10, 2009, accessed April 2, 2010, www.bloomberg.com/bw/magazine/content/09_46/b4155058815908.htm.

offering franchise opportunities, the franchisor—often the founder of what was once a small business—loses control over every aspect of the business. Not having control can make it difficult to select the right franchisees to carry out the company's mission.[38]

The franchisee has many cash expenses: the initial investment, franchise fees, supplies, maintenance, leases, and so on. The most expensive franchises are usually franchises that involve hotels and resorts. These franchises can cost millions of dollars.[39] It is not unusual for groups of businesspeople to purchase a franchise (or several franchise locations) together.[40] The franchisees' payments to the franchisor can add to the difficulty of keeping the business going until the owner begins to earn a profit. Choosing a low-cost startup may be a good alternative. But it's important for potential franchisees to check carefully how much profit they can make after they pay their expenses.

Franchises are closely linked to their brand, so franchisors and franchisees must work together to maintain standards of quality in their goods and services. If customers are unhappy with their experience at one franchise location, they might not stop at another location several kilometres away, even if the second location is owned and operated by someone else. This is especially true where food is involved. The discovery of bad meat or produce at one franchise restaurant can cause panic to spread throughout the entire chain of restaurants. A potential franchisee is smart to thoroughly research the financial performance and reputation of the franchisor. This research can be done using resources such as other franchisees, the Better Business Bureau, Industry Canada, the U.S. Federal Trade Commission, and the Canadian Franchise Association (CFA). The CFA is a trade association representing franchisors. CFA members agree to a review before they are accepted as members. They also agree to follow the association's code of ethics.

Some franchisees have found the franchising agreement to be too confining. As the saying goes, you can't add a tuna salad sandwich to the menu at McDonald's no matter how many stores you own. The agreements are usually strict, which helps to maintain the brand's good standing. Some franchise companies control promotional activities, select the site location, and might even get involved in hiring decisions. These activities may seem overly controlling to some franchisees, especially those who want more independence and freedom.

Controls can also cost franchisees more than they feel is fair. Recently, the National Franchise Association, a group that represents more than 80 percent of Burger King's U.S. franchisees, sued Burger King because Burger King forced its franchisees to offer consumers a $1 double cheeseburger, which supported the company's promotional efforts. While the $1 burger offering may seem like a great way to attract and serve hungry consumers, Burger King franchisees said the promotion has cost them a loss of at least 10 cents per burger. In other words, it costs most franchises $1.10 to make and serve a double cheeseburger, but the franchisor told them they must charge $1.[41]

> ✓ **ASSESSMENT CHECK**
>
> 5.6.1 What is the difference between a franchisor and a franchisee?
>
> 5.6.2 How does franchising benefit both parties?
>
> 5.6.3 What are the potential downsides of franchising for both parties?

LO 5.7 Outline the forms of private business ownership.

FORMS OF PRIVATE BUSINESS OWNERSHIP

No matter how big or small, most businesses are organized as one of three legal structures: sole proprietorship, partnership, or corporation. Each legal structure offers unique advantages and disadvantages. In addition to the three main legal structures, there is the option of creating and running a not-for-profit organization.

Sole Proprietorships

The most common, oldest, and simplest form of business ownership is the **sole proprietorship**. In a sole proprietorship, the sole proprietor's status as an individual is not legally separate from his or her status as a business owner. Although sole proprietorships are common in many industries, they are found mostly among small businesses such as repair shops, small retail stores, and service providers such as plumbers, hairstylists, and photographers.

sole proprietorship a business ownership structure in which the sole proprietor's status as an individual is not legally separate from his or her status as a business owner.

Sole proprietorships have some unique advantages. Because sole proprietorships have a single owner, they are easy to form *and* dissolve. A sole proprietorship gives the owner the most management flexibility. The owner also has the right to all profits after paying business-related bills and taxes. A highly motivated owner of a sole proprietorship directly receives all the benefits of his or her hard work.

It is easy to enter and exit a sole proprietorship because there are very few legal requirements. The owner registers the business or trade name to make sure that another firm does not use the same name. Next, the owner pays for any necessary licences. Local governments require certain licences for businesses, such as restaurants, motels or hotels, and retail stores. Some occupational licences require that business owners have specific insurance, such as liability coverage.

Sole proprietorships are also easy to dissolve. This factor is particularly important to temporary or seasonal businesses that set up for a limited period of time. It's also helpful if the owner needs or wants to close the business for any reason—for example, to relocate or to accept a full-time position with a larger firm.

Management flexibility is another advantage of a sole proprietorship. The owner can make decisions without reporting to a manager, take quick action, and keep trade secrets. A sole proprietorship always bears the individuality, or style, of its owner, whether it's a certain way of cutting hair or how a store window is decorated.

The greatest disadvantage of the sole proprietorship is the owner's personal financial liability for the business's debts. Also, the business must operate with financial resources that are limited to the owner's personal funds and to money that he or she can borrow. Such financing limitations can keep the business from expanding.

Another disadvantage is that the owner must handle a wide range of management and operational tasks. He or she may not have skills in every area, which may keep the firm from growth or may even cause the firm damage. Sole proprietors may also face a higher chance of being audited by the Canada Revenue Agency. Finally, a sole proprietorship usually lacks long-term continuity because a change in personal circumstances or finances can terminate the business on short notice.

Partnerships

Another option for organizing a business is to form a partnership. A **partnership** is an association of two or more persons who operate a business as co-owners by voluntary legal agreement. Many small businesses begin as partnerships between co-founders.

Partnerships are easy to form. The partners need to register the business name and obtain any necessary licences. Having a partner usually means greater financial capability and someone to share in the tasks and decision making. It's even better if one partner has a particular skill, such as design, while the other is good at finance.

Most partnerships have the downside of being exposed to unlimited financial liability. Each partner bears full responsibility for the debts of the firm, and each is legally liable for the actions of the other partners. If the firm fails and has debt, every partner is responsible for those debts; it doesn't matter if the debts are the fault of only one partner. If one partner defaults, the others are responsible for the firm's debts, even if they have to use their personal funds. To avoid these problems, many firms set up a limited-liability partnership. This type of partnership limits the liability of partners to the value of their interests in the company.

Breaking up a partnership is more complicated than dissolving a sole proprietorship. The partner who wants to leave cannot just withdraw his or her portion of the funds from the bank. Instead, the partner who wants out may need to find a new partner to buy his or her interest in the firm. The death of a partner also threatens the business. A new partnership must be formed, and the estate of the deceased can take a share of the firm's value. To ease the possible financial difficulties of this situation, business planners suggest life insurance coverage for each partner, combined with a buy-sell agreement. The insurance proceeds can be used to repay the deceased partner's heirs. That way, the surviving partners can retain control of the business.

Businesses that are based on partnerships also risk having personal conflicts. Partners need to choose each other carefully; best friends sometimes don't make the best partners. Good partners work hard and try to plan for the future.

> **partnership** an association of two or more persons who operate a business as co-owners by voluntary legal agreement.

Corporations

corporation a legal organization with assets and liabilities separate from the assets and liabilities of its owners.

A **corporation** is a legal organization that has assets and liabilities separate from the assets and liabilities of its owners. A corporation can be a large or small business—it can be Air Canada or a local auto repair shop.

Corporate ownership offers many advantages. Because a corporation is a separate legal entity, its shareholders have only limited financial risk. If the firm fails, the shareholders lose only the money they invested. The same goes for the firm's managers and executives. Because they are not the sole proprietors or partners in the business, their personal savings are not at risk if the company closes or goes bankrupt. This protection also extends to legal risk. Class action lawsuits against automakers, drug manufacturers, and food producers are filed against the companies, not the owners of those companies.[42]

Corporations offer other advantages. They can gain access to more funding because they can offer direct outside investments such as sales of shares. A large corporation can legally raise internal funds for projects by transferring money from one part of the corporation to another.

One major disadvantage for a corporation is the double taxation of corporate earnings. A corporation pays federal and provincial income taxes on its profits, but its owners (the shareholders) also pay personal taxes on dividends, the distributions of profits they receive from the corporation.

Not-for-Profit Corporations

not-for-profit corporations organizations whose goals do not include pursuing a profit.

The same business concepts that apply to commercial companies also apply to **not-for-profit corporations**—organizations whose goals do not include pursuing a profit. Canada has about 160,000 not-for-profits, including charitable groups, social-welfare organizations, government agencies, and religious congregations. Not-for-profit corporations also include museums, libraries, hospitals, conservation groups, and private schools.

Governments have separate legal provisions for organizational structures and operations of not-for-profit corporations. These organizations do not issue shares because they do not pay dividends to owners, and their ownership rarely changes. They are also exempt from paying income taxes. However, they must meet very strict guidelines to keep their not-for-profit status.

Montreal's Sun Youth Organization was founded in 1954 by a small group of kids tired of the few sports and recreational activities in the St. Lawrence Boulevard/Boulevard Saint Laurent area (now Le Plateau). The entrepreneurial kids created a handwritten newspaper called the *Clark Street Sun*. They sold the newspaper door to door to raise funds to pay for the sports activities. The children themselves organized most of the activities. Finally, they were able to purchase equipment and uniforms for the increasing number of children involved. As these early groups of children grew older, Sun Youth became the social services organization known to and supported by Montrealers of every language and ethnic background. Today, the organization works with schools, police officers, firefighters, medical professionals, corporations, and volunteers to deal with referrals from more than 170 social service agencies from the Greater Montreal area.[43]

✓ ASSESSMENT CHECK

5.7.1 What are the key differences between sole proprietorships and partnerships?

5.7.2 What is a corporation?

5.7.3 What is the main characteristic of a not-for-profit corporation?

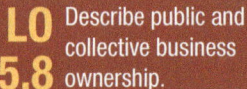

Describe public and collective business ownership.

PUBLIC AND COLLECTIVE OWNERSHIP OF BUSINESS

Most businesses in Canada are owned by the private sector, but some firms are owned and operated by local, provincial, or federal governments. For example, Manitoba Hydro, New Brunswick Power, and many other electricity utility companies are owned entirely or partially by governments.[44]

MEC (formerly Mountain Equipment Co-op) is a collectively owned retailer that sells outdoor gear and clothing.

In another type of ownership structure, groups of customers can collectively own a company. At the end of the year, after paying suppliers, employees, and operating costs, the co-op returns any remaining funds to members as patronage shares. In another collective ownership structure, smaller firms can group together to own a larger organization. Both types of collective ownership structures are called *cooperatives*.

Public (Government) Ownership

One alternative to private ownership is some form of *public ownership*. In public ownership, a government unit or agency owns and operates an organization. In Canada, local governments often own the city's bus companies, parking structures, and water systems. For example, the Toronto Transit Commission operates the network of buses, subways, and streetcars that serve the city of Toronto. People who support public ownership believe that services can be provided to more people when profits are turned back to the company to provide more services. However, some people disagree. These people say the supporters' belief has no proof. There is evidence to support parts of both sides of the argument.

Sometimes public ownership results when private investors are unwilling to invest in a high-risk project—or when operating an important service is simply unprofitable. VIA Rail Canada operates the national passenger rail service for the Government of Canada. VIA was established as an independent Crown corporation in 1977. It provides public transportation by operating trains that serve 450 communities across the country. Each year, VIA carries more than 4 million customers on a fleet of 400 passenger cars.[45]

Collective (Cooperative) Ownership

Collective ownership sets up an organization called a *cooperative* (or *co-op*). The owners work together to operate all or part of the activities in their firm or industry. Currently, about 100 million people are employed by cooperatives around the world.[46] Cooperatives allow small businesses to pool their resources for purchases, marketing, equipment, and distribution. Discount savings can be split among members, and cooperatives often share equipment and expertise. During difficult economic times, members of a cooperative find a variety of ways to support each other.

ASSESSMENT CHECK

5.8.1 What is public ownership?

5.8.2 What is collective ownership? Where are cooperatives typically found, and what benefits do they provide small businesses?

Canada has more than 8,400 co-ops. These co-ops employ more than 152,000 people: More than 87,000 work in nonfinancial cooperatives and more than 32,000 work in the agricultural sector. Canada has 5.9 million cooperative members, which means that four of every ten Canadians are members of a cooperative. At least seven co-ops are listed in the top 500 companies in Canada. Several financial cooperatives, such as Vancouver's Vancity Credit Union network, have been rated among the best places to work in Canada.[47]

LO 5.9 Discuss the organizational structure of corporations.

ORGANIZING A CORPORATION

A corporation is a legal structure. It also requires a more complex organizational structure than a sole proprietorship or a partnership. This complexity explains why we often think of a corporation as a large entity, even though it does not have to be a big company.

Where and How Businesses Incorporate

Businesses owners who want to incorporate must decide where to locate their headquarters. They must also follow the correct procedure for filling out the legal document that sets up the corporation.

Where to Incorporate

The business decision of where to incorporate—and establish headquarters—may be based on a number of factors. Most businesses want to be near their customers. Other factors are real estate prices, public transportation, and communications networks. Access to a good source of employees is another reason for choosing a location. Online businesses such as Amazon.ca and eBay don't need to worry about being located near their customers, but they should think about the local source of employees.

Most small and medium-sized businesses are incorporated in the provinces where they operate, but a Canadian firm can actually incorporate in any province it chooses. The founders of large corporations or the founders of corporations that do business nationwide often compare the benefits, such as tax incentives, of different locations. Some provinces are considered to be more "business friendly" than others. For example, Alberta has one of the lowest taxes for incorporated businesses in Canada.

The Corporate Charter

A corporation is like an artificial person created by law, with most of the legal rights of a real person. These rights include the rights to start and operate a business, to buy or sell property, to borrow money, to sue or be sued, and to enter into binding contracts.

Incorporation of a business can be done at the federal or provincial level. Legally, if you incorporate provincially your corporation has the right to carry on business only in the province where your business is incorporated. This rule is not a problem for restaurants and other businesses that have a fixed location, but it might be a problem for others. Federally incorporated businesses are permitted to operate everywhere in Canada.

Each province has a specific process for incorporating a business. For example, the individual or individuals who create the corporation must select a name that is different from the names used by other businesses. **Figure 5.1** lists the 10 elements that are typically required for chartering a corporation.

- Name and Address of the Corporation
- Corporate Objectives
- Type and Amount of Stock to Issue
- Expected Life of the Corporation
- Financial Capital at the Time of Incorporation
- Provisions for Transferring Shares of Stock among Owners
- Provisions for Regulating Internal Corporate Affairs
- Address of the Business Office Registered with the Province
- Names and Addresses of the Initial Board of Directors
- Names and Addresses of the Incorporators

FIGURE 5.1 Traditional Articles of Incorporation

The information in the articles of incorporation forms the basis on which a government grants a *corporate charter*. This charter is the legal document that formally establishes a corporation. After securing the charter, the owners prepare the company's bylaws, which set out the rules for operation.

Corporate Management

Every corporation, large or small, has levels of management and ownership. **Figure 5.2** illustrates the typical levels—although a smaller firm might not have all five levels. These levels range from shareholders down to supervisory management.

Stock Ownership and Shareholder Rights

At the top of Figure 5.2 are **shareholders**. They buy shares of stock in the corporation, which makes them part owners. Some companies, such as many family businesses, are owned by only a few shareholders and the shares are generally unavailable to outsiders. In such a firm, known as a *closed* or *closely held corporation*, the shareholders also control and manage all of the company's activities.

shareholders owners of a corporation as a result of their purchase of shares in the corporation.

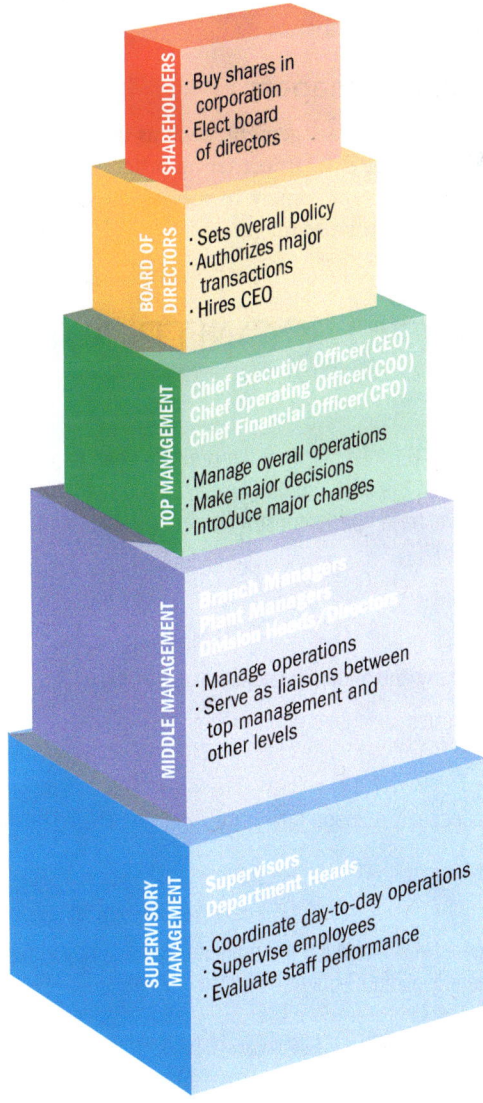

FIGURE 5.2 Levels of Management in a Corporation

An open corporation, also called a *publicly held corporation*, is different. It sells shares to the general public, which sets up a diversified ownership. This type of ownership often leads to a broader range of operations than in a closed corporation. Publicly held corporations usually hold annual shareholders' meetings. During these meetings, managers report on corporate activities, and shareholders vote on decisions that require their approval, including elections of officers.

The shareholders' role in the corporation depends on the class of shares they own. Shares are usually either common shares or preferred shares. Although owners of **preferred shares** have limited voting rights, they receive dividends before the holders of common shares. If the corporation is dissolved, the owners of preferred shares also have first claims on assets once all debtors are repaid. Owners of **common shares** have voting rights but only residual claims on the firm's assets. That means they are the last to receive any income distributions. Because one share is typically worth only one vote, small shareholders generally have little influence over corporate management actions.

> **preferred shares** shares that give owners limited voting rights and the right to receive dividends or assets before owners of common shares.
>
> **common shares** shares that give owners voting rights but only residual claims to the firm's assets and income distributions.

Board of Directors

Shareholders elect a **board of directors**—the governing body of a corporation. The board sets overall policy, authorizes the corporation's major transactions, and hires the chief executive officer (CEO). Most boards include both inside directors (corporate executives) and outside directors—people who are not employed by the organization. Sometimes the corporation's top executive also chairs the board. Generally, outside directors are also shareholders, so they have a financial stake in the company's performance.

> **board of directors** the governing body of a corporation.

Corporate Officers and Managers

The CEO and other members of top management, such as the chief operating officer (COO), the chief financial officer (CFO), and the chief information officer (CIO), make most major corporate decisions. Top executives get paid handsomely in most large organizations, as discussed in the "Solving an Ethical Controversy" feature. Managers at the next level down, the middle management,

---

SOLVING AN **ETHICAL** CONTROVERSY

Do Some CEOs Earn Too Much?

Median CEO pay reached $9.7 million in North America recently, up 6.5 percent from the previous year. Enormous pay packages are meant to reward stellar company performance, but this has not always been the case. Some CEOs in recent years have been paid large amounts of money as part of their compensation packages, yet their companies have not demonstrated strong business gains.

Is executive pay excessive?

PRO
1. CEO compensation should reflect the overall state of the company and should be adjusted accordingly.
2. CEOs do not merit high rewards when their company demonstrates lacklustre performance.

CON
1. CEOs must take huge personal and professional risks to successfully manage their firms, and they should be well rewarded.
2. High pay ensures that firms attract and keep talented CEOs.

Summary
CEO salaries have continued to skyrocket to more than 300 times the average North American worker's pay in recent years. Should there be a formula or set of rules to control the growing gap between executives and workers in a firm?

Sources: Daily Viewpoint, "GMI Ratings' 2013 CEO Pay Survey Reveals CEO Pay Is Still on the Rise," accessed January 17, 2014, www3.gmiratings.com/home; Rob Silverblatt, "New Report Condemns Trends in CEO Compensation," *U.S. News and World Report*, accessed January 17, 2014, http://money.usnews.com/money/personal-finance/mutual-funds/articles/2013/09/03/new-report-condemns-trends-in-ceo-compensation; Christina Rexrode, "Median CEO Pay Rises to $9.7 million in 2012," *USA Today*, accessed January 17, 2014, www.usatoday.com/story/money/business/2013/05/26/ceo-pay-rises-in-2012/2350545.

handle the ongoing operational functions of the company. At the bottom tier of management, supervisory personnel coordinate day-to-day operations, assign tasks to employees, and evaluate job performance.

Today's CEOs and CFOs work under stricter regulations than in the past. They must verify in writing the accuracy of their firm's financial statements. The process for nominating candidates for the board has also become more complex. In short, more checks and balances are in place for the governance of corporations.

ASSESSMENT CHECK

5.9.1 What are the two key elements of the incorporation process?

5.9.2 Identify the five main levels of corporate ownership and management.

LO 5.10 Describe mergers, acquisitions, and joint ventures.

WHEN BUSINESSES JOIN FORCES

Today's business environment includes many complex relationships among businesses and not-for-profit organizations. Two firms may team up to develop a product or to co-market products. One company may buy another company. Large corporations may split into smaller units. The list of alliances can be as varied as the organizations themselves, but the major trends in corporate ownership are mergers and acquisitions (M&A) and joint ventures.

Mergers and Acquisitions (M&A)

The terms *merger* and *acquisition* are often used interchangeably, but their meanings are different. In a **merger**, two or more firms combine to form one company. In an **acquisition**, one firm purchases the other. This purchase means that the buyer acquires the firm's property and assets *and* takes on the firm's debt. Acquisitions also occur when one firm buys a division or a subsidiary from another firm. A recent study looked at mergers and acquisitions in the global mining sector. The study suggests Canadian firms are major players in this sector. Canadian firms were involved in 36 percent of the almost 3,000 deals that represented more than $113 billion in value.[48]

Mergers can be classified as vertical, horizontal, or conglomerate. A **vertical merger** combines firms operating at different levels in the production and marketing process. For example, the combination of a manufacturer and a large retailer is a vertical merger. A vertical merger pursues one of two main goals: (1) to ensure adequate flows of raw materials and supplies needed for a firm's products, or (2) to increase distribution. Microsoft is well known for acquiring small firms that have developed products with strong market potential, such as Teleo, a provider of voice over Internet protocol (VoIP) software and services that can be used to make phone calls via the Internet.

A **horizontal merger** joins firms in the same industry. Firms use a horizontal merger to diversify, to increase their customer base, to cut costs, or to expand product lines. This type of merger is popular in the auto industry. India-based Tata Motors bought the Jaguar and Land Rover brands from Ford Motor Corp., and Volkswagen owns Audi and Porsche.

A **conglomerate merger** combines unrelated firms. The most common reasons for a conglomerate merger are to diversify, to increase sales, or to spend a cash surplus to avoid a takeover attempt. Conglomerate mergers may join firms in totally unrelated industries. General Electric is well known for its conglomerate mergers, including its ownership of healthcare services and household appliances. Experts debate whether conglomerate mergers are a good idea. Those in favour of such mergers say that a company can use its management expertise to succeed in a variety of industries. But the obvious downside is that a huge conglomerate can spread its resources too thin to be successful in any one market.

merger an agreement in which two or more firms combine to form one company.

acquisition an agreement in which one firm purchases another.

vertical merger a merger that combines firms operating at different levels in the production and marketing process.

horizontal merger a merger that joins firms in the same industry for the purpose of diversification, increasing customer bases, cutting costs, or expanding product lines.

conglomerate merger a merger that combines unrelated firms usually with the goal of diversification, increasing sales, or spending a cash surplus to avoid a takeover attempt.

Joint Ventures: Specialized Partnerships

A **joint venture** is a partnership between companies for a specific activity. Sometimes a company enters into a joint venture with a local firm to share the operation's costs, risks, management, and profits. This type of joint venture is common when a firm wants to start a business in a foreign market. A joint venture can also help companies solve a common problem.

joint venture a partnership between companies for a specific activity.

Joint ventures between for-profit firms and not-for-profit organizations provide great benefits for both parties. Becel has been the title sponsor for the Heart and Stroke Foundation's Ride for Heart for over 20 years, helping to raise funds supporting research and education on heart disease and stroke.

✓ **ASSESSMENT CHECK**

5.10.1 Distinguish between a merger and an acquisition.

5.10.2 What are the different kinds of mergers?

5.10.3 What is a joint venture?

Joint ventures between for-profit firms and not-for-profit organizations are becoming common. These partnerships provide benefits for both parties. Not-for-profit organizations receive the funding, marketing exposure, and sometimes the staff they might not have on their own. The CIBC, New Balance, East Side Mario's, The Running Room, Canpar, and Revlon are some of the Canadian businesses that have partnered with the Canadian Breast Cancer Foundation's Run for the Cure. The annual event raised $25 million in 2014 across the country.[49]

Joint ventures between not-for-profits and for-profit firms are often good for businesses, too. Firms that partner with environmental groups can cut costs, save energy, and reduce waste. For example, McDonald's partnered with the Environmental Defense Fund. McDonald's was then successful in phasing out harmful packaging, converting much of its cooking oil to biodiesel, getting rid of more than 136 million kilograms of packaging, and reducing restaurant waste by more than 30 percent.[50]

WHAT'S AHEAD

The next chapter focuses on the driving forces that lead to new businesses: entrepreneurs. It examines the differences between a small-business owner and an entrepreneur. It also identifies the personality traits common to most entrepreneurs. The chapter also describes the process of launching a new venture, including identifying opportunities, locating financing, and turning good ideas into successful businesses. Finally, the chapter explores a method for infusing the entrepreneurial spirit into established businesses—intrapreneurship.

RETURN TO INSIDE BUSINESS

Pi Athlete Management Inc.: Advising Athletes about Their Careers and More

According to Daniel Smajovits of Pi Athlete Management, the firm avoids "hustling" athletes. Instead, it relies on word-of-mouth referrals to attract new clients.

"Our short game is to represent professional athletes. The athletes come to us via word-of-mouth and through athletes whom we currently represent. We are not actively trying to poach other athletes from their agents for two reasons: (1) We are trying to eliminate the sleaze factor in this industry. I do not want to be the guy in the hotel lobby passing out business cards to currently represented players. (2) We do not want to take on more than we can handle. If an athlete comes to us, we will see what we can do for him: While it might sound nice to say that we represent 20 professional athletes, if I can't be there equally for each guy, then it's all smoke and mirrors. If we know that an athlete is unhappy with his current representation, we would love to speak with him as we know we can do better by him, but it's not something we actively pursue.

"Additionally, for our professional athletes, one unique selling point about us is that we can take care of all their off-field needs in house. We're working with one lawyer and one CA/CPA, both with a tremendous amount of experience and a vast international network, so all their legal, financial, and tax work can be handled by us. My background in marketing and PR is vital to provide media training, to seek out marketing opportunities, and [to] coordinate media appearances."

QUESTIONS FOR CRITICAL THINKING

1. What other professional consulting services would be helpful for Pi Athlete Management to offer to athletes?
2. What else can Pi Athlete Management do to increase its network of consultants and athletes?

SUMMARY OF LEARNING OBJECTIVES

LO 5.1 Describe the characteristics of a small business.

A small business is an independently owned business that has fewer than 100 employees and revenues less than $2 million. A small business is not usually the leading business in its field. It meets industry-specific size standards for income or number of employees. A business is classified as large when its number of employees or revenue exceeds these standards.

 **ASSESSMENT CHECK ANSWERS**

5.1.1 How does Industry Canada define *small business*? Industry Canada defines a small business as an independent business that has fewer than 100 employees and revenues not more than $2 million.

5.1.2 In what industries do small businesses play a significant role? Small businesses provide many jobs in construction, agriculture, wholesale trade, services, and retail trade.

LO 5.2 Discuss the contributions of small businesses to the economy.

Small businesses create new jobs and new industries. They often hire people who have difficulty finding jobs at larger firms. Small firms give businesspeople the opportunity and outlet for developing new ideas. Sometimes these new ideas become entirely new industries. Small businesses also develop new and improved goods and services.

 ASSESSMENT CHECK ANSWERS

5.2.1 What are the three key ways that small businesses contribute to the economy? Small businesses create new jobs, create new industries, and provide innovation.

5.2.2 How are new industries formed? New industries are formed when small businesses shift their focus to meet consumer interests and preferences. Innovation and new technology can play a significant role. In addition, new industries can be created when both the business world and consumers see a need for change.

LO 5.3 Discuss why small businesses fail.

About 96 percent of small businesses that enter the marketplace are in business for one full year, 85 percent are in business for three years, and 70 percent are in business for five years. Failure is often attributed to management inexperience, inadequate financing, and difficulty meeting government regulations.

 ASSESSMENT CHECK ANSWERS

5.3.1 What percentage of small businesses are still operating five years after starting? About 70 percent are in business after five years.

5.3.2 What are the three main causes of small-business failure? The three main causes of small-business failure are management inexperience, inadequate financing, and difficulty meeting government regulations.

LO 5.4 Describe the features of an effective business plan.

A complete business plan contains an executive summary, an introduction, financial and marketing sections, and résumés of the business principals. An effective business plan uses these five sections and includes the company's mission, an outline of what makes the company unique, identification of customers and competitors, financial evaluation of the industry and market, and an assessment of the risks.

✓ ASSESSMENT CHECK ANSWERS

5.4.1 What are the five main sections of a business plan? The five sections of a business plan are the executive summary, introduction, financial section, marketing section, and résumés of the principals.

5.4.2 Why is an effective business plan important to the success of a firm? The business plan puts in writing all the reasons the firm can be successful. It contains the company's mission and addresses many issues, including the vision of its founders and why the company is unique. It is the document that is needed to obtain financing. The business plan also creates a framework for the organization.

LO 5.5 Identify the assistance available to small businesses.

The Business Development Bank of Canada (BDC) is a government agency that assists, counsels, and protects the interests of small businesses in Canada. The BDC was created by an act of Parliament in 1944. It operates across Canada through offices and resource centres that provide long-term financial assistance and management counselling. The BDC also provides training, technical assistance, and education to help small businesses prepare for doing business in foreign markets. Statistics show that most failures in small businesses happen because of poor management. For this reason, the BDC works to improve the management skills of small-business owners and managers.

✓ ASSESSMENT CHECK ANSWERS

5.5.1 What are the various ways the BDC helps small businesses? The BDC provides long-term financial assistance and management counselling. It also provides business information, advice, and training to owners of small businesses.

5.5.2 What are business incubators? Business incubators are programs that community agencies set up to help small businesses get started. Their services can include low-cost rental space, shared clerical staff, and shared office equipment, such as computers.

5.5.3 Why are small businesses good opportunities for women? Women feel they can achieve more as small-business owners and can balance family and work more easily if they own their own firms.

LO 5.6 Explain franchising.

A franchisor is a large firm that allows a small-business owner (a franchisee) to market and sell the larger firm's products under its brand name in return for a fee. The franchisor's opportunities include the possibilities of expansion and greater profits. The franchisee's benefits include name recognition, quick startup, support from the franchisor, and the freedom of small-business ownership.

ASSESSMENT CHECK ANSWERS

5.6.1 What is the difference between a franchisor and a franchisee? A franchisor permits a small-business owner (the franchisee) to market and sell the franchisor's products under its brand name in return for a fee.

5.6.2 How does franchising benefit both parties? Benefits to the franchisor include opportunities for expansion and greater profits. Benefits to the franchisee include name recognition, quick startup, support from the franchisor, and the freedom of small-business ownership.

LO 5.7 Outline the forms of private business ownership.

The three legal forms of business ownership are sole proprietorships, partnerships, and corporations. A sole proprietorship is owned and operated by one person. Sole proprietorships are easy to set up and offer great operating flexibility, but the owner is personally liable for all of the firm's debts and legal responsibilities. In a partnership, two or more individuals share responsibility for owning and running the business. Partnerships are relatively easy to set up, but they do not protect either partner from liability. A corporation is a separate legal entity from its owners. Investors receive shares of stock in the firm, and owners have no legal and financial liability beyond their individual investments. The legal structure of a not-for-profit corporation requires that its goals do not include earning a profit.

ASSESSMENT CHECK ANSWERS

5.7.1 What are the key differences between sole proprietorships and partnerships? Sole proprietorships have more management flexibility and are easier to dissolve than partnerships. Partnerships require shared workload and decision making, whereas sole proprietorships are entirely the responsibility of one business owner.

5.7.2 What is a corporation? A corporation is a legal organization that has assets and liabilities separate from the assets and liabilities of its owners. A corporation can be a large or small business.

5.7.3 What is the main characteristic of a not-for-profit corporation? A not-for-profit corporation is an organization whose goals do not include pursuing a profit. Governments have separate legal provisions for organizational structures and operations of not-for-profit corporations. They are also exempt from paying income taxes.

LO 5.8 Describe public and collective business ownership.

In public ownership, a government unit or agency owns and operates an organization. Collective ownership sets up an organization called a cooperative. The owners join forces to operate all or part of the activities in their firm or industry.

✓ ASSESSMENT CHECK ANSWERS

5.8.1 What is public ownership? Public ownership occurs when a unit or agency of government owns and operates an organization.

5.8.2 What is collective ownership? Where are cooperatives typically found, and what benefits do they provide small businesses? Collective ownership sets up an organization called a *cooperative* (or *co-op*). The owners work together to operate all or part of the activities in their firm or industry. Cooperatives are frequently found among agricultural businesses. They can also occur in retail. Cooperatives allow small firms to pool their resources, share equipment and expertise, and help each other through difficult times.

LO 5.9 Discuss the organizational structure of corporations.

Shareholders are the owners of a corporation. In return for their financial investments, they receive shares of stock in the company. Shareholders elect a board of directors, who sets overall policy. The board hires the chief executive officer (CEO), who then hires the managers.

✓ ASSESSMENT CHECK ANSWERS

5.9.1 What are the two key elements of the incorporation process? The two key elements are where to incorporate and the corporate charter.

5.9.2 Identify the five main levels of corporate ownership and management. The five levels are the shareholders, the board of directors, top management, middle management, and supervisory management.

LO 5.10 Describe mergers, acquisitions, and joint ventures.

In a merger, two or more firms combine to form one company. A vertical merger combines firms operating at different levels in the production and marketing process. A horizontal merger joins firms in the same industry. A conglomerate merger combines unrelated firms. An acquisition occurs when one firm purchases another. A joint venture is a partnership between companies for a specific activity.

✓ ASSESSMENT CHECK ANSWERS

5.10.1 Distinguish between a merger and an acquisition. In a merger, two or more firms combine to form one company. In an acquisition, one firm purchases another company. The buyer acquires the firm's property and assets *and* takes on the firm's debt. Acquisitions also occur when one firm buys a division or a subsidiary from another firm.

5.10.2 What are the different kinds of mergers? Mergers can be classified as vertical, horizontal, or conglomerate. A vertical merger combines firms operating at different levels in the production and marketing process. A horizontal merger joins firms in the same industry. A conglomerate merger combines unrelated firms.

5.10.3 What is a joint venture? A joint venture is a partnership between organizations formed for a specific activity.

BUSINESS TERMS YOU NEED TO KNOW

acquisition 145	common shares 144	home-based businesses 125	preferred shares 144
board of directors 144	conglomerate merger 145	horizontal merger 145	shareholders 143
Business Development Bank of Canada (BDC) 133	corporation 140	joint venture 145	small business 124
	franchisee 136	merger 145	sole proprietorship 138
business incubator 133	franchising 135	not-for-profit corporations 140	venture capital 133
business plan 131	franchisor 136	partnership 139	vertical merger 145

REVIEW QUESTIONS

1. Describe how a small business might use innovation to create new jobs.

2. Why do so many small businesses fail before they reach their fifth year?

3. What are the benefits of developing and writing an effective business plan?

4. What is the Business Development Bank of Canada? How does it assist small companies, financially and in other ways?

5. Describe how local governments and business incubators help small firms to set up and grow.

6. Why are so many small-business owners attracted to franchising? When would it be better to start an entirely new business instead of purchasing a franchise?

7. What are the upsides and downsides of the traditional corporate structure?

8. Cooperatives appear frequently in agriculture. Describe another industry where collective ownership would work well, and explain why.

9. In a sole proprietorship and in partnerships, the owners and the managers are the same people. How are ownership and management separated in corporations?

10. How can a joint venture between a commercial firm and a not-for-profit organization help both parties achieve their goals?

PROJECTS AND TEAMWORK APPLICATIONS

1. Research a large firm to learn more about its beginnings as a small business. Who founded the company? Does the firm still produce its original product or service, or does it provide a new product or service?

2. Go to the Canadian Franchise Association website, www.cfa.ca, to research franchises. Choose a franchise that interests you and look up its startup requirements. Would you run a franchise in a partnership with someone you know? Why or why not? Present your findings in class.

3. Think of an idea for a small business. Research the industry and the major competition online. Draft a business plan. Will your firm be a sole proprietorship or a partnership? Include this decision in your business plan.

4. Identify an organization that is owned by a unit or agency of government, such as VIA Rail or BC Hydro. Imagine that you have been hired by as a consultant. You must decide whether the organization should remain publicly owned. Research its successes and failures. Write a memo to explain your conclusion.

5. Identify a business and a not-for-profit organization that could form a joint venture that would be good for both parties. Write a proposal or create an advertisement for the event or activity that the organizations could present.

WEB ASSIGNMENTS

1. **Small-business successes.** Visit the website www.inc.com/31-stories-of-small-business-success/index.html. Scroll through the success stories and choose one that interests you. Read the feature and prepare a brief report answering these questions:

    a. What does the firm do?

    b. Where did the idea come from?

    c. What expertise does the owner have?

    d. How did the business begin?

    e. Who are its competitors?

2. **Business Development Bank of Canada (BDC).** Go to the BDC's website at www.bdc.ca. Click on Articles and Tools and have a look at the articles. Identify one article that you believe provides the most useful information for a small-business owner. Write a summary of the article's highlights.

Note: Internet Web addresses change frequently. If you do not find the exact sites listed, you may need to access the organization's or company's home page and search from there.

6 | STARTING YOUR OWN BUSINESS: THE ENTREPRENEURSHIP ALTERNATIVE

LEARNING OBJECTIVES

LO 6.1 Describe what is an entrepreneur and the different types of entrepreneurs.

LO 6.2 Explain why people choose to become entrepreneurs.

LO 6.3 Discuss factors that support and expand opportunities for entrepreneurs.

LO 6.4 Identify the traits of successful entrepreneurs.

LO 6.5 Summarize the process of starting a new venture.

LO 6.6 Explain intrapreneurship.

INSIDE BUSINESS

Sharing Economy Sparks Start-Ups

Find a need and fill it is the age-old way to start a new business venture. New business opportunities are rapidly emerging in what is referred to as the "sharing economy" and technologies like smartphone apps are providing individual entrepreneurs the opportunity to participate like never before. Individuals are sharing their cars, apartments, clothes, tools, sports equipment—the list continues to grow daily. The business models that bring participants together usually include direct money payment and can include services as well. For example, the ride sharing service Uber allows anyone with a car to offer rides for a fee. Needless to say, Uber is facing complaints of unfair competition from the taxi industry across Canada, as Uber drivers do not pay the same licensing and other fees required of registered taxis.

Perhaps a shared transportation solution is at hand with FlightCar. For most travellers, parking at the airport is the easiest, although not the least expensive, option. If you head to a typical large airport, you will see parking lots filled with private cars. Upon closer inspection, you will also see lots filled with rental cars waiting for customers. What if the owners of these parked cars could be connected with travellers who want to rent cars? In this way, cars would not sit idle while travelers are away and there would be no need for large fleets of rental cars to own and maintain. In exchange for allowing FlightCar to rent their car to a traveller, the car owner is paid a small fee and is provided with free parking—hopefully the car is actually being rented by a fellow traveler. The rental charges are lower than what a traditional car rental firm would charge.

Airbnb is probably the best-known sharing business. Started a little more than five years ago, this firm offers a web-based service linking travellers who want to rent rooms with individuals who have space in their homes or apartments to rent. Airbnb charges owners 3 percent of the nightly room charge and renters 10 percent.

The company prescreens individuals to ensure guests and owners have a good experience and even suggests that individuals check each other's information on social media sites such as Facebook. For the room owners, it is a good deal because they can make some money from their unused rooms; for the travellers, they can stay in private homes for a fraction of the cost of a hotel room. More than 9 million people have used Airbnb's services, with more than a half a million listings worldwide.

Peer-to-peer sharing is part of a fast-growing trend toward renting and not owning. *Forbes* estimates that this new "share economy" will be greater than $3.5 billion and grow at over 25 percent per year. What is fuelling this trend? For one thing, it is the access to information via the Internet, which provides search engines, mobile devices, and social media pages and profiles. There is also the idea that spending money for little-used goods may not make much sense. So, the next time you drive by airport parking, open your closet, or store holiday decorations in an unused room, think about the items you own that could be shared with others—for a fee. You might be able to make a few dollars by renting these items out or, like FlightCar, Uber, and Airbnb founders, maybe make millions, by starting a company to help others do the same.[1]

CHAPTER 6 OVERVIEW

You think you want to start and run your own company. Like the founders of Uber, Airbnb, and other start-ups you have a great idea for a new business and you dream of fame and fortune. If you are entrepreneurial, you're not alone. More than ever, people like you, your classmates, and your friends are choosing to be entrepreneurs.

How do you become an entrepreneur? Experts advise people who want to be entrepreneurs to learn as much as possible about business. Take courses and complete academic programs such as the one you are currently taking. Try to gain practical experience by working part-time or full-time. Shoshana Finn learned about the fashion business while she was growing up. Both her grandfather and father ran successful garment manufacturing businesses. You can also learn about the upsides and downsides of entrepreneurship by reading newspaper and magazine articles and biographies of successful entrepreneurs. You will learn how entrepreneurs handle the challenges of starting their businesses. Need advice on how to launch and grow a new venture? Turn to magazines such as *Entrepreneur*, *Forbes*, *Fast Company*, *Success*, and *Inc*. You can also get assistance from entrepreneurship associations, such as the Canadian Federation of Independent Business (CFIB). Anyone who wants to be an entrepreneur should visit the websites listed in **Figure 6.1**.

Canada Business	www.canadabusiness.ca
Business Development Bank	www.bdc.ca
Entrepreneur.com	www.entrepreneur.com
Canadian Chamber of Commerce	www.chamber.ca
U.S. Chamber of Commerce	www.uschamber.com
Kauffman Foundation	www.kauffman.org
U.S. Small Business Administration	www.sba.gov
The Wall Street Journal Small Business	http://www.wsj.com/public/page/small-business.html

FIGURE 6.1 Internet Resources for Entrepreneurs

In this chapter, we focus on how to enter the world of entrepreneurship. This chapter describes the activities of entrepreneurs, the different kinds of entrepreneurs, and the reason more and more people are choosing to be entrepreneurs. We will discuss the business environment where entrepreneurs work, the characteristics that help entrepreneurs succeed, and how they start new ventures. The chapter ends with a discussion of how large companies try to keep the entrepreneurial spirit alive and well.

WHAT IS AN ENTREPRENEUR?

LO 6.1 Describe what is an entrepreneur and the different types of entrepreneurs.

entrepreneur a person who seeks a profitable opportunity and takes the necessary risks to set up and operate a business.

An **entrepreneur** is a risk taker in the private enterprise system, a person who seeks a profitable opportunity and takes the necessary risks to set up and operate a business. Think about Vancouver's Jim Pattison, founder of the Jim Pattison Group. He started by purchasing a car dealership in 1961. Today, he is head of a private Canadian corporation with over 39,000 employees worldwide and 2014 revenues of about $8.4 billion. The company works in the automotive, media, packaging, food sales and distribution, magazine distribution, entertainment, export, and financial industries. Today, the Jim Pattison Group is Canada's second-largest private company.[2]

Entrepreneurs differ from many small-business owners. Many small-business owners share the same drive, creative energy, and desire to succeed. But entrepreneurs are different because one of their major goals is expansion and growth. (Many small-business owners want to keep their businesses small.) Jim Pattison wasn't happy having just one successful business, so he purchased

Vancouver's Jim Pattison is founder of the Jim Pattison Group. In 1961, he purchased a car dealership. Today, he is head of Canada's second-largest private corporation.

and developed others. Entrepreneurs combine their ideas and drive with money, employees, and other resources to create a business that meets a need.

Entrepreneurs also differ from managers. Managers are employees who direct others to reach an organization's goals. Owners of some small startup firms work as owner-managers to carry out their plans for their businesses and to make up for human resource limitations at their new companies. Entrepreneurs may also perform a managerial role, but their main responsibility is to use the resources of their organizations—employees, money, equipment, and facilities—to accomplish their goals.

Studies have identified certain personality traits and behaviours common to entrepreneurs that differ from the traits and behaviours needed for managerial success. One of these traits is the willingness to take on the risks of starting a new venture. Some take that risk because they need to—they've left or lost their previous jobs or just need a way to make money. Others, like Jim Pattison, want a challenge or a different quality of life. Entrepreneurial characteristics are examined in detail later in this chapter.

Categories of Entrepreneurs

Entrepreneurs use their talents in different situations. These differences can be classified into three categories: classic entrepreneurs, serial entrepreneurs, and social entrepreneurs.

Classic entrepreneurs see business opportunities and set aside resources to gain access to those markets. Andrew Henle of TronSports.ca is a classic entrepreneur. As an avid amateur hockey player in Montreal-area leagues, he saw a niche in the sports equipment and accessories market and built an online storefront. The site caters mostly to teams and serious athletes looking for high caliber equipment such as hockey skates, sticks, protective padding, and other equipment at competitive prices and regular promotional deals.

A classic entrepreneur starts a new company by seeing a business opportunity and setting aside resources to gain access to a new market. **Serial entrepreneurs** are different. They start one business, run it, and then start and run more businesses, one after another. Elon Musk, the founder of such businesses as PayPal, Tesla Motors, Solar City, and SpaceX, is a serial entrepreneur. Jessica Herrin is also a serial entrepreneur. When Herrin graduated from college with an economics degree, she joined a software startup firm where she got hooked on the idea of "unlimited potential." At age 24, Herrin co-founded WeddingChannel.com in Los Angeles, which grew within a few

classic entrepreneur a person who sees a business opportunity and sets aside resources to gain access to that market.

serial entrepreneur a person who starts one business, runs it, and then starts and runs more businesses, one after another.

social entrepreneur a person who sees societal problems and uses business principles to develop new solutions.

 **ASSESSMENT CHECK**

6.1.1 What tools do entrepreneurs use to create a new business?

6.1.2 How do entrepreneurs differ from managers?

6.1.3 What do classic entrepreneurs and social entrepreneurs have in common?

6.1.4 Is a social entrepreneur simply a philanthropist who gives to good causes to help others?

LO 6.2 Explain why people choose to become entrepreneurs.

years to 100 employees and $21 million in revenues. When her firm was purchased by The Knot, Herrin went on to start Stella & Dot, a high-quality fashion jewellery business sold by more than 14,000 independent representatives at parties and online. Stella & Dot now has $200 million in revenues, and the jewellery has been featured in the business and fashion press—and perhaps more important, on celebrities.[3]

Some entrepreneurs focus on solving society's challenges through their businesses. **Social entrepreneurs** see a societal problem and use business principles to develop new solutions. Social entrepreneurs develop new solutions that help humanity. More than 50 years ago, a group of seven Indian women gathered one afternoon to roll out dough to make traditional crackers. They saw an opportunity to make and market these crackers for a wider audience. They set up a women's cooperative that was based on this idea. They called their business Lijjat Papad and hoped to empower Indian women entrepreneurs. Since then, the cooperative's president, Jyoti Naik, has led the cooperative to become one of India's most successful business ventures. The company now produces a wide variety of bakery products, spices, and flour. It has 62 branches across India. The cooperative brand is one of the most popular and trusted in India. It is viewed as the best-run small-village cooperative in the nation.[4]

REASONS TO CHOOSE ENTREPRENEURSHIP AS A CAREER PATH

If you want to run your own business, you have lots of company. During one recent year, about 10,000 new businesses were created each month in Canada. The United States has more people and created more businesses—there, 543,000 new businesses were created each month. In both countries, new businesses in services and the construction industry had the highest rates of activity.[5]

In the past few decades, more people have shown interest in entrepreneurial careers. They may have been encouraged in part by publicity around the successes of entrepreneurs such as Mark Zuckerberg. He launched the global social-networking website Facebook while he was a student at Harvard University.

As shown in **Figure 6.2**, people become entrepreneurs for one or more of four major reasons: a desire to be their own boss, a desire to succeed financially, a desire to attain job security, and a desire to improve their quality of life. Each of these reasons is described in more detail in the following sections.

Being Your Own Boss

One of the biggest reasons for becoming an entrepreneur is the chance to be your own boss. Entrepreneurs have the freedom to make all the decisions. In Montreal's West Island area, Carmine Petrillo has made Monster Gym an inviting community-oriented gym for people who are serious and not-so-serious about exercise. When gym clients need to decide whether to renew their memberships or join another club, they often consider the condition of the exercise equipment. For gym owners, deciding when to upgrade to new equipment is an expensive decision: a single exercise machine can cost thousands of dollars. Monster Gym clients are lucky. Carmine has made such decisions on his own since opening his doors in 1994. He is good at looking ahead to keep meeting the needs of his suburban clientele. After all, they have grown used to having the latest and best exercise equipment. Carmine's decision to upgrade equipment often and regularly has helped grow the client base to 4,500 people.[6]

FIGURE 6.2 Why People Become Entrepreneurs

Carmine Petrillo created Monster Gym, an inviting community-oriented gym for people who are serious and not-so-serious about exercise. For many people, the main reason for being an entrepreneur is to control when, where, and how they work.

CAREER KICKSTART

Communicating by Email, Text Message, or Social Networking Updates: You Don't Have to Be All Thumbs

Most entrepreneurs use email, texting, social networking updates, and other electronic communications to reach their customers, suppliers, distributors, employees, and others. That communication often takes place on the run; when you are your own boss, you are busy taking care of many tasks. You may think of yourself as being fast with the cellphone or smartphone keyboard, and maybe you can send off an email in no time. Still, it might be a good idea to review a few etiquette tips to make sure your messages sound professional.

- Don't write in all caps. Using all capital letters makes the message look frantic, or as if you are yelling.

- On the subject line, do *not* write "Important—Please Read." That kind of message is likely to end up in a "delete" box, unread. Also, try to avoid sending any kind of "forwarded" messages—for the same reason. Instead, use a short but descriptive subject line so the person you are emailing knows what the message is about. An example is "Review of Tuesday's Meeting."

- Avoid slang expressions and shorthand, such as "LOL," "ru," and "L8." Also don't use smiley or sad-face icons.

- Be friendly but not too familiar. Never include jokes in a business email or text message.

- Be brief. A short message is more helpful than a long message. If you need to say more, then end the email by saying you will follow up with a phone call.

- Remember that your computer and your phone are like a tape recorder. Messages can be saved and stored. You do *not* want to make an unprofessional comment that could cause problems later. Never add personal messages to professional messages. Avoid complaints or criticisms that could hurt your company's image or the reputation of others.

Sources: Mark Grossman, "Email Etiquette Is Important," Grossman Law Group, accessed March 16, 2010, www.ecomputerlaw.com; "Business Email Etiquette: What You Should Know BEFORE You Hit Send," accessed March 16, 2010, www.evancarmichael.com/Women-Entrepreneurs; Karl Stolley and Allen Brizee, "Email Etiquette," *Purdue Owl*, accessed March 16, 2010, http://owl.english.purdue.edu; Nina Kaufman, "Making it Legal," *Entrepreneur*, accessed March 16, 2010, http://legal.entrepreneur.com.

Being your own boss usually means having to make all the important decisions. It also means engaging in most—if not all—of the communication related to your business, including dealing with customers, suppliers, distributors, retailers, and others. The "Career Kickstart" feature offers tips for professional-style communication—even if you're on the run and using your thumbs.

In 1987, Cora Tsouflidou opened her first restaurant in Montreal. She offered a big-breakfast menu of crepes, omelettes, fruits, and cereals. Her recipe of high-quality, healthier food was a hit with customers. Today, the family-run company has 130 Chez Cora franchise locations across Canada. Family members actively manage the firm and enjoy their financial success.[7]

Financial Success

Entrepreneurs create wealth. Many start their ventures with the specific goal of becoming rich—or at least financially successful. Entrepreneurs often believe they have an idea for a better product. They want to be the first to bring it to market—and to receive the financial rewards as a result. Entrepreneurs believe they won't achieve their greatest success by working for someone else—and they're generally right. Of course, the downside is that when they fail, they become unemployed.

Job Security

The demand for skilled employees remains high in many industries. But working for a company, even a *Fortune* 500 firm, is no guarantee of job security. In fact, over the past 10 years, large companies have looked for efficiencies by downsizing and getting rid of more jobs than they created. As a result, more and more workers—both first-time job seekers and laid-off long-term employees—are deciding to create their own job security by starting their own businesses. Having your own business doesn't guarantee job security, but research has found that most newly created jobs come from small businesses. Many of those new jobs are in new companies.[8]

Economies are changing overseas. Workers there are discovering the benefits of entrepreneurship compared with being employed by big firms. In China, entire industries are government-owned, such as banking, steel, and telecommunications. Many young Chinese businesspeople are starting their own small firms. China has nearly 500 million people under the age of 30. Their role models are Bill Gates and Michael Dell, reports an entrepreneurship professor at the Europe International Business School in Shanghai.[9]

Quality of Life

Entrepreneurship is a good career option for people who want to improve their quality of life. Starting a business means independence and some freedom to decide when, where, and how to work. A **lifestyle entrepreneur** is a person who starts a business for two reasons: to gain flexibility in work hours and to gain control over his or her life. It does *not* mean working fewer hours or easier work. Generally it is the opposite—people who start their own businesses often work longer and harder than ever before, at least in the beginning. But they enjoy being successful, both materially and in the way they live their lives.

Zhena Muzyka, a single mom, needed a job that gave her flexibility and earning power. Her young son, "needed operations [for kidney disease], and the insurance wasn't going to cover them. I had to come up with a job where I could have him with me because he had special needs," Muzyka explains. So she combined her interest in herbal medicine with fair-trade practices. That's how she started her firm, Gypsy Tea. Today, Muzyka's son is healthy, and Gypsy Tea is a multimillion-dollar firm. It produces flavoured teas grown on fair-trade farms in Peru, India, and other countries. Workers at these farms receive health care, clean water, maternity leave, child care, and other benefits. New products have been added to the Gypsy Tea line, including candles and beads. "It's the most 'worth-it' thing I've ever done," says Muzyka of Gypsy Tea.[10] Another group of entrepreneurs also found a way to make their business fit their lifestyle and their creative interest in home fragrance products. Read about Fruits & Passion co-owners Jean Hurteau; his wife, France Menard; and brother, Guy Hurteau, in the "Hit & Miss" feature.

lifestyle entrepreneur a person who starts a business to reduce work hours and create a more relaxed lifestyle.

✓ ASSESSMENT CHECK

6.2.1 What are the four main reasons people choose to become entrepreneurs?

6.2.2 What factors affect the entrepreneur's job security?

HIT & MISS

Fruits & Passion for Lifestyle Products

Fruits & Passion is a popular beauty, body, and lifestyle products retailer. This business is the result of a great success story in a very competitive global marketplace. The firm creates unique fragrances for oils, candles, other personal care products. It uses ingredients gathered from around the world to make its products and then wraps them in attractive packaging.

Fruits & Passion was started in 1991 by Jean Hurteau; his wife, France Menard; and his brother, Guy Hurteau. The threesome believed that the "lifestyle market" for personal luxuries was beginning to grow, and they wanted to be part of it. Stores like The Body Shop were leading the way in the personal care market. But the partners sensed that people's desire for personal lifestyle quality would also lead to demand for other products for the home. For example, small decorative candles could enhance a room's quality if the design and fragrance were just right. Little things could make a big difference in their kitchens, bathrooms, and bedrooms.

Before long, the firm was selling its creative products through a dozen Canadian retail stores, which they still own and operate today. But, to truly realize the potential sales, the company needed a large retail distribution network to provide products to customers in more markets.

Currently, the firm sells its products through 175 Fruits & Passion retailers—93 are in Canada—and through more than 2,000 independent retailers around the world. Fruits & Passion franchise retailers can be found in England, Taiwan, China, Morocco, Mexico, France, the United States, and Canada. The company's website helps people to learn about the variety of products it sells and is set up for online sales.

Questions for Critical Thinking

1. Why do these products sell so well around the world?
2. What entrepreneurial characteristics do you think were needed to make this business a success?

Sources: Fruits and Passion, accessed April 8, 2015, www.fruits-passion.ca.

THE ENVIRONMENT FOR ENTREPRENEURS

LO 6.3 Discuss factors that support and expand opportunities for entrepreneurs.

Are you ready to start your own company? Do some research about the environment where you want to do business. You'll need to think about several important overall factors. First is the economy—whether it is stalled or booming, you may find opportunities. Think about where you want to locate your business.

The general attitude toward entrepreneurs in North America is positive. In addition to favourable public attitudes and more financing options, four additional factors also support and expand opportunities for entrepreneurs: globalization, education, information technology, and demographic and economic trends (see **Figure 6.3**). Each of these factors is discussed in the following sections.

Globalization

The rapid globalization of business has created many opportunities for entrepreneurs. Entrepreneurs market their products abroad and hire international talent. Most of the fastest-growing small Canadian companies have international sales—usually to the United States. For example, despite being based in Montreal, TronSports.ca sells hockey and other sports equipment to Americans through its dedicated U.S. site Besthockey.com.[11]

Entrepreneurship is growing around the world. The role of entrepreneurs is growing in most industrialized countries, in newly industrialized countries, and in the emerging free-market countries in central and eastern Europe. However, the level of entrepreneurship varies. Worldwide,

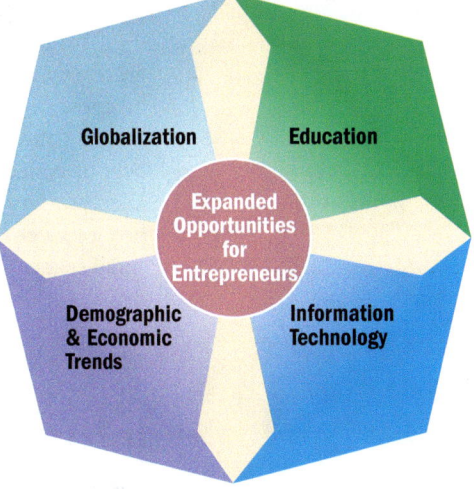

FIGURE 6.3 Factors Supporting and Expanding Opportunities for Entrepreneurs

more than 9 percent of adults are starting or managing a new business. Thailand leads in the number of adults engaged in entrepreneurial activity (27 percent), followed by Peru (26 percent), Colombia (23 percent), Venezuela (20 percent), Dominican Republic (17 percent), and China (16 percent).[12]

India has experienced a big increase in the number of female entrepreneurs. Shahnaz Husain knew the effects that chemical-based beauty care products can have on consumers—and on the environment. In 1971, she opened India's first professional herbal salon on the balcony of her house in Delhi. She now runs a respected beauty care empire called Ayurvedic. Husain's Ayurvedic products contain natural ingredients, ranging from vegetables to diamond dust. "The ancient Indian system of Ayurveda is the oldest and most organized system of herbal healing in the world. I was convinced that it could offer ideal answers to cosmetic care," explains Husain. "I entered highly competitive international markets, without commercial advertising or fancy packaging." Ayurvedic supplies its products to high-end stores in London, Paris, and Milan, and in shops located in Spain and Japan.[13]

Education

In the past 20 years, more educational opportunities have been offered for would-be entrepreneurs. Today, students at many colleges and universities can take a major in entrepreneurship. Dozens of other colleges and universities offer an emphasis in entrepreneurship, and hundreds more offer one or two courses in how to start a business.

Many schools offer opportunities to intern with a startup or to work toward launching a company. Most large universities in Canada, such as Simon Fraser University's Beedie School of Business, host entrepreneurial centres for research and development of new business. The school recently hosted an event that included two expert judges from the CBC program *Dragons' Den*, Jim Treliving and Bruce Croxon.[14]

In addition to schools, many other organizations have opened in recent years to teach entrepreneurship to young people. The Kauffman Center for Entrepreneurial Leadership offers training programs for learners from kindergarten through community college. The centre's Entreprep summer program is taught in cooperation with local colleges and universities. This summer program teaches high-school juniors how to start and manage a company. Students in Free Enterprise (SIFE) is a worldwide not-for-profit organization. College students work with faculty advisors to teach grade-school and high-school students and others the value of private enterprise and entrepreneurship.[15] The Association of Collegiate Entrepreneurs has chapters on many school campuses in Canada and the United States.

You don't have to major in business to become an entrepreneur, but students who major in entrepreneurship or take entrepreneurship courses are three times more likely to start their own business or to help someone else to start a business.[16] You don't have to wait for graduation to launch your first startup, and your business idea doesn't have to change the world. Record numbers of college students are launching their own businesses—while still in school. When Ryan Dickerson was a junior living in a small dorm room at university, he figured out how to turn his bed into a couch during the day. It was a good idea that gave him the furniture he needed for the small space. He designed a special bolster pillow that was the same length as his bed. During the day, this pillow became the "back" of the couch. He called his invention the Rylaxer. The pillows were first made locally and sold on campus. Dickerson immediately drew up a business plan for selling them nationwide.[17]

Information Technology

The explosion in information technology (IT) has been one of the biggest advances for entrepreneurs. Computer and communications technologies have merged, and their costs have dropped. Low-cost technology has given entrepreneurs the tools they need to help them compete with large companies. Information technology helps entrepreneurs to work quickly and efficiently and to provide immediate and helpful customer service. Information technology also increases sales and gives businesses a professional image. In fact, technology has made it possible for a dorm-room

HIT & MISS

Businesses Based at Home Are Booming

The idea itself makes perfect sense: you've been laid off from your full-time job, or you've recently moved to a new area, or you just had a baby. Working from home seems like the ideal solution. But until a few years ago, home-based businesses were not really considered to be real businesses by many in the business community. Most people viewed home-based work as no more challenging—or successful—than stuffing envelopes. All that has changed. Today, more than 6.6 million home-based businesses contribute at least half of their owners' household income. *Homepreneurs* are estimated to employ about one in every 10 private-sector workers—and their businesses are competitive. Technology has made all this possible.

Some homepreneurs run businesses that are entirely based on technology, such as Web development. Stephen Labuda is president of Agency3. He is a former programmer for Deutsche Bank, a large international banking firm. Labuda built websites on the side for several years. Then he quit his job and made Agency3 his full-time, home-based career. The firm's revenues are in the millions, and Labuda has about half a dozen employees. Labuda loves working from home. "I'm not intending to go rent office space," he notes.

Other homepreneurs rely on technology to reach customers, fulfill orders, ship goods, and provide other services. When Michael and Mary Ferrari retired, they realized they needed to supplement their savings—and they didn't want to stop working. So they formed UnusualThreads.com, a company that sells fashions worn by celebrities. The couple still only works the site part-time, but they earn enough money to add to their savings and can take time off to travel. Another homepreneur is Marco Barberini, who launched OvernightPetTags.com several years ago. He now grosses more than $8,000 a month. Barberini discovered how to manufacture and ship pet-identification tags cheaper than his competition. Barberini echoes the advice of every successful homepreneur. "Most people give up too quickly," he says. "Just make sure that [your product] is going to be something that's in demand, and do it."

Questions for Critical Thinking

1. Could any of these home-based businesses succeed without the heavy use of information technology? Why or why not?

2. Outline your own idea for a home-based business that relies on technology.

Sources: Steven Berglas, "Wake-up Call for Newly Hatched Entrepreneurs," *Forbes*, February 6, 2010, www.forbes.com/2010/02/06/baby-boomer-risk-entrepreneur-human-resources-berglas.html; Carol Tice, "Homepreneur Winners Keep Growing Despite Downturn," *Entrepreneur*, February 1, 2010, www.entrepreneur.com/article/218626; John Tozzi, "The Rise of the Homepreneur," *Businessweek*, October 23, 2009 accessed January 8, 2010, www.businessweek.com/smallbiz/content/oct2009/sb20091023_263258.htm.

---

innovator like Ryan Dickerson to compete with a much larger firm. Technology has also assisted in the huge increase of *homepreneurs*—entrepreneurs who run home-based businesses. These successful ventures are described in the "Hit & Miss" feature.

Social networking has also changed the business environment for entrepreneurs. According to a recent study, more than 90 percent of successful companies now use at least one social media tool. Many entrepreneurs have included the use of sites such as Twitter, LinkedIn, and Facebook in their business strategy. They believe that social media will help them reach more customers and grow faster. Social media will give these entrepreneurs a competitive edge. Eric Mattson, a researcher for *Inc.* magazine, believes that social networking is more useful to small firms run by entrepreneurs than to larger firms because "in smaller organizations, there is more room for innovation because it requires [fewer] processes to adopt."[18]

Demographic and Economic Trends

Who else is starting a business? Two groups are most likely to start their own businesses: immigrants to North America and people between the ages of 55 and 64.[19] As baby boomers continue to age and control a large share of North American wealth, the trend is expected to continue. Older entrepreneurs will also have access to their retirement funds and home equity for financing. Many boomers plan to work after retiring from their traditional jobs or careers. Some just want to keep working; others want to add to their income and savings.

As mentioned earlier, more college and university students are becoming entrepreneurs. Ted Livingston, the founder and chief executive officer (CEO) of Waterloo-based Kik Interactive Inc.,

ASSESSMENT CHECK

6.3.1 To what extent is entrepreneurship possible in different countries, and what opportunities does globalization create for today's entrepreneurs?

6.3.2 Identify the educational factors that help expand current opportunities for entrepreneurs.

6.3.3 Describe current demographic trends that suggest new goods and services for entrepreneurial businesses.

studied mechatronics engineering at the University of Waterloo between 2005 and 2009. He founded Kik (then called Unsynced) while in the VeloCity residence in the winter term of 2009. VeloCity is a student residence–based startup incubator that was set up in September 2008 at the University of Waterloo. VeloCity is a community that educates and connects talented, like-minded students with each other and with the surrounding startup community for support and mentorship. At age 23, Livingston showed his appreciation by donating $1 million to VeloCity.[20]

Demographic trends can create opportunities for entrepreneurs. For example, the aging of the population, the growth of ethnic groups, and two-income families can lead to new markets for products and services. Services designed for older consumers, foods that cater to ethnic preferences, and convenience products for busy parents all have an opportunity for success. As the economy rises and falls, entrepreneurs who are flexible and can adapt quickly have the best chance for success. When consumers are less willing to spend money, certain businesses do well. For example, a shoe-repair shop will likely see an increase in business. The Play It Again chain of North American stores sells used sports equipment. This retail chain's business will also likely increase. Skates and protective hockey gear are often used for only one or two seasons before a child has outgrown them. The slightly used equipment will be a great bargain for another family looking to outfit the next Sidney Crosby in their family.[21]

LO 6.4 Identify the traits of successful entrepreneurs.

CHARACTERISTICS OF ENTREPRENEURS

People who start a business of their own are true innovators. They aren't satisfied with things the way they are but want to achieve certain goals on their own terms. Successful entrepreneurs often have parents who were entrepreneurs—or who had dreams of starting their own business. Most entrepreneurs share some specific personality traits. Researchers have studied successful entrepreneurs and report that they are more likely to be curious, passionate, self-motivated, honest, courageous, and flexible. The eight traits shown in **Figure 6.4** are especially important for people who want to succeed as entrepreneurs.

FIGURE 6.4
Characteristics of Entrepreneurs

Entrepreneurial Personality

- Vision
- High Energy Level
- Need to Achieve
- Self-Confidence and Optimism
- Tolerance for Failure
- Creativity
- Tolerance for Ambiguity
- Internal Locus of Control

© 4x6/iStockphoto.com

Vision

Entrepreneurs generally begin with a *vision*—an overall idea for how to make their business idea a success. Then they follow this vision with energy and excitement. Bill Gates and Paul Allen launched Microsoft with the vision of a computer on every desk and in every home, all running Microsoft software. Their vision helped Microsoft become the world's largest marketer of computer software. It guided the company and provided clear direction for employees. This kind of direction was especially helpful as Microsoft grew, adapted, and prospered during huge technological changes.

It can be said that every invention, from the light bulb to the cellphone, started with someone having a vision—viewing the world in a slightly different way. Some inventions have been created out of need or because of a mistake. True entrepreneurs can turn these situations into opportunities. In the healthcare field, penicillin was created by accident. Products with narrower markets have also found success. Jodi Pliszka has an autoimmune disorder that causes baldness. She's an athlete who spent years searching for a product that would keep her head cool and dry under helmets and during exercise. She couldn't find anything, but instead of giving up, she invented what she needed. The result is called HeadlineIt, a thin, lightweight disposable liner worn under helmets, wigs, and hats. Within a few years, Pliszka received a design patent for her product, and sales hit the $1 million mark. Pliszka was first a clinical therapist and an author. Now she is also a successful entrepreneur.[22]

High Energy Level

Entrepreneurs work long and hard to make their visions a reality. Many entrepreneurs work full-time at their regular day jobs and spend weeknights and weekends launching their startups. Many entrepreneurs work alone or with a very small staff. That means that the entrepreneurs themselves do most—if not all—of the work needed to get the business going. This work includes tasks related to the startup's design, marketing, sales, and finances. Most entrepreneurs spend at least 70 hours a week on their new business. This time can affect their other job (if they have one) and their personal life—at least in the beginning.[23] Thus, entrepreneurs need a high level of energy if they want to succeed.

Need to Achieve

Entrepreneurs work hard because they want to do well. Their strong desire to compete helps them to enjoy the challenge of reaching difficult goals. It also promotes a commitment to personal success. A poll by About.com showed Oprah Winfrey as the most admired entrepreneur among adults. She is the first African-American woman to become a billionaire. Winfrey has built an empire that includes television, magazines, and radio. Her own words best illustrate her strong drive: "I don't think of myself as a poor, deprived ghetto girl who made good. I think of myself as somebody who from an early age knew I was responsible for myself, and had to make good."[24] But when teens were polled by Junior Achievement, they picked Apple founder Steven Jobs as their most admired entrepreneur. Teens said that Jobs "made a difference in/improved people's lives or made the world a better place."[25] Both of these entrepreneurs have achieved very high goals.

Self-Confidence and Optimism

Entrepreneurs believe that they can succeed, and their self-confidence and excitement leads to optimism in others. Their optimism can seem like fearlessness in the face of difficult odds. They see opportunities where others see danger. Ishita Khanna founded her not-for-profit organization, Ecosphere, in one of the harshest living areas on the planet, the Spiti valley in Tibet. But this valley is also one of the most beautiful—and searched for—locations for eco-travellers. Khanna believed that if small entrepreneurial businesses in Tibet—especially those run by women—could be linked, they would have more power. She knew it wouldn't be easy. "Spiti's geographical isolation and poor communication infrastructure has been one of the major hurdles," Khanna now admits. But Khanna didn't give up, and Ecosphere recently received the Green Livelihoods Achievement Award from The Sierra Club. "There are numerous doubts that plague one before one takes the plunge," Khanna says. "But if you are passionate about what you want to do, that is half the battle won already."[26]

Tolerance for Failure

Entrepreneurs often succeed because of their strong will and because they continue to try again and again when others would give up. They also view setbacks and failures as learning experiences. They are not easily discouraged or disappointed when things don't go as planned. Bobbi Brown has built a big name in the cosmetics industry. Estée Lauder bought her company, and Brown stayed on in an active role. The brand faced some setbacks after its acquisition. Sales decreased, but Brown never gave up. She met with the CEO, who said the problem was that the cosmetics were not setting themselves apart from the competition. Brown tried to understand the criticism, learned from the setback, and decided to change the culture of the company. She made the advertising photographs more editorial, and approached the cosmetics business as if it were a magazine. The company's numbers improved and today the Bobbi Brown empire is valued at over a billion dollars.[27]

Entrepreneurs often succeed simply because they won't give up. When sales of Bobbi Brown's cosmetics line slowed, she moved the company to a new location and updated its advertising. In the process, she successfully made her company stand out from the competition.

SOLVING AN **ETHICAL** CONTROVERSY

Entrepreneurs and Ethics: It's Good Business

When you're starting a new business, it's easy to get caught up in the excitement: a fresh start, a new idea, visions of fame and fortune. It might seem harmless to present an overly optimistic sales picture or to be a bit vague about where and how your product will be produced. After all, once your invention hits the stores, sales will skyrocket and everyone will forgive what you said before. But experts in every industry warn against unclear communication and decision making. Your business could fall flat, and failure may come in the form of a damaged image or legal problems. You might be someone who can tolerate some failures, but a wise entrepreneur knows how to prevent other failures—such as a failure of ethics.

Should every new business have a formal code of ethics?

PRO

1. A code of ethics "embodies the ethical commitments of your organization," writes business author Chris MacDonald. "It tells the world who you are, what you stand for, and what to expect when conducting business with you." It also shows leadership.
2. A code of ethics is a necessity in today's business environment. Without it, when a difficult incident or event happens, a small firm may be exposed to "greater risk from regulatory and prosecutorial authorities," observes Michael Connor, publisher of *Business Ethics*.

CON

1. Not every entrepreneurial enterprise, particularly those run by one person, needs a formal code of ethics. A person's word or a handshake is just as effective. The important thing is to convey honesty and integrity about the way your firm will do business.
2. There are too many stories in the media about businesspeople who have failed to make ethical decisions—and not enough stories about the many entrepreneurs who conduct business every day in an ethical manner. A code of ethics will not make a bad person good; nor will lack of a code turn a good person bad.

Summary

Some people argue that writing a formal code of ethics takes too much time; others recommend outsourcing the task to a consultant or another third party. However, the overwhelming majority of business experts advise taking the time and effort to develop a code of ethics. If a company has more than one employee, then all employees should be required to become familiar with the code. As an entrepreneur, you will face many challenges and probably a few failures; but none should be a failure of ethics.

Sources: "Business Ethics," Small Business Administration, accessed March 16, 2010, www.sba.gov; Carter McNamara, "Complete Guide to Ethics Management," *Management Help*, accessed March 16, 2010, www.managementhelp.org; Chris MacDonald, "Considerations for Writing a Code of Ethics," *Streetwise Small Business Book of Lists*, accessed March 16, 2010, www.ethicsweb.ca/codes/writing-a-code-of-ethics.htm; Josh Spiro, "How To Write a Code of Ethics for Business," *Inc.*, February 24, 2010, www.inc.com/guides/how-to-write-a-code-of-ethics.html; Don Knauss, "The Role of Business Ethics in Relationships with Customers," *Forbes*, January 19, 2010, www.forbes.com/2010/01/19/knauss-clorox-ethics-leadership-citizenship-ethics.html.

When things go well, it's easy to take personal credit. But when poor business decisions result in failure, it's more difficult. Truly successful entrepreneurs are willing to take responsibility for their mistakes. That is why an important part of launching any new business is establishing a code of ethics, as discussed in the "Solving an Ethical Controversy" feature.

Creativity

Entrepreneurs think of new ideas for goods and services. They also devise new ways to overcome difficult problems and situations. When we look at the top entrepreneurs in the world, we can see that creativity is a common trait. *Inc.* magazine presents an annual list of the 500 top small businesses, most of which were started by entrepreneurs. The word *solution* is one of the most common words in the names of these companies.

Some entrepreneurs find creative solutions to problems; others find creative ways to complete a task or provide a service. Still others create entirely new products. Aaron Patzer started Mint.com because he and his friends and family were frustrated with Intuit's Quicken products. He believed that he could develop a more user-friendly personal-finance software—and he did. Two years later, Patzer sold his website to Intuit for $170 million.[28]

Tolerance for Ambiguity

Entrepreneurs take in stride the uncertainties of launching a business. Dealing with unexpected events is normal for most entrepreneurs. Tolerance for ambiguity is different from the love of risk taking that many people relate to entrepreneurship. Successful entrepreneurship is not at all like gambling. Entrepreneurs look for strategies that they believe have a good chance of success. When a strategy isn't working, they quickly make changes. An important way entrepreneurs manage ambiguity is by staying close to customers so that they can change their offerings to match customer desires. One such entrepreneur is Kevin Mitnick. In the mid-1990s, Mitnick was arrested by the FBI for computer hacking, after which he served five years in prison. When he was released, Mitnick could have hidden his identity and started a new life—or gone on to further crimes. Instead, Mitnick went legitimate, opening his own computer security consulting company. He maintains a solid relationship with the businesses whose systems he once might have compromised. "The lifestyle of an entrepreneur is not so different from that of a hacker," quips Mitnick. "The only thing lacking is the sneakiness, the seduction of adventure." His firm, Mitnick Security Company, is earning more than $750,000 a year.[29]

Internal Locus of Control

Entrepreneurs have an internal locus of control. That means they believe that they control their own future. You won't find entrepreneurs blaming others or outside events for their successes or failures—they own it all.

Ralph Braun was diagnosed with a degenerative illness when he was 6 years old. By the time he was 14, he was in a wheelchair. Braun attended college but for only one year. He had to drop out because he couldn't get around the large campus in his wheelchair. So he decided to design his own transportation. Within about four months, he had built his first scooter. Then he got a job at a local automotive supply factory. There, he was able to get around easily on his scooter. People noticed and told him about friends or family members who needed a scooter like that. He started building them to order. Braun then began to focus on the van he was driving. He redesigned the interior to include a wheelchair/scooter lift that is now standard on buses and other mass transit. Again, he received requests to convert the vans of other wheelchair-bound drivers. Eventually Braun quit his factory job to focus on his business full-time. BraunAbility is now a $200 million empire. When he began building scooters, Braun recalls, "everyone told me it wasn't going to work. But when it comes to commonsense engineering, I'm very blessed. I think it is a [natural] ability." Braun is clearly in charge of his fate.[30]

> **ASSESSMENT CHECK**
>
> 6.4.1 What do we mean when we talk about an entrepreneur's vision?
>
> 6.4.2 Why is it important for an entrepreneur to have a high energy level and a strong need for achievement?
>
> 6.4.3 How do entrepreneurs generally feel about the possibility of failure?

STARTING A NEW VENTURE

> **LO 6.5** Summarize the process of starting a new venture.

Entrepreneurs can start a business in many different ways. This section discusses how to choose an idea for a new venture and how to turn a good idea into a working business.

Selecting a Business Idea

When choosing an idea for your business, remember the two most important things: (1) find something you love to do and are good at doing and (2) find an idea that meets a need in the marketplace. People willingly work hard doing something they love, and the experience will bring personal fulfillment. The old sayings "Do what makes you happy" and "Be true to yourself" are the best guidelines for deciding on a business idea.

Success also depends on customers. Would-be entrepreneurs need to be sure that the idea they choose will interest customers in the marketplace. The most successful entrepreneurs tend to work in industries where lots of change is taking place. These are usually the same industries where customers have difficulty deciding on their exact needs. In these industries,

Corin and Brian Mullins are the founders of Hapi Foods Group. Their company uses organic ingredients to make two artisan cereals, Holy Crap and Skinny B. The mom-and-pop startup business is located in Sechelt, on the Sunshine Coast of British Columbia. This startup is doing well in the very competitive breakfast cereal market. Read their story in the "Going Green" feature.

entrepreneurs can make use of their strengths, such as creativity, hard work, and tolerance of ambiguity. They can use these strengths to build customer relationships. But outstanding entrepreneurial success happens in every industry. Maybe you want to build a business based on your grandmother's cookie recipes, or maybe you have a better idea for tax-preparation software. Whatever your idea is, you are more likely to succeed if you ask yourself the right questions from the beginning.

Consider the guidelines in **Figure 6.5** as you think about your business ideas.

Many entrepreneurs invent new products or new ways of doing things. The inventor–entrepreneur needs to protect the rights to his or her invention by obtaining a patent. In Canada, the Patent Office is part of the Canadian Intellectual Property Office (CIPO), an agency of Industry Canada. The U.S. Patent and Trademark Office provides information about this process from an American perspective.

- List your interests and abilities. Include your values and beliefs, your goals and dreams, things you like and dislike doing, and your job experiences.
- Make another list of the types of businesses that match your interests and abilities.
- Read newspapers and business and consumer magazines. Learn about demographic and economic trends that discuss future needs for products that no one yet offers.
- Carefully evaluate existing goods and services. Look for ways to improve them.
- Decide on a business that matches what you want and offers profit potential.
- Do marketing research to decide whether your business idea will attract enough customers to earn a profit.
- Learn as much as you can about the industry in which your new venture will operate, your product or service, and your competitors. Read surveys that project growth in different industries.

FIGURE 6.5 Guidelines for Selecting a Business Idea

Buying an Existing Business

Some entrepreneurs prefer to buy established businesses instead of taking on the risks of starting new businesses. Buying an existing business brings many advantages: employees are already in place to serve regular customers and to deal with familiar suppliers, the good or service is already known in the marketplace, and the necessary permits and licences have already been obtained. It is easier to get financing for an existing business than for most startups. Some sellers may even help the buyers by providing financing and by offering to stay on as consultants. Most people want to buy a healthy business so that they can build on its success. But an experienced entrepreneur might buy a struggling business with the idea of turning it around. Entrepreneurs who are thinking about buying a business can use many resources, ranging from information provided by government agencies to websites listing actual companies for sale.

Buying a franchise is similar to buying an established business. Both are a less risky way to begin a business than starting an entirely new firm. But franchising (which was discussed in detail in Chapter 5) involves risks. It is a good idea to do thorough research before making any decision to start a new business.

GOING GREEN

HOLY CRAP: CORIN AND BRIAN MULLINS SURE KNOW HOW TO PICK A NAME FOR THEIR ORGANIC CEREALS

They named their cereals "Holy Crap" and "Skinny B." Everyone remembered these names when the couple appeared on the CBC's *Dragons' Den*. But the brand name was only one of several smart business decisions made by the Mullins. Their product is a good choice for customers who want a good-tasting organic cereal that (to be polite) helps with digestion and moving things along on the inside. Holy Crap has no genetically modified organisms (GMOs). It is made from all-natural ingredients: organic chia, hulled hemp hearts, organic buckwheat, organic cranberries, organic raisins, organic apple bits, and organic cinnamon.

The recipe is perfect for physically active young adults who want foods that fit with their lifestyle and taste good. Customers post "taste-imonials" on the company's website. Their comments show how much they believe in the products. For example, Will Kelsay is a professional XTERRA triathlete from Boulder, Colorado. His profile is titled "Holy Crap Cereal Is Rocket Fuel for Triathletes." It shows photos of Will in competition and bylines like "Will loves Holy Crap and the benefits of its super food ingredients." Will describes his belief in the product this way:

"The key ingredient of Holy Crap is chia, or Salvia Hispanica L. This oil seed crop is considered a perfect food because it's one of the few vegetarian sources of complete protein. The Aztecs valued it more highly than gold. Holy Crap cereal is a chia based wheat free, gluten free, lactose free breakfast cereal. The Tarahumara Indians in Copper Canyon, Mexico, the greatest long distance runners on the planet, have had a long history of using this slow burning rocket fuel for both athletes and warriors alike. The main cereal ingredient is Chia or Salvia Hispanica L., which typically contains 20% protein, 34% oil, and 25% dietary fiber. Salvia Hispanica L. contains the highest Omega-3 nutrient source found in nature with perfectly balanced Omega 3, 6, 9 profiles and ratios. The next most abundant ingredient is hulled hemp hearts, which are low in carbohydrates, contain more protein than milk, meat or eggs and are suitable for those unable to digest gluten, sugar, milk, nuts and meat." This kind of comment helps promote the cereals to serious athletes and to not-so-serious athletes that want to be like serious athletes—at least in what they eat.

The company has a warm relationship with its customers. It continues to do well because of brand name recognition. The company has retail distribution across North America at health food stores, specialty grocery stores, and through online shopping from their website.

Questions for Critical Thinking

1. Will the brand name help or hurt the company as it tries to grow further?
2. What are some other products that the company should consider developing and what names would you give them?

Sources: Holy Crap, accessed April 8, 2015, http://holycrap.ca; Julie Greco, "Is Holy Crap Cereal Milking the Hype?" *St. Catharines Standard*, November 26, 2010, accessed April 13, 2012, www.stcatharinesstandard.ca/ArticleDisplay.aspx?e=2862817; Allison Cross, "Sales Explode for Cereal with Cheeky Name," *Toronto Star*, November 23, 2010, accessed April 13, 2012, www.thestar.com/living/article/895792--sales-explode-for-cereal-with-cheeky-name; Remy Scalza, "Holy Crap: Local Cereal with Funny Name Goes Global," December 27, 2011, accessed April 13, 2012, www.insidevancouver.ca/2011/12/27/holy-crap-local-cereal-goes-global.

Creating a Business Plan

In the past, many entrepreneurs launched their businesses without writing formal business plans. Planning is an important part of managing in contemporary business. But entrepreneurs often go after opportunities as they arise and then they change course when they need to. Flexibility seems to be the key to business startups, especially in rapidly changing markets. But starting a business has many risks. Doing at least some planning is not just advisable but necessary, especially when an entrepreneur needs to look for funds from outside sources.

Appendix E discusses business plans in more detail. The Internet also offers a variety of resources for creating business plans. **Table 6.1** lists some of these online resources.

Table 6.1 Online Resources for Preparing a Business Plan

AllBusiness.com www.allbusiness.com	Under the "Finance" tab, select "Business Planning" for links to business plan examples, templates, and tips.
Inc. www.inc.com	Search for "business plans" to get access to articles on how to structure a business plan and how to write a mission statement.
MoreBusiness.com www.morebusiness.com	To see sample plans, select "Business Plans" under "Startup."

Finding Financing

seed capital the initial funding needed to launch a new venture.

A key issue in any business plan is financing. The need for **seed capital**, the funds used to launch a company, depends on the nature of the business. Seed capital can range as high as several million—say, for the purchase of a McDonald's franchise in a lucrative area—or as low as $1,000 for a website design. Many entrepreneurs use personal savings. Some ask for loans from business associates, family members, or even friends to use as startup funds. In fact, 82 percent of startups are self-financed, the greatest source by far.[31]

Debt Financing

debt financing borrowed funds that entrepreneurs must repay.

Entrepreneurs sometimes use **debt financing**, borrowed money that they must repay. Debt financing includes loans from banks, finance companies, credit-card companies, and family or friends. Some entrepreneurs charge business expenses to their personal credit cards, which are relatively easy to obtain. But high interest rates on credit cards mean that this source of funding is expensive. It is usually better to find other methods of funding.

Many banks turn down people who apply for loans to fund startups. The banks are fearful of the high risk of starting a new business. Over the last several years, more and more banks have turned down loan requests. Only a small percentage of startups raise seed capital through bank loans. Much planning and preparation is needed when applying for a bank loan. Bank loan officers want to see a business plan and will evaluate the entrepreneur's credit history. Because a startup has not yet established a business credit history, banks often base lending decisions on the entrepreneurs' personal credit histories. Banks are more willing to make loans to three kinds of entrepreneurs: those who have been in business for a while, those whose businesses show a profit on rising revenues, and those who need funds to finance expansion. Some entrepreneurs find that local community banks or credit unions are more interested in their loan applications than are the major national banks.

Even entrepreneurs who have previously received funding from banks—and have maintained a good relationship with their lenders—have experienced credit difficulties in recent years. A line of credit is an approved loan that a business can borrow from when funds are needed. Without that money, some businesses would not be able to pay for the materials they need to make the products that customers have already ordered. The 2008–10 economic slowdown was made worse by the reduction in credit and (in many cases) the refusal to offer more credit to businesses that could no longer function without normal levels of credit.

equity financing funds invested in new ventures in exchange for part ownership.

venture capitalists business firms or groups of individuals that invest in new and growing firms in exchange for an ownership share.

Equity Financing

In **equity financing**, entrepreneurs exchange a share of ownership in their company for money supplied by one or more investors. Entrepreneurs invest their own money and the funds supplied by the other people and firms that become co-owners of the startups. An entrepreneur does not have to repay equity funds. Instead, the investors share in the success of the business. Sources of equity financing include family and friends, business partners, venture capital firms, and private investors.

Some entrepreneurs team up with a partner who has funds to invest. This arrangement may be good for an entrepreneur who has a great business idea and skills but little or no money. Some investors also have business experience. These investors will be eager to share their knowledge because if the company succeeds, they will succeed. But, like borrowing, equity financing has its downsides. For example, investment partners may not agree on the future direction of the business. When the disagreement happens in a partnership, and the partners cannot resolve their differences, one partner may have to buy out the other to keep operating.

Venture capitalists are business organizations or groups of private individuals that invest in early stage, high-potential, growth companies. Venture capitalists usually back companies

Some entrepreneurs find creative ways to obtain equity financing. Gavin McClurg's venture, Offshore Odysseys, is a sailing expedition aboard a catamaran named *Discovery*. Investors buy timeshare segments for between $20,000 and $30,000. During the journey, they might swim across the equator or paraglide above Tahiti.

in high-technology industries such as biotechnology. In exchange for taking a risk with their own funds, these investors expect high rates of return and a share of the company. Typical terms for accepting venture capital include agreeing on how much the company is worth, how much stock both the investors and the founders will retain, control of the company's board, payment of dividends, and the period of time during which the founders are prohibited from "shopping" for further investments.[32] Venture capitalists want to invest in companies that have a combination of extremely rare qualities: the use of innovative technology, a potential for rapid growth, a well-developed business model, and an impressive management team.

Angel investors are wealthy individuals who invest money directly in new ventures in exchange for an equity share. These investors are a larger source of investment capital for startup firms. In contrast to venture capitalists, angels focus mostly on new ventures. Many angel investors are successful entrepreneurs who want to help would-be business owners get through the familiar difficulties of launching their businesses. Angel investors fund a wide variety of new ventures. Most entrepreneurs have trouble finding wealthy private investors. Angel networks have formed to match business angels with startups in need of capital.

You can learn about entrepreneurship and angel investors by watching CBC's television program *Dragons' Den*.

angel investors wealthy individuals who invest directly in a new venture in exchange for an equity stake.

Government Support for New Ventures

All levels of government support new ventures in many ways, as discussed in Chapter 5. Various local agencies and business incubators offer information, resources, and sometimes even access to financing for entrepreneurs.

Another way to encourage entrepreneurship is through *enterprise zones*, specific geographic areas set aside for economic renewal. Enterprise zones encourage investment, often in troubled areas, by offering tax advantages and incentives to businesses locating within the zone.

Long Plain First Nation's second urban reserve is located in Winnipeg at 480 Madison Street. An *urban reserve* is an economic zone within a municipality. It is an area that the federal government has set aside as First Nation reserve land. This economic zone allows for Aboriginal commercial ventures that enjoy tax exemptions offered to traditional reserves. Yellowquill College moved into a converted two-storey, 25,000-square-foot former Manitoba Hydro office building on the Long Plain urban reserve. Plans for the urban reserve include a gas station, a convenience store, and a five-storey, 80,000-square-foot office tower. Also in the plans is a depot for First Nations buyers to take delivery of tax-free goods purchased in the city.

Many First Nations are located in rural and remote areas. These areas are usually some distance from cities and towns where jobs and wealth are created. The distance creates challenges for First Nations who are trying to be economically self-sufficient. The federal government reports that Canada had 120 urban reserves as of 2008. The Winnipeg urban reserve is Long Plain's second urban reserve. Long Plain has operated an urban reserve in Portage la Prairie since the 1980s.[33]

✓ **ASSESSMENT CHECK**

6.5.1 What are the two most important considerations when choosing an idea for a new business?

6.5.2 What is the difference between debt financing and equity financing?

6.5.3 What is seed capital?

INTRAPRENEURSHIP

LO 6.6 Explain intrapreneurship.

Established companies try to keep the entrepreneurial spirit alive by encouraging **intrapreneurship**, the process of promoting innovation within their organization. In today's business world, things can change very quickly. Established firms need to innovate continually to hold onto their competitive advantages.

Many companies encourage intrapreneurship. In fact, 30 percent of large firms now set aside funds to support intrapreneurship.[34] Perhaps no business has benefited more from intrapreneurship than 3M. To foster creativity, 3M encourages engineers to "bootleg," or borrow, up to 15 percent of their time from other assignments to explore new product ideas of their choosing. Bootlegging has led to some of 3M's most successful products, including Scotch tape and Post-it notes.[35]

intrapreneurship the process of promoting innovation within the structure of an existing organization.

ASSESSMENT CHECK

6.6.1 Why do large companies support intrapreneurship?

6.6.2 What is a skunkworks?

Established companies such as 3M support intrapreneurial activity in varied ways. In addition to allowing bootlegging time for traditional product development, 3M implements two intrapreneurial approaches: skunkworks and pacing programs. A *skunkworks* project is initiated by an employee who has an idea and then recruits resources from within 3M to turn it into a commercial product. *Pacing programs* are company-initiated projects. They focus on a few products and technologies that 3M sees as having potential for success. The company provides financing, equipment, and people to support such pacing projects.[36]

WHAT'S AHEAD

In upcoming chapters, we look at other trends that are shaping the business world of the twenty-first century. In the next part of *Contemporary Business*, we explore the critical issues of how companies organize, lead, and manage their work processes; manage and motivate their employees; empower their employees through teamwork and enhanced communication; handle labour and workplace disputes; and create and produce world-class goods and services.

RETURN TO INSIDE BUSINESS

Sharing Economy Sparks Start-Ups

Entrepreneurial success is like a recipe for success. Given the right ingredients and business conditions, the entrepreneur is more likely to succeed. Those ingredients include the character of the entrepreneur, the uniqueness of the product, and the price customers are willing to pay. Many small businesses are successful at filling a unique need, or a spot in an industry, similar to the way FlightCar, Uber, and Airbnb have in the "share economy."

QUESTIONS FOR CRITICAL THINKING

1. Develop a "shared economy" business idea that follows the patterns established by FlightCar, Uber, and Airbnb.
2. How would your idea be better than the existing competition?

SUMMARY OF LEARNING OBJECTIVES

LO 6.1 Describe what is an entrepreneur and the different types of entrepreneurs.

Unlike many small-business owners, entrepreneurs typically own and run their businesses with the goal of building significant firms that create wealth and add jobs. Entrepreneurs are visionaries. They see opportunities and take the initiative to gather the resources they need to start their businesses quickly. Both managers and entrepreneurs use the resources of their companies to achieve the goals of their organizations.

A classic entrepreneur sees a business opportunity and sets aside resources to gain access to that market. A serial entrepreneur starts one business, runs it, and then starts and runs more businesses, one after another. A social entrepreneur uses business principles to solve social problems.

ASSESSMENT CHECK ANSWERS

6.1.1 What tools do entrepreneurs use to create a new business? Entrepreneurs combine their ideas and drive with money, employees, and other resources to create a business that meets a need.

6.1.2 How do entrepreneurs differ from managers? Managers direct others to reach an organization's goals. Entrepreneurs have the drive and impatience that make their companies successful. These qualities may hurt their ability to manage.

6.1.3 What do classic entrepreneurs and social entrepreneurs have in common? They both see opportunities and then set aside resources to develop new solutions.

6.1.4 Is a social entrepreneur simply a philanthropist who gives to good causes to help others? A philanthropist usually supports human welfare through charitable donations. A social entrepreneur develops new ways to advance social causes and thus enhance social welfare.

LO 6.2 Explain why people choose to become entrepreneurs.

People choose to become entrepreneurs for many reasons. Four of the common reasons are a desire to be one's own boss, a desire to achieve financial success, a desire for job security, and a desire to improve one's quality of life.

✓ ASSESSMENT CHECK ANSWERS

6.2.1 What are the four main reasons people choose to become entrepreneurs? People usually choose to become entrepreneurs because they want to be their own boss, they believe they will achieve greater financial success, they believe they have more control over job security, and they want to enhance their quality of life.

6.2.2 What factors affect the entrepreneur's job security? An entrepreneur's job security depends on the decisions of customers and investors. It also depends on the cooperation and commitment of the entrepreneur's own employees.

LO 6.3 Discuss factors that support and expand opportunities for entrepreneurs.

Several factors provide support and opportunities for entrepreneurs: a favourable public perception, availability of financing, the falling cost and widespread availability of information technology, globalization, entrepreneurship education, and changing demographic and economic trends.

✓ ASSESSMENT CHECK ANSWERS

6.3.1 To what extent is entrepreneurship possible in different countries, and what opportunities does globalization create for today's entrepreneurs? More than 9 percent of adults worldwide are starting or managing a new business. Globalization makes it possible for entrepreneurs to market their products abroad and to hire international talent. Many of the fastest-growing small Canadian companies have international sales, especially to the United States.

6.3.2 Identify the educational factors that help expand current opportunities for entrepreneurs. Many universities offer majors in entrepreneurship, dozens of others offer an entrepreneurship emphasis, and hundreds more offer courses in how to start a business. Some organizations encourage and teach entrepreneurship, such as the Kauffman Center for Entrepreneurial Leadership, Entreprep, and Students in Free Enterprise.

6.3.3 Describe current demographic trends that suggest new goods and services for entrepreneurial businesses. The aging of the North American population and the growth of two-income families are creating opportunities for entrepreneurs to market new goods and services.

LO 6.4 Identify the traits of successful entrepreneurs.

Successful entrepreneurs share several typical traits, including vision, high energy levels, the need to achieve, self-confidence and optimism, tolerance for failure, creativity, tolerance for ambiguity, and an internal locus of control.

✓ ASSESSMENT CHECK ANSWERS

6.4.1 What do we mean when we talk about an entrepreneur's vision? Entrepreneurs begin with a vision, which is an overall idea for how to make their business idea a success. They then follow this vision with energy and excitement.

6.4.2 Why is it important for an entrepreneur to have a high energy level and a strong need for achievement? Start-up companies usually have a small staff and have a difficult time raising enough capital. The entrepreneur needs to make up the difference by working long hours. A strong need for achievement helps entrepreneurs to enjoy the challenge of reaching difficult goals. It also promotes dedication to personal success.

6.4.3 How do entrepreneurs generally feel about the possibility of failure? They view failure as a learning experience and are not easily discouraged or disappointed when things don't go as planned.

LO 6.5 Summarize the process of starting a new venture.

Entrepreneurs must choose an idea for their business, develop a business plan, obtain financing, and organize the resources they need to operate their startups.

✓ ASSESSMENT CHECK ANSWERS

6.5.1 What are the two most important considerations when choosing an idea for a new business? The two most important considerations are finding something you love to do and are good at doing, and finding an idea that meets a need in the marketplace.

6.5.2 What is the difference between debt financing and equity financing? Debt financing is money borrowed that must be repaid. Equity financing is an exchange of ownership shares in a company for money supplied by one or more investors.

6.5.3 What is seed capital? Seed capital is the money that is used to start a company.

LO 6.6 Explain intrapreneurship.

Organizations encourage intrapreneurial activity within the company in a variety of ways, including through hiring practices, dedicated programs such as skunkworks, providing access to resources, and giving employees freedom to innovate within established firms.

✓ **ASSESSMENT CHECK ANSWERS**

6.6.1 Why do large companies support intrapreneurship? Large firms support intrapreneurship to keep an entrepreneurial spirit alive and to promote innovation and change.

6.6.2 What is a skunkworks? A skunkworks project is initiated by an employee who has an idea and then recruits resources from within the company to turn the idea into a commercial product.

BUSINESS TERMS YOU NEED TO KNOW

angel investors 169
classic entrepreneur 155
debt financing 168
entrepreneur 154
equity financing 168
intrapreneurship 169
lifestyle entrepreneur 158
seed capital 168
serial entrepreneur 155
social entrepreneur 156
venture capitalists 168

REVIEW QUESTIONS

1. Identify the three categories of entrepreneurs. How are they different from each other? How might an entrepreneur belong to more than one category?

2. People often become entrepreneurs because they want to be their own boss, and they want to be in control of most or all of the major decisions related to their business. How might these desires relate to potential financial success? Are there any downsides? If so, what are they?

3. How have globalization and information technology created new opportunities for entrepreneurs? Describe current demographic trends that suggest new goods and services for entrepreneurial businesses.

4. Identify the eight characteristics that are attributed to successful entrepreneurs. Which trait or traits do you believe are the most important for success? Why? Are there any traits that might contribute to potential failure? If so, which traits? Why might they contribute to failure?

5. When selecting a business idea, why is it important to follow the advice to "do what makes you happy" and "be true to yourself"?

6. Suppose an entrepreneur is considering buying an existing business or franchise. Which of the eight entrepreneurial traits would most likely apply to this person, and why?

7. Imagine that you and a partner are planning to launch a business that sells backpacks, briefcases, and soft luggage made from recycled materials. You'll need seed capital for your venture. Outline how you would use that seed capital.

8. Describe the two main types of financing that entrepreneurs may seek for their businesses. What are the risks and benefits of each?

9. What is an enterprise zone? Describe what types of businesses might benefit from opening in an enterprise zone. How might their success be interconnected?

10. What is intrapreneurship? How does it differ from entrepreneurship?

PROJECTS AND TEAMWORK APPLICATIONS

1. Interview an entrepreneur. You can do the interview in person, by email, or by phone. The person can be a local shop or restaurant owner, a hair salon owner, a pet groomer, a consultant—any field is fine. Find out why that person decided to become an entrepreneur. Ask whether his or her viewpoint has changed since starting the business. Decide whether the person is a classic, serial, or social entrepreneur. Present your findings to the class.

2. Certain demographic trends can represent opportunities for entrepreneurs—the aging of the North American population,

the increasing diversity of the population, the growth in population of some areas, and the large number of two-income families, to name a few. On your own or with a classmate, choose a demographic trend and brainstorm for business ideas that can profit from the trend. Create a poster or a PowerPoint presentation to present your idea—and its relationship to the trend—to your class.

3. Review the eight characteristics of successful entrepreneurs. Which characteristics do you have? Do you think you would be a good entrepreneur? Why or why not? Create an outline of the traits you believe are your strengths—and the traits that might be your weaknesses.

4. Many entrepreneurs turn a hobby or an area of interest into a business idea. Others get their ideas from situations or daily problems when they believe they have a solution—or a better solution than those already tried. Think about an area of personal interest or a problem you think you can solve with a new good or service. Create the first part of a potential business plan, which is the introduction to your new company and its offerings. Outline briefly what kind of financing you think would work best for your business, and what steps you would take to obtain the funds.

5. Enterprise zones are designed to revitalize economically distressed areas. Choose an area you are familiar with. It may be as close as a local neighbourhood, or as far away as a city where you might like to live. Do some online research about the area. Outline your own plan for an enterprise zone. Include businesses that you think would do well in the area, jobs that might be created, housing creation, and other factors.

WEB ASSIGNMENTS

1. **Tools for entrepreneurs.** American Express has established what it calls "Open Forum" to allow entrepreneurs and small-business owners to communicate with one another and share ideas. Visit the Open Forum website and review the material. Prepare a short report on how Open Forum can help an entrepreneur to start and grow a business.

    www.openforum.com

2. **Venture capitalists.** Venture capital firms are an important source of financing for entrepreneurs. Most actively look for funding proposals. Go to the website shown below to learn more about venture capital. What are some of the famous businesses that were originally financed by venture capitalists?

    www.nvca.org

3. **Getting started.** Visit the website of *Entrepreneur* magazine. Explore the information on how to research a business idea. What are the steps involved in getting a product to market?

    www.entrepreneur.com

Note: Internet Web addresses change frequently. If you don't find the exact sites listed, you may need to access the organization's home page and search from there or use a search engine such as Bing or Google.

PART 2: CASE STUDY Beau's All Natural Brewing Company
Getting Started: Choosing a Location, Building the Plant, and Hiring Employees

In 2006, two years after their initial discussions and a year after seriously starting to put things together, Steve and Tim Beauchesne were ready to begin brewing operations for the key summer sales season. Their business plan initially included a bank loan from the Business Development Bank of Canada along with $150,000 from an investor who would not be involved in operations. When the investor backed out, the Beauchesnes scrambled to pool $100,000 of funds from friends and family along with funds from the mortgaged leather plant to total around $300,000. This was perhaps half the funds needed that would have made starting up easier to handle. But the desire to succeed in their business meant that the decision to move ahead and get busy building the business was carried forward. Beer recipes were tried and tested, and relationships with local restaurants and bars were established. Provincial government approval was granted to sell their beer in the highly regulated industry. Beau's was allowed to sell through the LCBO (Liquor Control Board of Ontario) retail system as well as in bars and restaurants throughout Ontario. The only thing holding things up now was acquiring the equipment for production on a larger scale.

By the spring of 2006, Tim's leather finishing plant was prepared and ready to receive machinery and equipment for its new life as a brewery. Months of searching for equipment was finally rewarded when a full brew system complete with a brew house, fermenters, and brite tanks were sourced from a location in New Hampshire. The brand name of the system was CENTURY, a manufacturer that the Beauchesne's later discovered was no longer in business and perhaps explained the reason they had gotten such a good deal. The whole system was in pristine condition and had the desired 15-barrels capacity the Beauchesne's wanted. There were six fermenting and brite tanks that Steve and Tim felt would do the job of getting Beau's off the ground. They hired truckers specially equipped to move the 10-feet-tall tanks in an upright position to their new home in Vankleek Hill.

Steve and Tim recognized the limitations of their knowledge and skills. Making a small batch of beer in their kitchen was one thing; knowing how to operate large-scale machinery that would produce hundreds of litres was something else. Beau's lucked out when one of the most talented brew masters in the country, Matthew O'Hara, joined them. Matthew gained his knowledge of brewing by working his way up the ranks of well-respected breweries, including Upper Canada Brewing (now owned by Sleeman Breweries), Dennison's Brewing in Toronto, and Montreal's McAuslan Brewing. He developed the unique recipe for Beau's flagship beer, a lagered ale called Lug-Tread. Along with family members and a handful of employees, the Beauchesne's were ready.

To Steve, the local market in the Ottawa region seemed particularly receptive to a new craft beer. He was confident he could succeed in serving the younger beer drinkers he sensed he understood well. Ottawa had a young demographic with two large universities and colleges throughout the trading region. Besides being home, Vankleek Hill, located about 45 minutes south-east of Ottawa, was a good location that would allow for short delivery runs to pubs and restaurants and other venues where their brew would be sold. The Beauchesnes received encouragement from local businesses, government officials, and the Ontario Craft Brewers Association. Vankleek Hill's population of 2,000 appreciated the jobs created and the entrepreneurial risk that was being taken. This all fit with the philosophy guiding the Beauchesnes' business thinking, which focused on building relationships with customers and giving back to their community.

Questions for Critical Thinking

1. Evaluate each of the primary risks discussed in Chapter 5 that Beau's faced as a new business.

2. Why was Vankleek Hill a good location choice?

3. How do Steve and Tim Beauchesne fit the textbook description of entrepreneurs?

2 LAUNCHING YOUR...

ENTREPRENEURIAL CAREER

In Part 2, "Starting and Growing Your Business," you learned the many ways that business owners have achieved their dreams of owning their own company and being their own boss. The two chapters in Part 2 introduced the wide variety of entrepreneurial or small businesses; the forms these businesses can take (sole proprietorship, partnership, or corporation); and the reasons that some new ventures succeed and others fail. You learned that entrepreneurs are visionaries who build firms that create wealth. They share qualities such as vision and creativity, high energy, optimism, a strong need to achieve, and a tolerance for failure. You might wonder how you can use this information. Here are some career ideas and opportunities in the small-business and ebusiness areas.

First, think about the field that attracts you as a future business owner. Try to gain experience in the industry by first working for someone else. The information and skills you learn will be valuable when you start out on your own. Remember that lack of experience is often the leading reason for small-business failure.[1]

Next, look for a good fit between your own skills, abilities, and qualities and a market need, or niche. For example, the number of older people in the population is increasing, and more and more young families find themselves running short on time. As a result, the need for childcare and eldercare services will increase—and so will the opportunities for new businesses in those areas. Watch these trends to find ideas that you can use or adapt.

Do you like the idea of being your own boss but worry about risking your savings to start a new and untried business? Then you might want to think about owning a franchise, such as Quiznos or Tim Hortons. Franchising can be less risky than starting a new business from scratch, but it still means hard work. You need to understand the franchise resources you can access and the franchise responsibilities you will take on. Filling a market need is important for success. To find more information about franchising, access the Business Development Bank of Canada's review of franchising at www.bdc.ca/EN/articles-tools/start-buy-business/buy-business/Pages/making-right-choice.aspx.

Are you skilled in a certain area of business, technology, or science? Consulting firms offer their expertise to clients in private, government, not-for-profit, and foreign business operations. Business consultants influence clients' decisions in marketing, finance, manufacturing, information systems, ebusiness, human resources, and many other areas, including corporate strategy and organization. Technology consultants support businesses in all fields. They might set up a secure website, train employees in the use of new software, manage an off-site help desk, or plan for disaster recovery. Science consulting firms find work in the field of environmental consulting. They help businesses to deal with pollution cleanup and control, habitat protection, and help them to meet government environmental regulations and standards.

But maybe you prefer to tinker with gears and machinery or with computer graphics and code. If you think you have the ideas and creativity to invent something completely new, you need to learn about patents, trademarks, and copyright laws to protect your ideas.[2] Patents, trademarks, and copyright each offer different protections for your work, but none will guarantee success. Again, hard work, persistence, and a little bit of luck will help you succeed.

CAREER ASSESSMENT EXERCISES IN ENTREPRENEURSHIP AND BUSINESS OWNERSHIP

1. Find out whether you have what it takes to be an entrepreneur. Review the material on the Business Development Bank of Canada's website: www.bdc.ca/EN/articles-tools/entrepreneur-toolkit/business-assessments/Pages/self-assessment-test-your-entrepreneurial-potential.aspx

   Answer the questions there. After you've finished, use the scoring guides to see how ready you are to start your own business. What weak areas did your results show? What can you do to strengthen those areas?

2. Find an independent business or franchise in your area. Make an appointment to talk to the owner about his or her startup experience. Prepare a list of questions for a 10- to 15-minute interview. Remember to ask about details, such as the number of hours worked per week, the approximate startup costs, the goals of the business, the available resources, the lessons learned since opening, and the rewards of owning the business. How do the owner's answers differ from what you expected?

3. Search online for information about how to file for a patent, trademark, or copyright. A good starting point is the BDC's website: www.bdc.ca/EN/articles-tools/business-strategy-planning/innovate/Pages/patents-trademarks-copyright-an-overview.aspx

    Assume you have an invention you want to protect. Find out what forms are required; what fees are needed; how much time is usually needed to complete the legal steps; and the rights and protections you will gain from the patent, trademark, or copyright.

Chapter 5
E-Business and E-Commerce

[LEARNING OBJECTIVES]	[CHAPTER OUTLINE]	[WEB RESOURCES]
1. Describe the six common types of electronic commerce; provide specific personal examples of how you have used or could use B2C, C2C, G2C, and mobile commerce; and offer a specific example of B2B and G2B.	5.1 Overview of E-Business and E-Commerce	**Student Companion Site**
2. Discuss the five online services of business-to-consumer electronic commerce, provide a specific example of each service, and state how you have used or would use each service.	5.2 Business-to-Consumer (B2C) Electronic Commerce	wiley.com/go/rainercanada
3. Describe the three business models for business-to-business electronic commerce, and provide a specific example of each model.	5.3 Business-to-Business (B2B) Electronic Commerce	• Student PowerPoints for note taking
4. Describe the four types of electronic payments and provide a specific example of each one.	5.4 Electronic Payments	• Interactive Case: Ruby's Club Assignments
5. Illustrate the ethical and legal issues relating to electronic commerce with two specific examples of each issue.	5.5 Ethical and Legal Issues in E-Business	• Complete glossary

WileyPLUS

All of the above and **WileyPLUS**

- E-book
- Mini-lecture by author for each chapter section
- Practice quizzes
- Flash Cards for vocabulary review
- Additional "What's in IT for Me?" cases
- Video interviews with managers
- Lab Manuals for Microsoft Office 2010 and 2013
- How-to Animations for Microsoft Office 2010 and 2013

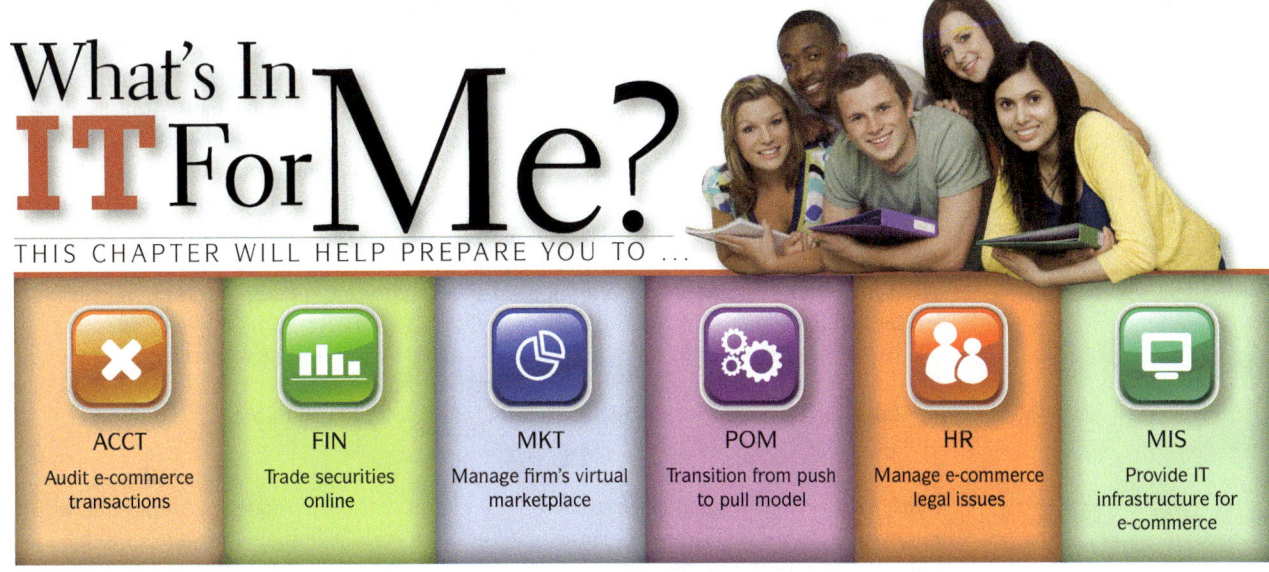

What's In IT For Me?

THIS CHAPTER WILL HELP PREPARE YOU TO ...

ACCT	FIN	MKT	POM	HR	MIS
Audit e-commerce transactions	Trade securities online	Manage firm's virtual marketplace	Transition from push to pull model	Manage e-commerce legal issues	Provide IT infrastructure for e-commerce

[Case 5.1 From Social Networks to Social Commerce]

The Problem

We're all familiar with national advertising campaigns for big brands that spend millions on 30-second television commercials, as an example. But did you know that local advertising is also big business? In Canada alone, for example, advertisers spend about $13 billion every year to try to reach local customers. Much of that money is wasted, because local commerce is highly segmented and inefficient. A small company cannot acquire customers or advertise with the efficiency of a large chain that has multiple locations in the same town. The problem, therefore, is how to make local advertising more efficient and effective for small businesses.

VLADGRIN/Shutterstock

The Solution

The solution may lie in the emerging area of social commerce, as illustrated by Groupon (*www.groupon.com*). Every day, Groupon e-mails its subscribers—more than 200 million globally and growing—discounts on goods and services, but only if a minimum of people sign up for the deals. The discount could be up to 90 percent off on a hotel room, a restaurant meal, a cooking class, dental work, or just about any product or service available in dozens of cities in 48 countries where Groupon operates. Groupon's social commerce model pays off in three ways: (1) The subscriber gets a better price; (2) the merchant gets additional business and potential new customers; and (3) Groupon receives a share of the revenues generated by the deals.

When Groupon started it merely connected local merchants with local customers, advertising one deal per day because it did not have any merchant relationships. As you can imagine, such e-mail blasts were not targeted. As Groupon became more popular, however, merchants were approaching the company to form relationships and offer deals. Demand became so great that merchants were waiting months for their deal to be featured. To solve this problem, Groupon created Groupon Stores and the Deal Feed.

Instead of waiting for Groupon to organize and publicize a deal, Groupon Stores lets businesses create and launch their own deals whenever they want, without waiting to be featured as the deal of the day. Merchants create Groupon stores without any upfront fee. Groupon then promotes their deals via e-mail, Twitter, and Facebook, while the merchants collect 70 percent of the revenue from each promoted Groupon deal. As part of the promotion, Groupon members can sign up for the Deal Feed, which acts similar to a Twitter feed. Merchants can use the Deal Feed to inform their followers about new deals or special offers. Using software it developed, Groupon selects the best deals from Groupon Stores each day and matches them with customers.

Groupon then refined its business model even further, moving into a phase it calls *hyperlocal*. This involves knowing where subscribers live and what their interests are, becoming familiar with their shopping and leisure experiences, and sharing these experiences with their friends. Groupon then tailors its e-mail blasts to subscribers' cell phones based on what they might like. It also can integrate and popularize deals through social networking sites such as Twitter and Facebook.

The next phase of its business model is *Groupon Now*, offering subscribers two choices: "I'm hungry" and "I'm bored." When you click the "I'm hungry" button, Groupon displays a list of deals from nearby restaurants. Similarly, when you click "I'm bored," Groupon displays a list of nearby events and deals.

Groupon Now works by reducing inefficiencies in the market: by selling off food, labour hours, or anything else that is "perishable," merchants can make money on things that would otherwise go to waste. Groupon claims that Groupon Now will enable businesses to become more like airlines selling off empty seats, matching supply against demand to maximize revenues. For example, a spa could send out a deal on a massage because a customer cancelled, or a gym could run several days of coupons to fill the class of a new yoga instructor.

The Results

Groupon's business model has been wildly successful. The company has about 10,000 employees and sends out more than 900 deals each day in over 550 markets. The company, which launched in 2008, gained 1 million subscribers within a year and went from zero to $500 million in sales within 18 months. In 2014, Groupon's global sales rose to just over US$3 billion.

While it was a pioneer in the field, today Groupon faces competition from more than 500 companies around the world offering similar services. And that burgeoning market has attracted the interest of Internet giants that want a foothold in social commerce, including Google and LivingSocial, Groupon's biggest rival.

In addition to competition, Groupon has other problems. Running a discounted deal can attract so many customers that the deal can actually cost small businesses money. In a survey of 150 small to mid-size businesses that had used Groupon, two thirds said that their Groupon deal was profitable, while the other third found it unprofitable. And in a blow to a service that should rely on repeat business, 40 percent of the respondents stated that they would not use Groupon again, mostly because they did not know what to expect from each Groupon deal; they could be overwhelmed with customers, or not have any customers at all.

What We Learned from This Case

A profound change in the modern world of business is the emergence of electronic commerce, also known as *e-commerce*. E-commerce is transforming all business functional areas and their fundamental tasks, from advertising to paying bills. Its impact is so widespread that it is affecting almost every organization. This means that, regardless of where you work, your organization likely is practising electronic commerce.

Electronic commerce affects organizations in many significant ways. First, it increases an organization's reach, defined as the number of potential customers to whom the company can market its products. In fact, e-commerce provides unparalleled opportunities for companies to expand worldwide at a small cost, to increase market share, and to reduce costs. By using electronic commerce, many small businesses now can operate and compete in market spaces once dominated by larger companies.

Another major impact of electronic commerce has been to remove many of the barriers that previously kept entrepreneurs from starting their own businesses. E-commerce offers amazing opportunities for you to open your own business by developing an e-commerce website.

Electronic commerce also is drastically changing the nature of competition, due to the development of new online companies, new business models, and the diversity of electronic commerce-related products and services. Recall your study of competitive strategies in Chapter 2, particularly the impact of the Internet on Porter's five forces. You learned that the Internet can both endanger and enhance a company's position in a given industry.

Case 5.1 on Groupon demonstrated how the company uses social networking to build its social commerce business model. That is, Groupon realized that social networking technologies can provide a direct link between businesses and their customers.

You need to have a working knowledge of electronic commerce because your organization almost certainly will employ e-commerce applications that affect the firm's strategy and business model. This knowledge will make you more valuable to your organization and will enable you to quickly contribute to e-commerce applications in your functional area. When you read the What's in IT for Me? feature at the end of the chapter, envision yourself performing the activities discussed in your functional area.

Going further, you may decide to become an entrepreneur and start your own business. In that case, an understanding of electronic commerce is even more essential for you because e-commerce, with its broad reach, will probably be critical for your business to survive and thrive.

Social commerce is a type of electronic commerce that uses social media to assist in the online buying and selling of products and services. Social commerce taps into a community of enthusiasts, builds relationships, anticipates needs, and promotes products with special deals for the community's members. Social commerce efforts include shareable coupons, refer-a-friend programs, loyalty incentives, group promotions, and time-sensitive offers.

The biggest advantage that social commerce enjoys over traditional e-commerce, and even Google Search, is the ability to predict buying habits based on real-time information as opposed to historical data. Google Search cannot anticipate any one person's needs very well; in contrast, that person's friends would know, for example, that she is going to be a grandmother and probably will be shopping for baby products. Social commerce focuses squarely on one-to-one relationships. Still another advantage of social commerce is that it analyzes relationships and interactions within a social community, enabling companies to bring exciting new products to the market more effectively.

In this chapter you will discover the major applications of e-business, and you will be able to identify the services necessary for its support. You then will study the major types of electronic commerce: business-to-consumer (B2C), business-to-business (B2B), consumer-to-consumer (C2C), business-to-employee (B2E), and government-to-citizen (G2C). You conclude by examining several legal and ethical issues that have arisen as a result of the rapid growth of e-commerce.

5.1 Overview of E-Business and E-Commerce

Any entrepreneur or company that decides to practise electronic commerce must develop a strategy to do so effectively. The first step is to determine exactly *why* you want to do business over the Internet using a website. There are several reasons for employing websites:

- To sell goods and services
- To induce people to visit a physical location
- To reduce operational and transaction costs
- To enhance your reputation

A website can accomplish any and all of these goals. Unless a company (or you) has substantial resources, however, it is difficult to accomplish all of them at the same time. The appropriate website for achieving each goal will be somewhat different. When setting up your website, you must consider how the site will generate and retain traffic, as well as a host of other issues. The point here is that, when you are considering electronic commerce, keeping the strategy of the organization or entrepreneur in mind will give you a good idea as to the type of website to use.

This section examines the basics of e-business and e-commerce. First, these two concepts are defined, and then you become familiar with pure and partial electronic commerce. You then take a look at the various types of electronic commerce. Next, you focus on e-commerce mechanisms, which are the ways in which businesses and people buy and sell over the Internet. The section concludes by considering the benefits and limitations of e-commerce.

Definitions and Concepts

Electronic commerce (**EC** or **e-commerce**) describes the process of buying, selling, transferring, or exchanging products, services, or information via computer networks, including the Internet. **E-business** is a somewhat broader concept. In addition to the buying and selling of goods and services, e-business also refers to servicing customers, collaborating with business partners, and performing electronic transactions within an organization.

Sources: Compiled from B. Stone and D. MacMillan, "Are Four Words Worth $25 Billion for Groupon?" *Bloomberg BusinessWeek*, March 17, 2011; B. Saporito, "The Groupon Clipper," *Time*, February 21, 2011; L. Indvik, "Groupon Goes from Local to Hyperlocal with New Ad Campaign," *Forbes*, January 25, 2011; J. O'Dell, "The History of Groupon," *Forbes*, January 7, 2011; E. Anderson, "Groupon Getting It Right," *Forbes*, January 7, 2011; S. Purewal, "Groupon Nightmares (and How to Avoid Them)," *Entrepreneur*, December 10, 2010; S. Gaudin, "Google Expected to Buy or Eclipse Groupon," *Computerworld*, December 6, 2010; K. Burnham, "Groupon 2.0: More Deals and a Personalized Feed," *CIO*, December 1, 2010; J. Galante, "Groupon Coupons: The Small-Biz Challenge," *Bloomberg BusinessWeek*, June 10, 2010; www.groupon.com, www.livingsocial.com, accessed February 21, 2015; I. Lunden, "Groupon Q4 Beats Street On Sales Of $925.4M, EPS Of $0.06, But Posts Weaker Outlook For Q1," www.techcrunch.com, accessed February 12, 2015; "Global revenue of Groupon from 2008 to 2014 (in million U.S. dollars)," www.statista.com, accessed February 24, 2015; "Statistics and Facts about the Advertising Industry in Canada," www.statista.com, accessed February 24, 2015.

Electronic commerce can take several forms depending on the degree of digitization involved. The *degree of digitization* is the extent to which the commerce has been transformed from physical to digital. This concept can relate to both the product or service being sold and the delivery agent or intermediary. In other words, the product can be either physical or digital, and the delivery agent can be either physical or digital.

In traditional commerce, both dimensions are physical. Purely physical organizations are referred to as **brick-and-mortar organizations**. (You may also see the term "bricks-and-mortar.") In contrast, in *pure EC* all dimensions are digital. Companies engaged only in EC are considered **virtual** (or *pure-play*) **organizations**. All other combinations that include a mix of digital and physical dimensions are considered *partial* EC (but not pure EC). **Clicks-and-mortar organizations** are those that conduct some e-commerce activities, yet carry out their primary business in the physical world. (A common alternative to the term "clicks-and-mortar" is "clicks-and-bricks." You will encounter both terms.) Therefore, clicks-and-mortar organizations are examples of partial EC. E-commerce now is so well established that people generally expect all companies to offer this service in some form.

Purchasing a shirt at Walmart.ca or a book from Amazon.ca is partial EC because the merchandise, although bought and paid for digitally, is physically delivered by courier. In contrast, buying an e-book from Amazon.ca or a software product from Buy.com is pure EC because the product itself as well as its delivery, payment, and transfer are digital. To avoid confusion, we use the term "electronic commerce" to denote both pure and partial EC.

Types of E-Commerce

E-commerce can be conducted between and among various parties. In this section, you will identify the six common types of e-commerce, and you will learn about three of them—C2C, B2E, and e-government—in detail. You then consider B2C and B2B in separate sections because they are very complex.

- **Business-to-consumer (B2C):** In B2C, the sellers are organizations, and the buyers are individuals. You learn about B2C electronic commerce in Section 5.2.
- **Business-to-business (B2B):** In B2B transactions, both the sellers and the buyers are business organizations. The vast majority of EC volume is of this type. You see B2B electronic commerce in Section 5.3.
- **Consumer-to-consumer (C2C):** In C2C (also called "customer-to-customer"), an individual sells products or services to other individuals. The major strategies for conducting C2C on the Internet are auctions and classified ads.

In dozens of countries, C2C e-commerce on auction sites is exploding. Most auctions are conducted by intermediaries like eBay (*www.ebay.ca*). Consumers can select general sites such as *www.auctionanything.com*, a company that sells software and services that help individuals and organizations conduct their own auctions. In addition, many individuals are conducting their own auctions. You will learn about reverse auctions, in which buyers solicit bids from sellers, later in this section.

The major categories of online classified ads are similar to those found in print ads: vehicles, real estate, employment, pets, tickets, and travel. Classified ads are available through most Internet service providers (such Rogers, Bell, and SaskTel), at some portals (such as Yahoo!), and from Internet directories and online newspapers. Many of these sites contain search engines that help shoppers narrow their searches. Craigslist (*www.craigslist.org*) is the largest online classified ad provider.

Internet-based classified ads have one big advantage over traditional types of classified ads: They provide access to an international, rather than a local, audience. This wider audience greatly increases both the supply of goods and services and the number of potential buyers. It is important to note that the value of expanded geographic reach depends greatly on what is being bought or sold. For example, you might buy software from a company located 1,000 kilometres away from you, but you would not buy firewood from someone at such a distance.

- **Business-to-employee (B2E):** In B2E, an organization uses EC internally to provide information and services to its employees. For example, companies allow employees to manage their benefits and to take training classes electronically. In addition, employees can buy discounted insurance, travel packages, and tickets to events on the corporate intranet. They also can order supplies and materials electronically. Finally, many companies have electronic corporate stores that sell the company's products to its employees, usually at a discount.

- **E-government:** E-government is the use of Internet technology in general and e-commerce in particular to deliver information and public services to citizens (called *government-to-citizen* or *G2C EC*) and to business partners and suppliers (called *government-to-business* or *G2B EC*). G2B EC is much like B2B EC, usually with an overlay of government procurement regulations. That is, G2B EC and B2B EC are similar conceptually. However, the functions of G2C EC are different from anything that exists in the private sector (e.g., B2C EC).

    E-government is also an efficient way of conducting business transactions with citizens and businesses and within the governments themselves. E-government makes government more efficient and effective, especially in the delivery of public services. An example of G2C electronic commerce is electronic benefits transfer, in which governments transfer benefits, such as employment insurance and Canada Pension Plan payments, directly to recipients' bank accounts.

- **Mobile commerce (m-commerce):** The term *m-commerce* refers to e-commerce that is conducted entirely in a wireless environment. An example is using cell phones to shop over the Internet. You will learn about m-commerce in Chapter 6.

Each of the above types of EC is executed in one or more business models. A **business model** is the method by which a company generates revenue to sustain itself. Table 5.1 summarizes the major EC business models. Other classifications of EC business models include Michael Rappa's Business Models on the Web (*http://digitalenterprise.org/models*).

E-Commerce and Search

The development of e-commerce has proceeded in phases. Initial e-commerce efforts consisted of flashy brochure sites with rudimentary shopping carts and checkout systems. They were then replaced with systems that tried to anticipate customer needs and accelerate checkout.

However, one of the biggest changes in recent times has been the growing importance of search in the overall e-commerce experience. For example, Google justifies the importance of online searches because a higher number of purchases follow successful web searches compared to nonproductive searches where online shoppers tend to abandon their shopping carts. In other words, if you are able to quickly find that product you are looking for and the information you need to make a decision, then you are more likely to buy it in that online session. If, on the other hand, you are not able to find the product and/or the information you need to make an informed decision about your purchase, you are more likely to abandon your shopping cart even though you might have initially decided to buy it.

Google is confident that in the future, retailers will post tremendous amounts of additional details. Merchants will pour continuous structured feeds of data—including product listings, daily inventory, and hours of operation—into public search engines such as Google. Google currently is using Google Base, the company's online database, to work on this process. This process would allow customers to access much more specific and relevant search results.

Major E-Commerce Mechanisms

There are many mechanisms through which businesses and customers can buy and sell on the Internet. The most widely used are electronic catalogues, electronic auctions, e-storefronts, e-malls, and e-marketplaces.

Catalogues have been printed on paper for generations. Today, however, they are available on CD-ROM and the Internet. Electronic catalogues consist of a product database, directory and search capabilities, and a presentation function. They are the backbone of most e-commerce sites.

An **auction** is a competitive process in which either a seller solicits consecutive bids from buyers or a buyer solicits bids from sellers. The primary characteristic of auctions is that prices are determined dynamically by competitive bidding. Electronic auctions (e-auctions)

TABLE 5.1

E-Commerce Business Models

EC Model	Description
Online direct marketing	Manufacturers or retailers sell directly to customers. Very efficient for digital marketing of products and services. Can allow for product or service customization (*www.dell.ca*).
Electronic tendering system	Businesses request quotes from suppliers. Uses B2B with a reverse auction mechanism.
Name-your-own-price	Customers decide how much they are willing to pay. An intermediary (for example, *www.priceline.com*) tries to match a provider.
Find-the-best-price	Customers specify a need; an intermediary (for example, *www.hotwire.com*) compares providers and shows the lowest price. Customers must accept the offer in a short time or they may lose the deal.
Affiliate marketing	Vendors ask partners to place logos (or banners) on partners' sites. If customers click on the logo, go to the vendor's site, and buy, then the vendor pays commissions to partners.
Viral marketing	Receivers send information about your product to their friends.
Group purchasing (co-ops)	Small buyers aggregate demand to get a large volume. The group then conducts tendering or negotiates a low price.
Online auctions	Companies run auctions of various types on the Internet. Very popular in C2C, but gaining ground in other types of EC (*www.ebay.ca*).
Product customization	Customers use the Internet to self-configure products or services. Sellers then price them and fulfill them quickly (*build-to-order*) (*www.jaguar.com*).
Electronic marketplaces and exchanges	Transactions are conducted efficiently (more information to buyers and sellers, lower transaction costs) in electronic marketplaces (private or public).
Bartering online	Intermediary administers online exchange of surplus products and/or company receives "points" for its contribution, which can be used to purchase other needed items (*www.bbu.com*).
Deep discounters	Companies (for example, *www.half.ebay.com*) offer deep price discounts. Appeals to customers who consider only price in their purchasing decisions.
Membership	Only members can use the services provided, including access to certain information and conducting trades (for example, *www.qtrade.ca*).

generally increase revenues for sellers by broadening the customer base and shortening the cycle time of the auction. Buyers generally benefit from e-auctions because they can bargain for lower prices. In addition, they don't have to travel to an auction at a physical location.

The Internet provides an efficient infrastructure for conducting auctions at lower administrative costs and with many more involved sellers and buyers. Individual consumers and corporations alike can participate in auctions. There are two major types of auctions: forward and reverse.

Forward auctions are auctions that sellers use as a channel to many potential buyers. Usually, sellers place items at sites for auction, and buyers bid continuously for them. The highest bidder wins the items. Both sellers and buyers can be individuals or businesses. The popular auction site eBay.com is a forward auction.

In **reverse auctions**, one buyer, usually an organization, wants to buy a product or a service. The buyer posts a request for quotation (RFQ) on its website or on a third-party site. The RFQ provides detailed information on the desired purchase. The suppliers study the RFQ and then submit bids electronically. Everything else being equal, the lowest-price bidder wins the auction. The reverse auction is the most common auction model for large purchases (in terms of either quantities or price). Governments and large corporations frequently use this approach, which may provide considerable savings for the buyer.

Auctions can be conducted from the seller's site, the buyer's site, or a third party's site. For example, eBay, the best-known third-party site, offers hundreds of thousands of different items in several types of auctions. Overall, more than 300 major companies, including Amazon.com and Dellauction.com, offer online auctions.

An *electronic storefront* is a website that represents a single store. An *electronic mall*, also known as a *cybermall* or *e-mall*, is a collection of individual shops under one Internet address. Electronic storefronts and electronic malls are closely associated with B2C electronic commerce. You will study each one in more detail in Section 5.2.

An **electronic marketplace (e-marketplace)** is a central, virtual market space on the web where many buyers and many sellers can conduct e-commerce and e-business activities. Electronic marketplaces are associated with B2B electronic commerce. You will learn about electronic marketplaces in Section 5.3.

Benefits and Limitations of E-Commerce

Few innovations in human history have provided as many benefits to organizations, individuals, and society as e-commerce has. E-commerce benefits organizations by making national and international markets more accessible and by lowering the costs of processing, distributing, and retrieving information. Customers benefit by being able to access a vast number of products and services, around the clock. The major benefit to society is the ability to easily and conveniently deliver information, services, and products to people in cities, rural areas, and developing countries.

Despite all these benefits, EC has some limitations, both technological and non-technological, that have restricted its growth and acceptance. One major technological limitation is the lack of universally accepted security standards. Also, in less-developed countries, telecommunications bandwidth often is insufficient, and accessing the web is expensive. Non-technological limitations include the perceptions that EC is insecure, has unresolved legal issues, and lacks a critical mass of sellers and buyers. As time passes, the limitations, especially the technological ones, will diminish or be overcome.

before you go on..

1. Define e-commerce, and distinguish it from e-business.
2. Differentiate among B2C, B2B, C2C, and B2E electronic commerce.
3. Define e-government.
4. Describe the key characteristics of forward and reverse auctions.
5. Identify some benefits and limitations of e-commerce.

5.2 Business-to-Consumer (B2C) Electronic Commerce

B2B EC is much larger than B2C EC by volume, but B2C EC is more complex. The reason is that B2C involves a large number of buyers making millions of diverse transactions per day with a relatively small number of sellers. As an illustration, consider Amazon, an online retailer that offers thousands of products to its customers. Each customer's purchase is relatively small, but Amazon must manage that transaction as if that customer were its most important one. Each order must be processed quickly and efficiently, and the products must be shipped to the customer in a timely manner. In addition, returns must be managed. Multiply this simple example by millions, and you get an idea of the complexity of B2C EC. Overall, B2B complexities tend to be more business related, whereas B2C complexities tend to be more technical and volume related.

This section addresses the primary issues in B2C EC. You begin by studying the two basic mechanisms that customers use to access companies on the web: electronic storefronts and electronic malls. In addition to purchasing products over the web, customers also access online services. Therefore, the next section covers several online services, such as banking, securities trading, job searching, and travel. The complexity of B2C EC creates two major challenges for sellers: channel conflict and order fulfillment. You will examine these two topics in detail. Finally, companies engaged in B2C EC must "get the word out" to prospective customers. Therefore, this section concludes with a look at online advertising.

Electronic Storefronts and Malls

For several generations, home shopping from catalogues, and later from television shopping channels, has attracted millions of customers. Today, shopping online offers an alternative to catalogue and television shopping. **Electronic retailing (e-tailing)** is the direct sale of products and services through electronic storefronts or electronic malls, usually designed around an electronic catalogue format and/or auctions.

Like any mail-order shopping experience, e-commerce enables you to buy from home 24 hours a day, 7 days a week. However, EC also offers a wider variety of products and services, including unique items, often at lower prices. Further, within seconds, shoppers can access very detailed

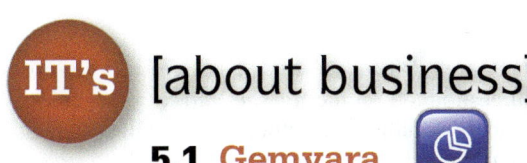

IT's [about business]

5.1 Gemvara

When Matt Lauzon was a senior at Babson College in Wellesley, Massachusetts, he created an interesting business plan. He developed a website, Gemvara (www.gemvara.com), that enables consumers to design custom, high-end jewelry without ever having to visit a jewelry store.

Lauzon signed 50 jewelers onto a network that lets clients customize items both in their stores and online. He found that customers liked customizing from home, because they had more control over the process. Lauzon's business plan concentrated on the concept of electronic commerce for what Lauzon calls "Generation Me."

Gemvara's website allows its customers to custom-design the piece of jewelry they want. Gemvara then sends the design specifications to one of its brick-and-mortar jewelry store partners. Each design is made to order by integrating the customer's vision with gemstones, precious metals, and processes.

Lauzon launched Gemvara in February 2011. Since that time, the website has experienced monthly revenue growth in the double digits, had more than 1 million page views per month, and recorded an average order price of about $1,000.

Lauzon attributes much of Gemvara's success to its superb customer service, which his company provides 24/7 via phone, e-mail, or live chat. He notes that establishing customers' trust is essential, especially for expensive purchases like fine jewelry. Nearly half of Gemvara's customers have never purchased a piece of jewelry online before, and 24/7 customer service goes a long way toward overcoming the trust barrier.

Questions

1. Access the Gemvara website. What are its strengths? Its weaknesses? Would you design and purchase jewelry on the site? Why or why not?
2. Search out websites for Gemvara competitors. Discuss each site's strengths and weaknesses. In light of your findings, do you think Gemvara will be successful in the long term? Why or why not?
3. How would a traditional brick-and-mortar jewelry store compete against Gemvara and other similar websites?

Sources: Compiled from "Gemvara Welcomes Summer with Launch of Black and White Collection," *12News.com*, June 19, 2013; J. Brooks, "Oprah names Gemvara Earrings to 'Favorite Things' List," *Boston Business Journal*, 2012; "America's Most Promising Companies: Gemvara," *Forbes*, November 30, 2011; L. Indvik, "How Gemvara Is Changing the Way Fine Jewelry Is Bought Online," *Mashable*, March 27, 2011; J. Holland, "The Bling King," *Entrepreneur*, March, 2011; www.gemvara.com, accessed March 2, 2013.

supplementary product information. In addition, they can easily locate and compare competitors' products and prices. Finally, buyers can find hundreds of thousands of sellers. Two popular online shopping mechanisms are electronic storefronts and electronic malls.

Electronic Storefronts. As noted earlier, an **electronic storefront** is a website that represents a single store. Hundreds of thousands of electronic storefronts can be found on the Internet. Each has its own uniform resource locator (URL), or Internet address, at which buyers can place orders. Some electronic storefronts are extensions of physical stores, such as Future Shop, Chapters, and Sears. Others are new businesses started by entrepreneurs who discovered a niche on the web (e.g., TigerDirect.ca and Abebooks.com). Manufacturers (e.g., *www.dell.ca*) and retailers (e.g., *www.staples.ca*) also use storefronts.

Despite the proliferation of e-businesses, questions have lingered about whether selling luxury goods online would be successful. IT's About Business 5.1 offers one successful example.

Electronic Malls. Whereas an electronic storefront represents a single store, an **electronic mall**, also known as a *cybermall* or an *e-mall*, is a collection of individual shops grouped under a single Internet address. The basic idea of an electronic mall is the same as that of a regular shopping mall—to provide a one-stop shopping place that offers a wide range of products and services.

There are two types of cybermalls. In the first type, known as *referral malls* (e.g., *http://yahoo.shoptoit.ca*), you cannot buy anything. Instead, you are transferred from the mall to a participating storefront. In the second type of mall (e.g., *www.shop.ca*), you can actually make a purchase (see Figure 5.1). At this type of mall, you might shop at several stores, but make only one purchase transaction at the end. You use an *electronic shopping cart* to gather items from various vendors and then pay for them all together in a single transaction. The mall organizer, such as Yahoo! or Shop.ca, takes a commission from the sellers for this service.

Online Service Industries

In addition to purchasing products, customers can also access needed services via the web. Selling books, toys, computers, and most other products on the Internet can reduce vendors' selling costs by 20 to 40 percent. Further reduction is difficult to achieve because the products must be delivered physically. Only a few products, such as software or music, can be digitized and then delivered online for additional savings. In contrast, services, such as buying an airline ticket and purchasing stocks or insurance, can be delivered entirely through e-commerce, often with considerable cost reduction. Not surprisingly, then, online delivery of services is growing very rapidly, with millions of new customers being added each year.

One of the most pressing EC issues relating to online services (as well as in marketing tangible products) is disintermediation. Intermediaries, also known as *middlemen*, have two functions: (1) they provide information, and (2) they perform value-added services such as

FIGURE 5.1 Electronic malls include products from many vendors. (*Source*: Google and the Google logo are registered trademarks of Google Inc., used with permission.)

consulting. The first function can be fully automated and most likely will be assumed by e-marketplaces and portals that provide information for free. When this occurs, the intermediaries who perform only (or primarily) this function are likely to be eliminated. This process is called **disintermediation**.

In contrast, performing value-added services requires expertise. Unlike the information function, therefore, this function can be only partially automated. Thus, intermediaries who provide value-added services not only are likely to survive, but may actually prosper. The web helps these employees in two situations: (1) when the number of participants is enormous, as with job searches, and (2) when the information that must be exchanged is complex.

In this section, you will examine some leading online service industries: banking, trading of securities (stocks, bonds), job matching, travel services, and online advertising.

Cyberbanking. *Electronic banking*, also known as **cyberbanking**, involves conducting various banking activities from home, at a place of business, or on the road instead of at a physical bank location. Electronic banking has capabilities ranging from paying bills to applying for a loan. For customers, it saves time and is convenient. For banks, it offers an inexpensive alternative to branch banking—for example, about 2 cents cost per transaction versus $1.07 at a physical branch. It also enables banks to attract remote customers. In addition to regular banks with added online services, **virtual banks**, which are dedicated solely to Internet transactions, are emerging. An example of a virtual bank is Tangerine (*www.tangerine.ca*) (see Figure 5.2).

International banking and the ability to handle trading in multiple currencies are critical for international trade. Transfers of electronic funds and electronic letters of credit are important services in international banking. For example, banks and companies such as OANDA (*www.oanda.com*) provide conversions of more than 160 currencies.

Online Securities Trading. Many Canadians use computers to trade stocks, bonds, and other financial instruments. Around the world, several well-known securities companies, including E*Trade and Charles Schwab, offer only online trading. In South Korea, more than half of stock traders are already using the Internet for that purpose. Why? Because it is cheaper than a full-service or discount broker. Further, on the web, investors can find a considerable amount of information regarding specific companies or mutual funds in which to invest (via, for example, *www.bnn.ca* and *www.bloomberg.com*).

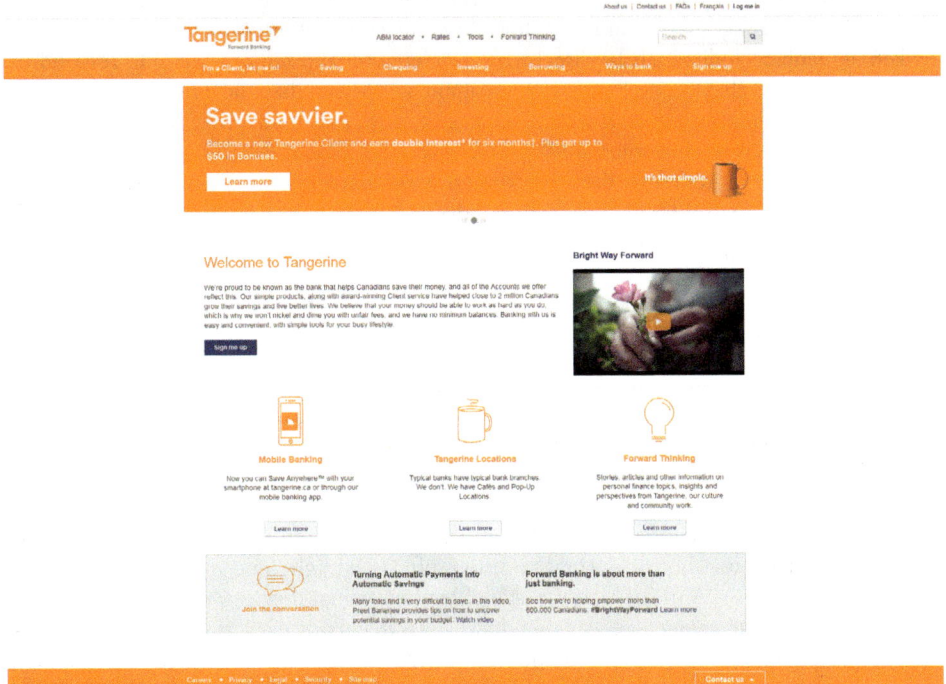

FIGURE 5.2 Tangerine (www.tangerine.ca). Courtesy of Tangerine.

For example, let's say you have an account with TDwaterhouse.ca. You access the *www.tdwaterhouse.ca* website from your personal computer or your Internet-enabled mobile device, enter your account number and password to access your personalized web page, and then click on "stock trading." Using a menu, you enter the details of your order—buy or sell, margin or cash, price limit, market order, and so on. The computer informs you of the current "ask" and "bid" prices, much as a broker would do over the telephone. You then can approve or reject the transaction.

The Online Job Market.
The Internet offers a promising new environment for job seekers and for companies searching for hard-to-find employees. Thousands of companies and government agencies advertise available positions, accept resumés, and take applications via the Internet.

Job seekers use the online job market to reply to employment ads, to place resumés on various job sites and social networking sites, and to use recruiting firms (e.g., *www.monster.ca* and *www.linkedin.com*). Companies that have jobs to offer advertise these openings on their websites, and they search the bulletin boards of recruiting firms. In many countries, governments must advertise job openings on the Internet.

Travel Services.
The Internet is an ideal place to plan, explore, and arrange almost any trip economically. Online travel services allow you to purchase airline tickets, reserve hotel rooms, and rent cars. Most sites also offer a fare-tracker feature that sends you e-mail messages about low-cost flights. Examples of comprehensive online travel services are Expedia.ca, Travelocity.ca, and itravel2000.com. Online services are also provided by all major airline vacation services, large conventional travel agencies, car rental agencies, hotels (e.g., *www.hotels.ca*), and tour companies. In a variation of this process, Priceline.com allows you to set a price you are willing to pay for an airline ticket or hotel accommodations. It then attempts to find a vendor that will match your price.

One costly problem that e-commerce can cause is "mistake fares" in the airline industry. For example, over the weekend of May 4–6, 2007, United Airlines offered a $1,221 fare for a round trip from the United States to New Zealand in business class. This price was incorrect; the actual price was much higher. By the time United noticed the mistake and pulled the fare, however, hundreds of tickets had been sold, thanks in part to online travel discussion groups.

Online Advertising.
Advertising is the practice of disseminating information in an attempt to influence a buyer–seller transaction. Traditional advertising on TV or in newspapers is impersonal, one-way mass communication. In contrast, direct-response marketing, or telemarketing, contacts individuals by direct mail or telephone and requires them to respond in order to make a purchase. The direct-response approach personalizes advertising and marketing. At the same time, however, it can be expensive, slow, and ineffective. It also can be extremely annoying to the consumer.

Internet advertising redefines the advertising process, making it media-rich, dynamic, and interactive. It improves on traditional forms of advertising in a number of ways. First, Internet ads can be updated any time at minimal cost and therefore can be kept current. In addition, these ads can reach very large numbers of potential buyers all over the world. Further, they are generally cheaper than radio, television, and print ads. Finally, Internet ads can be interactive and targeted to specific interest groups and/or individuals.

Advertising Methods. The most common online advertising methods are banners, pop-ups, and e-mail. **Banners** are simply electronic billboards. Typically, a banner contains a short text or graphical message that promotes a product or a vendor. It may even contain video clips and sound. When customers click on a banner, they are transferred to the advertiser's home page. Banner advertising is the most commonly used form of advertising on the Internet (see Figure 5.3).

A major advantage of banners is that they can be customized to the target audience. If the computer system knows who you are or what your profile is, it might send you a banner targeted to match your interests. A major disadvantage of banners is that they can convey only limited information due to their small size. Another drawback is that many viewers simply ignore them.

Pop-up and pop-under ads are contained in a new browser window that is automatically launched when you enter or exit a website. A **pop-up ad** appears in front of the current browser

FIGURE 5.3 When customers click on a banner ad, they are transferred to the vendor's homepage. (*Source*: Google and the Google logo are registered trademarks of Google Inc., used with permission.)

window. A **pop-under ad** appears underneath the active window, and when the active window is closed, the ad appears. Many users strongly object to these ads, which they consider intrusive. Modern browsers let users block pop-up ads, but this feature must be used with caution because some websites depend on pop-up capabilities to present content other than advertising. For example, when customers log on to their Verizon e-mail page, they also see brief (one-line) summaries of recent news stories. If you hover your mouse over one of them, a pop-up window appears with an extended summary (a few paragraphs) of that story. Another example is the WebCT Vista software for online instruction, where discussion group posts appear in pop-up windows. Blocking pop-ups would make the first of these two examples less useful and would eliminate important functionality from the second example.

E-mail is emerging as an Internet advertising and marketing channel. It is generally cost effective to implement, and it provides a better and quicker response rate than other advertising channels. Marketers develop or purchase a list of e-mail addresses, place them in a customer database, and then send advertisements via e-mail. A list of e-mail addresses can be a very powerful tool because the marketer can target a group of people or even individuals.

As you have probably concluded by now, there is a potential for misuse of e-mail advertising. In fact, some consumers receive a flood of unsolicited e-mail, or *spam*. **Spamming** is the indiscriminate distribution of electronic ads without the permission of the receiver. Unfortunately, spamming is becoming worse over time.

Two important responses to spamming are permission marketing and viral marketing. **Permission marketing** asks consumers to give their permission to voluntarily accept online advertising and e-mail. Typically, consumers are asked to complete an electronic form that asks what they are interested in and requests permission to send related marketing information. Sometimes, consumers are offered incentives to receive advertising.

Permission marketing is the basis of many Internet marketing strategies. For example, thousands of users periodically receive e-mails from airlines such as Air Canada and WestJet. Users of this marketing service can ask to be notified of low fares from their hometown or to their favourite destinations. Significantly, they can easily unsubscribe at any time. Permission marketing is also extremely important for market research (for example, see the Media Metrix suite at *www.comscore.com*).

In one particularly interesting form of permission marketing, companies such as CashSurfers.com have built customer lists of millions of people who are happy to receive advertising messages whenever they are on the web. These customers are paid $0.25 to $0.50 an hour to view messages while they do their normal surfing.

Viral marketing is online "word-of-mouth" marketing. The strategy behind viral marketing is to have people forward messages to friends, family members, and other acquaintances suggesting they "check this out." For example, a marketer can distribute a small game program embedded with a sponsor's e-mail that is easy to forward. The marketer releases only a few thousand copies, with the expectation that the recipients, in turn, will forward the program to many more thousands of potential customers. In this way, viral marketing enables companies to build brand awareness at a minimal cost without having to spam millions of uninterested users.

Online Advertising on Social Networks. Online advertising on social networks has become more successful over time. This type of advertising takes several forms, including self-service advertising, brand advertising, performance-based advertising, and impression-based advertising.

Self-service advertising is advertising purchased without the assistance of a sales representative. By eliminating the expense of a sales representative, a social networking company can offer smaller minimum ad buys than would otherwise be practical or profitable. Also, using text ads rather than banner ads makes self-service advertising easier for small businesses that do not have compelling graphical ads. Self-service advertising enables companies to carefully target very small groups. For example, Facebook allows advertisers to target "Americans who are married or engaged and are avid flyfishers."

Brand advertising relies on large advertising campaigns that emphasize the company's brand and use special features like fan pages that are unique to Facebook and other social networking sites. Typically, a company that runs a brand advertising campaign on a social networking site will create a fan page for free. The advertising company pays the social networking site for premium ad placement that drives users to the fan page, where they can interact with the brand.

With *performance-based advertising*, the advertising company pays only for measurable results; that is, when someone clicks on a company's ad and goes on to purchase something. For example, today many universities place precisely targeted ads on Facebook because the right sorts of people view the ads, click on them, and sign up for online courses. Facebook is paid only when customers actually enroll for classes.

Impression-based advertising occurs when a company purchases a set amount of impressions. An *impression* is a single instance of an ad appearing on a website. Impression-based advertising is typically cheaper than *click-through advertising*, where a company pays only when someone clicks on its ad.

Issues in E-Tailing

Despite e-tailing's increasing popularity, many e-tailers continue to face serious issues that can restrict their growth. Perhaps the two major issues are channel conflict and order fulfillment.

Clicks-and-mortar companies may face a conflict with their regular distributors when they sell directly to customers online. This situation, known as **channel conflict**, can alienate the distributors. Channel conflict has forced some companies to avoid direct online sales. For example, Walmart, Lowe's, and Home Depot would rather have customers come to their stores. Therefore, although all three companies maintain e-commerce websites, their sites place more emphasis on providing information—products, prices, specials, and store locations—than on online sales.

Channel conflict can arise in areas such as pricing and resource allocation; for example, how much money to spend on advertising. Another potential source of conflict involves the logistics services provided by the off-line activities to the online activities. For example, how should a company handle returns of items purchased online? Some companies have completely separated the "clicks" (the online portion of the organization) from the "mortar" or "bricks" (the traditional physical part of the organization). However, this approach can increase expenses and reduce the synergy between the two organizational channels. As a result, many companies are integrating their online and off-line channels, a process known as **multichannelling**.

The second major issue confronting e-commerce is order fulfillment, which can create problems for e-tailers as well. Any time a company sells directly to customers, it is involved in various order-fulfillment activities: quickly finding the products to be shipped; packing them; arranging for the packages to be delivered speedily to the customer's door; collecting the money from every customer, either in advance or by individual bill; and handling the return of unwanted or defective products.

It is very difficult to accomplish these activities both effectively and efficiently in B2C, because a company has to ship small packages to many customers and do it quickly. For this reason, companies involved in B2C activities often experience difficulties in their supply chains.

In addition to providing customers with the products they ordered and doing it on time, order fulfillment also provides all related customer services. For example, the customer must receive assembly and operation instructions for a new appliance. In addition, if the customer is not happy with a product, an exchange or return must be arranged. (Visit *www.fedex.com* to see how returns are handled via FedEx.)

In the late 1990s, e-tailers faced continuous problems in order fulfillment, especially during the holiday season. These problems included late deliveries, delivering wrong items, high delivery costs, and compensation to unhappy customers. For e-tailers, taking orders over the Internet is the easy part of B2C e-commerce. Delivering orders to customers' doors is the hard part. In contrast, order fulfillment is less complicated in B2B. These transactions are much larger, but they are fewer in number. In addition, these companies have had order fulfillment mechanisms in place for many years.

before you go on...

1. Describe electronic storefronts and malls.
2. Discuss various types of online services, such as cyberbanking, securities trading, job searches, and travel services.
3. Discuss online advertising, its methods, and its benefits.
4. Identify the major issues relating to e-tailing.
5. What are spamming, permission marketing, and viral marketing?

5.3 Business-to-Business (B2B) Electronic Commerce

In *business to business (B2B)* e-commerce, the buyers and sellers are business organizations. B2B comprises about 85 percent of EC volume. It covers a broad spectrum of applications that enable an enterprise to form electronic relationships with its distributors, resellers, suppliers, customers, and other partners. Organizations can use B2B to restructure their supply chains and their partner relationships.

There are several business models for B2B applications. The major ones are sell-side marketplaces, buy-side marketplaces, and electronic exchanges.

Sell-Side Marketplaces

In the **sell-side marketplace** model, organizations attempt to sell their products or services to other organizations electronically from their own private e-marketplace website and/or from a third-party website. This model is similar to the B2C model in which the buyer is expected to come to the seller's site, view catalogues, and place an order. In the B2B sell-side marketplace, however, the buyer is an organization.

The key mechanisms in the sell-side model are electronic catalogues that can be customized for each large buyer and forward auctions. Sellers such as Dell Computer (*www.dellauction.com*) use auctions extensively. In addition to conducting auctions from their own websites, organizations can use third-party auction sites, such as eBay, to liquidate items. Companies such as Ariba (*www.ariba.com*) are helping organizations auction old assets and inventories.

The sell-side model is used by hundreds of thousands of companies. It is especially powerful for companies with superb reputations. The seller can be either a manufacturer (e.g., Dell, IBM), a distributor (e.g., *www.avnet.com*), or a retailer (e.g., *www.grandandtoy.com*). The seller uses EC to increase sales, reduce selling and advertising expenditures, increase delivery speed, and lower administrative costs. The sell-side model is especially suitable to customization. Many companies allow their customers to configure their orders online. For example, at Dell (*www.dell.ca*), you can determine the exact type of computer that you want. You can choose the type of chip (e.g., Itanium 2), the size of the hard drive (for example, 1 terabyte), the type of monitor (e.g., 22-inch flat screen), and so on. Similarly, the Jaguar website (*www.jaguar.com*) allows you to customize the Jaguar you want. Self-customization greatly reduces any misunderstandings concerning what customers want, and it encourages businesses to fill orders more quickly.

Buy-Side Marketplaces

The **buy-side marketplace** is a model in which organizations attempt to buy needed products or services from other organizations electronically. A major method of buying goods and services in the buy-side model is the reverse auction.

The buy-side model uses EC technology to streamline the purchasing process. The goal is to reduce both the costs of items purchased and the administrative expenses involved in purchasing them. In addition, EC technology can shorten the purchasing cycle time. Procurement includes purchasing goods and materials as well as sourcing (finding goods), negotiating with suppliers, paying for goods, and making delivery arrangements. Organizations now use the Internet to accomplish all of these functions.

Purchasing by using electronic support is referred to as **e-procurement**. E-procurement uses reverse auctions, particularly group purchasing. In **group purchasing**, multiple buyers combine their orders so that they constitute a large volume and therefore attract more seller attention. In addition, when buyers place their combined orders on a reverse auction, they can negotiate a volume discount. Typically, the orders of small buyers are aggregated by a third-party vendor, such as the United Sourcing Alliance (*www.usa-llc.com*).

Electronic Exchanges

E-marketplaces, called **public exchanges** or just **exchanges**, are independently owned by a third party and connect many sellers and many buyers. Public exchanges are open to all business organizations. They frequently are owned and operated by a third party. Public exchange managers provide all the necessary information systems to the participants. Thus, buyers and sellers merely have to "plug in" in order to trade. B2B public exchanges often are the initial point for contacts between business partners. Once the partners make contact, they may move to a private exchange or to the private trading rooms provided by many public exchanges to conduct their subsequent trading activities. IT's About Business 5.2 offers the example of Biddingo.com, an Canadian electronic exchange for municipalities and other government agencies.

IT's [about business]

5.2 A New Electronic Exchange for the City of Kingston

Canadian municipalities have long embraced the web as a means of informing residents of important policies and offering online transactions, such as telling them when garbage pick-up day is or letting them reserve a book at their local library branch. But some municipalities are taking the web to the next level, leveraging its ability to procure products and services at the best cost for taxpayers.

The City of Kingston in Ontario is one such municipality. The city of 125,000 people recently underwent an updating of its website. The project objectives were to provide easier navigation and improved functionality on computers and mobile devices.

The new site includes the traditional tools for residents such as Kingston Transit's trip planner, online pay services, and the waste sorting look-up. But probably most importantly, the new website also incorporates a section for businesses to do business with the City of Kingston. This new system, called Biddingo (*www.biddingo.com*), is aimed at streamlining the city's purchasing process. Anything from buying a truck or cleaning products, to catering for events can be done through the Biddingo e-commerce platform.

This system is already used by multiple government agencies and other cities around Canada. It is becoming the industry standard for businesses interested in providing various goods and services to public sector buyers.

Whenever a customer, such as the City of Kingston, needs to buy a vehicle or computers, for example, it uses the Biddingo platform to issue a request for information, if they only want to find out about possible products and services and their cost, or they issue a request for proposal, which is the formal tender document seeking specific products and services. Suppliers can only win the contracts that they know about, and Biddingo ensures that they are made aware of the proposals. Suppliers get a daily e-mail alert of all the bids that match their profile, submit bid responses, and often win them! They have access to detailed reports that provide crucial business decision-making information, such as invitation lists, document taker's lists, mandatory site meetings, amendment notices, bid results, and awarded contracts. Biddingo.com helps both sides: It assists buyers with fulfilling their purchasing requirements and it assists suppliers with bidding on work that can help their businesses grow.

Questions

1. What type of B2B e-commerce exchange website is Biddingo?
2. Visit the Biddingo website (*www.biddingo.com*) and view some of the goods and services being tendered by the City of Kingston or any other city in Canada. What types of goods and services are tendered through Biddingo.com?
3. Are there any goods or services that might not be suitable to be tendered on Biddingo? Why or why not?
4. What reasons would lead the City of Kingston to set up its own buy-side marketplace instead of using Biddingo?

Sources: Compiled from D. Mathison, "City of Kingston Website Launches New Design," *Kingston Herald*, February 21, 2013; *www.biddingo.com*, accessed May 2013.

Some electronic exchanges deal in direct materials, and others in indirect materials. *Direct materials* are inputs to the manufacturing process, such as safety glass used in automobile windshields and windows. *Indirect materials* are items, such as office supplies, that are needed for maintenance, repairs, and operations (MRO). There are three basic types of public exchanges: vertical, horizontal, and functional. All three types offer diversified support services, ranging from payments to logistics.

Vertical exchanges connect buyers and sellers in a given industry. Vertical exchanges are frequently owned and managed by a *consortium*, a term for a group of major players in an industry. For example, Marriott and Hyatt own a procurement consortium for the hotel industry, and ChevronTexaco owns an energy e-marketplace. The vertical e-marketplaces offer services that are particularly suited to the community they serve.

Horizontal exchanges connect buyers and sellers across many industries and are used primarily for MRO materials. Examples of horizontal exchanges are Worldbid.com (*www.worldbid.com*), Global Sources (*www.globalsources.com*), and Alibaba (*www.alibaba.com*).

In *functional exchanges*, needed services such as temporary help or extra office space are traded on an "as-needed" basis. For example, Employease (*www.employease.com*) can find temporary labour by searching employers in its Employease Network.

before you go on...

1. Briefly differentiate between the sell-side marketplace and the buy-side marketplace.
2. Briefly differentiate among vertical exchanges, horizontal exchanges, and functional exchanges.

5.4 Electronic Payments

Implementing EC typically requires electronic payments. **Electronic payment systems** enable you to pay for goods and services electronically rather than by writing a cheque or using cash. Payments are an integral part of doing business, whether in the traditional manner or online. Traditional payment systems typically have involved cash and/or cheques.

In most cases, traditional payment systems are not effective for EC, especially for B2B. Cash cannot be used because there is no face-to-face contact between buyer and seller. Further, not everyone accepts credit cards or cheques, and some buyers do not have credit cards or chequing accounts. Finally, contrary to what many people believe, it may be *less* secure for the buyer to use the telephone or mail to arrange or send payments, especially from another country, than to complete a secured transaction on a computer. For all of these reasons, a better way is needed to pay for goods and services in cyberspace. This better method is electronic payment systems. We now take a closer look at four types of electronic payment: electronic cheques, electronic credit cards, purchasing cards, and electronic cash.

Electronic Cheques

Electronic cheques (*e-cheques*) are similar to regular paper cheques. They are used primarily in B2B. A customer who wishes to use e-cheques first must establish a chequing account with a bank. Then, when the customer buys a product or a service, he or she e-mails an encrypted electronic cheque to the seller. The seller deposits the cheque in a bank account, and funds are transferred from the buyer's account into the seller's account.

Like regular cheques, e-cheques carry a signature (in digital form) that can be verified (see *www.authorize.net*). Properly signed and endorsed e-cheques are exchanged between financial institutions through electronic clearinghouses. (Visit the Canadian Payments Association *www.cdnpay.ca* to learn more about electronic clearinghouses.)

FIGURE 5.4 How e-credit cards work. The numbers 1–9 indicate the sequence of activities. (*Source:* Drawn by E. Turban)

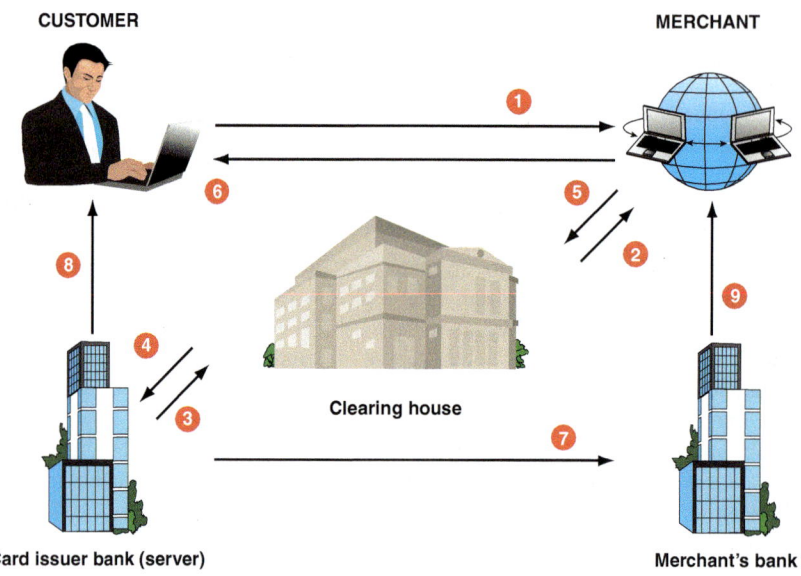

Electronic Credit Cards

Electronic credit (*e-credit*) cards allow customers to charge online payments to their credit card account. These cards are used primarily in B2C and in shopping by small-to-medium enterprises (SMEs). Here is how e-credit cards work (see Figure 5.4).

- Step 1: When you buy a book from Amazon, for example, your credit card information and purchase amount are encrypted in your browser. This way, the information is safe while it is "travelling" on the Internet to Amazon.
- Step 2: When your information arrives at Amazon, it is not opened. Rather, it is transferred automatically (in encrypted form) to a *clearinghouse*, where it is decrypted for verification and authorization.
- Step 3: The clearinghouse asks the bank that issued you your credit card (the card issuer bank) to verify your credit card information.
- Step 4: Your card issuer bank verifies your credit card information and reports this to the clearinghouse.
- Step 5: The clearinghouse reports the result of the verification of your credit card to Amazon.
- Step 6: Amazon reports a successful purchase and amount to you.
- Step 7: Your card issuer bank sends funds in the amount of the purchase to Amazon's bank.
- Step 8: Your card issuer bank notifies you (either electronically or in your monthly statement) of the debit on your credit card.
- Step 9: Amazon's bank notifies Amazon of the funds credited to its account.

Several major credit card issuers are offering customers the option of shopping online with *virtual, single-use credit card numbers* (see Figure 5.5). The goal is to thwart criminals by using a different random card number every time you shop online. This virtual number is good only on the website where you make your purchase. An online purchase made with a virtual card number shows up on your bill just like any other purchase.

Purchasing Cards

The B2B equivalent of electronic credit cards is *purchasing cards* (see Figure 5.6). In some countries, purchasing cards are the primary form of payment between companies. Unlike credit cards, where credit is provided for 30 to 60 days (for free) before payment is made to the merchant, payments made with purchasing cards are settled within a week.

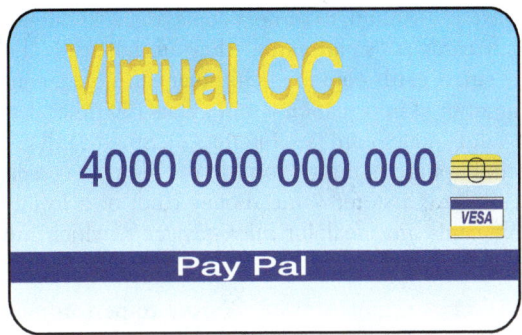

FIGURE 5.5 Example of virtual credit card.

FIGURE 5.6 Purchasing card. (*Source*: Mike Clarke/AFP/GettyImages/NewsCom)

Purchasing cards typically are used for unplanned B2B purchases, and corporations generally limit the amount per purchase, usually $1,000 to $2,000. Purchasing cards can be used on the Internet, much like regular credit cards.

Electronic Cash

Despite the growth of credit cards, cash remains the most common mode of payment in off-line transactions. Many EC sellers, and some buyers, however, prefer electronic cash. *Electronic cash* (*e-cash*) appears in three major forms: stored-value money cards, smart cards, and person-to-person payments.

Stored-Value Money Cards.
Although **stored-value money cards** resemble credit cards, they actually are a form of e-cash. The cards that you use to pay for photocopies in your library, for transportation, and for telephone calls are stored-value money cards. They are called "stored-value" because they allow you to store a fixed amount of prepaid money and then spend it as necessary. Each time you use the card, the amount is reduced by the amount you spent. Figure 5.7 shows a stored-value money card for use at York University in Toronto.

FIGURE 5.7 York University stored-value money card. (*Source*: © York University)

FIGURE 5.8 Smart cards are frequently multipurpose.
(*Source*: © MARKA/Alamy Limited)

Smart Cards. Although some people refer to stored-value money cards as "smart cards," they are not really the same. True **smart cards** contain a chip that can store a considerable amount of information—more than 100 times that of a stored-value money card (see Figure 5.8). Smart cards are frequently multipurpose; that is, you can use them as a credit card, a debit card, a stored-value money card, or a loyalty card. Smart cards are ideal for *micropayments*, which are small payments of a few dollars or less.

Person-to-Person Payments. **Person-to-person payments** are a form of e-cash that enables two individuals, or an individual and a business, to transfer funds without using a credit card. Person-to-person payments can be used for a variety of purposes, such as sending money to students at university, paying for an item purchased at an online auction, or sending a gift to a family member.

One of the first companies to offer this service was PayPal. Most recently, a new company called Stripe (*http://stripe.com/ca*) started offering similar online payment services as PayPal, but for small and medium businesses, as IT's About Business 5.3 describes.

All of these person-to-person payment services work in a similar way. First, you select a service and open up an account. Basically, this process entails creating a user name, selecting a password, and providing the service with a credit card or bank account number. Next, you

 **[about business]**

5.3 Stripe, an Online Payment System for Small Businesses

Stripe is a new online payment system for small businesses developed by two brothers from Ireland, Patrick and John Collison. They turned their hobby of developing software applications into a growing business by raising over $38 million in cash from investors in order to expand to other countries, including Canada.

The new payment system is geared toward small and medium businesses that want to sell their products online. It provides them with a quick way to accept credit card payments without a lot of technical complexity or overhead costs. An e-tailer can set up an account within minutes and it charges its customers a flat fee of 2.9 percent plus 30 cents for every transaction. Stripe has already spent several months of beta testing with companies such as Ottawa-based Shopify, one of Canada's leading e-commerce players.

But what is the difference between Stripe and online payment methods such as PayPal? The first difference when you visit Stripe's website is that it is easy to navigate and with a well-designed GUI. But the main difference is that Stripe doesn't require e-tailers to set up an account with them first before using their platform. Stripe stands out from its rivals because of its simplicity and easy of use. For example, it allows a company to quickly incorporate the Stripe payment features into its e-commerce website and mobile apps without lengthy programming modifications, and to start processing credit-card payments in 139 different currencies, bank transfers, and even bitcoins in less than five minutes. This offers new e-tailers a cost advantage when setting up their payment systems on their websites.

Today, Stripe handles millions of dollars of payments per day from thousands of businesses, many of them small but some of them enormous, such as Walmart and NBC. As for the highly encrypted security system used by the company, it is certified as a Level 1 provider, which is the highest level available by the payment card industry.

Questions

1. Would Stripe be able to maintain its current competitive advantage based on ease of payment and costs? Why or why not?
2. Would Stripe be a good payment system to pay for small purchases? Why or why not? As a hint, discuss the payment of an online newspaper article that would cost 20 cents.
3. What are the main differences between person-to-person payment systems such as Stripe and PayPal and the use of credit cards?

Sources: Compiled from M. Evans, "Stripe 'Disrupts' Payment-Processing Market with Its Simplicity," *The Globe and Mail,* September 24, 2012; D. Kucera, "Payments Startup Stripe Expands to Canada in Challenge to PayPal," go.bloomberg.com, September 19, 2012; C. Wong, "Online Payment Startup Stripe Hits Canada," ITbusiness.ca, September 19, 2012; D. Weir, "Stripe Is the Payment System Under the Hood at Lots of Your Favorite Sites and Apps," 7x7SF, *www.7x7.com*, April 4, 2013; O. Kharif and S. Saitto, "Stripe Lands Apple in Quest for $720 Billion in Payments," *www.bloomberg.com,* September 17, 2014.

transfer funds from your credit card or bank account to your new account. Now you're ready to send money to someone over the Internet. You access the service—for example, PayPal—with your user name and password, and you specify the e-mail address of the person to receive the money, along with the dollar amount that you want to send. The service then sends an e-mail to the payee's e-mail address. The e-mail contains a link back to the service's website. When the recipient clicks on the link, he or she is taken to the service. There, the recipient is asked to set up an account to which the money that you sent will be credited. The recipient can then credit the money from this account to either a credit card or a bank account. The service charges the payer a small amount, roughly $1 per transaction.

An attractive security feature of PayPal is that you have to put only enough money in the account to cover any upcoming transactions. Therefore, if anyone should gain access to your account, they he or she not have access to all of your money.

Digital Wallets.   Digital wallets (or e-wallets) are not proper online payment systems but are software mechanisms that provide security measures, combined with convenience, to EC purchasing. The wallet stores the financial information of the buyer, such as credit card number, shipping information, and so on. Thus, the buyer does not need to re-enter sensitive information for each purchase. In addition, if the wallet is stored at the vendor's website, then it does not have to travel on the Internet for each purchase, making the information more secure. Examples of popular digital wallets are Skrill (*www.skrill.com*), Yahoo! Wallet (*http://ca.wallet.yahoo.com/*), and Google Checkout (*http://checkout.google.com/*). Convenience is the main advantage of digital wallets; however, they are not totally secured systems.

before you go on...

1. List the various electronic payment mechanisms. Which of these mechanisms are most often used for B2B payments?
2. What are micropayments?

5.5 Ethical and Legal Issues in E-Business

Technological innovation often forces a society to re-examine and modify its ethical standards. In many cases the new standards are incorporated into law. In this section, you will learn about two important ethical considerations—privacy and job loss—as well as various legal issues arising from the practice of e-business.

Ethical Issues

Many of the ethical and global issues related to IT also apply to e-business. Here you will learn about two basic issues, privacy and job loss.

By making it easier to store and transfer personal information, e-business presents some threats to privacy. To begin with, most electronic payment systems know who the buyers are. It may be necessary, then, to protect the buyers' identities. Businesses frequently use encryption to provide this protection.

Another major privacy issue is tracking. For example, individuals' activities on the Internet can be tracked by cookies, discussed in Chapter 13. Cookies store your tracking history on your personal computer's hard drive, and any time you revisit a certain website, the server recognizes the cookie. In response, antivirus software packages routinely search for potentially harmful cookies.

In addition to compromising individual privacy, the use of EC may eliminate the need for some of a company's employees, as well as brokers and agents. The manner in which these unneeded workers, especially employees, are treated can raise ethical issues: How should the company handle the layoffs? Should companies be required to retrain employees for new positions? If not, how should the company compensate or otherwise assist the displaced workers?

Legal and Ethical Issues Specific to E-Commerce

There are many legal issues that are related specifically to e-commerce. When buyers and sellers do not know one another and cannot even see one another, there is a chance that dishonest people will commit fraud and other crimes. During the first few years of EC, the public witnessed many such crimes. These illegal actions ranged from creating a virtual bank that disappeared along with the investors' deposits to manipulating stock prices on the Internet. In the following section, you explore some of the major legal issues that are specific to e-commerce.

Fraud on the Internet.
Internet fraud has grown even faster than Internet use itself. In one case, stock promoters falsely spread positive rumours about the prospects of the companies they touted in order to boost the stock price. In other cases, the information provided might have been true, but the promoters did not disclose that they were paid to talk up the companies. Stock promoters specifically target small investors who are lured by the promise of fast profits.

Stocks are only one of many areas where swindlers are active. Auctions also are especially conducive to fraud, by both sellers and buyers. Other types of fraud include selling bogus investments and setting up phantom business opportunities. Due to the growing use of e-mail, financial criminals now have access to many more people. The Royal Canadian Mounted Police (RCMP) (*www.rcmp-grc.gc.ca/scams-fraudes*) regularly publishes examples of scams that are most likely to be spread via e-mail or to be found on the web. Later in this section you will see some ways in which consumers and sellers can protect themselves from online fraud. One of the most common types of e-commerce fraud is website "phishing." IT'S About Business 5.4 describes one case of phishing of the Canada Renenue Agency main web page.

Domain Names.
Another legal issue is competition over domain names. Domain names are assigned by central non-profit organizations that check for conflicts and possible infringement of trademarks. Obviously, companies that sell goods and services over the Internet want customers to be able to find them easily. In general, the more closely the domain name matches the company's name, the easier the company is to locate.

A domain name is considered to be legal when the person or business who owns the name has operated a legitimate business under that name for some period of time. Companies such as Christian Dior, Nike, Deutsche Bank, and even Microsoft have had to fight or pay to get the domain name that corresponds to their company's name. Consider the case of Delta Air Lines. Delta originally could not obtain the Internet domain name delta.com because Delta Faucet had purchased it first. Delta Faucet had been in business under that name since 1954 and therefore had a legitimate business interest in the domain name. Delta Air Lines had to settle for delta-airlines.com until it bought the domain name from Delta Faucet. Delta Faucet is now at deltafaucet.com. Several cases of disputed domain names have been before the courts.

Cybersquatting.
Cybersquatting is the practice of registering or using domain names for the purpose of profiting from the goodwill or the trademark that belongs to someone else.

Some practices that could be considered cybersquatting, however, are not illegal, although they may well be unethical. One of these practices, known as *domain tasting*, lets registrars profit from the complex money trail of pay-per-click advertising. The practice can be traced back to the policies of the organization responsible for regulating web names, the Internet Corporation for Assigned Names and Numbers (ICANN) (*www.icann.org*). In 2000, ICANN established the "create grace period," a five-day period when a company or person can claim a domain name and then return it for a full refund of the $6 registry fee. ICANN implemented this policy to allow anyone who mistypes a domain name to return it without cost.

Domain tasters exploit this policy by claiming Internet domains for five days at no cost. These domain names frequently resemble those of prominent companies and organizations. The tasters then jam these domains full of advertisements that come from Google and Yahoo!. Because this process involves zero risk and 100 percent profit margins, domain tasters register millions of domain names every day—some of them over and over again. Experts estimate that registrants ultimately purchase less than 2 percent of the sites they sample. In the vast majority of cases, they use the domain names for only a few days to generate quick profits. IT's About

IT's [about business]

5.4 Domain Name Slamming

Ever since there has been an Internet, there have been Internet scams. A new one involves owners of dot-ca top-level domains. The Canadian Internet Registration Authority (CIRA) recently warned these owners of an online scam involving fake renewal notices sent via e-mail from Renewdomain.ca, which was not a CIRA-certified registrar, that tried to collect payment from dot-ca site owners.

The fraudulent site sent an e-mail to legitimate dot-ca domain owners and told them that they need to renew their domain. The e-mail sender fraudulently posed as the dot-ca registrar, telling them to make a payment though PayPal in order to keep the ownership of their domain name.

Although it might seem a rather simple way of misleading businesses that operate on the Internet, this type of fraud seems to be effective, especially with small businesses since owners may not remember who their original registrar is in the first place.

In response to the scam, the Renewdomain.ca website was shut down and CIRA revoked the licence of the company that owned it. In addition, CIRA also worked with PayPal to close the fraudulent web page to process the payments. However, one of today's most common e-commerce scams is phishing—using a fake web page that pretends to be from a legitimate business. This is what happened to the Canada Revenue Agency (CRA) in 2014, when a fake website that looked just like the CRA website asked visitors for their social insurance number, date of birth, and credit card number right after the fake CRA main page loaded.

Questions

1. What are the differences between cybersquatting and domain name slamming?
2. Why would it be so difficult to detect domain slamming cases?
3. How could a company protect itself against this kind of scam?

Sources: Compiled from B. Jackson, "CIRA Investigating dot-ca Phishing Scammers," *ITbusiness.ca*,, August 13, 2012; B. Jackson, "Canadian Web Site Owners Targeted by New Scam," *ITbusiness.ca,* August 10, 2012; "Online Scam Warning for Internet Users," CIRA news release, 2012, www.cira.ca, accessed May 29, 2013; K. Murray, "Fake Revenue Canada Agency website used in online scam," *CBC News, www.cbc.ca*, October 28, 2014.

Business 5.4 relates another recent fraudulent way of using domain names called *domain name slamming*.

Taxes and Other Fees. In off-line sales, most provinces and localities collect taxes on business transactions conducted within their jurisdiction. For online sales in Canada we must pay a federal tax on most items we purchase. In most provinces of Canada, we must also pay a provincial tax such as the QST in Québec. Some provinces however federal and provincial taxes are combined into a single, harmonized tax (HST), this is the case of provices such as Ontario or Nova Scotia.

In addition to the sales tax, in many jurisdictions around the world, there is a question about where—and in some cases, whether—electronic sellers should pay business licence taxes, franchise fees, gross-receipts taxes, excise taxes, privilege taxes, and utility taxes. Furthermore, how should tax collection be controlled?

Copyright. As you will learn in Chapter 12, intellectual property is protected by copyright laws and cannot be used freely. This point is significant because many people mistakenly believe that once they purchase a piece of software, they have the right to share it with others. In fact, what they have bought is the right to *use* the software, not to *distribute* it. That right remains with the copyright holder. Similarly, copying material from websites without permission is a violation of copyright laws. Protecting intellectual property rights in e-commerce is extremely difficult, however, because it involves hundreds of millions of people who have access to billions of web pages in about 200 countries with differing copyright laws.

before you go on...

1. List and explain some ethical issues in EC.
2. Discuss the major legal issues of EC.

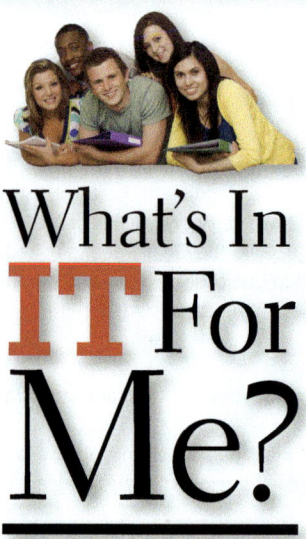

What's In IT For Me?

For the Accounting Major
Accounting personnel are involved in several EC activities. Designing the ordering system and its relationship with inventory management requires accounting attention. Billing and payments also are accounting activities, as are determining cost and profit allocation. Replacing paper documents with electronic means will affect many of the accountant's tasks, especially the auditing of EC activities and systems. Finally, building a cost-benefit and cost-justification system to determine which products and services to take online and creating a chargeback system are critical to the success of EC.

For the Finance Major
The worlds of banking, securities and commodities markets, and other financial services are being re-engineered due to EC. Online securities trading and its supporting infrastructure are growing more rapidly than any other EC activity. Many innovations already in place are changing the rules of economic and financial incentives for financial analysts and managers. Online banking, for example, does not recognize political boundaries, and it may create a new framework for financing global trades. Public financial information now is accessible in seconds. These innovations will dramatically change the manner in which finance personnel operate.

For the Marketing Major
A major revolution in marketing and sales is taking place due to EC. Perhaps its most obvious feature is the transition from a physical to a virtual marketplace. Equally important, though, is the radical transformation to one-on-one advertising and sales and to customized and interactive marketing. Marketing channels are being combined, eliminated, or recreated. The EC revolution is creating new products and markets and significantly altering existing ones. Digitization of products and services also has implications for marketing and sales. The direct producer-to-consumer channel is expanding rapidly and is fundamentally changing the nature of customer service. As the battle for customers intensifies, marketing and sales personnel are becoming the most critical success factor in many organizations. Online marketing can be a blessing to one company and a curse to another.

For the Production/Operations Management Major
EC is changing the manufacturing system from product-push mass production to order-pull mass customization. This change requires a robust supply chain, information support, and re-engineering of processes that involve suppliers and other business partners. Suppliers can use extranets to monitor and replenish inventories without the need for constant reorders. In addition, the Internet and intranets help reduce cycle times. Many production/operations problems that have persisted for years, such as complex scheduling and excess inventories, are being solved rapidly with the use of web technologies. Companies now can use external and internal networks to find and manage manufacturing operations in other countries much more easily. Also, the web is re-engineering procurement by helping companies conduct electronic bids for parts and subassemblies, thus reducing cost. All in all, the job of the progressive production/operations manager is closely tied in with e-commerce.

For the Human Resources Management Major
HR majors need to understand the new labour markets and the impacts of EC on old labour markets. Also, the HRM department may use EC tools for such functions as procuring office supplies. Also, becoming knowledgeable about new government online initiatives and online training is critical. Finally, HR personnel must be familiar with the major legal issues related to EC and employment.

For the MIS Major

The MIS function is responsible for providing the information technology infrastructure necessary for electronic commerce to function. In particular, this infrastructure includes the company's networks, intranets, and extranets. The MIS function also is responsible for ensuring that electronic commerce transactions are secure.

[Summary]

1. **Describe the six common types of electronic commerce; provide specific personal examples of how you have used or could use B2C, C2C, G2C, and mobile commerce; and offer a specific example of B2B and G2B.**

   In *business-to-consumer* (B2C) electronic commerce, the sellers are organizations, and the buyers are individuals. In *business-to-business* (B2B) electronic commerce, the sellers and the buyers are businesses. In *consumer-to-consumer* (C2C) electronic commerce, an individual sells products or services to other individuals. In *business-to-employee* (B2E) electronic commerce, an organization uses EC internally to provide information and services to its employees. *E-government* is the use of Internet technology in general and e-commerce in particular to deliver information and public services to citizens (called *government-to-citizen* or *G2C EC*), and business partners and suppliers (called *government-to-business* or *G2B EC*). *Mobile commerce* is e-commerce that is conducted entirely in a wireless environment.

   We leave the examples of each type to you.

2. **Discuss the five online services of business-to-consumer electronic commerce, provide a specific example of each service, and state how you have used or would use each service.**

   Electronic banking, also known as *cyberbanking*, involves conducting various banking activities from home, at a place of business, or on the road instead of at a physical bank location.

   Online securities trading involves buying and selling securities over the web.

   Online job matching over the web offers a promising environment for job seekers and for companies searching for hard-to-find employees. Thousands of companies and government agencies advertise available positions, accept resumés, and take applications via the Internet.

   The Internet is an ideal place to plan, explore, and arrange almost any trip economically. *Online travel services* allow you to purchase airline tickets, reserve hotel rooms, and rent cars. Most sites also offer a fare-tracker feature that sends you e-mail messages about low-cost flights.

   Online advertising over the web makes the advertising process media-rich, dynamic, and interactive.

   We leave the examples to you.

3. **Describe the three business models for business-to-business electronic commerce, and provide a specific example of each model.**

   In the *sell-side marketplace* model, organizations attempt to sell their products or services to other organizations electronically from their own private e-marketplace website and/or from a third-party website. Sellers such as Dell Computer (*www.dellauction.com*) use sell-side auctions extensively. In addition to auctions from their own websites, organizations can use third-party auction sites, such as eBay, to liquidate items.

   The *buy-side marketplace* is a model in which organizations attempt to buy needed products or services from other organizations electronically.

E-marketplaces, in which there are many sellers and many buyers, are called *public exchanges*, or just exchanges. Public exchanges are open to all business organizations. They frequently are owned and operated by a third party. There are three basic types of public exchanges: vertical, horizontal, and functional. *Vertical exchanges* connect buyers and sellers in a given industry. *Horizontal exchanges* connect buyers and sellers across many industries. In *functional exchanges*, needed services such as temporary help or extra office space are traded on an "as-needed" basis.

4. **Describe the four types of electronic payments and provide a specific example of each one.**

   Electronic cheques (*e-cheques*) are similar to regular paper cheques. They are used mostly in B2B.

   Electronic credit (*e-credit*) cards allow customers to charge online payments to their credit card account. Electronic credit cards are used primarily in B2C and in shopping by small-to-medium enterprises.

   The B2B equivalent of electronic credit cards is *purchasing cards*. Unlike credit cards, where credit is provided for 30 to 60 days (for free) before payment is made to the merchant, payments made with purchasing cards are settled within a week. Purchasing cards typically are used for unplanned B2B purchases, and the amount per purchase generally is limited (usually $1,000 to $2,000).

   Electronic cash (*e-cash*) appears in three major forms: stored-value money cards, smart cards, and person-to-person payments. Although they resemble credit cards, *stored-value money cards* allow you to store a fixed amount of prepaid money and then spend it as necessary. Each time you use the card, the amount is reduced by the amount you spent. *Smart cards* contain a chip that can store a considerable amount of information. You can use them as a credit card, a debit card, or a stored-value money card. *Person-to-person payments* enable two individuals or an individual and a business to transfer funds without using a credit card.

   We leave the examples to you.

5. **Illustrate the ethical and legal issues relating to electronic commerce with two specific examples of each issue.**

   E-business presents some threats to privacy. To begin with, most electronic payment systems know who the buyers are. It may be necessary, therefore, to protect the buyers' identities with encryption. Another major privacy issue is tracking, where individuals' activities on the Internet can be tracked by cookies.

   The use of EC may eliminate the need for some of a company's employees, as well as brokers and agents. The manner in which these unneeded workers, especially employees, are treated can raise ethical issues: How should the company handle the layoffs? Should companies be required to retrain employees for new positions? If not, how should the company compensate or otherwise assist the displaced workers?

[Chapter Glossary]

auction A competitive process in which either a seller solicits consecutive bids from buyers or a buyer solicits bids from sellers, and prices are determined dynamically by competitive bidding.

banners Electronic billboards, which typically contain a short text or graphical message to promote a product or a vendor.

brick-and-mortar organizations Organizations in which the product, the process, and the delivery agent are all physical.

business-to-business electronic commerce (B2B) Electronic commerce in which both the sellers and the buyers are business organizations.

business-to-consumer electronic commerce (B2C) Electronic commerce in which the sellers are organizations and the buyers are individuals; also known as *e-tailing*.

business-to-employee electronic commerce (B2E) An organization that uses electronic commerce internally to provide information and services to its employees.

business model The method by which a company generates revenue to sustain itself.

buy-side marketplace B2B model in which organizations buy needed products or services from other organizations electronically, often through a reverse auction.

channel conflict The alienation of existing distributors when a company decides to sell to customers directly online.

clicks-and-mortar organizations Organizations that do business in both the physical and digital dimensions.

consumer-to-consumer electronic commerce (C2C) Electronic commerce in which both the buyer and the seller are individuals (not businesses).

cyberbanking Various banking activities conducted electronically from home, a business, or on the road instead of at a physical bank location.

cybersquatting Registering domain names in the hope of selling them later at a higher price.

digital wallets (e-wallets) software mechanisms that stores the financial information of the buyer, such as credit card number, shipping information so the buyer does not need to re-enter this information for each purchase.

disintermediation Elimination of intermediaries in electronic commerce.

e-government The use of electronic commerce to deliver information and public services to citizens, business partners, and suppliers of government entities, and those working in the public sector.

e-procurement Purchasing by using electronic support.

electronic business (e-business) Electronic commerce, more broadly defined to include buying and selling of goods and services as well as servicing customers, collaborating with business partners, conducting e-learning, and conducting electronic transactions within an organization.

electronic commerce (EC or e-commerce) The process of buying, selling, transferring, or exchanging products, services, or information via computer networks, including the Internet.

electronic mall A collection of individual shops under one Internet address.

electronic marketplace (e-marketplace) A virtual market space on the web where many buyers and many sellers conduct electronic business activities.

electronic payment systems Computer-based systems that allow customers to pay for goods and services electronically, rather than writing a cheque or using cash.

electronic retailing (e-tailing) The direct sale of products and services through storefronts or electronic malls, usually designed around an electronic catalogue format and/or auctions.

electronic storefront The website of a single company, with its own Internet address, at which orders can be placed.

exchange (see **public exchange**)

forward auctions An auction that sellers use as a selling channel to many potential buyers; the highest bidder wins the items.

group purchasing The aggregation of purchasing orders from many buyers so that a volume discount can be obtained.

mobile commerce (m-commerce) Electronic commerce conducted in a wireless environment.

multichannelling A process in which a company integrates its online and off-line channels.

permission marketing Method of marketing that asks consumers to give their permission to voluntarily accept online advertising and e-mail.

person-to-person payments A form of electronic cash that enables the transfer of funds between two individuals, or between an individual and a business, without the use of a credit card.

pop-under ad An advertisement that is automatically launched by some trigger and appears underneath the active window.

pop-up ad An advertisement that is automatically launched by some trigger and appears in front of the active window.

public exchange (exchange) Electronic marketplace in which there are many sellers and many buyers, and entry is open to all; it is frequently owned and operated by a third party.

reverse auction An auction in which one buyer, usually an organization, seeks to buy a product or a service, and suppliers submit bids; the lowest bidder wins.

sell-side marketplace B2B model in which organizations sell to other organizations from their own private e-marketplace and/or from a third-party site.

smart card A card that contains a microprocessor (chip) that enables the card to store a considerable amount of information (including stored funds) and to conduct processing.

social commerce type of electronic commerce that uses social media to assist in the online buying and selling of products and services.

spamming Indiscriminate distribution of e-mail without the receiver's permission.

stored-value money card A form of electronic cash on which a fixed amount of prepaid money is stored; the amount is reduced each time the card is used.

viral marketing Online word-of-mouth marketing.

virtual bank A banking institution dedicated solely to Internet transactions.

virtual organizations Organizations in which the product, the process, and the delivery agent are all digital; also called *pure-play organizations*.

[Discussion Questions]

1. Discuss the major limitations of e-commerce. Which of these limitations are likely to disappear? Why?
2. Discuss the reasons for having multiple EC business models.
3. Distinguish between business-to-business forward auctions and buyers' bids for requests for quotations (RFQs).
4. Discuss the benefits to sellers and buyers of a B2B exchange.

5. What are the major benefits of G2C electronic commerce?
6. Discuss the various ways to pay online in B2C. Which one(s) would you prefer and why?
7. Why is order fulfillment in B2C considered difficult?
8. Discuss the reasons for EC failures.
9. Should BMW or Honda sell cars online? (Hint: Take a look at the discussion of channel conflict in this chapter.)
10. In some cases, individuals engage in cybersquatting so that they can sell the domain names to companies expensively. In other cases, companies engage in cybersquatting by registering domain names that are very similar to their competitors' domain names in order to generate traffic from people who misspell web addresses. Discuss each practice in terms of its ethical nature and legality. Is there a difference between the two practices? Support your answer.

[Problem-Solving Activities]

1. Suppose that you are interested in buying a brand new car. You can find information about cars at numerous websites from car manufacturers. Access three of these sites and write a report analyzing the different types of online advertising methods they use on their main website.
2. Compare the various electronic payment methods. Specifically, collect information from the vendors cited in the chapter, and find additional vendors using Google.ca. Pay attention to security level, speed, cost, and convenience. What type of payment method has the lowest cost for the seller? Which one is the most convenient for the buyer?
3. Conduct a study on selling diamonds and gems online. Access such sites as *www.peoplesjewellers.com*, *www.tiffany.ca*, and *www.charmdiamondcentres.com/*
   a. What features do these sites use to educate buyers about gemstones?
   b. How do these sites attract buyers?
   c. How do these sites increase customers' trust in online purchasing?
   d. What customer service features do these sites provide?
4. Access Canadian payment association *www.cdnpay.ca*. What is its role? What is their vision for the year 2020?
5. Access *www.tsn.com*. Identify at least five different ways the site generates revenue.
6. Access *www.queendom.com*. Examine its offerings and try some of them. What type of electronic commerce is this? How does this website generate revenue?
7. Access *www.ediets.com*. Prepare a list of all the services the company provides. Identify its revenue model.
8. Access *www.theknot.com*. Identify the site's revenue sources.
9. Access *www.mint.com*. Identify the site's revenue model. What are the risks of giving this website your credit and debit card numbers, as well as your bank account number?
10. Research the case of *www.nissan.com*. Is Uzi Nissan cybersquatting? Why or why not? Support your answer. How is Nissan (the car company) reacting to the *www.nissan.com* website?

[Web Activities]

1. Access the Stock Market Game Worldwide (*www.smgww.org*). You will be bankrolled with $100,000 in a trading account every month. Play the game, and relate your experiences with regard to information technology. Identify the site's revenue sources.
2. Enter *www.alibaba.com*. Identify the site's capabilities. Look at the site's private trading room. Write a report. How can such a site help a person who is making a purchase?
3. Enter *www.dineoncampus.ca/* Explore the site. Why is the site so successful? Could you start a competing site? Why or why not?
4. Enter *www.dell.ca* and configure a desktop system. Register to "my account" (no obligation). What calculators are used there? What are the advantages of this process as compared with buying a computer in a physical store? What are the disadvantages?
5. Enter *www.fiserv.com/* and *www.digitalriver.com/*, and compare and contrast their product and service offerings. Prepare a report comparing the two sites' offerings.
6. Access various travel sites such as *www.travelocity.ca*, *www.orbitz.com*, *www.expedia.ca*, and *www.kayak.com*. Compare these websites for ease of use and usefulness. Note differences among the sites. If you ask each site for the itinerary, which one gives you the best information and the best deals?
7. Access *www.outofservice.com*, and answer the musical taste and personality survey. When you have finished, click on Results and see what your musical tastes say about your personality. How accurate are the findings about you?

[Spreadsheet Activity: Building Charts and Graphs]

STEP 1 – Background

Any time you store data, you should take steps to secure those data. Spreadsheets frequently contain private or personal data that employees and/or customers do not want to be lost or released.

To prevent data loss, it is a good idea to understand spreadsheet protection at three levels: workbook protection, worksheet protection, and range protection (including a single cell). *Workbook protection* requires the user to enter a password to access the entire workbook. This is an effective strategy to prevent unauthorized parties from accessing the data. *Worksheet* protection within a protected workbook maintains the consistency of all of the data in the worksheet. Perhaps there are a few pages of data that do NOT need to be altered. Protecting those worksheets while allowing others to be modified will ensure that those data will not be changed. Finally, *range protection* allows users to modify data in some cells on a worksheet without affecting the data in other cells.

It is important to note that protecting a workbook does not encrypt the workbook. Rather, the data are stored in traditional spreadsheet files. The underlying idea in protecting a workbook is either to lock out unauthorized people completely or to keep authorized users from modifying something they should not.

STEP 2 – Activity

Recently, Juanita signed up for a Debt Management course, but she didn't want her family, friends, and coworkers to know that she had problems with debt. However, the course manager's computer was hacked, and the spreadsheet—which was not protected—was posted on the Internet. Research the three methods of protecting spreadsheets, and be prepared to give advice on which method would have been the most appropriate for the course manager: workbook, worksheet, or range.

STEP 3 – Deliverable

Charles is the teacher whose computer was hacked in the example in Step 2. Visit www.wiley.com/go/rainercanada, and download Charles's spreadsheet. The workbook will include instructions to guide you in helping Charles to protect his data so that even if his computer is hacked, at least the spreadsheet will be inaccessible. Submit your protected workbook to your professor with another document of notes that contains your passwords so that your professor will be able to access your work.

Follow the instructions in the spreadsheet and submit your final work to your instructor.

[Case Assignment]

Bellwood College has switched to using electronic readers rather than paper-based textbooks. Students are issued a reader that gives them access to the textbooks that are listed as required for their courses at no additional charge. The publishing fee for the texts, paid to one Canadian publisher, means that the college is now using textbooks from only that publisher. It also means that the college will be spending less on new library acquisitions, since the licence fee for the books is coming from the college library budget.

Students at the college also have access to the college's e-mail systems, websites, and a computer lab with a variety of software, as well as a wireless network.

The College Store sells a variety of products in addition to books: these include uniforms, stationery, and art supplies. There is also a full-service restaurant on campus, which is open to the public, run by students. Recently, the college has started a campaign for students to bring non-students to the restaurant, by offering free desserts to students who bring a new person to the restaurant.

The college student council has set up a website where students can sell their art work or other products that they have developed or created. Five percent of the sale price goes to the student council and the rest goes to the student.

Required

a. Provide examples of how Bellwood College could engage in or provide the following types of e-commerce:

  (Note: Your examples must indicate a clear understanding of the type of e-commerce listed.)
  - Business-to-consumer (B2C)
  - Business-to-business (B2B)
  - Consumer-to-consumer (C2C)

b. For the following four e-commerce business models, describe the business model and explain how the college or the student council could use the business model.
  - Online direct marketing
  - Electronic tendering system
  - Viral marketing
  - Electronic marketplace or exchange

c. Describe three different types of electronic payments that Bellwood College could accept.

[Team Assignments]

1. Assign each team to one industry vertical. An industry vertical is a group of industries in the "same" business, such as financial services, insurance, manufacturing, retail, telecommunications, pharmaceuticals and chemicals, and so on. Each team will find five real-world applications of the major business-to-business models listed in the chapter. (Try success stories of vendors and EC-related magazines.) Examine the problems they solve or the opportunities they exploit.

2.  Have teams investigate how B2B payments are made in global trade. Consider instruments such as electronic letters of credit and e-cheques. Visit Global Payments Canada *www.globalpaymentsinc.com/Canada*, and examine its services to small and medium-size enterprises (SMEs). Also, investigate what Visa and MasterCard are offering. Finally, write a report summarizing your findings.

[Case 5.2 The Future of Shopping]

Once considered a retail pioneer, by late 2011 eBay (*www.ebay.com*) had become an auction wasteland and was mired in obsolete technology. In order to save the company, John Donahoe, eBay's new CEO, completely remodelled the company's business practices. He removed layers of bureaucracy between engineers and management, opened PayPal to outside developers, created a website that consumers could experiment with and comment on, and invested in new e-commerce technology. Donahoe also worked to reduce eBay's dependence on auctions as a source of revenue. By mid-2012, only 24 percent of eBay's revenue came from auctions, compared with 35 percent in previous years.

Donahoe also shifted eBay's focus as a website. He realized that the increased use of mobile devices was closing the gap between online and off-line shopping, and he wanted to locate eBay at the centre of the hybrid online/off-line shopping experience. According to Forrester Research, the financial potential in this new hybrid experience is much greater than that of simple e-commerce (i.e., browsing and buying online), which represents just 9 percent of all retail sales. Donahoe's vision for eBay's future is for the company to provide its customers with the ability to shop wherever they want, however they want, for the best price, and with the greatest convenience.

How did eBay go about accomplishing this goal and transitioning into a hybrid online/off-line shopping experience? The retailer followed the progression outlined below:

- Step 1: eBay purchased RedLaser (*www.redlaser.com*). RedLaser is a company whose technology allows consumers to scan bar codes, vehicle identification numbers, gift cards, asset tags, and QR codes with their mobile devices.
- Step 2: eBay purchased Milo (*www.milo.com*), a company that enables shoppers to view the inventory of off-line stores online 24/7. Although Milo had been able to sign on major retailers, the company was still relatively small. eBay, however, had the designers and developers who could help Milo overcome its technical challenges. In addition, eBay had more than 30 million merchants and sellers in its marketplace, many of whom had off-line inventory that Milo could incorporate into its inventory network. As a result, Milo's technology could help eBay list far more products than was previously possible.
- Step 3: eBay purchased GSI Commerce (*www.gsicommerce.com*), a company that builds e-commerce platforms for several hundred off-line retailers. GSI concentrates on customer care and on interactive marketing for its clients. This purchase helped eBay to improve its online customer interactions, strengthen its customer relationships, and provide superior customer service.
- Step 4: eBay purchased Where (*www.where.com*). Where builds location-based mobile apps for every major mobile device platform, including Android, iPhone, and BlackBerry. The company boasts 4 million active users per month. Where provides local listings for restaurants, bars, merchants, and events, and it suggests places and deals for its users based on their location and past behaviour. The absorption of Where into eBay allowed eBay customers to shop from any location. Further, Where enabled eBay to suggest additional products to customers based on their location.
- Step 5: eBay purchased Fig Card (*http://figcard.com*, bought by PayPal in 2011). Fig Card allows merchants to accept payments from mobile devices in stores by using a simple USB device that plugs into the cash register or point-of-sale terminal. To participate, customers simply need to download the Fig app onto their smartphone. Going further, once consumers set up their payment information and designate PayPal as a payment option, Fig Card is able to integrate with PayPal. This new functionality allowed eBay to expand the options that its customers could use to pay for purchases.
- Step 6: Since eBay already owned PayPal (www.paypal.com), it would drive every transaction to end with PayPal.

Consider these scenarios:

- You have met a friend for lunch, and you like her new handbag. You want to get one too. You take a picture of her purse with your smartphone. Your smartphone then uses an eBay app to identify all of the boutiques within a Three-mile radius that have the same colour and style of bag in stock, along with the price that each store charges. You then decide which store has your ideal combination of price and location, and you order the bag via your phone. After lunch, you visit that store, and you bypass the checkout lines by showing the salesperson the digital receipt on your phone.

- The local Starbucks "sees" you (i.e., it senses your smartphone's location) when you are two blocks away, and it offers you a dollar toward your next Frappuccino purchase. Starbucks puts the dollar into your PayPal account, where it sits for an hour, after which it is removed.
- What about the new Canon camera you are thinking about, but are not yet able to purchase? Scan the bar code (or RFID tag or QR code) into your PayPal "wish list." Then, when you walk by a retailer who has the camera in stock, that store can make you a special pricing offer that is better than you have found anywhere else.

Here is the model: eBay + RedLaser + Milo + GSI + PayPal + Fig Card + Where = Success!

Recall that eBay's new CEO wants to establish a complete shopping experience for the company's customers. With each piece of the puzzle, eBay has made it easier, faster, and more convenient for its customers to shop. Furthermore, the company's customers have more choices than ever before, and many of those choices are relevant to the customer's location. eBay's new model appears to be working. The company claims that, although all the pieces are not yet integrated, the model still facilitated nearly $4 billion in mobile transactions in 2011.

Questions

1. What are the advantages of eBay's hybrid shopping experience vision for the customer?
2. What are potential disadvantages of eBay's hybrid shopping experience vision for the customer?

Sources: Compiled from I. Steiner, "eBay's New X.Commerce Is Getting Some Legs," *eCommerce Bytes*, July 23, 2012; P. Demery, "eBay Turns to Technology," *Internet Retailer*, June 1, 2012; R. Kim, "With X.Commerce, eBay Eyes a Bigger Prize as Sales Enabler," *GigaOM*, October 12, 2011; D. Sacks, "How Jack Abraham Is Reinventing eBay," *Fast Company*, June 22, 2011; L. Rao, "eBay Closes $2.4 Billion Acquisition of GSI Commerce," *TechCrunch*, June 20, 2011; S. Kirsner, "eBay Buys Mobile Payments Start-up Fig Card, Second Boston Acquisition in April," *Boston.com*, April 28, 2011; www.milo.com, www.ebay.com, accessed March 20, 2013.

[Interactive Case]

Planning E-commerce Applications for Ruby's Club

Go to the Ruby's Club link at the Student Companion website or *WileyPLUS* for information about your current internship assignment. You will evaluate opportunities for e-commerce at Ruby's and build a spreadsheet application that will help Ruby's managers make decisions about e-commerce options.

APPENDIX E
DEVELOPING A BUSINESS PLAN

What's Next? A New Business Model for Restaurants

You're probably familiar with buying airline tickets and concert tickets in advance—but what about a restaurant meal? We're not talking about a fast-food chain; we're talking about a fine dining restaurant. Usually, restaurant customers walk in the door and hope to find a vacant table; if they plan ahead, they might call for a reservation. But the idea of purchasing advance tickets for a restaurant is new to most of us.

Grant Achatz is a well-known chef and restaurant owner. He has a new restaurant called Next—based on a new kind of business plan. Instead of taking reservations, the restaurant sells tickets. The plan makes sense. Next will probably be as popular as Achatz's other restaurant, Alina, which is sold out many weeks in advance. "We now pay three or four reservationists all day long to basically tell people they can't come to the restaurant," explains Achatz. When customers purchase tickets in advance, they are assured of a ready table just as they would with a reservation. Achatz and his partner, Nick Kokonas, will be able to save the costs of the full-time reservation staff. They plan to pass along savings like this to their diners. Selling tickets "allows us to give an experience that is actually a great value," notes Achatz.

Diners who want a meal at Next simply visit the restaurant's website. They can look at the menu, which changes four times a year, and then lock into the fixed price for the entire six-course meal. They can also choose to dine at peak or off-peak hours, which will be reflected in the ticket price. For example, a table at 9:30 on a Tuesday night will cost less than a table at 8:00 on Saturday night. Meals range from $45 to $75, with wine and other beverages costing extra. A service charge—instead of a traditional tip—is included in the ticket price. This way, Achatz and Kokonas can distribute the gratuities among the staff as they see fit.

Achatz is known to offer unique dining experiences that many customers are willing to pay for. Next offers patrons a total experience in the cuisine of a specific place and time. It isn't just a theme; it's an experience that re-creates an era, with everything researched by Achatz and his team. The first offering was based on Paris in 1912, with Escoffier-era cuisine prepared, cooked, and served down to the last detail. When the menu changes, every three months, the chef may choose recipes that take diners to postwar Sicily or a fantasy of Chinese cuisine in the year 2020.

In the same way that sports fans buy season tickets, customers of Next can purchase a year's subscription to Next. That way they lock in the price and are guaranteed a reserved table for each of the seasonal menus. Achatz believes that once people get used to the idea of a prepaid meal, they will enjoy the experience. The dinner is paid for, and there's no fumbling for the wallet. "There's no transaction in the restaurant at all," Achatz points out. "So you can literally come in, sit down, start your experience, and when you're done, you just get up and leave."[1]

APPENDIX E OVERVIEW

Many entrepreneurs and small-business owners write business plans to help them organize their businesses, get them up and running, and raise money for expansion. In this appendix, we cover the basics of business planning: what business plans are, why they're important, and who needs them. We also explain the steps involved in writing a good plan and the major elements it should include. Finally, we cover additional resources to get you started with your own business plan—to help you bring your unique ideas to reality with a business of your own.

WHAT IS A BUSINESS PLAN?

You may wonder how the millions of different businesses operating throughout the world today got their start. Many of them got started with a formal business plan. A *business plan* is a written document that defines what a company's objectives are, how these objectives will be achieved, how the business will be financed, and how much money the company expects to bring in. In short, it describes where a company is, where it wants to go, and how it intends to get there.

Why a Business Plan Is So Important

A well-written business plan serves two key functions:

1. It organizes the business and validates (or gives justification for) its central idea.
2. It summarizes the business and its strategy to obtain funding from lenders and investors.

First, a business plan gives a business formal direction, whether it is just starting, going through a phase of growth, or struggling. The business plan forces the principals—the owners—to do some thorough planning, to think through the realities of running and financing a business. In their planning, they consider many details. How will inventory be stored, shipped, and stocked? Where should the business be located? How will the business use the Internet? And most important, how will the business make enough money to make it all worthwhile?

A business plan also gives the owners a well-thought-out blueprint, or plan, to refer to when daily challenges come up. It also acts as a benchmark by which successes and disappointments can be measured. A solid business plan will sell the potential owner on the real possibilities of the idea. In some cases, the by-product of developing the plan is demonstrating to a dreamy person that he or she is trying to start a business that won't work. In other words, the process of writing a plan benefits a would-be businessperson as much as the final plan benefits potential investors.

Finally, a business plan communicates the business's strategy to financiers who may fund the business. A business plan is usually required to obtain a bank loan. Lenders and venture capitalists need to see that the business owner has thought through the critical issues and has presented a promising idea before they will consider investing. After all, they're really interested in whether investing in the business will bring them significant returns.

Who Needs a Business Plan?

Every business owner who expects to be successful needs a business plan. Some people mistakenly believe that they need a business plan only if it will land on the desk of a venture capitalist or the loan committee of a bank. Others think that writing a plan is unnecessary if their bank or lending institution doesn't need it. But these people miss the point of planning. A business plan acts as a map to guide the way through the often tangled roads of running a business. Every small-business owner should develop a business plan because it empowers that person to take control.

> **Take a few minutes to read and answer these questions. Don't worry about answering in too much detail at this point. The questions are preliminary and intended to help you think through your venture.**
>
> 1. In general terms, how would you explain your idea to a friend?
> 2. What is the purpose or objective of your venture?
> 3. What service are you going to provide, or what goods are you going to manufacture?
> 4. Is there any significant difference between what you are planning and what already exists?
> 5. How will the quality of your product compare with competitive offerings?
> 6. What is the overview of the industry or service sector you are going to enter? Write it out.
> 7. What is the history, current status, and future of the industry?
> 8. Who is your customer or client base?
> 9. Where and by whom will your good or service be marketed?
> 10. How much will you charge for the product you are planning?
> 11. Where is the financing going to come from to initiate your venture?
> 12. What training and experience do you have that qualifies you for this venture?
> 13. Does such training or experience give you a significant edge?
> 14. If you lack specific experience, how do you plan to gain it?

FIGURE E.1 Self-Evaluation Questions

proper information, they will quickly move on to the next business plan in the stack. The executive summary is also important to people funding the business with their own resources. The business plan channels their motivations into a clear, well-written mission statement. It is a good idea to write the executive summary last because it will almost always be revised again, when the business plan takes its final shape.

To write an effective executive summary, focus on the issues that are most important to your business's success, and save the supporting information for the body of the business plan. The executive summary should describe the firm's strategy and goals, the good or service it is selling, and the advantages it has over the competition. It should also give a quick overview of how much money will be required to launch the business, how the money will be used, and how the lenders or investors will recoup their funds.

Introduction

The introduction follows the executive summary. After the executive summary has offered an attractive overview, the introduction should begin to discuss the fine details of the business. It should include any material the upcoming marketing and financing sections do not cover. The introduction should describe the company, the management team, and the product in detail. If one

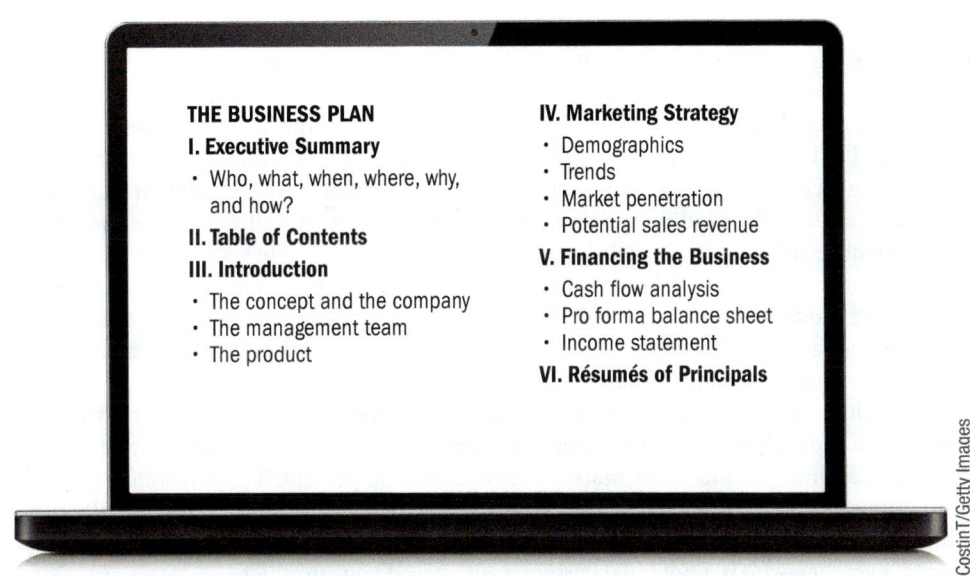

FIGURE E.2 Outline of a Business Plan

of these topics is particularly noteworthy for your business, you may want to present that topic as its own section. Listen to what you write and respond as the plan takes shape.

Include basic information about the company—its past, present, and future. What are the company's roots, what is its current status, and what actions does it need to take to achieve its goals? If you are starting a company, include a description of the evolution of the concept. Be sure to tie all of the business's goals and plans to the industry it will operate in, and describe the industry itself.

A business doesn't run itself, of course. People are the heart of a business, so write an interesting profile of the business's management team. Who are the key players and how does their experience support the company's goals? Describe their—or your, if you are a sole proprietor (an owner–operator)—education, training, and experience, and highlight and refer to résumés included later in the plan. Be honest—not all businesses are started by experts. If you lack demonstrated experience in a certain area, explain how you plan to gain experience.

Also describe the product, which is the driving force behind the venture. What are you offering, and why is it special? What are the costs of the service or the price tag on the good? Analyze the features of the offering and the effect these features have on the overall cost.

Marketing Strategy

Next comes the marketing strategy section. The *marketing strategy* describes the market's need for the item and the way the business will fulfill it. Marketing strategies are not based on informal projections or observations. They are the result of a careful market analysis. Putting together a marketing strategy allows the business owner to become familiar with every aspect of the particular market. If done properly, it will allow you to define your target market and position your business within that sector to get its share of sales.

The marketing strategy will include discussing the size of the customer base that will want to purchase your good or service and the projected rate of growth for the product or category. Highlight information on the demographics of your customers. *Demographics* are statistical characteristics of the segment of the market, such as income, gender, and age. What types of people will purchase your product? How old are they, and where do they live? What is their lifestyle like? For example, someone starting an interior design business will want to report how many homeowners live within a certain distance from the firm and their median income. Of course, this section of the marketing analysis will be quite different for a company that does all of its business online. You will want to know the types of people who will shop at your website, but your discussion won't be limited to one geographic area. It is also a good idea to describe the trends in your product category. Trends are consumer and business tendencies or patterns that business owners can use to gain market share.

The marketing strategy should also detail your distribution, pricing, and promotional goals. Discuss the average price of your offering and the reasons behind the price you have chosen. How do you intend to let your potential customers know that you have a product to sell? How will you sell it—through a catalogue, in a retail location, online, or maybe a combination of all three? The effectiveness of your distribution, pricing, and promotional goals will determine the extent to which you will be able to gain market share.

Competitors are another important part of your marketing strategy. What companies are already selling products similar to yours? Include a list of your competitors to show that you know exactly who they are and what you are up against. Describe what you think are their major strengths and weaknesses and how successful they have been within your market.

Also include the *market penetration,* which is the percentage of total customers who have purchased a company's product. For example, if there are 10,000 people in your market, and 5,000 have purchased your product, your market penetration is 50 percent. The *potential sales revenue,* also an important figure to include, is the total revenue of a company if it captured 100 percent market penetration. In other words, this figure represents the total dollar value of sales you would bring in if everyone who is a potential customer purchased your product.

Financing the Business

The goal of a business is to make money. Everything in the business plan lays the foundation for the *financing section.* Business owners should not skip this section even if they are not seeking outside money. It is crucial to have an accurate financial analysis to get financing, but it also is a necessary exercise for business owners funding the venture themselves. The financing section shows the cost of the product, operating expenses, expected sales revenue and profit, and the amount of the business owner's personal funds that will be invested to get the business up and running. The financial projections should be encouraging but also accurate and based on realistic assumptions. The owner should be able to defend the numbers projected.

Any assumptions made in the body of the business plan should be tied into the financial section. For example, if you think you will need a staff of five, your cash flow analysis should explain how you are going to pay them. A cash flow analysis, a required section of a financial analysis, shows how much money will flow through your business throughout the year. It helps you plan for staggered purchasing, high-volume months, and slow periods. Your business may be cyclical or seasonal; the cash flow projection lets you know whether you need to arrange a line of credit to cover periodic shortfalls. An income statement is another critical document. The income statement is a statement of income and expenses your company has taken on over a period of time.

Remember that leaving out important details can reduce your credibility, so be thorough. The plan must include your assumptions about the conditions under which your business will operate. It should cover details such as market strength; date of startup; sales buildup; gross profit margin; equipment, furniture, and fixtures required; and payroll and other key expenses that will affect the financial plan. In addition, a banker will want a pro forma balance sheet, which provides an estimate of what the business owns (its assets), what it owes (its liabilities), and what it is worth (the owner's equity). Refer to chapters 15, 16, and 17 of *Contemporary Business* for additional details on accounting, financial statements, and financial management.

Résumés of Principals

The final element of the business plan is the inclusion of the résumés of the principals behind the business: the management team. Each résumé should include detailed employment information and accomplishments. Consider expanding on the traditional résumé by including business affiliations, professional memberships, hobbies, and leisure activities, but only if this information applies to your business.

Whichever method you choose to develop a business plan, make sure that *you* develop the plan. It should sound as though it was written by the entrepreneur, not by some outside "expert."

RESOURCES

Whether a person has been in business for decades or is just starting out, many resources are available. A tremendous amount of material can help business owners write effective business plans. The biggest task is narrowing down the resources to the ones that are right for you. The Internet offers many sound business-planning tools and advice, much of which are free. You can look up different examples and opinions, which is important. Remember that no one source will match your situation exactly. Your library and career centre also offer many resources. Following are some helpful resources for business planning.

Books

Dozens of books describe how to write a business plan. Examples include the following:

- Edward Blackwell, *How to Prepare a Business Plan*, 5th ed. (London: Kogan Page Ltd., 2011).
- Michael Gerber, *The E-Myth Enterprise: How to Turn a Great Idea into a Thriving Business* (New York: Harper Collins, 2010).
- Mike McKeever, *How to Write a Business Plan*, 11th ed. (Berkeley, CA: Nolo Press, 2012).
- John W. Mullins, *The New Business Road Test: What Entrepreneurs and Executives Should Do Before Writing a Business Plan*, 3rd ed. (Financial Times/Prentice Hall, 2012).
- Steven D. Peterson, Peter E. Jaret, and Barbara Findlay Schenck, *Business Plans Kit for Dummies*, 4th ed. (Wiley, 2013).
- Hal Shelton, *The Secrets to Writing a Successful Business Plan: A Pro Shares a Step-by-Step Guide to Creating a Plan That Gets Results* (Rockville, MD: Summit Valley Press, 2014).
- Paul Tiffany, Steven D. Peterson, and Nada Wagner, *Business Plans for Canadians for Dummies*, 2nd ed. (Wiley, 2012).

Websites

- *Entrepreneur, Inc.* and *BusinessWeek* magazines offer knowledgeable guides to writing a business plan. *Entrepreneur*'s website also contains sample business plans.

    www.entrepreneur.com

    www.inc.com

    www.bloomberg.com

- If you are hoping to obtain funding with your business plan, it is a good idea to become familiar with what investors are looking for. The following are professional associations for the venture capital industry:

    www.cvca.ca/ (Canadian Venture Capital & Private Equity Association)

    www.nvca.org (National Venture Capital Association)

    www.sbia.org (Small Business Investor Alliance)

    www.bdc.ca/EN/bdc-capital/venture-capital/Pages/venture-capital.aspx (Business Development Bank of Canada - BDC Capital)

Software

Business-planning software can help to give an initial shape to your business plan. But a word of caution if you write a business plan using a software template—bankers and potential investors, such as venture capitalists, read so many business plans that the plans that are based on templates may sink to the bottom of the pile. Also, if you aren't looking for funding, using software can undercut a chief purpose of writing a plan—learning about your unique idea. Think twice before you deprive yourself of that experience. Remember, software is a tool. It can help you get started, stay organized, and build a professional-looking business plan, but it can't actually write the plan for you.

Associations and Organizations

Many government and professional organizations provide assistance to would-be business owners. Here is a partial list:

- The Business Development Bank of Canada (BDC) is Canada's business development bank providing Canadian businesses with flexible financing, venture capital, and consulting services.

    www.bdc.ca/Pages/SplashPage.aspx

- The U.S. Small Business Administration offers planning materials, along with other resources.

    www.sba.gov/category/navigation-structure/starting-managing-business

- The SBA also has a centre specifically designed for female entrepreneurs.

    www.sba.gov/content/women-owned-businesses

PROJECTS AND TEAMWORK APPLICATIONS

1. Visit the website for Next Restaurant at www.nextrestaurant.com to learn more about the restaurant's innovative method of selling tickets in advance. Think of another business that doesn't usually sell tickets in advance—yet. Write a brief plan for converting that business to the pre-selling business model. Why do you think this business would be successful? What might be the drawbacks?

2. Do you dream of starting your own business? Take your idea and answer as many of the self-evaluation questions in **Figure E.1** as you can. Share your answers with the class. Then file your answers away to read at a future date—either when you have graduated from college or university or when you think you are ready to pursue your own business.

3. Write the executive summary portion of the business plan for your potential business. You may use the answers to the questions in **Figure E.1** to help you get started.

APPENDIX G
CAREERS IN CONTEMPORARY BUSINESS

You'll be hitting the job market soon—if you haven't already. Regardless of what industry you want to work in—financial services, marketing, travel, construction, hospitality, manufacturing, wireless communications—you need an education. Attending college or university and taking a business course like this one will help you in your job search. Business skills and knowledge are needed in many different fields. But education comes in many forms. In addition to taking classes, you should try to gain related real-life experience. A summer job, an internship, or even a volunteer opportunity can give you excellent experience that you can build on after you graduate. Cooperative education programs and work–study programs can also give you hands-on experience while you pursue your education. Many students across the country will be doing the same thing, but you can set yourself apart through your work ethic and initiative.

Once you leave school, you will need to earn a living—if you aren't already doing so. Your level of education will probably affect your earnings. There is a wide gap between earnings for high-school graduates and earnings for college or university graduates. And there is still a gap between earnings for men and women.[1]

Keep in mind that a degree may help you get in the door for certain job interviews and may put you on a path for advancement, but a degree doesn't guarantee success—you have to achieve that yourself.

Companies plan their hiring strategies carefully to attract and keep the most productive, creative employees and to avoid the cost of rehiring. So, soon-to-be graduates need to be on their toes. But creativity is common among business students. By the time you finish this class—and your college or university education—you will be well equipped to take on the challenge. You can think of your job hunt as a course in itself; at the end of it, you will have a job. And you will be well on your way toward a rewarding business career.

This course exposes you to all the functional areas of business. You learn how firms are organized and operated. You find out who does what in a company. Gradually, you identify industries and disciplines—such as sales, finance, or product design—that interest you. And you learn about many organizations, large and small—who founded them, what products they offer, how they serve their customers, and what types of decisions they make. In short, you gain knowledge about business that you can apply to your career search and life.

Choosing a career is an important life decision. It sets you on a path that will influence where you live, how much money you earn, what type of people you meet, and what you do every day. Whether your goal is to operate an organic farm or to rise high in the ranks of a major corporation, you'll need to understand the principles of business. Even if you think you're headed down a different path, business skills almost always prove to be helpful. Also, many fields are beginning to recognize the importance of a broader base of knowledge than specialized technical skills—and business knowledge is part of that base.

For example, engineers once relied almost solely on a foundation of technical skill and expertise. But experts in the industry now report a trend toward a more well-rounded education. Engineers still need a strong technical foundation, but they need additional skills. "There's no question that the employee who can do five things is harder to get rid of than the one who can only do one or two," says an engineer who held onto his job during the economic downturn. "The more diverse your toolset, the more stable your job will be."[2] That's why this appendix discusses the best way to approach career decisions and to prepare for an *entry-level job*—your first permanent employment after leaving school. We then look at a range of business careers and discuss employment opportunities in a variety of fields.

It's important to remember that you'll be looking for a job regardless of the state of the overall economy, whether it's slow or booming. You'll read about job cuts and unemployment rates, hiring freezes and wage increases. But if you stay flexible and are ready to work—just about any time and anywhere—you'll succeed.[3]

INTERNSHIPS—A GREAT WAY TO ACQUIRE REAL-WORLD EXPERIENCE

Many business students complete one or more *internships* prior to completing their academic careers. Some arrange internships during the summer, while others work at an internship during a semester away from school. An internship gives you hands-on experience in a real business environment, whether it's in banking, the hotel industry, or retailing. An internship does two helpful things: it teaches you how a business runs and can help you decide whether you want to pursue a career in that industry. You might spend a summer interning in the admissions department of a hospital and then graduate with your job search focused on hospital administration. Or you might decide you'd much rather work for a magazine publisher or a construction company.

When you apply for an internship, don't expect to be paid much, if at all. The true value of an internship lies in its hands-on experience. An internship bridges the theory–practice educational gap. It will help carry you from your academic experience to your professional future. Keep in mind that, as an intern, you will not be running a department. People may not ask for your input or ideas. You may work in the warehouse or copy centre. You might be answering phones or entering data. But it is important to make the most of your internship. Many companies make permanent job offers—or offers to enter paid training programs—to the best interns, so you'll want to stand out.

Internships can serve as critical networking and job-hunting tools. They often lead to future employment opportunities, allowing students to demonstrate their technical skills while providing cost-effective employee training for the company. Even if you aren't hired by the company where you interned, the experience is valuable to your job hunt. One study estimates that almost one-third of all entry-level hires had internships prior to being hired. In a recent year, PricewaterhouseCoopers hired 91 percent of its entry-level employees from those who had interned.[4]

With this information in mind, start thinking the way a professional does. Here are some tips for a successful internship experience. These guidelines are also helpful for your first job.

- **Dress like a professional.** Dress appropriately for your future career. During an interview visit, look around to see what the employees are wearing. If you have any questions, ask your supervisor.

- **Act like a professional.** Arrive on time to work. Be punctual for any meetings or assignments. Ask questions and listen to the answers carefully. Complete your work thoroughly and on time. Maintain good etiquette. Be polite on the phone, in meetings, and in all interactions with other people.

- **Stand out.** Work hard and show initiative, but behave appropriately. Don't try to use authority that you do not have. Show that you are willing to learn.

- **Be evaluated.** Even if your internship does not include a formal evaluation, ask your employer how you are doing so you can learn about your strengths and weaknesses.

- **Keep in touch.** Once you complete your internship, stay in touch periodically with the firm so that people know what you are currently doing.

Internships provide college and university students with critical hands-on experience. It is important for students to make the most of the opportunities that internships provide both in terms of experience and a future job hunt once they have completed their schooling.

An excellent source of information to begin your search for an internship can be found at the Canadian government's Youth Canada website, www.youth.gc.ca/eng/topics/career_planning/index.shtml.

In addition to an internship, you can build your résumé with work and life experience through volunteer opportunities, extracurricular activities, and summer or off-campus study programs. *Cooperative education* also provides valuable experience. Cooperative education programs are similar to internships, but the jobs themselves usually pay more. These programs may take place during the summer or during the school year. Students typically take classes one semester and hold jobs the next semester. Most cooperative programs are specific to a major field of study, such as retailing or information technology. At your cooperative job, you'll be treated like a real full-time employee, meaning you'll work long hours and probably have more responsibility than you would as an intern. And depending on how these programs are scheduled, you might add a semester or two to your college education. But in the long run, you will gain knowledge and work experience that will serve you well as you build your career.[5]

SELF-ASSESSMENT FOR CAREER DEVELOPMENT

You are going to spend much of your lifetime working, so why not find a job—or at least an industry—that interests you? To choose the line of work that suits you best, you must first understand yourself. Self-assessment involves looking in the mirror and seeing the real you—with all your strengths and weaknesses. It means answering some tough questions. But being honest with yourself pays off because it will help you find a career that will be challenging, rewarding, and meaningful. As you get to know yourself better, you may discover that helping other people really makes you happy. You may realize that to feel secure, you need to earn enough to put away substantial savings. Or you might learn that you are drawn to risks and the unknown, which might point you toward owning your own business. Each of these discoveries provides you with valuable information in choosing a career.

Many resources are available to help you in selecting a career. They include school libraries, career guidance and placement offices, counselling centres, and online job-search services. They include alumni from your college, friends, family, and neighbours. Don't forget the contacts you make during an internship—they can help you in many ways. Ask questions of anyone you know—a local retailer, banker, or restaurant owner. Most people will be happy to speak with you or arrange a time to do so.

If you are interested in a particular industry or company, you might be able to arrange an informational interview—an appointment with someone who can provide you with more knowledge about an industry or career path. This type of interview is different from an interview after you've applied for a specific job, although it may ultimately lead to a job. The informational interview can help you decide whether you want to pursue a particular type of work. It also gives you some added experience in the interview process—without the pressure. To arrange an interview, talk to anyone you know—friends of your parents, local businesspeople, or coordinators of not-for-profit organizations. Your school may have a database of graduates who are working in various fields and who are willing to talk with students on an informational basis—so be sure to start your search right at your own school.

To help you get started asking and answering the questions that will help you begin looking in the right direction, you can visit a number of websites that offer online career assessment tests. Career Explorer, at www.careerexplorer.net is one such site; LiveCareer at https://ww2.livecareer.com is another. These sites and others, such as Monster's Career Tools and Career Advice areas at http://english.monster.ca/geo/siteselection, help you identify your interests, strengths, and weaknesses—including some that may surprise you.[6] In addition, follow the self-assessment process outlined in the next section to learn more about yourself.

The Self-Assessment Process

For a thorough assessment of your goals and interests, follow these steps:

1. **Outline your career interests.** What field or work activities interest you? What rewards do you want to gain from work?

2. **Outline your career goals.** What do you want to achieve through your career? What type of job can you see yourself doing? Where do you see yourself in a year? In five years? Do you have an ultimate dream job? How long are you willing to work to reach it? Write your goals down so that you can refer to them later.

3. **Make plans to reach your goal.** Do you need more education? Does the career require an apprenticeship or a certain number of years on the job? Outline the requirements you'll need to meet to reach your goal.

4. **List your skills and specific talents.** Write down your strengths—job skills you already have and skills you have developed in life. For example, you might know how to use financial software, and you might be good at negotiating with people. In addition, your school's career development office probably has standardized tests that can help test your aptitude for specific careers. However, take these only as a guideline. If you really want to pursue a certain career, go for it.

5. **List your weaknesses.** This can be tough—but it can also be fun. If you are shy about meeting new people, put shyness on your list. If you are quick to argue, admit it. If you aren't the best business-letter writer or think you're terrible at math, confess to yourself.

This list gives you an opportunity to see where you need improvement—and take steps to turn weaknesses into strengths.

6. **Briefly sketch out your educational background.** Write down the schools, colleges, universities, and special training programs you have attended, along with any courses you plan to complete before starting full-time employment. Make an honest assessment of how your background matches up with the current job market. Then make plans to complete any further education you may need.

7. **List the jobs you have held.** Include jobs that paid, internships, and volunteer opportunities. They all gave you valuable experience. As you make your list, think about what you liked and disliked about each. Maybe you liked working with the general public as a supermarket cashier. Perhaps you enjoyed caring for animals at a local shelter.

8. **Consider your hobbies and personal interests.** Many people have turned hobbies and personal pursuits into rewarding careers. Mick Jagger, lead singer of the Rolling Stones, has a master's degree from the London School of Economics. Without it, he probably wouldn't have been able to manage his rock group's vast business dealings. Jake Burton Carpenter earned a bachelor's degree in economics, but he loved winter sports. So he started a snow-board manufacturing company—and revolutionized the way people get from the top of a snowy mountain to the bottom. Cooking and catering star Paula Deen needed to support her young family. She loved the cooking from her own region—the South—so she opened a small business where she and her boys delivered freshly made bag lunches to local businesses. She went on to become a celebrity chef with her own television show. Today she has cookbooks, a website, retail products, and more.[7] Turning a hobby into a career doesn't happen overnight, and it's not easy. It requires the same amount of research and hard work as any other business. But for many people, it is a labour of love—and it ultimately succeeds because they refuse to give up.

JOB SEARCH GUIDELINES

Once you have narrowed your choice of career possibilities to two or three that seem right for you, get to work on your job search. Think about the qualities that made these career choices attractive to you. The same qualities also likely caught the attention of others, so you must expect competition. Locate available positions that interest you; then be resourceful! Your success depends on gathering as much information as possible.

Register at Your Career Centre

Register at your school's career centre. Set up an applicant file, including letters of recommendation and supporting personal information. Most placement offices send out periodic lists of new job vacancies by email, so be sure to get your name and email address on the list. Visit the office regularly, and become a familiar face. Find out how the office arranges interviews with company representatives who visit campus. If your school has a career event, make sure you attend.

Preparing Your Job Credentials

Most placement or credential files include the following information:

1. Letters of reference from people who know you well—instructors and employers
2. Transcripts of course work to date
3. Personal data form to report factual information
4. Statement of career goals.

The career centre will provide you with special forms to help you to develop your file. Often, these forms can be completed online. Prepare the forms carefully because employers are always interested in your written communication skills. Keep a copy of the final file for later use in preparing similar information for other employment sources. Check back with the career centre to make sure your file is in order. Update it whenever necessary to reflect additional academic accomplishments and added work experiences.

Letters of reference are very important because they give prospective employers some personal and professional insights about you. They can influence a hiring decision. Make a careful list of people who might be willing to write letters of reference. Your references should not be family members or close friends. Instead, choose a coach, an instructor, a former employer, or someone else whose knowledge could help your job application. A soccer coach could vouch for your hard work and determination. A music teacher might be able to detail how well you accept instruction. A former employer might describe your punctuality and ability to get along with others. If possible, include someone from your school's business faculty on your list of references, or at least one of your current instructors.

Always ask people personally for letters of reference. Be prepared to give them a brief outline of your academic preparation and information about your job interests and career goals. This information will help them prepare their letters quickly and efficiently. It also shows that you are serious about the task and respect their time. Remember that these people are very busy. Allow them at least a couple of weeks to prepare their reference letters; then follow up politely if you haven't heard back. Always call or write to thank them for writing the letters.

Finding Employment through the Internet

The Internet plays an important role in connecting employers and job seekers. Companies of all sizes post their job opportunities on the Web, both on their own sites and on job sites such as Monster.ca, HotJobsCanada.ca, and CareerBuilder.ca. Specialized, or niche, sites such as AccountingJobs.ca and TechJobsCanada.com are also gaining popularity. Some sites are free to applicants, while others charge a subscription fee. **Figure G.1** provides a sampling of general and focused career sites.

Career websites typically offer job postings, tips on creating an effective résumé, a place to post your résumé, and advice on interviews and careers. If this sounds easy, keep in mind that these sites may receive hundreds of thousands of hits each day from job hunters, which means you have lots of competition. You can still use one of these sites as part of your job search; just don't

General and Staffing Sites
Monster.ca
HotJobsCanada.ca
CareerBuilder.ca
KellyServices.ca

Government Sites
http://jobs-emplois.gc.ca/index-eng.htm
www.govjobs.ca

Industry
Health care—www.healthcarejob.ca
Business & finance—www.accountingjobs.ca/en; www.efinancialcareers-canada.com/
Marketing—www.marketing-jobs.ca
Sales—www.cpsa.com/recruit/index.aspx
Technology—www.techjobscanada.com

FIGURE G.1 Internet Job Sites

make it your only source. Smart job seekers often find that their time is better spent on specialized job boards that offer more focused listings. Naturally, if a particular company interests you, go to the firm's website, where available positions will be posted. If you are interested in applying for a job at the accounting firm Ernst & Young, go to www.ey.com. If you are looking for a job with Whole Foods Market, visit www.wholefoodsmarket.com. And if you fancy yourself working for an outdoor retailer, go to MEC (Mountain Equipment Co-op) at www.mec.ca.

Newspapers, the source for traditional classified want ads, also post their ads on the Web. Job seekers can even visit sites that merge ads from many different newspapers into one searchable database, such as CareerBuilder (www.careerbuilder.ca). Some sites go a step farther and create separate sections for each career area. For example, entire sections may be devoted to accounting, marketing, and other business professions. Searches can then be narrowed according to geographic location, entry level, company name, job title, job description, and other categories.

As mentioned earlier, you can connect with potential employers by posting your résumé on job sites. Employers search the résumé database for prospects with the right qualifications. One commonly used approach is for an employer to list one or more *keywords* to select candidates for personal interviews—for example, "retail sales experience," "network architecture," or "spa management"—and then browse the résumés that contain all the required keywords. Employers also scan résumés into their human resource database. Then, when a manager requests, for example, 10 candidates, the database can be searched by keywords that apply to the request. Job seekers need to respond to this type of computer screening of applicants by ensuring that right keywords appear on their résumés.

Finding Employment through Other Sources

Earlier, we mentioned the importance of registering at your school's career planning or placement office. If you have completed formal academic coursework at more than one institution, you may be able to set up a placement file at each school. In addition, you may want to contact private and public employment services available in your location or in the area where you would like to live.

Private Employment Agencies

These firms often specialize in certain types of jobs, such as marketing, finance, sales, or engineering. They help both employers and job candidates by offering services that are not available elsewhere. Many private agencies interview, test, and screen job applicants so that potential employers do not have to. Job candidates benefit from the service by being accepted by the agency and because the agency makes the first contact with the potential employer.

A private employment agency usually charges the employer a fee for finding a suitable employee. Other firms charge job seekers a fee for helping find them a job. Make sure that you understand the terms of any agreement you sign with a private employment agency.

Employment Offices

Don't forget to check the government employment offices in your area. Because of the mix of duties, some people view government employment agencies as providing services for semiskilled or unskilled workers. However, these agencies *do* list jobs in many professional categories and are often intimately involved with identifying job finalists for major new facilities moving to your area. In addition, many of the jobs listed at government employment offices may be with government agencies and may include professionals such as accountants, attorneys, healthcare professionals, and scientists.

Learning More about Job Opportunities

Carefully study the various employment opportunities you have identified. Obviously, you will like some more than others, but you can examine a variety of factors when assessing each job possibility:

- Actual job responsibilities
- Industry characteristics

- Nature of the company
- Geographic location
- Salary and opportunities for advancement
- How it supports your long-range career objectives.

Too many job applicants consider only the most striking features of a job, such as its location or the salary offer. But a comprehensive review of job openings should provide a balanced view of the overall employment opportunity, including both long-term and short-term factors.

BUILDING A RÉSUMÉ

Regardless of how you locate job openings, you must learn how to prepare and submit a *résumé*, a written summary of your personal, educational, and professional achievements. The résumé is a personal document covering your educational background, work experience, career preferences and goals, and any related major interests. It also includes such basic contact information as your home and email addresses and your telephone number. It should *not* include information on your age, marital status, race, or ethnic background.

Your résumé is usually your formal introduction to an employer, so it should present you in the best light, highlighting your strengths and your ability to contribute to a firm. But it should *never* contain inflated statements or wrong information. You don't want to begin your career with unethical behaviour, and an employer is bound to discover any conflicts in fact—either immediately or during the months following your employment. Either event will disrupt your career path.

Organizing Your Résumé

The primary purpose of a résumé is to highlight your qualifications for a job, usually on a single page. An attractive layout makes it easier for the employer to review your qualifications. You can prepare your résumé in several ways. You may use narrative sentences to explain job duties and career goals, or you may present information in outline form. A résumé included as part of your credentials file at the career centre on campus should be quite short. Remember to design it around your specific career objectives.

Figures G.2, G.3, and **G.4** illustrate different ways to organize your résumé—by *reverse chronology*, or time; by *function*; and by *results*. Regardless of which format you select, you will want to include the following: a clearly stated objective, your work or professional experience, your education, your personal interests such as sports or music, and your volunteer work. While all three formats are acceptable, one study showed that 78 percent of employers preferred the reverse chronological format—with the most recent experience listed first—because it was the easiest to follow.

Tips for Creating a Strong Résumé

Your résumé should help you stand out from the crowd, just as your college or university admissions application did. A company may receive hundreds or even thousands of résumés, so you want yours to be on the top of the stack. Here are some do's and don'ts:

Do:

- State your immediate objective clearly. If you are applying for a specific job, say so. State why you want the job and why you want to work at this company.
- Use terms related to your field, so that a human resource manager can spot those terms quickly. If you are submitting your résumé online, use words that will create an automatic "match" with a job description or field. If you are applying for an entry-level job in marketing, the phrase

"communication skills" is likely to generate a match. You can identify such words and phrases by reading job descriptions online.

- Provide facts about previous jobs, internships, cooperative education programs, or volunteer work, including results or specific achievements. Include any projects or tasks you undertook through your own initiative.
- Emphasize your education if you are a recent graduate. Place it closer to the top of your résumé instead of near the bottom.
- Highlight your strengths and skills, such as research, writing, or organizing.
- Write clearly and concisely.
- Proofread your résumé carefully for grammar, usage, and typographical errors. Refer to a dictionary or style manual.
- Keep your résumé to a single page.

FELICIA SMITH-WHITEHEAD
4265 Popular Lane
Toronto, ON, M4Y 2K2,
416-555-3296
FeliciaSW@gmail.com

OBJECTIVE
Challenging office management position in a results-oriented company where my organizational and people skills can be applied; leading to an operations management position.

WORK EXPERIENCE
ADM Distribution Enterprises, Toronto, ON   2015–Present
Office Manager of leading regional soft-drink bottler. Coordinate all bookkeeping, correspondence, scheduling of 12-truck fleet to serve 300 customers, promotional mailings, and personnel records, including payroll. Install computerized systems.

Merriweather, Hicks & Bradshaw Attorneys, Toronto, ON   2013–2015
Office Supervisor and Executive Assistant for Douglas H. Bradshaw, Managing Partner. Supervised four clerical workers and two paraprofessionals, automated legal research and correspondence functions, and assisted in coordinating outside services and relations with other firms and agencies. Promoted three times from Secretary to Office Supervisor.

Conner & Sons Custom Coverings, Toronto, ON   2009–2013
Secretary in father's upholstery and awning company. Performed all office functions over the years, running the office when the owner was on vacation.

EDUCATION
Humber College, Business Studies Certificate   2013
North Toronto Collegiate, Honours   2009

COMPUTER SKILLS
Familiar with Microsoft Office and Adobe Acrobat

LANGUAGE SKILLS
Fluent in French (speaking and writing)
Adequate speaking and writing skills in Portuguese

PERSONAL
Member of various community associations; avid reader; enjoy sports such as camping and cycling; enjoy volunteering in community projects.

FIGURE G.2 Chronological Résumé

FIGURE G.3 Functional Résumé

Eric Greene
Five Oceanside Drive, Apt. 6B
Cavendish, Prince Edward Island
902-444-3838
egreene87@gmail.com

Objective
Joining a growth-oriented company that values highly productive employees. Seeking an opportunity that leads to senior merchandising position.

Professional Experience
Administration
Management responsibilities in a major retailing buying office, coordinated vendor-relation efforts. Supervised assistant buyers.

Category Management
Experience in buying home improvement and sport and recreation categories.

Planning
Chaired a team charged with reviewing the company's annual vendor evaluation program.

Problem Solving
Successfully developed a program to improve margins in the tennis, golf, and fishing lines.

Work Experience
Senior Buyer for Island Department Store	2015–Present
Merchandiser for Maritime Inc.	2012–2015

Education
Master's Degree in Business Administration
McGill University, Montreal   2010–2012

Bachelor's Degree
Dalhousie University, Halifax   2006–2010

Don't:

- Offer any misleading or inaccurate information.
- Make vague statements, such as "I work well with others," or "I want a position in business."
- State your objective as, "to run this company" or to "advance as quickly as possible."
- Include a salary request.
- Make demands about vacation time, work hours, or excessive benefits.
- Highlight your weaknesses.
- Submit a résumé with typos or grammatical errors.
- Use slang or other inappropriate phrases or comments.
- Include pictures or graphics, or use fancy fonts.[8]

Take your time with your résumé; it is one of the most important documents you'll create during your career. If you need help, go to your school's career centre. If you are dealing with an employment agency, a counsellor there can help.

ANTONIO PETTWAY
101 Beverly Road
Victoria, BC V8N 1S3
778-224-5764
apettway@yahoo.com

OBJECTIVE
To apply my expertise as a construction supervisor to a management role in an organization seeking improvements in overall production, long-term employee relationships, and the ability to attract the best talent in the construction field.

PROFESSIONAL EXPERIENCE
DAL Construction Company, Victoria, BC   2015–Present
  Established automated, on-site recordkeeping system improving communications and morale between field and office personnel, saving 400 work hours per year, and reducing the number of accounting errors by 20 percent. Developed a crew selected as "first choice crew" by most workers wanting transfers. Completed five housing projects ahead of deadline and under budget.

Alberta Housing Authority, Lethbridge, AB   2013–2015
  Created friendly, productive atmosphere among workers enabling first on-time job completion in 4 years and one-half of usual materials waste. Initiated pilot materials delivery program with potential savings of 3.5 percent of yearly maintenance budget.

Essex County Housing Authority, Windsor, ON   2013
  Produced information pamphlets increasing applications for county housing by 22 percent. Introduced labor-management discussion techniques saving jobs and over $29,000 in lost time.

Payton, Durnbell & Associates Architects, London, ON   2012–2013
  Developed and monitored productivity improvements, saving 60 percent on information transfer costs for firm's 12 largest jobs.

EDUCATION
University of Windsor, Bachelor's degree in Business   2008–2012

COMPUTER SKILLS
Familiar with Microsoft Office and Adobe Acrobat

PERSONAL
Highly self-motivated. Willing to relocate. Enjoy tennis and hiking.

FIGURE G.4 Results-Oriented Résumé

Keep in mind that you will probably need to tailor your résumé to each company or job. Again, take the time to do this; it may mean the difference between standing out and being lost in a sea of other applicants.

Preparing Your Cover Letter

In most cases, your résumé will be sent with a *cover letter*. This letter should introduce who you are, explain why you are submitting a résumé (cite the specific job opening if possible), and inform the recipient where you can be reached for an interview. An effective cover letter will make the recipient want to take the next step and read your résumé. Here are a few tips for preparing an outstanding letter:

- Write the letter to a specific person, if possible. A letter addressed to "to whom it may concern" may never reach the right person. Call the company or check its website for the name of the person you should address your letter to. It might be someone in human resources or a person in the department where you'd actually be working. Be sure to obtain the person's title if possible (such as general manager or director)—and spell the person's name correctly.

- Introduce yourself and explain the purpose of your letter—to apply for a job.
- Describe briefly an example of your best work or your most ambitious project.
- Keep it short—a page is acceptable, half a page even better.
- Request an interview.
- Thank the person for his or her time and consideration.
- Make sure all your contact information is in the letter—name, address, home phone number, cellphone number, and email address.
- Proofread your letter carefully.[9]

Submitting Your Online Résumé

You may write a sparkling cover letter and an expert résumé. But if your online submission is blocked or tossed aside by an automated processing system, you'll never have a chance to impress the person it was intended for. Here are a few tips for making certain your letter and résumé reach their destination.

- Review the formatting of your résumé to make sure it will appear the same to the recipient as it does to you. Delete any unusual symbols or fonts.
- Use keywords that create a match and allow your résumé through the company's filter. This tip also applies to the subject line of your email, which should be specific and contain keywords such as "application for sales trainee job."
- Include your cover letter in the email.
- Send your résumé in the body of the email—not as an attachment. This is more convenient for the recipient. It also avoids the disaster of having your attachment automatically deleted by an antivirus system.
- Do not send graphics, because they may be blocked or deleted.
- If you are answering an ad, read the instructions for application and follow them exactly.[10]

THE JOB INTERVIEW

Congratulations! You've prepared an effective résumé, and you've been contacted for an interview. An interview is more than a casual conversation. During an interview, at least one manager will learn about you, and you'll learn more about the company and the job. Although you may feel nervous about the interview, you can control some of its outcome by doing your homework: planning and preparing for this important encounter with your potential employer. Before you meet with an interviewer, learn everything you can about the firm. The simplest way to do this is to visit the company's website. You can also check with your school's career centre. If you know anyone who works for the company, ask that person about the firm. Try to learn the answers to the following questions about the organization:

- What does the firm do—manufacture clothing, market snack foods, produce films, sell cars? If you are applying for a job at a large corporation, zero in on the division where you would be working.
- What is the company's mission? Many firms include a statement about their purpose in the business world—to supply affordable energy to communities, to serve fresh food, to make communication easier. Understanding why the company exists will help you grasp where it is headed and why.
- Where, when, and by whom was the company founded? Learn a little about the history of the firm.
- What is its position in the marketplace? Is it a leader or is it trying to gain a competitive advantage? Who are its main competitors?

- Where is the firm based? Does it have operations located around the country and the world, or is it purely local?
- How is the company organized? Are there multiple divisions and products?
- Learning about the firm shows the interviewer that you have initiative and motivation, and an interest in the firm's culture and history. You have taken the time and effort to find out more about the organization, and your enthusiasm shows.

Tips for Successful Interviewing

An interview is your personal introduction to the company. You want to make a good impression. But you also want to learn whether you and the firm are a good fit. Although the interviewer will be asking most of the questions, you will also want to ask some questions. People who conduct interviews say that the most important qualities candidates can exhibit are self-confidence, preparedness, and an ability to communicate clearly.

When you are contacted for an interview, find out the name(s) of the person or people who will be interviewing you. You can also ask whether the initial interview will be with a human resource manager or with the person to whom you would be reporting on the job, or both. Many people who conduct initial job interviews work in their firms' human resource divisions. These interviewers act as gatekeepers and can make recommendations to managers and supervisors about which individuals to interview further, or hire. Managers who head the units where an applicant will be employed may get involved later in the hiring process. Some hiring decisions come from human resource personnel together with the immediate supervisor of the prospective employee. In other cases, immediate supervisors make the decision alone. At your interview, keep in mind the following tips.

Do:

- **Dress appropriately.** Dress as if it is your first day of work at the firm. Conceal any tattoos or body piercings and wear simple jewellery.
- **Arrive a few minutes early.** These few minutes will give you time to relax and take in the surroundings. It also shows that you are punctual and care about other people's time.
- **Introduce yourself with a smile and a handshake.** Be friendly, but not overly familiar.
- **Be yourself—at your best.** Don't suddenly adopt a new personality. Be confident, polite, respectful, and interested in the people who are spending time with you. Be sure to thank each person who interviews you.
- **Listen.** Pay attention to what the interviewer is saying. If something is unclear, ask for clarification. Turn off your cellphone. Your full attention should be on the conversation you are having in the interview.
- **Use appropriate language.** As in your résumé and cover letter, be sure to use correct English. You don't need to be stiff or formal, but avoid slang or phrases that you know are inappropriate for the situation.
- **Be positive in your outlook.** Be enthusiastic about the firm and the job, but don't go overboard.

Don't:

- **Talk too much.** Avoid telling the interviewer a lot about your personal life, or why you left a particular job. Answer questions honestly and thoroughly, but don't dip into meaningless details.
- **Be arrogant or aggressive.** Self-confidence is a good trait, but don't go overboard by behaving in a superior or snobbish manner. Never be aggressive. Do not demand that the interviewer offer you the job or even another interview.

- **Act indifferent or bored.** This may not be the job you ultimately want, but treat the interview and the interviewer with respect and attention. If you make a good impression, the firm is likely to keep your name on file—and that dream job may appear after all.
- **Don't get ahead of yourself.** This is not the time to discuss salary, vacation, or benefits.[11]

Answering and Asking Questions

In a typical format, the interviewer gives you enough time to talk about yourself and your goals. You want to present your thoughts clearly and concisely, in an organized fashion, without rambling on to unrelated topics. The interviewer may wait until you are finished or prompt you to talk about certain subjects by asking questions. Be as specific as possible when answering questions. The questions that interviewers ask often include the following:

- "Why do you want this job?"
- "Why do you want to work in this field?"
- "What are your short-term goals? Long-term objectives?"
- "Where do you see yourself in five years? In 10 years?"
- "What are your strengths? What are your weaknesses?"
- "What motivates you?"
- "Describe a situation in which you made a tough decision or solved a problem."
- "What did you like best about your last job? What did you like least?"
- "Why did you leave your last job?"
- "Why should my firm hire you?"
- "Are you considering other jobs or companies?"

Some of these questions may seem tougher than others, but you can reduce your anxiety by preparing for them. First, think about which questions you fear the most. Then think about possible answers that are both truthful and positive. Rehearse your delivery in front of a mirror or with a friend.[12]

At some point, the interviewer will probably ask you whether you have any questions of your own. It's a good idea to come prepared with some questions, but you may think of other questions during the interview. Try to keep your list short, to three or four of your most important questions. The questions you ask show who you are—just as you revealed yourself when you answered the interviewer's questions. Here is a sample of appropriate questions for the initial interview:

- "Could you clarify a certain aspect of the job responsibilities for me?"
- "Do people who start in entry-level jobs at this company tend to develop their careers here?"
- "In what ways could I perform above and beyond the job requirements?"

At some point during your conversation, the interviewer may give you an idea of the salary range for the job. If not, he or she will do so during a subsequent interview. You may ask about the range, but do not ask exactly how much you will be paid if you get the job. Keep in mind that usually there is little or no negotiation for an entry-level salary. You can ask whether there is a probationary period with a review at the end of the period. Here are a few other questions *not* to ask:

- "When will I be promoted?"
- "How much time off do I get?"
- "When will I get my first raise?"
- "How many people are applying for this job?"
- "What are my chances of getting this job?"

At the end of the interview, be sure to thank the interviewer with a smile and a handshake, even if you both know the job is not for you. Again, another opportunity may come along in the future and you want to leave the door open. When you get home, write a note or email the interviewer, thanking him or her for the time spent with you. Thank-you notes really do make a lasting impression on a person, and it gives you another chance to reinforce your interest.

A successful first interview will often lead to a second interview. The purpose of this interview is to learn more about your specific qualifications and fit with the company. You may be introduced to more people—potential co-workers, people in other divisions, or sales staff. You may have another meeting with human resource staff, where you'll learn more about salary, employee benefits, and the firm's code of ethics. Depending on the type of job, you might be asked to take some skills tests. If you are entering a training program for a bank, you might be required to take some math-oriented tests. If you are going to work for a publisher, you might be asked to take an editing test or do some proofreading. If you are applying for a job as a sales representative, you may be given a test that assesses your personality traits. Don't be intimidated by these tests—you are not expected to know everything or be perfect—just do your best.

Making the Employment Decision

After receiving your résumé, conducting one or two interviews, and administering a skills test, a potential employer knows a lot about you. You should also know a lot about the company. If the experience has been positive on both sides, you may be offered a job. If you have interviewed at several companies and are offered more than one job, congratulations! You may receive a phone call, followed by a letter outlining the offer in writing. Whether you receive one offer or several, thank the person making the offer. If you choose to accept immediately, feel free to do so. If you have doubts about the job or need to decide between two, feel free to ask for 24 hours to respond. If you must decline an offer, do so promptly and politely. After all, you may end up working for that firm sometime in the future. If you get a few rejections before you receive an offer, don't give up. Every application and interview adds to your experience.

As you think about an offer, consider the parts of the job that are most important. You'll want to choose a job that comes closest to your career interests and objectives. But don't rule out the element of surprise—you might wind up with a job you like in an industry you'd never considered before. Don't worry too much about the salary. The point of an entry-level job is to get moving on a forward path. And keep in mind that your first job won't be your last. Once you have accepted an offer, you'll be given a start date and the name of the person to report to. Congratulations, you are now a member of the workforce!

Congratulations! You've accepted an offer for your first job. You are now a member of the workforce.

Nontraditional Students

Take a quick glance around your class. You'll likely see classmates of all ages. Some will fall into the traditional college age group of 18 to 22, but many don't. Perhaps you are a Canadian Armed Forces recruit returning from military duty overseas. Maybe you have been working in a full-time career but want to broaden your education. Students who fall outside the 18- to 22-year-old age group are often referred to as *nontraditional students,* but these students have become the norm on many campuses. Other examples of nontraditional students are homemakers returning to school to freshen up their résumés before returning to the workforce and workers who have been laid off due to an economic downturn. As diverse as this group is, they share one thing in common: they are older than traditional students. That means they face different challenges—but also enjoy some advantages over their younger classmates.

One major challenge faced by nontraditional students is scheduling. Often they are juggling the responsibilities of work, school, and family. They may have to study at odd times—during meals, while commuting, or after putting the kids to bed. If they are switching careers, they may also be learning an entirely new set of skills. But nontraditional students have an important advantage: experience. Even experience in an unrelated field is a plus. Older students know how organizations operate. Often, they have developed useful skills in human relations, management, budgeting, and communications. Even a former stay-at-home parent has skills in all of these areas. By observing other people's successes and failures—and by living through a few of their own—they have developed a knowledge of what to do and what not to do. So, in some ways, these students have a head start on their younger counterparts. But they also face the reality that they have fewer years for developing a career.

THE JOB MARKET: WHERE DO YOU FIT IN?

The industry you choose, and the career path you follow within it, are part of a bigger picture. They reflect the needs of society, changing populations, developing technology, and the overall economy. For example, the North American population is expected to increase at a slower rate of growth for the near future than during the previous two decades.

As the North American baby-boom generation ages, the age group between 55 and 64 will increase by about one-third. Thus, we will need more healthcare services and other services for an aging population, such as assisted living facilities and leisure and hospitality. Today's younger workers are receiving more education and training to fill the need for professional and business service workers. These projections affect both the workforce and the types of goods and services needed to satisfy consumers. So jobs in education and healthcare services and in professional and business services will increase substantially.

Careers in service-providing industries continue a long-term rise. Service jobs in healthcare and social assistance will increase while manufacturing jobs will continue to shrink. But industries that produce certain types of goods, such as those related to the needs of an aging population and those related to green technologies or products, will probably increase.

The good news is that even in a weaker job market, employers are looking to hire recent college and university graduates. In fact, some continue to offer signing bonuses and other incentives to recruit the best workers. Why? Continuing to hire entry-level employees makes good business sense. Some of the hot jobs can be found in accounting, sales, management training, engineering, and business services. So celebrate your graduation. Keep your résumé current and your outlook positive: a job is out there for you.

A LONG-RANGE VIEW OF YOUR CAREER

Choosing a career is an important life decision. A career is a professional journey—whether you want to run a small restaurant or a bank branch, whether you are fascinated by language or math, whether you prefer to work with animals or people. In the end, you hope to contribute something good to society while enjoying what you do—and make a reasonable living at it.

Throughout your career, it is important to stay flexible and to continue learning. Challenging new skills will be required of managers and other businesspeople during these first decades of the twenty-first century. Remain open to unexpected changes and opportunities that can help you learn and develop new skills. Keep in mind that your first job will not be your last. But tackle that first job with the same energy and excitement you'd have if someone asked you to run the company itself. Everything you learn on that job will be valuable at some point during your career, and who knows—someday, you may actually run the company.

Finally, if you haven't already started your career search, begin now. Start by talking with various people, lining up an internship, looking for a part-time job on or off campus, or volunteering for an organization. Register with the campus career centre long before you graduate. Then, when you reach your final semester, you'll be well on your way to beginning the career you want.

We are confident that this textbook presents a selection of career options. Whatever you decide, be sure it is right for you—not your friends, your instructors, or your parents. As the old saying goes, "You pass this way just once." Enjoy the journey!

PROJECTS AND TEAMWORK APPLICATIONS

1. Visit one of the job websites such as CareerBuilder.ca or Monster.ca and research an industry you think you might be interested in. Prepare a report on what you learned about the field. Was the site helpful? What types of jobs were available in the field? Based on your report, do you plan to pursue this industry or select another field?

2. Prepare your résumé following the procedures outlined earlier in this section. Exchange your résumé with a classmate so you can critique each other's resume. Then revise and proofread your résumé.

3. Go online to the website for a specific company that you might be interested in working for. Click on the "Careers" or "Job Opportunities" section of the site, and read carefully the job descriptions for any entry-level positions and the procedure for applying for them. Also review any general information about career development at the firm. Write a cover letter as if you were actually applying for one of the jobs.

4. With a classmate, practise interviewing for the job you selected in the previous question. Prepare questions for each other and take turns interviewing and being interviewed. What parts of the interview did you handle well? What can you improve?

5. Think about where you would like to be in your career in five years and write about your plans. Share your plans with the class, then seal them in an envelope. Keep the envelope and open it in five years to see how close you came to your predictions.

NOTES

1. U.S. Census Bureau, "Average Earnings of Year-Round, Full-Time Workers by Educational Attainment: 2009," *Current Population Reports*, accessed May 10, 2010, www.census.gov/compendia/statab/2012/tables/ 12s0703.pdf.

2. *San Diego News Network*, April 27, 2010, www.sdnn.com.

3. "College Grad Job Search Strategies," *The Job Doc Blog*, March 15, 2010, www.boston.com/jobs/news/jobdoc/2010/03/college_grad_job_search_strate.html.

4. Lindsey Gerdes, "Best Places to Intern," *Bloomberg Business*, December 10, 2009, www.bloomberg.com.

5. "The Cooperative Education Model," *National Commission for Cooperative Education*, accessed May 10, 2010, www.co-op.edu.

6. "More Free Assessment Tests," *Career Explorer*, accessed May 10, 2010, www.careerexplorer.net; "Assessment Exercises," *Monster Careers*, accessed May 10, 2010, www.monstercareeres.com.

7. "Paula's Story," Paula Deen.com, accessed May 10, 2010, www.pauladeen.com.

8. Kim Isaacs, "Five Résumé Tips for College Students," *Monster College*, accessed May 10, 2010, http://college.monster.com/benefits-entry-level-resume/articles/193-five-resume-tips-for-college-students; "Top 10 Professional Resume Writing Tips for 2010," *Elite Résumés*, accessed May 10, 2010, http://aneliteresume.com/resume-writing/top-10-professional-resume-writing-tips-for-2010; "Five Tips for Better Resume Writing," *Job Hunting for Dummies*, accessed May 10, 2010, www.dummies.com/how-to/content/five-tips-for-better-resume-writing.html.

9. Kat Neville, "What Makes a Great Cover Letter, According to Companies?" *Smashing Magazine,* March 25, 2010, www.smashingmagazine.com/2010/03/what-makes-a-great-cover-letter-according-to-companies.

10. "Tips for Submitting Your Online Resume," *Elite Résumés,* accessed May 10, 2010, http://aneliteresume.com/resume-writing/tips-for-submitting-your-online-resume.

11. Carole Martin, "Ten Tips to Boost Your Interview Skills," *Daily News,* accessed October 15, 2013, www.nydailynews.com/jobs/ten-tips-boost-interview-skills-article-1.1486141.

12. Jerome Young, "How to Answer the Hard Interview Questions," *Forbes,* April 9, 2010, www.forbes.com/2010/04/09/hard-interview-questions-leadership-careers-employment.html.

GLOSSARY

accounting the process of measuring, interpreting, and communicating financial information to support internal and external business decision making.

accounting cycle the set of activities involved in converting information and individual transactions into financial statements.

accounting equation the relationship that should reflect a firm's financial position at any time: assets should always equal the sum of liabilities and owners' equity.

Accounting Standards Board (AcSB) the organization that interprets and modifies GAAP in Canada for private and not-for-profit businesses.

accrual accounting an accounting method that records revenues and expenses when they occur, not when cash actually changes hands.

acquisition an agreement in which one firm purchases another.

advertising paid nonpersonal communication usually targeted at large numbers of potential buyers.

affective conflict a disagreement that focuses on individuals or personal issues.

affinity program a marketing effort sponsored by an organization that targets people who share common interests and activities.

angel investors wealthy individuals who invest directly in a new venture in exchange for an equity stake.

application service provider (ASP) an outside supplier that provides both the computers and the application support for managing an information system.

asset anything with future benefit owned or controlled by a firm.

balance of payments the overall money flows into and out of a country.

balance of trade the difference between a nation's exports and imports.

balance sheet a statement of a firm's financial position—what it owns and claims against its assets—at a particular point in time.

balanced budget a situation where total revenues raised by taxes and fees equal the total proposed government spending for the year.

Bank of Canada (the Bank) the central bank of Canada.

bankruptcy the legal nonpayment of financial obligations.

benchmarking the process of looking at how well other companies perform business functions or tasks and using their performance as a standard for measuring another company's performance.

board of directors the governing body of a corporation.

botnet a network of PCs that have been infected with one or more data-stealing viruses.

brand a name, term, sign, symbol, design, or some combination that identifies the products of one firm and shows how they differ from competitors' offerings.

brand equity the added value that a respected and successful name gives to a product.

brand name the part of a brand that is made up of words or letters that form a name. It is used to identify a firm's products and show how they differ from the products of competitors.

branding the process of creating in consumers' minds an identity for a good, service, or company; a major marketing tool in contemporary business.

breakeven analysis the pricing-related technique used to calculate the minimum sales volume a product must generate at a certain price level to cover all costs.

budget an organization's plan for how it will raise and spend money during a specific period of time.

budget deficit a situation where the government spends more than it raises through taxes.

budget surplus the excess funding when government spends less than it raises through taxes and fees.

business all profit-seeking activities and enterprises that provide goods and services necessary to an economic system.

Business Development Bank of Canada (BDC) a governmental agency that assists, counsels, and protects the interests of small businesses in Canada.

business ethics standards of conduct and moral values regarding right and wrong actions in the business environment.

business incubator a local program designed to provide low-cost, shared business facilities to small startup companies.

business intelligence a field of research that uses activities and technologies for gathering, storing, and analyzing data to make better competitive decisions.

business law those parts of law that most directly influence and regulate the management of business activity.

business plan a formal document that details a company's goals, methods, and standards.

business product or business-to-business (B2B) product a good or service purchased to be used, either directly or indirectly, in the production of other goods for resale.

Canada Deposit Insurance Corporation (CDIC) the federal agency that insures deposits at commercial and savings banks.

capital production inputs consisting of technology, tools, information, and physical facilities.

capital structure the mix of a firm's debt and equity capital.

capitalism an economic system that rewards firms for their ability to perceive and serve the needs and demands of consumers; also called the private enterprise system.

category advisor the individual that the business customer assigns as the major supplier to deal with all the other suppliers for a project. The category advisor also presents the entire package to the business buyer.

cause advertising a form of institutional advertising that promotes a specific viewpoint on a public issue as a way to influence public opinion and the political process.

cause marketing marketing that promotes a cause or social issue, such as preventing child abuse, anti-littering efforts, and stop-smoking campaigns.

Central America–Dominican Republic Free Trade Agreement (CAFTA-DR) an agreement among the United States, Costa Rica, the Dominican Republic, El Salvador, Guatemala, Honduras, and Nicaragua to reduce tariffs and trade restrictions.

chief information officer (CIO) the executive responsible for managing a firm's information systems and related computer technologies.

classic entrepreneur a person who sees a business opportunity and sets aside resources to gain access to that market.

cloud computing the use of powerful servers that store applications software and databases that users access by using any Internet-connected device, such as a PC or a smartphone.

co-branding a cooperative arrangement where two or more businesses team up to closely link their names on a single product.

code of conduct a formal statement that defines how an organization expects its employees to resolve ethical issues.

cognitive conflict a disagreement that focuses on problem- and issue-related differences of opinion.

collective bargaining the process of negotiation between management and union representatives.

co-marketing a cooperative arrangement where two businesses jointly market each other's products.

common law laws that result from judicial decisions, some of which can be traced to early England.

common shares the basic form of company ownership; shares that give owners voting rights but only residual claims to the firm's assets and income distributions.

communication a meaningful exchange of information through messages.

communism an economic system where all property is shared equally by the people in a community under the direction of a strong central government.

compensation the amount employees are paid in money and benefits.

competition the battle among businesses for consumer acceptance.

competitive differentiation the unique combination of organizational abilities, products, and approaches that sets one company apart from its competitors in the minds of customers.

competitive pricing a strategy that tries to reduce the emphasis on price competition by matching other firms' prices and by focusing their own marketing efforts on the product, distribution, and promotional elements of the marketing mix.

computer-aided design (CAD) a process used by engineers to design parts and entire products on the computer. Engineers who use CAD can work faster and with fewer mistakes than those who use traditional drafting systems.

computer-aided manufacturing (CAM) a computer tool that a manufacturer uses to analyze CAD output and the steps that a machine must take to produce a needed product or part.

computer-based information systems information systems that use computer and related technologies to store information electronically in an organized, accessible manner.

computer-integrated manufacturing (CIM) an integrated production system that uses computers to help workers design products, control machines, handle materials, and control the production function.

conflict the outcome when one person's, or one group's, needs do not match those of another, and one side may try to block the other side's intentions or goals.

conflict of interest a situation in which an employee must choose between a business's welfare and personal gain.

conglomerate merger a merger that combines unrelated firms, usually with the goal of diversification, increasing sales, or spending a cash surplus to avoid a takeover attempt.

consumer behaviour end consumers' activities that are directly involved in obtaining, consuming, and disposing of products, and the decision processes before and after these activities.

consumer orientation a business philosophy that focuses first on consumers' unmet wants and needs, and then designs products to meet those needs.

Consumer Price Index (CPI) a measurement of the monthly average change in prices of goods and services.

consumer product or business-to-consumer (B2C) product a good or service that is purchased by end users.

consumerism public demand that a business consider the wants and needs of its customers when making decisions.

contract a legally enforceable agreement between two or more parties regarding a specified act or thing.

controlling the function of assessing an organization's performance against its goals.

cooperative advertising allowances that marketers provide to share with channel partners the cost of local advertising of their firm's product or product line.

copyright legal protection of written or printed material such as books, designs, cartoons, photos, computer software, music, and videos.

core inflation rate the inflation rate after energy prices and food prices are removed.

corporate culture an organization's collection of principles, beliefs, and values.

corporate philanthropy an organization's contribution to the communities where it earns profits.

corporation a legal organization with assets and liabilities separate from the assets and liabilities of its owners.

Corruption of Foreign Public Officials Act a federal law that prohibits Canadian citizens and companies from bribing foreign officials to win or continue business.

cost-based pricing calculating total costs per unit and then adding markups to cover overhead costs and generate profits.

countertrade a barter agreement whereby trade between two or more nations involves payment made in the form of local products instead of currency.

creative selling a persuasive type of promotional presentation.

creativity the capacity to develop novel solutions to perceived organizational problems.

credit receiving money, goods, or services on the basis of an agreement between the lender and the borrower that the loan is for a specified period of time with a specified rate of interest.

critical thinking the ability to analyze and assess information to pinpoint problems or opportunities.

cross-functional team a team made up of members from different functions, such as production, marketing, and finance.

cyclical unemployment the joblessness of people who are out of work because of a cyclical contraction in the economy.

data raw facts and figures that may or may not be meaningful to a business decision.

data mining the use of computer searches of customer data to detect patterns and relationships.

data warehouse a customer database that allows managers to combine data from several different organizational functions.

database a centralized integrated collection of data resources.

debt financing borrowed funds that entrepreneurs must repay.

decision making the process of seeing a problem or opportunity, assessing possible solutions, selecting and carrying out the best-suited plan, and assessing the results.

decision support system (DSS) an information system that gives direct support to businesspeople during the decision-making process.

deflation the opposite of inflation, occurs when prices continue to fall.

delegation the managerial process of assigning work to employees.

demand the willingness and ability of buyers to purchase goods and services.

demand curve a graph of the amount of a product that buyers will purchase at different prices.

demographic segmentation dividing markets on the basis of various demographic or socioeconomic characteristics, such as gender, age, income, occupation, household size, stage in family life cycle, education, or ethnic group.

departmentalization the process of dividing work activities into units within the organization.

devaluation a reduction in a currency's value in terms of other currencies or in terms of a fixed standard.

directing guiding and motivating employees to accomplish organizational goals.

discrimination biased treatment toward a job candidate or employee.

distribution channels the paths that products—and their legal ownership—follow from producer to consumers or business users.

distribution strategy a plan that deals with the marketing activities and institutions that get the right good or service to the firm's customers.

diversity the blending of individuals of different genders, ethnic backgrounds, cultures, religions, ages, and physical and mental abilities to enhance a firm's chances of success.

divestiture the sale of assets by a firm.

double-entry bookkeeping the process used to record accounting transactions; each individual transaction is always balanced by another transaction.

downsizing the process of reducing the number of employees within a firm by eliminating jobs.

dumping selling products in other countries at prices below production costs or below typical prices in the home market to capture market share from domestic competitors.

economics the social science that studies the choices people and governments make when dividing up their scarce resources.

embargo a total ban on importing specific products or a total stop to trading with a particular country.

employee benefits additional compensation—such as vacation time, retirement savings plans, profit-sharing, health insurance, gym memberships, child and elder care, and tuition reimbursement—paid entirely or in part by the company.

employee separation a broad term for the loss of an employee for any reason, voluntary or involuntary.

Employment Equity Act (EEA) an act created (1) to increase job opportunities for women and members of minority groups and (2) to help end discrimination based on race, colour, religion, disability, gender, or national origin.

empowerment giving employees shared authority, responsibility, and decision making with their managers.

end-use segmentation a marketing strategy that focuses on the precise way a B2B purchaser will use a product.

entrepreneur a person who seeks a profitable opportunity and takes the necessary risks to set up and operate a business.

entrepreneurship the willingness to take risks to create and operate a business.

equilibrium price the current market price for an item.

equity financing funds invested in new ventures in exchange for part ownership.

equity theory an individual's perception of fair and equitable treatment.

European Union (EU) a 28-nation European economic alliance.

event marketing marketing or sponsoring of short-term events such as athletic competitions and cultural and charitable performances.

everyday low pricing (EDLP) a strategy of maintaining continuous low prices instead of using short-term price cuts such as cents-off coupons, rebates, and special sales.

exchange control a restriction on importing certain products or a restriction against certain companies to reduce trade and the spending of foreign currency.

exchange process an activity in which two or more parties trade something of value (such as goods, services, or cash) that satisfies each other's needs.

exchange rate the value of one country's currency in terms of the currencies of other countries.

executive support system (ESS) an information system that lets senior executives access the firm's primary databases, often by touching the computer screen, pointing and clicking a mouse, or using voice recognition.

expansionary monetary policy a plan to increase the money supply to try to decrease the cost of borrowing. Lower interest rates encourage businesses to make new investments, which leads to employment and economic growth.

expectancy theory the process people use to evaluate the likelihood that their efforts will lead to the results they want and the degree to which they want those results.

expert system a computer program that imitates human thinking through complicated sets of "if-then" rules.

exports domestically produced goods and services sold in other countries.

external communication a meaningful exchange of information through messages sent between an organization and its major audiences.

factors of production four basic inputs for effective operation: natural resources, capital, human resources, and entrepreneurship.

fair trade a market-based approach of paying higher prices to producers for goods exported from developing countries to developed countries in an effort to promote sustainability and to ensure the people in developing countries receive better trading conditions.

finance the business function of planning, obtaining, and managing the company's funds to accomplish its objectives as effectively and efficiently as possible.

finance charge the difference between the amount borrowed and the amount repaid on a loan.

Financial Accounting Standards Board (FASB) the organization that interprets and modifies GAAP in the United States.

financial institutions intermediaries between savers and borrowers that collect funds from savers and then lend the funds to individuals, businesses, and governments.

financial managers the executives who develop and carry out their firm's financial plan and decide on the most appropriate sources and uses of funds.

financial markets markets where securities are issued and traded.

financial plan a document that specifies the funds needed by a firm for a period of time, the timing of cash inflows and outflows, and the most appropriate sources and uses of funds.

financial system the process by which money flows from savers to users.

firewall a type of security system for computers that limits data transfers to certain locations; it also tracks system use so that managers can identify threats to the system's security, including attempts to log on with invalid passwords.

fiscal policy a plan of government spending and taxation decisions designed to control inflation, reduce unemployment, improve the general welfare of citizens, and encourage economic growth.

flexible manufacturing system (FMS) a production facility that workers can quickly change to manufacture different products.

foreign licensing agreement an international agreement in which one firm allows another firm to produce or sell its product, or use its trademark, patent, or manufacturing processes, in a specific geographical area, in return for royalties or other compensation.

franchise a contract-based agreement in which a franchisee can produce and/or sell the franchisor's products under that company's brand name if the franchisee agrees to the operating terms and requirements.

franchisee the individual or business firm purchasing a franchise.

franchising a contract-based business arrangement between a manufacturer or other supplier, and a dealer, such as a restaurant operator or retailer.

franchisor the firm whose products are sold to customers by the franchisee.

frequency marketing a marketing initiative that rewards frequent purchases with cash, rebates, merchandise, or other premiums.

frictional unemployment the joblessness of people in the workforce who are temporarily not working but are looking for jobs.

General Agreement on Tariffs and Trade (GATT) an international trade accord that has greatly reduced worldwide tariffs and other trade barriers.

generally accepted accounting principles (GAAP) principles that outline the conventions, rules, and procedures for deciding on the acceptable accounting practices at a particular time.

geographical segmentation dividing an overall market into similar groups on the basis of their locations.

global business strategy the offering of a standardized, worldwide product and the selling of it in basically the same way throughout a firm's domestic and foreign markets.

goal-setting theory the idea that people will be motivated to the extent to which they accept specific, challenging goals and receive feedback that shows their progress toward goal achievement.

grapevine an internal information channel that passes information from unofficial sources.

green marketing a marketing strategy that promotes environmentally safe products and production methods.

grid computing a network of smaller computers that run special software.

gross domestic product (GDP) the sum of all goods and services produced within a country during a specific time period, such as a year.

guerrilla marketing innovative, low-cost marketing efforts designed to get consumers' attention in unusual ways.

hardware all tangible, or physical, elements of a computer system.

health insurance insurance that pays for losses due to illness or injury.

home-based businesses firms operated from the residence of the business owner.

horizontal merger a merger that joins firms in the same industry for the purpose of diversification, increasing customer bases, cutting costs, or expanding product lines.

human resource management the function of attracting, developing, and retaining employees who can perform the activities needed to meet organizational objectives.

human resources production inputs consisting of anyone who works, including both the physical labour and the intellectual inputs contributed by workers.

hyperinflation an economic situation marked by soaring prices.

imports foreign goods and services purchased by domestic customers.

income statement a financial record of a company's revenues, expenses, and profits over a specific period of time.

inflation rising prices caused by a combination of excess consumer demand and higher costs of raw materials, component parts, human resources, and other factors of production.

infomercials a form of broadcast direct marketing; 30-minute programs resemble regular TV programs, but sell goods or services.

information knowledge gained from processing data.

information system an organized method for collecting, storing, and communicating past, present, and projected information on internal operations and external intelligence.

infrastructure the basic systems of a country's communication, transportation, and energy facilities.

insider trading use of material nonpublic information about a company to make investment profits.

institutional advertising messages that promote concepts, ideas, or philosophies. It can also promote goodwill toward industries, companies, organizations, or government entities.

insurance a contract in which the insurer, for a fee, agrees to reimburse an insured firm or individual a sum of money if a loss occurs.

integrated marketing communications (IMC) the coordination of all promotional activities—media advertising, direct mail, personal selling, sales promotion, and public relations—to produce a unified customer-focused message.

integrity behaving according to one's deeply felt ethical principles in business situations.

International Accounting Standards Board (IASB) the organization that promotes worldwide consistency in financial reporting practices.

International Financial Reporting Standards (IFRS) the standards and interpretations adopted by the IASB.

international law the numerous regulations that govern international trade.

International Monetary Fund (IMF) an organization created to promote trade, eliminate barriers, and make short-term loans to member-nations that are unable to meet their budgets.

International Organization for Standardization (ISO) an international organization whose mission is to develop and promote international standards for business, government, and society. The aim is to improve and encourage global trade and cooperation.

intranet a computer network that is similar to the Internet but limits access to authorized users.

intrapreneurship the process of promoting innovation within the structure of an existing organization.

inventory control a function that balances the costs of storing inventory with the need to have stock on hand to meet demand.

joint venture a partnership between companies for a specific activity.

judiciary the branch of government that is responsible for applying laws to settle disagreements; also known as the court system.

just-in-time (JIT) system a broad management philosophy that reaches beyond the narrow activity of inventory control to affect the entire system of production and operations management.

labour union a group of workers who organize themselves to work toward common goals in the areas of wages, hours, and working conditions.

law the standards set by government and society in the form of either legislation or custom.

law of large numbers the idea that seemingly random events will follow predictable patterns if enough events are observed.

leadership the ability to direct or inspire people to reach goals.

LEED (Leadership in Energy and Environmental Design) a voluntary certification program administered by the Canada Green Building Council, aimed at promoting the most sustainable construction processes available.

leverage increasing the rate of return on funds invested by borrowing funds.

leveraged buyouts (LBOs) transactions where public shareholders are bought out and the firm reverts to private status.

liability a claim against a firm's assets by creditors.

life insurance a type of insurance that protects people against the financial losses that occur with premature death.

lifestyle entrepreneur a person who starts a business to reduce work hours and create a more relaxed lifestyle.

lifetime value of a customer the revenues and intangible benefits (such as referrals and customer feedback) from a customer over the life of the relationship, minus the amount the company must spend to acquire and serve that customer.

listening receiving a message and interpreting its intended meaning by grasping the facts and feelings the message conveys.

local area networks (LANs) computer networks that connect machines within limited areas, such as a building or several nearby buildings.

logistics the process of coordinating flow of goods, services, and information among members of the supply chain.

macroeconomics the study of a nation's overall economic issues, such as how an economy maintains and divides up resources and how a government's policies affect its citizens' standards of living.

make, buy, or lease decision choosing whether to manufacture a needed product or part in-house, buy it from an outside supplier, or lease it.

malware any malicious software program designed to infect computer systems.

management the process of achieving organizational goals through people and other resources.

management by objectives (MBO) a structured approach that helps managers to focus on reachable goals and to achieve the best results based on the organization's resources.

management information system (MIS) an information system designed to produce reports for managers and other professionals.

management support systems information systems that are designed to provide support for effective decision making.

market segmentation the process of dividing a total market into several relatively similar groups.

marketing an organizational function and set of processes for creating, communicating, and delivering value to customers and for managing customer relationships in ways that benefit the organization and its stakeholders.

marketing concept a companywide consumer focus on promoting long-term success.

marketing mix a blending the four elements of marketing strategy—product, distribution, promotion, and pricing—to satisfy chosen customer segments.

marketing research the process of collecting and evaluating information to support marketing decision making.

Maslow's hierarchy of needs a theory of motivation proposed by Abraham Maslow. According to the theory, people have five levels of needs that they try to satisfy: physiological, safety, social, esteem, and self-actualization.

mass production a system for manufacturing products in large quantities by using effective combinations of employees with specialized skills, mechanization, and standardization.

materials requirement planning (MRP) a computer-based production planning system that ensures a firm has all the parts and materials it needs to produce its output at the right time and place and in the right amounts.

merger an agreement in which two or more firms combine to form one company.

microeconomics the study of small economic units, such as individual consumers, families, and businesses.

mission statement a written description of an organization's overall business purpose and aims.

missionary selling an indirect form of selling where the representative promotes goodwill for a company or provides technical or operational assistance to the customer.

mixed market economy an economic system that draws from both private enterprise economies and planned economies, to different degrees.

monetary policy a government plan to increase or decrease the money supply and to change banking requirements and interest rates to affect bankers' willingness to make loans.

monopolistic competition a market structure where large numbers of buyers and sellers exchange distinct and differentiated (dissimilar) products so each participant has some control over price.

monopoly a market situation where a single seller controls trade in a good or service, and buyers can find no close substitutes.

multidomestic business strategy a plan to develop and market products to serve different needs and tastes in separate national markets.

multinational corporation (MNC) a firm with many operations and marketing activities outside its home country.

national debt the money owed by government to individuals, businesses, and government agencies who purchase Treasury bills, Treasury notes, and Treasury bonds.

natural resources all production inputs that are useful in their natural states, including agricultural land, building sites, forests, and mineral deposits.

nearshoring the outsourcing of production or services to locations near a firm's home base.

net worth the difference between an individual's or a household's assets and liabilities.

nonpersonal selling forms of selling such as advertising, sales promotion, direct marketing, and public relations.

North American Free Trade Agreement (NAFTA) an agreement among the United States, Canada, and Mexico to break down tariffs and trade restrictions.

not-for-profit corporations organizations whose goals do not include pursuing a profit.

not-for-profit organizations organizations whose primary aims are public service, not returning a profit to their owners.

objectives guideposts by which managers define the organization's desired performance in such areas as new-product development, sales, customer service, growth, environmental and social responsibility, and employee satisfaction.

odd pricing a pricing method that uses uneven amounts to make prices appear to be less than they really are.

offshoring the relocation of business processes to lower-cost locations overseas.

oligopoly a market situation where relatively few sellers compete and high startup costs act as barriers to keep out new competitors.

on-demand computing the use of software time from application providers; firms pay only for their usage of the software, not for purchasing or maintaining the software.

operational support systems information systems designed to produce a variety of information on an organization's activities for both internal and external users.

order processing a form of selling used mostly at the wholesale and retail levels; involves identifying customer needs, pointing out products that meet those needs, and completing orders.

organization a structured group of people working together to achieve common goals.

organization marketing a marketing strategy that influences consumers to accept the goals of and organization, receive the services of an organization, or contribute in some way to an organization.

organizing the process of blending human and material resources through a formal structure of tasks and authority: arranging work, dividing tasks among employees, and coordinating them to ensure plans are carried out and goals are met.

outsourcing using outside vendors to produce goods or fulfill services and functions that were previously handled in-house or in-country.

owners' equity the funds that owners invest in the business plus any profits not paid to owners in the form of cash dividends.

partnership an association of two or more persons who operate a business as co-owners by voluntary legal agreement.

patent legal protection that guarantees an inventor exclusive rights to an invention for 20 years.

penetration pricing a strategy that sets a low price as a major marketing tactic.

performance appraisal evaluation of and feedback on an employee's job performance.

person marketing efforts that are designed to attract the attention, interest, and preference of a target market toward a person.

personal financial management the study of the economic factors and personal decisions that affect a person's financial well-being.

personal financial plan a guide to help a person reach his or her desired financial goals.

personal selling the most basic form of promotion: a direct person-to-person promotional presentation to a potential buyer.

physical distribution the actual movement of products from producer to consumers or business users.

place marketing an attempt to attract people to a particular area, such as a city, state, or country.

planned economy an economic system where business ownership, profits, and resource allocation are shaped by a plan to meet government goals, not goals set by individual firms.

planning the process of looking forward to future events and conditions and deciding on the courses of action for achieving organizational goals.

point-of-purchase (POP) advertising displays or demonstrations that promote products when and where consumers buy them, such as in retail stores.

positioning a concept whereby marketers try to establish their products in the minds of customers by communicating to buyers the meaningful differences about the attributes, price, quality, or use of a good or service.

preferred shares shares that give owners limited voting rights and the right to receive dividends or assets before owners of common shares.

prestige pricing setting a relatively high price to develop and maintain an image of quality and exclusiveness.

price the exchange value of a good or service.

primary markets financial markets where firms and governments issue securities and sell them initially to the general public.

private enterprise system an economic system that rewards firms for their ability to identify and serve the needs and demands of customers.

private property the most basic freedom under the private enterprise system; the right to own, use, buy, sell, and hand down land, buildings, machinery, equipment, patents, individual possessions, and various intangible kinds of property.

privatization the conversion of government-owned and -operated companies to privately held businesses.

problem-solving team a temporary combination of workers who gather to solve a specific problem and then disband.

process control systems operational support systems that monitor and control physical processes.

product a bundle of physical, service, and symbolic attributes designed to satisfy buyers' wants.

product advertising messages designed to sell a particular good or service.

product liability the responsibility of manufacturers for injuries and damages caused by their products.

product life cycle the four basic stages in the development of a successful product—introduction, growth, maturity, and decline.

product line a group of related products that share physical similarities or are targeted toward a similar market.

product mix the assortment of product lines and individual goods and services that a firm offers to consumers and business users.

product placement a form of promotion where marketers pay placement fees to have their products featured in various media, from newspapers and magazines to television and movies.

production the use of resources, such as workers and machinery, to convert materials into finished goods and services.

production and operations management the process of overseeing the production process by managing the people and machinery that convert materials and resources into finished goods and services.

production control creating well-defined procedures for coordinating people, materials, and machinery to provide the greatest production efficiency.

productivity the relationship between the number of units produced and the number of human and other production inputs needed to produce them.

product-related segmentation dividing consumer markets into groups that are based on benefits sought by buyers, usage rates, and loyalty levels.

profitability objectives common goals that are included in the strategic plans of most firms.

profits rewards for businesspeople who take the risks involved to offer goods and services to customers.

promotion the function of informing, persuading, and influencing a purchase decision.

promotional mix the combination of personal and nonpersonal selling that marketers use to meet the needs of a firm's target customers and to effectively and efficiently communicate its message to them.

property and liability insurance a general category of insurance that protects against losses due to a number of perils, such as fire, accident, and theft.

psychographic segmentation dividing consumer markets into groups with similar attitudes, values, and lifestyles.

public accountant an accountant who provides accounting services to other organizations.

public relations an organization's communications and relationships with its various public audiences.

publicity the nonpersonal stimulation of demand for a good, service, place, idea, event, person, or organization by unpaid placement of information in print or broadcast media.

pulling strategy promotion of a product by generating consumer demand for it, mainly through advertising and sales promotion appeals.

pure competition a market structure where large numbers of buyers and sellers exchange similar products, and no single participant has a large influence on price.

pushing strategy personal selling to market an item to wholesalers and retailers in a company's distribution channels.

quality the state of being free of deficiencies or imperfections.

quality control measuring output against quality standards.

quota a limit set on the amounts of particular products that can be imported.

recession a cycle of economic contraction that lasts for six months or longer.

recycling reprocessing of used materials for reuse.

regulated monopoly a firm that is granted exclusive rights in a specific market by a local, provincial, or federal government.

relationship era the business era where firms seek to actively promote customer loyalty by carefully managing every interaction.

relationship management the collection of activities that build and maintain ongoing, mutually beneficial ties with customers and others.

relationship marketing developing and maintaining long-term, cost-effective exchange relationships with partners.

restrictive monetary policy a plan to reduce the money supply to control rising prices, overexpansion, and concerns about overly rapid economic growth.

retailers distribution channel members that sell goods and services to individuals for their own use, not for resale.

risk uncertainty about loss or injury.

risk management calculations and actions a firm takes to recognize and deal with real or potential risks to its survival.

risk–return tradeoff the process of maximizing the wealth of the firm's shareholders by striking the right balance between risk and return.

rule of indemnity the requirement that the insured cannot collect more than the amount of the loss and cannot collect for the same loss more than once.

salary pay calculated on a periodic basis, such as weekly or monthly.

sales law the law governing the sale of goods or services for money or on credit.

sales promotion forms of promotion such as coupons, product samples, and rebates that support advertising and personal selling.

Sarbanes-Oxley Act of 2002 U.S. federal legislation designed to deter and punish corporate and accounting fraud and corruption. It is also designed to protect the interests of workers and shareholders by requiring enhanced financial disclosures, criminal penalties for CEOs and CFOs who defraud investors, and safeguards for whistle-blowers. The act also established a new regulatory body for public accounting firms.

seasonal unemployment the joblessness of workers in a seasonal industry.

secondary market a collection of financial markets where previously issued securities are traded among investors.

securities financial instruments that represent the obligations of the issuers to provide the purchasers with the expected stated returns on the funds invested or loaned.

seed capital the initial funding needed to launch a new venture.

self-managed team a work team that has the authority to decide how its members complete their daily tasks.

serial entrepreneur a person who starts one business, runs it, and then starts and runs more businesses, one after another.

server the heart of a midrange computer network.

sexism discrimination against members of either sex, but usually against women.

sexual harassment unwelcome and inappropriate actions of a sexual nature.

shareholders owners of a corporation as a result of their purchase of shares in the corporation.

skimming pricing a strategy that sets an intentionally high price relative to the prices of competing products.

small business an independent business with fewer than 100 employees and revenues less than $2 million, not dominant in its market.

social audits formal procedures that identify and evaluate all company activities that relate to social issues, such as conservation, employment practices, environmental protection, and philanthropy.

social entrepreneur a person who sees societal problems and uses business principles to develop new solutions.

social era the business era in which firms seek ways to connect and interact with customers using technology.

social responsibility business's consideration of society's well-being and consumer satisfaction, in addition to profits.

socialism an economic system where the government owns and operates the major industries, such as communications.

software all the programs, routines, and computer languages that control a computer and tell it how to operate.

sole proprietorship a business ownership in which the sole proprietor's status as an individual is not legally separate from his or her status as a business owner.

specialty advertising promotional items that prominently display a firm's name, logo, or business slogan.

sponsorship providing funds for a sporting or cultural event in exchange for a direct association with the event.

spyware software that gathers user information through the user's Internet connection without his or her knowledge, usually for advertising purposes.

stakeholders customers, investors, employees, and public affected by or with an interest in a company.

standard of living the necessities, comforts, and luxuries a person wants to achieve or maintain.

statement of cash flows a record of the sources and uses of cash during a period of time.

statement of changes in equity a record of the change in equity from the end of one fiscal period to the end of the next fiscal period.

statutory law written law that includes provincial and federal constitutions; legislative enactments; treaties of the federal government; and ordinances of local governments.

stock markets (exchanges) markets where shares of stock are bought and sold by investors.

strategic alliance a partnership formed to create a competitive advantage for the businesses involved; in international business, the business strategy of one company partnering with another company in the country where it wants to do business.

structural unemployment the joblessness of people who remain unemployed for long periods of time, often with little hope of finding a job.

subcontracting an agreement that involves hiring other companies to produce, distribute, or sell goods or services; in international subcontracting, local companies in a specific country or geographical region are hired to produce, distribute, or sell goods or services.

supply the willingness and ability of sellers to provide goods and services.

supply chain the complete sequence of suppliers that help to create a good or service and deliver it to business users and final consumers.

supply curve a graph that shows the relationship between different prices and the amount of goods that sellers will offer for sale, regardless of demand.

sustainable the capacity to endure in ecology.

SWOT analysis SWOT is a short form for *strengths, weaknesses, opportunities,* and *threats*. By assessing all four factors one by one, a firm can then develop the best strategies for gaining a competitive advantage.

target market a group of people that an organization markets its goods, services, or ideas toward, using a strategy designed to satisfy this group's specific needs and preferences.

tariffs taxes imposed on imported goods.

tax an assessment by a governmental unit.

team a group of people with certain skills who share a common purpose, approach, and performance goals.

team cohesiveness the extent to which team members feel attracted to the team and motivated to remain part of it.

team diversity the team's differences in ability, experience, personality, or any other factor.

team level the team's average level of ability, experience, personality, or any other factor.

team norm a standard of conduct shared by team members that guides their behaviour.

technology the business application of knowledge based on scientific discoveries, inventions, and innovations.

telemarketing personal selling by telephone, which provides marketers with a high return on their expenses, an immediate response, and an opportunity for a personalized two-way conversation.

tender offer a proposal made by a firm to the target firm's shareholders specifying a price and the form of payment.

test marketing the introduction of a new product and a complete marketing campaign to a selected city or TV coverage area.

tort a civil wrong inflicted by one person on another person or on another person's property.

trade promotion sales promotion geared to marketing intermediaries, not to final consumers.

trademark a brand that has been given legal protection; words, symbols, or other designations used by firms to identify their products.

transaction management building and promoting products in the hope that enough customers will buy them to cover costs and earn profits.

transaction processing systems operational support systems that record and process data from business transactions.

Trojan horse a program that claims to do one thing but in reality does something else, usually something malicious.

unemployment rate the percentage of the total workforce actively seeking work but currently unemployed.

utility the power of a good or service to satisfy a want or need.

vendor-managed inventory the process in which the producer and the retailer agree that the producer (or the wholesaler) will decide how much of a product a buyer needs and automatically ship new supplies when needed.

venture capital money invested in a business by another business firm or group of individuals in exchange for an ownership share.

venture capitalists business firms or groups of individuals that invest in new and growing firms in exchange for an ownership share.

vertical merger a merger that combines firms operating at different levels in the production and marketing process.

virtual private networks (VPNs) secure connections between two points on the Internet.

virtual teams groups of geographically or organizationally separated co-workers who use a combination of telecommunications and information technologies to accomplish an organizational task.

viruses malicious software programs that secretly attach themselves to other programs (called *hosts*) and change them or destroy data.

vision the ability to perceive marketplace needs and what an organization must do to satisfy them.

VoIP an alternative to traditional telecommunication services provided by companies such as Bell Canada and Telus; uses the Internet instead of telephone lines to transmit messages.

volume objectives pricing decisions that are based on market share, the percentage of a market controlled by a certain company or product.

wage pay based on an hourly rate or the amount of work accomplished.

whistle-blowing disclosure to company officials, government authorities, or the media of illegal, immoral, or unethical practices committed by an organization.

wholesaler a distribution channel member that sells primarily to retailers, other wholesalers, or business users.

wide area networks (WANs) computer networks that tie larger geographical regions together by using telephone lines and microwave and satellite transmission.

WiFi a wireless network that connects various devices and allows them to communicate with one another through radio waves.

work teams relatively permanent groups of employees with complementary skills who perform the day-to-day work of organizations.

World Bank an organization established by industrialized nations to lend money to less developed countries.

World Trade Organization (WTO) a 157-member international institution that monitors GATT agreements and mediates international trade disputes.

worm a small piece of software that uses a security hole in a network to replicate itself.

NOTES

Chapter 1

1. Official Website for Justin Bieber, accessed March 20, 2015, www.justinbiebermusic.com; Justin Bieber Facebook, accessed March 20, 2015, www.facebook.com/JustinBieber; Justin Bieber Twitter, accessed March 20, 2015, http://twitter.com/justinbieber; Justin Bieber Zone, accessed March 20, 2015, www.justinbieberzone.com; Caitlin Dewey, "From Startup to Pop Culture Conqueror," *Montreal Gazette*, February 18, 2015, C8; Marcus Hondro, "Bieber Hits 16 Million Twitter Followers on New Year's Day," *Digital Journal*, January 3, 2012, accessed January 3, 2012, www.digitaljournal.com/article/317183#ixzz1iP4EpfDS; Michael Paterniti, "How to Drake It in America," GQ, June 2013, accessed June 11, 2015, www.gq.com/entertainment/celebrities/201307/rapper-drake-in-america-july-2013?currentPage=1; YouTube video, "Drake before He Got famous!!" produced 2004, posted July 23, 2013, accessed June 11, 2015, www.youtube.com/watch?v=DKqmXJtDh7Y.

2. "Summary of the Findings of the National Survey of Nonprofit and Voluntary Organizations (NSNVO)," Statistics Canada, accessed January 23, 2011, www.statcan.gc.ca/pub/61-533-s/61-533-s2005001-eng.htm#5.

3. "Facts, Figures and Funding," Hospital for Sick Children (SickKids), accessed January 25, 2011, www.sickkids.ca/Research/AbouttheInstitute/Facts-Figures-and-Funding/Fact-Figures-and-Funding.html.

4. Doctors Without Borders, "Nepal," accessed May 23, 2015, www.doctorswithoutborders.org/country-region/nepal; "Powerful Earthquake Hits Nepal," CNN, May 3, 2015, accessed May 23, 2015, www.cnn.com/2015/04/25/world/gallery/nepal-earthquake; World Health Organization, "Nepal Earthquake 2015," accessed May 23, 2015, www.searo.who.int/entity/emergencies/nepal-earthquake-2015/en.

5. "SickKids Book Series," Hospital for Sick Children, accessed January 25, 2011, www.sickkids.ca/Learning/PatientsandFamilies/SickKids-book-series/index.html.

6. Livestrong Foundation, www.livestrong.org.

7. Netflix, "Company Overview," accessed January 10, 2014, https://pr.netflix.com/WebClient/loginPageSalesNetWorksAction.do?contentGroupId=10476&contentGroup=Company+Facts.

8. Beyond the Rack, accessed January 25, 2011, www.beyondtherack.com.

9. "Tech's Top Ten," *Financial Post*, December 29, 2011, FP12; Iain Marlow, "Small ISPs Lament CRTC Fee Change, Look to Invest in Own Infrastructure," *Globe and Mail*, January 13, 2011, accessed January 27, 2011, www.theglobeandmail.com/news/technology/tech-news/small-isps-lament-crtc-fee-change-look-to-invest-in-own-infrastructure/article1868429.

10. "Small Business Forum 2010," *Canadian Business Journal*, November 10, 2010, accessed January 27, 2011, www.canadianbusinessjournal.ca/business_in_action/november_10/small_business_forum_2010.html.

11. Industry Canada, *Key Small Business Statistics: July 2010*, Small Business and Tourism Branch, accessed January 27, 2011, www.ic.gc.ca/eic/site/061.nsf/vwapj/KSBS-PSRPE_July-Juillet2010_eng.pdf/$FILE/KSBS-PSRPE_July-Juillet2010_eng.pdf.

12. Ciara, "Vibe by Ciara," accessed February 18, 2015, www.ciaravibe.com/index-en.html; Jason Magder, "Homegrown Tablet, the Vibe, Takes on iPad," *Montreal Gazette*, January 27, 2011, accessed February 18, 2011, www.montrealgazette.com/technology/Homegrown+tablet+Vibe+takes+iPad/4175127/story.html; ExoPC, accessed February 18, 2011, www.exopc.com/en/index.php; TMC, "At Dumoulin Électronique First! The CIARA VIBE Tablet, Powered by ExoPC, Now Available to the Public," *TMCnet*, January 26, 2011, accessed February 18, 2011, www.tmcnet.com/usubmit/ 2011/01/26/5269403.htm.

13. Patrick May, "So Many Apps, So Little Time," *San Jose Mercury News*, February 7, 2010, www.mercurynews.com.

14. Home Depot, accessed February 4, 2010, http://ir.homedepot.com.

15. Andreas Kaplan and Michael Haenlein, "Users of the World, Unite! The Challenges and Opportunities of Social Media," *Business Horizons* 53 (2010): 59–68.

16. Jennifer Van Grove, "Why Facebook Is Giving Out Free Wi-Fi for Check-In," CNET, October 2, 2013, accessed January 10, 2014, www.cnet.com/news/why-facebook-is-giving-out-free-wi-fi-for-check-ins.

17. Overstock.com, accessed February 9, 2010, www.overstock.com.

18. Canada Newswire, "Endura Energy Begins Construction of Inaugural Rooftop Solar Power System," March 4, 2011, accessed

January 2, 2012, http://cnw.ca/UO3x; Endura Energy, accessed January 2, 2012, www.enduraenergy.ca.

19. John Teresko, "Ford's Light Idea," *Industry Week*, November 1, 2007, www.industryweek.com.

20. Endura Energy, accessed January 2, 2012, www.enduraenergy.ca.

21. "A Change in Climate," *Economist*, January 17, 2008, www.economist.com.

22. "The Diversity Inc. Top 50 Companies for Diversity," Diversity Inc., accessed February 4, 2010, www.diversityinc.com.

23. "Survey: Workplace Discrimination Still Prevalent," *Inc.*, March 1, 2007, accessed March 2, 2010, www.inc.com/news/briefs/200703/0301survey.html.

24. James Cameron Online: The Home of James Cameron Fans, accessed February 18, 2011, www.jamescamerononline.com.

25. Michael Wilson, "Flight 1549 Pilot Tells of Terror and Intense Focus," *New York Times*, February 8, 2009, accessed May 8, 2015, www.nytimes.com/2009/02/09/nyregion/09interview.html?_r=0.

26. "World's Most Admired Companies 2014," *Fortune*, accessed April 11, 2014, http://fortune.com/worlds-most-admired-companies.

Chapter 2

1. Best of Vegas, "O—Cirque du Soleil," accessed February 15, 2011, www.bestofvegas.com/Shows-Tickets/O/; Cirque du Soleil, accessed February 15, 2011, www.cirquedusoleil.com/en/home.aspx#/en/home/about/details/cirque-du-soleil-at-a-glance.aspx; One Drop Foundation, "Who We Are," accessed February 15, 2011, www.onedrop.org/en/DiscoverOneDrop_Canada/WhoWeAre.aspx; One Drop Foundation, "Project Haiti: Water, a Source for Rebuilding," accessed August 14, 2014, www.onedrop.org/en/projects/projects-overview/haiti.aspx; BSR, accessed February 15, 2011, www.bsr.org; Ellen Barry, "What a Dump!," *Metropolis Magazine*, April 1998, accessed February 15, 2011, www.metropolismag.com/html/content_0498/ap98dump.htm; "Global Warming Fast Facts," *National Geographic News*, June 14, 2007, accessed February 15, 2011, http://news.nationalgeographic.com/news/2004/12/1206_041206_global_warming.html; Couvre Planchers Labrosse Inc., "Cirque du Soleil," accessed August 14, 2014, http://cplsolutions.ca/en/goods-and-service/achievements/cirque-du-soleil/.

2. Industry Canada, "New Standard on Social Responsibility Launched," accessed February 17, 2011, www.ic.gc.ca/eic/site/csr-rse.nsf/eng/rs00583.html.

3. "The List," *Maclean's*, accessed August 11, 2014, www.macleans.ca/general/266237/.

4. Johnson & Johnson, "Our Credo," accessed August 11, 2014, www.jnj.com/sites/default/files/pdf/jnj_ourcredo_english_us_8.5x11_cmyk.pdf; "Most Admired 2015," *Fortune*, accessed July 29, 2014, http://fortune.com/worlds-most-admired-companies/apple-1/.

5. Walmart Canada, "2013 Corporate Responsibility Leadership Council," accessed July 29, 2014, www.walmartcanada.ca/Pages/Corporate%20Responsibility%20Leadership%20Council/224/254/254.

6. Cliff Kuang, "The GOOD 100: Wal-Mart's Sustainability Push," *Good*, October 7, 2009; Michael Garry, "Wal-Mart Cites Progress on Sustainability Index," *Supermarket News*, November 23, 2009; SEIA, "Solar Means Business 2013: Top U.S. Commercial Solar Users," accessed July 29, 2014, www.seia.org/research-resources/solar-means-business-2013-top-us-commercial-solar-users.

7. National Business Ethics Survey, "About the National Business Ethics Survey of the U.S. Workforce 2013," accessed July 29, 2014, www.ethics.org/nbes/about.

8. Daniel Franklin, "Just Good Business," *Economist*, January 17, 2008.

9. Ethics Resource Center, "2009 National Business Ethics Survey," November 2009.

10. Tom Kemp, "Despite Privacy Concerns, It's Time to Kill the Password," *Forbes*, accessed August 18, 2014, www.forbes.com/sites/frontline/2014/07/18/despite-privacy-concerns-its-time-to-kill-the-password; Symantec, "2013 Cost of Data Breach Study: United States," accessed July 30, 2014, www.symantec.com/content/en/us/about/media/pdfs/b-cost-of-a-data-breach-us-report-2013.en-us.pdf?om_ext_cid=biz_socmed_twitter_facebook_marketwire_linkedin_2013Jun_worldwide_CostofaDataBreach.

11. Jim Dwyer, "H&M Says It Will Stop Destroying Unworn Clothing," *New York Times*, January 6, 2010; Jim Dwyer, "A Clothing Clearance Where More Than Just the Prices Have Been Slashed," *New York Times*, January 5, 2010.

12. "Obama Renews Ban on Ruby, Jade from Myanmar," *National Jeweler*, July 30, 2009, www.nationaljewelernetwork.com.

13. Jessica Murphy, "One in Five Job Seekers Lie on Resume: Poll," *Toronto Sun*, October 27, 2010, accessed January 15, 2011, www.torontosun.com/news/canada/2010/10/27/15855051.html; Dale Brazao, "Osgoode Hall Law School Vows to Weed out Fakes," *Toronto Star*, December 30, 2008, accessed February 12, 2011, www.thestar.com/news/gta/article/559484.

14. Heather Tooley, "Personal Internet Usage in the Workplace—A Serious Epidemic," *Associated Content*, January 17, 2010, www.associatedcontent.com; Jeffrey R. Smith, "No 'LOL' over Misuse of Email and Internet at Work," *Canadian HR Reporter*, September 28, 2009, http://chrremploymentlaw.wordpress.com.

15. Canadian Press, "University of Saskatchewan Dean Fired, Banned for Life from Campus after Speaking out about Cuts," *National Post*, May 14, 2014, accessed August 11, 2014, http://news.nationalpost.com/2014/05/14/dean-who-spoke-out-about-university-of-saskatchewan-cuts-fired-banned-for-life-from-campus; Canadian Press, "'We Want to See the Current Leadership . . . Gone': Protest Calls for University of Saskatchewan Resignations over Firing," *National Post*, May 21, 2014, accessed August 11, 2014, http://news.nationalpost.com/2014/05/21/we-want-to-see-the-current-leadershipgone-protest-calls-for-university-of-saskatchewan-resignations-over-firing; Josh Visser, "University of Saskatchewan 'Reconsiders' Decision on Fired Prof, Will Offer Him a New Position," *National Post*, May 15, 2014, accessed August 11, 2014, http://news.nationalpost.com/2014/05/15/university-of-saskatchewan-reconsiders-lifetime-ban-of-fired-prof-will-offer-him-a-new-position; Canadian Press, "University of Saskatchewan Provost Resigns Amid Controversy over Firing of Outspoken Professor," *National Post*, May 19, 2014, accessed August 11, 2011, http://news.nationalpost.com/2014/05/19/university-of-saskatchewan-provost-resigns-amid-controversy-over-firing-of-outspoken-

professor; Canadian Press, "University of Saskatchewan Fires President Ilene Busch-Vishniac Amid Controversy over Professor's Dismissal," *National Post*, May 22, 2014, accessed August 11, 2014, http://news.nationalpost.com/2014/05/22/university-of-saskatchewan-fires-president-ilene-busch-vishniac-amid-controversy-over-professors-dismissal.

16. "Whistleblower Legislation Bill C-25, Disclosure Protection," *CBC News*, April 28, 2004, accessed February 23, 2011, www.cbc.ca/news/background/whistleblower.

17. "Alberta Whistleblower Faces $10M Lawsuit from Gaming Company," *CBC News*, October 27, 2006, accessed February 23, 2011, www.cbc.ca/news/canada/edmonton/story/2006/10/27/alberta-gaming.html.

18. Air Canada, "Corporate Policy and Guidelines on Business Conduct," accessed February 27, 2011, www.aircanada.com/en/about/media/codeofconduct.pdf.

19. The Skald Group, "Ethical Awareness and Leadership," accessed February 17, 2011, www.skaldgroup.com.

20. SAI Global, "Compliance and Rish," accessed March 20, 2012, www.saiglobal.com/compliance.

21. Umaimah Mendhro and Abhinav Sinha, "Three Keys to Staying Ethical in the Age of Madoff," *Forbes*, February 6, 2009.

22. Pricewaterhouse Coopers Canada, "PricewaterhouseCoopers Canada Foundation," accessed August 11, 2014, www.pwc.com/ca/en/foundation/index.jhtml.

23. Tim Horton Children's Foundation, "One Dream Transforming Many Lives," accessed February 17, 2011, www.timhortons.com/ca/en/difference/childrens_about.html.

24. Brendan Kennedy, "Smoking Ban Sparks Drop in Hospitalization, Study Finds," *Toronto Star*, accessed February 23, 2011, www.thestar.com/life/health_wellness/2010/04/13/smoking_ban_sparks_drop_in_hospitalization_study_finds.html.

25. Childhood Obesity Foundation, www.childhoodobesityfoundation.ca, accessed February 17, 2011.

26. Coca-Cola Company, "New Program Puts Veterans to Work Teaching Physical Fitness to Youths and Families," April 23, 2015, www.coca-colacompany.com/press-center/press-releases/new-program-puts-veterans-to-work-teaching-physical-fitness-to-youths-and-families; Boys & Girls Clubs of America, "Triple Play: A Game Plan for Mind, Body and Soul," www.bgca.org/whatwedo/SportsFitnessRecreation/Pages/TriplePlayResources.aspx.

27. "Ben Johnson: Canada's Shame," *CBC Digital Archives*, September 26, 1988, accessed February 17, 2011, http://archives.cbc.ca/sports/drugs_sports/clips/8702; "1988: Johnson Stripped of Olympic Gold," *BBC on This Day*, accessed February 17, 2011, http://news.bbc.co.uk/onthisday/hi/dates/stories/september/27/newsid_2539000/2539525.stm.

28. "Mount Polley Mine Tailings Spill: Imperial Metals Could Face $1M Fine," *CBC News*, accessed August 18, 2014, www.cbc.ca/news/canada/british-columbia/mount-polley-mine-tailings-spill-imperial-metals-could-face-1m-fine-1.2728832.

29. US Environmental Protection Agency, "Where Can I Donate or Recycle My Old Computer and Other Electronic Products?" accessed February 4, 2010, www.epa.gov; Best Buy, "We Now Offer Electronics Recycling at All Best Buy Stores Nationwide," accessed February 4, 2010, www.bestbuy.com.

30. Recycling Council of Ontario, "Take Back the Light," accessed February 17, 2011, www.takebackthelight.ca.

31. William J. Watkins, Jr., "Rethinking Patent Enforcement: Tesla Did What?" *Forbes*, accessed August 12, 2014, www.forbes.com/sites/realspin/2014/07/17/rethinking-patent-enforcement-tesla-did-what.

32. Statistics Canada, "Waste Management Industry: Business and Government Sectors," *The Daily*, December 22, 2010, accessed February 17, 2011, www.statcan.gc.ca/daily-quotidien/101222/dq101222b-eng.htm.

33. Ontario Ministry of Finance, "Ontario Electronic Stewardship Fees," accessed February 17, 2011, www.rev.gov.on.ca/en/notices/rst/74.html.

34. Competition Bureau, *Environmental Claims: A Guide for Industry and Advisors*, June 2008, accessed February 18, 2011, www.competitionbureau.gc.ca/eic/site/cb-bc.nsf/eng/02701.html.

35. Martin LaMonica, "Bill Gates Investing in Vinod Khosla Green-Tech Fund," *CNET News*, January 25, 2010.

36. Natural Resources Canada, "ecoACTION," accessed August 12, 2014, www.nrcan.gc.ca/ecoaction.

37. Tim Hortons, "Tim Hortons Coffee Partnership," accessed February 18, 2011, www.timhortons.com/ca/en/difference/coffee-partnership.html.

38. Tim Hortons, "Our Scholarship Program," accessed February 18, 2011, www.timhortons.com/ca/en/join/scholarship.html.

39. COSTI Immigrant Services, "Programs and Services," accessed February 18, 2011, www.costi.org/programs/service_details.php?stype_id=53.

40. Coca-Cola, "Diversity," accessed February 12, 2010, www.thecoca-colacompany.com.

41. Canadian Breast Cancer Foundation CIBC Run for the Cure, accessed February 22, 2011, www.runforthecure.com/site/PageServer?pagename=about_the_run.

42. Marlene Rego, "Tickled Pink: Top Breast Cancer Products," *Chatelaine*, accessed February 22, 2011, www.chatelaine.com/en/article/3972--tickled-pink-top-breast-cancer-products; Cook for the Cure, accessed August 12, 2014, www.cookforthecure.ca/about.html.

43. "UPS Pilots Volunteer to Help Haiti Relief Effort," *Forbes*, January 14, 2010.

44. Consumers' Association of Canada, "About Us," accessed February 18, 2011, www.consumer.ca/1480.

45. "15th Listeria Death Linked to Maple Leaf Foods," *CBC News*, September 10, 2008, accessed February 18, 2011, www.cbc.ca/consumer/story/2008/09/10/listeria-ontario.html; "How Maple Leaf Foods Is Handling the Listeria Outbreak," *CBC News*, accessed February 18, 2011, www.cbc.ca/money/story/2008/08/27/f-crisisresponse.html; "Maple Leaf Settles Class Action Listeriosis Lawsuits for $27M," *CBC News*, accessed August 12, 2014, www.cbc.ca/news/canada/maple-leaf-settles-class-action-listeriosis-lawsuits-for-27m-1.696972.

46. Sharon Oosthoek, "Rogers Faces $10M Fine over Dropped-Call Ads," *CBC News*, November 19, 2010, accessed February 21, 2011,

www.cbc.ca/news/business/story/2010/11/19/consumer-chatr-rogers-competition-bureau.html; Canadian Press, "Ontario Court Fines Rogers $500,000 over Chatr Ads," *CBC*, accessed August 12, 2014, www.cbc.ca/news/technology/ontario-court-fines-rogers-500-000-over-chatr-ads-1.2550590.

47. Department of Justice, Food and Drugs Act, accessed February 21, 2011, http://laws.justice.gc.ca/en/f-27/.
48. "Ontario Seeks Appeal of Private-Label Drug Ruling," *CBC News*, February 19, 2011, accessed February 21, 2011, www.cbc.ca/news/health/story/2011/02/19/ontario-drug-ruling-appeal.html.
49. eBay, "eBay Rules and Policies Overview," accessed February 14, 2010, http://pages.ebay.com/help/policies/overview.html.
50. Human Resources and Skills Development Canada, "Work—Work-Related Injuries," accessed February 21, 2011, http://www4.hrsdc.gc.ca/.3ndic.1t.4r@-eng.jsp?iid=20.
51. "Canada's Top 100 Employers," accessed August 12, 2014, www.canadastop100.com/national/.
52. Robert Smithson, "Is Unlimited Vacation Time a Recipe for Business Success?" *Kelowna Capital News*, February 16, 2010.
53. Research In Motion, "Search Full Time Opportunities: Explore the World of RIM," accessed January 31, 2012, www.rim.com/careers/search/index.shtml; WestJet, "Great Jobs," accessed January 3, 2012, www.westjet.com/guest/en/jobs.shtml.
54. Canadian Charter of Rights and Freedoms, accessed February 22, 2011, http://laws.justice.gc.ca/en/charter/1.html#anchorbo-ga:l_I-gb:s_15.
55. "Exotic Dancer Files Age Discrimination Complaint," *CBC News*, accessed February 22, 2011, www.cbc.ca/news/canada/story/2008/11/03/dancer-ohrt-complaint.html.
56. Liz Wolgemuth, "20 Ways Older Workers Can Sell Themselves," *U.S. News & World Report*, November 26, 2008.
57. "Baby Boomers Swell Ranks of Retirement-Aged Canadians," *CBC News*, July 17, 2007, accessed February 21, 2011, www.cbc.ca/news/canada/story/2007/07/17/census-canada.html; Jamie Sturgeon, "Retiring Boomers Could Cost Economy $11,500 a Head in Lost Growth," *Global News*, accessed August 12, 2014, http://globalnews.ca/news/1240976/the-number-of-working-age-canadians-is-plummeting-report/.
58. Pay Equity Commission, "Gender Wage Gap," accessed August 12, 2014, www.payequity.gov.on.ca/en/about/pubs/genderwage/wagegap.php.
59. Gail Zoppo, "Why Are Women Still Earning Less than Men?" *Diversity Inc.*, April 28, 2009.
60. "Livent Co-founders Drabinsky, Gottlieb Convicted of Fraud and Forgery," *CBC News*, March 25, 2009, accessed February 23, 2011, www.cbc.ca/news/business/story/2009/03/25/livent-decision-fraud.html.

Chapter 3

1. Kent Spencer, "Signs of Life in Olympic Village," *The Province*, December 28, 2011, www.theprovince.com/technology/Signs+life+Olympic+Village/5917801/story.html; Kent Spencer, "Vancouver Drops Prices on Olympic Condo Units," *National Post*, February 11, 2011, p. A6; Canada Mortgage and Housing Corporation (CMHC), "Housing Market Information, Housing Market Outlook—Fourth Quarter 2010," accessed February 15, 2011, www.cmhc-schl.gc.ca/odpub/esub/61500/61500_2010_Q04.pdf?fr=1297379904219; CMHC, "Housing Market Information, Housing Market Outlook—Fall 2010," accessed February 15, 2011, www.cmhc-schl.gc.ca/odpub/esub/64363/64363_2010_B02.pdf?lang=en; CMHC, "Housing Market Information, Housing Market Outlook—Vancouver and Abbotsford CMAs, Date Released: Fourth Quarter 2007," accessed February 15, 2011, http://dsp-psd.pwgsc.gc.ca/collection_2007/cmhc-schl/nh12-56/NH12-56-2007-2E.pdf; CMHC, "Canadian Housing at a Glance 2010," accessed February 15, 2011, www.cmhc-schl.gc.ca/en/corp/about/cahoob/upload/dashboard_en.pdf.
2. Nathan Eddy, "Video Game Sales Down 8 Percent in 2009," *TechWeek Europe*, January 18, 2010, accessed May 14, 2015, www.techweekeurope.co.uk/cloud/datacenter/computer-games-sales-down-8-percent-3053.
3. Jeff Bercovici, "Soon, You'll Have to Pay for Hulu," *Daily Finance*, June 3, 2009, accessed May 14, 2015, www.dailyfinance.com/2009/06/03/soon-youll-have-to-pay-for-hulu; Dawn C. Chmielewski and Alex Pham, "At Hulu, 'Free' May Turn to 'Fee,'" *Los Angeles Times*, January 21, 2010, accessed May 14, 2015, http://articles.latimes.com/2010/jan/21/business/la-fi-ct-newhulu21-2010jan21.
4. Jad Mouawad, "Demand for Oil Set to Rise Anew," *New York Times*, February 15, 2010, accessed May 14, 2015, www.nytimes.com/2010/02/15/business/energy-environment/15renoil.html?_r=0.
5. David P. Schulz, "Top 100 Retailers," *Stores*, NRF Stores, accessed February 4, 2010, www.stores.org.
6. Pascal Fletcher, "Freeze Mauls Florida Citrus, Significant Damage Seen," Reuters, January 11, 2010, accessed May 14, 2015, http://mobile.reuters.com/article/idUSTRE60913020100111.
7. Sustainable Produce Urban Delivery, accessed March 26, 2012, www.spud.ca,; Eat Local, accessed March 26, 2012, www.eatlocal.org.
8. Bettina Wassener, "Fed's Move Prompts Drop in Asian Stocks, Oil and Gold, but Dollar Rises," *New York Times*, February 20, 2010, www.nytimes.com; Lewa Pardomuan, "Gold Slips 1 Percent after Fed Raises Discount Rate," Reuters, February 18, 2010, accessed March 26, 2012, www.reuters.com/article/2010/02/19/markets-precious-idUSSGE61I04C20100219.
9. Gold Price, "10 Year Gold Price in CAD/oz," accessed March 21, 2015, http://goldprice.org/charts/history/gold_10_year_o_cad.png.
10. William Spain, "Fast-Food Outlook: Intense Competition, Margin Pressures," *MarketWatch*, January 14, 2010, accessed May 14, 2015, www.marketwatch.com/story/fast-food-2010-stiff-competition-margin-pressure-2010-01-14.
11. Larissa MacFarquhar, "When Giants Fall," *The New Yorker*, May 14, 2012, accessed January 18, 2014, www.newyorker.com/magazine/2012/05/14/when-giants-fail.
12. "CRTC Issues Video-on-Demand Licence Conditions," *The Wire Report*, January 31, 2011, accessed February 11, 2011, www.thewirereport.ca/reports/content/11903-crtc_issues_video_on_demand_licence_conditions.

13. Air Canada, accessed February 4, 2010, www.aircanada.com.
14. Central Intelligence Agency, *World Factbook*, accessed January 24, 2014, www.cia.gov.
15. Alexis Leondis, "U.S. Millionaires' Ranks Rose 16% in 2009, Study Says," *BusinessWeek*, March 9, 2010, www.businessweek.com.
16. Statistics Canada, *Canada Year Book 2010*, p. 278, Table 21.7, "Employment, by Industry, 1995 to 2009," CANSIM table 282-0008, accessed February 3, 2011, www.statcan.gc.ca/pub/11-402-x/2010000/pdf/labour-travail-eng.pdf.
17. World Bank, accessed February 4, 2010, http://web.worldbank.org; "Disaster Experts Share Lessons for Haiti," http://web.worldbank.org; Jack Ewing, "Emerging Economies Gain a Voice at Davos," *New York Times*, January 26, 2010, accessed May 14, 2015, www.nytimes.com/2010/01/27/business/global/27global.html.
18. DaveManuel.com, "Canadian Debt Clock March 2015," accessed March 25, 2015, www.davemanuel.com/canada-debt-clock.php; Brillig.com, "U.S. National Debt Clock," accessed March 25, 2015, www.brillig.com/debt_clock.
19. U.S. and World Population Clocks, U.S. Census Bureau, accessed February 4, 2010, www.census.gov.
20. Justin Pritchard, "U.S. Agency Goes after Cadmium in Children's Jewelry," *ABC News*, January 11, 2010, http://abcnews.go.com.

Chapter 4

1. PotashCorp, accessed March 25, 2015, www.potashcorp.com; Yahoo Finance Canada, "PotashCorp," accessed March 25, 2015, https://ca.finance.yahoo.com/q/ks?s=POT.TO; "Reaction to Conference Board Report on Potash," Business News Network, October 4, 2010, accessed February 18, 2011, http://watch.bnn.ca/the-close/october-2010/the-close-october-4-2010/#clip356483; Brenda Bouw and Boyd Erman, "PotashCorp Value Tops $170/share: CEO," *Globe and Mail*, October 7, 2010, accessed February 11, 2011, www.bnn.ca/News/2010/10/7/PotashCorp-value-tops-170-share-CEO.aspx; Brenda Bouw, "Potash Corp. Doubles Profit, Vows to Avoid Dramatic Price Spike," *Globe and Mail*, January 28, 2011, accessed February 11, 2011, www.theglobeandmail.com/globe-investor/potash-corp-doubles-profit-vows-to-avoid-dramatic-price-spike/article1884428/.
2. Statistics Canada, "Imports, Exports and Trade Balance of Goods on a Balance-of-Payments Basis, by Country or Country Grouping," accessed March 25, 2015, www.statcan.gc.ca/tables-tableaux/sum-som/l01/cst01/gblec02a-eng.htm; Statistics Canada, "Exports of Goods on a Balance-of-Payments Basis, by Product," accessed February 27, 2011, www40.statcan.ca/l01/cst01/gblec04.htm; Central Intelligence Agency, "Canada," *World Factbook*, accessed February 27, 2011, www.cia.gov; Statistics Canada, "International Trade," *Canada Year Book*, pp. 255–266, accessed February 27 2011, www.statcan.gc.ca/pub/11-402-x/2010000/pdf/international-eng.pdf.
3. U.S. Census Bureau, "International Database," accessed January 6, 2014, www.census.gov; "You Think! But Do You Know?" World Bank, accessed January 6, 2014, http://youthink.worldbank.org.
4. World Bank, accessed January 6, 2014, http//worldbank.org.
5. Walmart, "International," accessed January 6, 2014, http://corporate.walmart.com.
6. Sahar Saffron, accessed March 8, 2010, http://safarsaffron.com; Spice Advice, accessed March 8, 2010, www.spiceadvice.com.
7. Steve Hamm, "Big Blue's Global Lab," *Businessweek*, August 27, 2009, www.bloomberg.com/bw/magazine/content/09_36/b4145040683083.htm.
8. Statistics Canada, "Imports, Exports and Trade Balance of Goods on a Balance-of-Payments Basis, by Country or Country Grouping," accessed March 25, 2015, www.statcan.gc.ca/tables-tableaux/sum-som/l01/cst01/gblec02a-eng.htm.
9. CIA, "Canada," *World Factbook*, accessed March 2, 2011, www.cia.gov/library/publications/the-world-factbook/geos/ca.html.
10. Illinois Oil and Gas Association, "History of Illinois Basin Posted Crude Oil Prices," accessed March 2, 2011, www.ioga.com/Special/crudeoil_Hist.htm.
11. Statistics Canada, "Table 380-00701, Exports and Imports of Goods and Services," accessed March 27, 2015, www5.statcan.gc.ca/cansim/pick-choisir?lang=eng&p2=33&id=3800070.
12. U.S. Census Bureau, "Annual Trade in Goods and Services, 1960–2012," accessed January 30, 2014, www.cencus.gov; U.S. Bureau of Economic Analysis, "U.S. International Trade in Goods and Services," press release, accessed January 30, 2014, www.bea.gov.
13. Bank for International Settlements, accessed March 26, 2015, www.bis.org.
14. Vivian Wai-yin Kwok, "How Kraft Won in China," *Forbes*, December 8, 2009, accessed March 26, 2015, www.forbes.com/2009/12/08/china-oreo-tang-cmo-network-kraft.html.
15. Tanya Mohn, "Going Global, Stateside," *New York Times*, March 8, 2010, accessed March 26, 2015, www.nytimes.com/2010/03/09/business/global/09training.html?_r=0.
16. "India Needs 400 Airports to Cater to People's Needs," LiveMint, March 3, 2010, www.livemint.com; Samar Halarnkar, "Delhi Airport's T3: Bags Packed, Ready to Go," LiveMint, February 28, 2010, www.livemint.com.
17. Transparency International, "Foreign Bribery and OECD Countries: A Hollow Commitment? Progress Report 2009," www.transparency.org, June 22, 2009.
18. Joe Ayling "'Made in Italy' Thrives without EU Label Law," *Just Style*, accessed January 6, 2014, www.just-style.com.
19. Canada Border Services Agency, "Fact Sheet," accessed March 2, 2011, www.cbsa-asfc.gc.ca/media/facts-faits/060-eng.html.
20. Louis Uchitelle, "Glassmaking Thrives Offshore, but Is Declining in U.S.," *New York Times*, January 19, 2010, accessed May 28, 2015, www.nytimes.com/2010/01/19/business/19glass.html.
21. World Trade Organization, "Lamy Calls for March Stocktaking to 'Inject Political Energy and Momentum' in the Negotiations," February 22 and 23, 2010, www.wto.org.
22. "G7 to Forgive Haiti Foreign Debt," *ABC News*, February 7, 2010; World Bank, "World Bank Statement on Haiti Debt," press release, January 21, 2010, www.worldbank.org.
23. CIA, "North America," *World Factbook*, accessed February 8, 2014, www.cia.gov; Office of the United States Trade Representative,

"North American Free Trade Agreement," accessed January 6, 2014, www.ustr.gov.

24. Ibid.

25. Ibid.

26. U.S. Census Bureau, "2013: Trade in Good with CAFTA-DR," accessed January 6, 2014, www.census.gov.

27. European Union, "Countries," accessed January 6, 2014, http://europa.eu/about-eu/countries/index_en.htm; CIA, "European Union," *World Factbook*, accessed January 6, 2014, www.cia.gov.

28. Pete Evans, "Tim Hortons, Burger King Agree to Merger Deal," *CBC News*, August 26, 2014, accessed March 25, 2015, www.cbc.ca/news/business/tim-hortons-burger-king-agree-to-merger-deal-1.2746948; "The Story of Tim Hortons," Tim Hortons, accessed January 14, 2012, www.timhortons.com/ca/en/about/index.html.

29. Morinaga & Company, accessed March 9, 2010, www.morinagamilk.co.jp.

30. Kate O'Sullivan, "Best Buys in Offshore Manufacturing," CFO.com, February 18, 2010, accessed May 28, 2015, http://ww2.cfo.com/technology/2010/02/best-buys-in-offshore-manufacturing.

31. "Target Buys Zellers Leases for $1.8B," *CBC News*, January 13, 2011, accessed March 3, 2011, www.cbc.ca/news/business/story/2011/01/13/target-zelles-takeover.html; Hollie Shaw, "Target Corp to Exit Canada after Racking up Billions in Losses," *Financial Post*, January 15, 2015, accessed March 27, 2015, http://business.financialpost.com/2015/01/15/target-corp-calls-it-quits-in-canada-plans-fair-and-orderly-exit.

32. Alcoa, accessed March 17, 2010, www.alcoa.com.

Part 1 Case Study: Beau's All Natural Brewing Company: Building a Craft Brewery in a Competitive Canadian Industry

Based on interviews with Steve Beauchesne at Beau's All Natural Brewery Company offices, Vankleek Hill, Ontario, on March 30, 2015; Beau's All Natural Brewery Company, accessed April 3, 2015, www.beaus.ca; Beau's Beer Blog, "How to Start a Brewery in 1 Million Easy Steps," January 9, 2007, accessed April 3, 2015, http://beausbeer.blogspot.ca/2007/01/brewery-measurements.html; Small Business Accelerator, "Industry Overview: Craft Breweries & Microbreweries," accessed April 3, 2015, www.sba-bc.ca/blog/industry-overview-craft-breweries-microbreweries; Glen Hodgson, "From Farm to Glass: The Value of Beer in Canada," November 5, 2013, accessed April 3, 2015, www.beercanada.com/sites/default/files/13-11-03-from_farm_to_glass.pdf; IBISWorld, "Breweries in Canada: Market Research Report," January 2015, accessed April 3, 2015, www.ibisworld.ca/industry/default.aspx?indid=288; Statistics Canada, Agriculture and Agri-Food Canada, "The Canadian Brewing Industry," accessed April 3, 2015, www.agr.gc.ca/eng/industry-markets-and-trade/statistics-and-market-information/by-product-sector/processed-food-and-beverages/the-canadian-brewery-industry/?id=1171560813521#s1; Beer Canada, "Industry Statistics," accessed April 3, 2015, www.beercanada.com/industry-statistics; Tracey Lindeman, "The Entrepreneurs: Beau's Beers to Flow in Quebec," *Montreal Gazette*, August 10, 2014, accessed April 3, 2015, www.montrealgazette.com/life/Entrepreneurs+Beau+beers+flow+Quebec/10109168/story.html.

Part 1: Launching Your Global Business and Economics Career

1. U.S. Department of Labor, "Tomorrow's Jobs," *Occupational Outlook Handbook*, 2010–2011 edition, U.S. Bureau of Labor Statistics, www.bls.gov.

2. U.S. Department of Labor, "Economists," *Occupational Outlook Handbook*, 2010–2011 edition, U.S. Bureau of Labor Statistics, www.bls.gov.

3. Adapted from Michael R. Czinkota, Ilkka A. Ronkainen, and Michael H. Moffett, "Criteria for Selecting Managers for Overseas Assignments," in *International Business*, 7th ed. (Mason, OH: SouthWestern, 2005), Table 19.2, p. 634.

4. Ursula Milton, "MBA Still Packs a Punch," *Financial Times*, January 28, 2008, accessed March 17, 2010, www.ft.com/intl/cms/s/0/0b99d4de-cd42-11dc-9b2b-000077b07658.html#axzz3bXYEJ9H9.

5. Sattar Bawany, "Transition Coaching Helps Ensure Success for Global Assignments," *Today's Manager*, January 2008, accessed March 17, 2010, entrepreneur.com.

Chapter 5

1. Pi Athlete Management Inc., accessed April 4, 2015, www.piathlete.com; interviews with Martin Bindman and Daniel Smajovits of Pi Athlete Management Inc., January 2012; "Pro Baseball Player Marc Bourgeois Visits Home Base in Granby," *CTV Montreal*, Pi Athlete Management Inc., accessed January 6, 2012, http://vimeo.com/31769085; National Collegiate Athletic Association, accessed January 6, 2012, http://ncaa.org; Ron Sirak, "The Golf Digest 50: Golf's Top Earners," *Golf Digest*, February 2012, accessed January 13, 2012, www.golfdigest.com/golf-tours-news/2012-02/top-earners#intro; Kurt Badenhausen, "Sports' First Billion-Dollar Man," Forbes, September 29, 2009, accessed January 13, 2012, www.forbes.com/2009/09/29/tiger-woods-billion-business-sports-tiger.html; "The Average NFL Player," *Businessweek*, January 27, 2011, accessed January 13, 2012, www.businessweek.com/magazine/content/11_06/b4214058615722.htm; Steve Aschburner, NBA.com, "NBA's 'Average' Salary—$5.15M—A Trendy, Touchy Subject," August 11, 2011, accessed January 13, 2012, www.nba.com/2011/news/features/steve_aschburner/08/19/average-salary/index.html; National Hockey League Players' Association, "NHL Player Compensation," accessed January 13, 2012, www.nhlpa.com/Players/compensation; "MLB Salaries," *CBS Sports*, accessed January 13, 2012, www.cbssports.com/mlb/salaries/avgsalaries.

2. Statistics Canada, "Self-Employment, Historical Summary," accessed April 4, 2015, www.statcan.gc.ca/tables-tableaux/sum-som/l01/cst01/labor64-eng.htm.

3. Industry Canada, Small Business Branch, "Key Small Business Statistics," July 2011, accessed March 21, 2012, www.ic.gc.ca/eic/site/sbrp-rppe.nsf/vwapj/KSBS-PSRPE_July-Juillet2011_eng.pdf/$FILE/KSBS-PSRPE_July-Juillet2011_eng.pdf.

4. Paul Delean, "Riding the Health Wave," *Montreal Gazette*, February 28, 2011, p. A16; Nutrisoya, accessed April 4, 2015, www.nutrisoya,ca.

5. Mary Teresa Bitti, "Running on the Fitness Regimen," *Financial Post*, Canada's 50 Best Special Report, February 22, 2011, p. SR 28; Running Room, accessed April 4, 2015, www.runningroom.com.

6. Industry Canada, "Small Business Research and Statistics: Key Small Business Statistics—August 2013," accessed April 4, 2015, www.ic.gc.ca/eic/site/061.nsf/eng/h_02800.html.

7. Statistics Canada, "The Financial Picture of Farms in Canada," *2006 Census of Agriculture*, accessed March 9, 2011, www.statcan.gc.ca/ca-ra2006/articles/finpicture-portrait-eng.htm#A1.

8. Industry Canada, "Small Business Research and Statistics: Key Small Business Statistics—August 2013: What Is the Contribution of Small Businesses to Canada Gross Domestic Product?" accessed April 5, 2015, www.ic.gc.ca/eic/site/061.nsf/eng/02812.html.

9. Industry Canada, "Small Business Research and Statistics: Key Small Business Statistics—August 2013: What Is the Contribution of Small Businesses to Canada's Exports?" accessed April 5, 2015, www.ic.gc.ca/eic/site/061.nsf/eng/02811.html.

10. Industry Canada, "Small Business Research and Statistics: Key Small Business Statistics—August 2013: How Many Jobs Do Small Businesses Create?" accessed April 6, 2015, www.ic.gc.ca/eic/site/061.nsf/eng/02806.html.

11. Facebook, accessed April 6, 2015, www.facebook.com/press.

12. John Tozzi, Stacy Perman, and Nick Leiber, "2009 Finalists: America's Best Young Entrepreneurs," *Businessweek*, October 12, 2009, accessed April 6, 2015, www.bloomberg.com/sSs/09/10/1009_entrepreneurs_25_and_under/21.htm.

13. Industry Canada, "Small Business Research and Statistics: Key Small Business Statistics—August 2013: How Many Jobs Do Small Businesses Innovate?" accessed April 6, 2015, www.ic.gc.ca/eic/site/061.nsf/eng/02810.html.

14. "Advocacy Small Business Statistics and Research," U.S. Small Business Administration, accessed April 2, 2010, http://web.sba.gov/faqs.

15. Industry Canada, "Small Business Research and Statistics: Key Small Business Statistics—July 2010: How Many Businesses Appear and Disappear Each Year?" accessed March 9, 2011, www.ic.gc.ca/eic/site/sbrp-rppe.nsf/eng/rd02494.html.

16. Carol Kopp, "The Tragedy of Krispy Kreme," *Yahoo! Finance*, October 13, 2009, http://finance.yahoo.news.

17. Patricia Schaefer, "The Seven Pitfalls of Business Failure and How to Avoid Them," BusinessKnowHow.com, accessed April 2, 2010, www.businessknowhow.com/Startup/business-failure.htm.

18. Ibid.

19. "Advocacy Small Business Statistics and Research."

20. Leona Liu, "Meet the Celebrity Gardener," *Businessweek*, October 13, 2009, accessed April 2, 2010, www.bloomberg.com/bw/stories/2009-10-13/meet-the-celebrity-gardenerbusinessweek-business-news-stock-market-and-financial-advice.

21. Statistics Canada, "Survey of Regulatory Compliance Costs, 2008," *The Daily*, July 9, 2010, accessed March 10, 2011, www.statcan.gc.ca/daily-quotidien/100709/dq100709c-eng.htm.

22. Canada Business Network, "Small Business Investor Tax Credit," accessed March 21, 2012, www.canadabusiness.ca/eng/summary/6038.

23. TOMS Shoes, "One for One," accessed April 2, 2010, www.tomsshoes.com/Our-Movement.

24. "Top 10 Tips for Writing Your Business Plan," *AllBusiness*, accessed April 2, 2010, www.allbusiness.com/business-planning-structures.

25. Business Development Bank of Canada (BDC), accessed March 10, 2011, www.bdc.ca/EN/Pages/home.aspx.

26. Industry Canada, "Canada Small Business Financing Program," accessed March 10, 2011, www.ic.gc.ca/eic/site/csbfp-pfpec.nsf/eng/home.

27. Robert Joseph, Michael Bordt, and Daood Hamdani, "Characteristics of Business Incubation in Canada, 2005," Statistics Canada, accessed March 10, 2011, http://dsp-psd.pwgsc.gc.ca/Collection/Statcan/88F0006X/88F0006XIE2006007.pdf.

28. Canada's Venture Capital and Private Equity Association, "2014 Canadian Venture Market Capital Overview," accessed April 6, 2015, www.cvca.ca/wp-content/uploads/2014/07/2014-CDN-VC-market-activity-infographic-FINAL.pdf; John Tozzi, "Venture Capital's Favorite Startups," *Businessweek*, December 19, 2008, www.bloomberg.com/bw/stories/2008-12-19/venture-capitals-favorite-startupsbusinessweek-business-news-stock-market-and-financial-advice.

29. Arlene Dickinson, accessed January 15, 2012, http://arlenedickinson.com; CBC, "The Dragons: Arlene Dickinson," accessed January 15, 2012, www.cbc.ca/dragonsden/dragons_arlene.html.

30. Industry Canada, "Small Business Research and Statistics: Sustaining the Momentum: An Economic Forum on Women Entrepreneurs—Summary Report," accessed March 9, 2011, www.ic.gc.ca/eic/site/sbrp-rppe.nsf/eng/rd01309.html.

31. Franchiselink.com, "Canadian Franchise Statistics & Info," accessed April 8, 2015, www.franchiselink.ca/canadian-franchise-faqs/canadian-franchise-statistics-info/.

32. International Franchise Association, "The Economic Impact of Franchised Businesses," accessed February 10, 2014, www.franchise.org; IHS Global Insight, *Franchise Business Economic Outlook 2014*, January 13, 2014, accessed February 10, 2014, http://franchiseeconomy.com/wp-content/uploads/2014/01/Franchise_Business_Outlook_January_2014-1-13-13.pdf.

33. Marina Strauss, "Tim Hortons Borrows Burger King's Global Expansion Plan," *Business News Network*, March 27, 2015, accessed April 8, 2015, www.bnn.ca/News/2015/3/27/Tim-Hortons-borrows-Burger-Kings-global-expansion-plan.aspx.

34. Subway Restaurants, "Franchising FAQs," accessed April 8, 2015, www.subway.com/subwayroot/Own_a_Franchise/FranchiseFAQs.aspx.

35. Edward N. Levitt, "What's so Great about Franchising?" *Franchise Know How*, accessed April 2, 2010, www.franchiseknowhow.com/articles/franchising-benefits.htm.

36. Ibid.

37. "Why People Are Drawn to Franchising," FranChoice, accessed April 2, 2010, www.franchoice.com/resources/Why_People_Are_Drawn_To_Franchising.

38. Levitt, "What's so Great about Franchising?"

39. "How Much Does a Franchise Cost?" AllBusiness.com, accessed April 2, 2010, www.allbusiness.com.

40. Levitt, "What's so Great about Franchising?"

41. Ashley M. Heher, "Food Fight: Burger King Franchisees Sue Chain," *USA Today*, November 12, 2009, accessed April 2, 1010, http://usatoday30.usatoday.com/money/industries/food/2009-11-12-burger-king-franchises-lawsuit_N.htm.

42. Laura Northrup, "Recent Class Action Lawsuits: Are You Eligible?" *Consumerist*, May 22, 2009, accessed April 2, 2010, http://consumerist.com/2009/05/22/recent-class-action-lawsuits-are-you-eligible.

43. Sun Youth Organization, accessed March 13, 2011, http://sunyouthorg.com.

44. The Electricity Forum, "Canadian Electricity Generation, Transmission and Distribution Company Sites," accessed March 13, 2011, www.electricityforum.com/links/cdautil.html.

45. VIA Rail Canada, accessed March 13, 2011, www.viarail.ca.

46. "Cooperatives around the World," accessed February 3, 2014, http://usa2012.coop.

47. Government of Canada, Co-operatives Secretariat, "About Co-ops in Canada," accessed March 13, 2011, www.coop.gc.ca/COOP/display-afficher.do?id=1232131333489&lang=eng.

48. Peter Koven and Kim Covert, "Canada Leads in Mining M&As, China Well Back," *Calgary Herald*, March 4, 2011, accessed March 13, 2011, www.calgaryherald.com/business/Canada+leads+mining+China+well+back/4382198/story.html.

49. Canadian Breast Cancer Foundation, "CIBC Run for the Cure," accessed May 23, 2015, www.cbcf.org/ontario/GetInvolved/Events/Pages/CIBC-Run-for-the-Cure.aspx, accessed May 23, 2015.

50. Barbara Quinn, "Partnering on Sustainability," *Pollution Engineering*, January 2009, p. 17.

Chapter 6

1. N.R. Kleinfield, "Airbnb Host Welcomes Travelers from All Over," The New York Times, accessed April 28, 2014, www.nytimes; company website, "About Us," www.airbnb.com, accessed April 28, 2014; company website, "How FlightCar Works," https://flightcar.com, accessed April 28, 2014; Ryan Lawler, "Airport Car Rental Startup FlightCar Launches at LAX, Unveils Mobile App," Tech Crunch, accessed February 4, 2014, http://techcrunch.com; Tamara Warren, "Peer-to-Peer Car Sharing at the Airport," The New York Times, accessed February 4, 2014, www.nytimes.com; Tomio Geron, "Airbnb and the Unstoppable Rise of the Share Economy," Forbes, accessed February 4, 2014, www.forbes.com; Alan Farnham, "Rental Car Co. Run by Teenagers Undercuts Hertz, Avis," ABC News, accessed February 4, 2014, http://abcnews.go.com.

2. The Jim Pattison Group, "About Us," accessed April 8, 2015, www.jimpattison.com/about/our-story.

3. Stella & Dot, accessed January 19, 2014, http://stelladot.com; Jefferson Graham, "Stella and Dot Brings Tech to At-Home Jewellery Parties," *USA Today*, accessed January 19, 2014, www.usatoday.com/story/tech/columnist/talkingtech/2013/11/03/stella-dot-bring-tech-women-parties/3004733/; Vikram Alexei Kansara, "Jessica Herrin of Stella & Dot on Remaking Direct Sales to the Digital Age," *Business of Fashion*, accessed January 19, 2014, www.businessoffashion.com/articles/founder-stories/jessica-herrin-stella-dot-sequoia-capital.

4. Navkirat Sodhi, "Meet India's Leading Ladies," *Women Entrepreneur*, September 22, 2009, www.womenentrpreneur.com.

5. Industry Canada, "Small Business Research and Statistics: Key Small Business Statistics—August 2013," accessed April 8, 2015, www.ic.gc.ca/eic/site/061.nsf/eng/h_02800.html; "Kauffman Index of Entrepreneurial Activity," accessed January 19, 2014, www.kauffman.org.

6. Monster Gym, accessed April 8, 2015, www.monstergym.net.

7. Coramark Inc., "Our History," accessed April 8, 2015, www.chezcora.com/our-company/history.

8. Industry Canada, "Small Business Research and Statistics: Key Small Business Statistics—August 2013," accessed April 8, 2015, www.ic.gc.ca/eic/site/061.nsf/eng/h_02800.html; Office of Advocacy, U.S. Small Business Administration, "The Facts about Small Businesses," accessed January 19, 2014, www.sba.gov/content/small-business-facts.

9. Hannah Seligson, "Nine Young Chinese Entrepreneurs to Watch," Forbes, February 28, 2010, www.forbes.com/2010/02/26/young-chinese-entrepreneurs-to-watch-entrepreneurs-technology-china.html.

10. Eve Gumpel, "Gypsy Tea Steeped in Health and Fun," *Women Entrepreneur*, January 24, 2010, www.womenentrepreneur.com.

11. TronSports.ca, accessed October 28, 2015, http://tronsports.ca.

12. Niels Bosma, Kent Jones, Erkko Autio, and Jonathan Levie, "Global Entrepreneurial Monitor: Executive Report," accessed March 11, 2010, www.gemconsortium.org.

13. Sodhi, "Meet India's Leading Ladies."

14. Simon Fraser University, "Beedie School of Business News: Beedie Looks Back at Extraordinary Year at Surrey," accessed January 18, 2012, http://beedie.sfu.ca/blog/tag/sfu-student-entrepreneur-of-the-year.

15. Students in Free Enterprise, "Leadership and Career Connections," accessed March 11, 2010, www.sife.org.

16. Mark Henricks, "Honor Roll," *Entrepreneur*, accessed March 11, 2010, www.entrepreneur.com.

17. "Cool College Startups 2010," *Inc.*, accessed March 10, 2010, www.inc.com/ss/cool-college-start-ups-2010.

18. Tamara Schweitzer, "Study: Inc. 500 CEOs Aggressively Use Social Media for Business," *Inc.*, November 25, 2009, www.inc.com/news/articles/2009/11/inc500-social-media-usage.html.

19. "Kauffman Index of Entrepreneurial Activity," accessed January 20, 2014.

20. Newswire, "23-Year-Old Donates US$1 Million to Support University of Waterloo Student Entrepreneurs," accessed March 29, 2011, www.newswire.ca/en/releases/archive/March2011/29/c7314.html.

21. Play It Again, accessed April 8, 2015, www.playitagainsports.com.
22. Eve Gumpel, "The Accidental Inventor," *Women Entrepreneur*, August 18, 2009, www.womenentrepreneur.com.
23. "A Day in the Life of an Entrepreneur," *Princeton Review*, accessed March 14, 2010, www.princetonreview.com.
24. "Oprah Winfrey—About.com Readers' Most Admired Entrepreneur," accessed March 14, 2010, www.entrepreneurs.about.com.
25. Dan Moren, "Forget Oprah: Jobs Is Teens' Most Admired Entrepreneur," About.com, October 13, 2009, http://pcworld.about.com.
26. Sodhi, "Meet India's Leading Ladies."
27. Bobbi Brown, accessed January 20, 2014, www.bobbibrowncosmetics.co.uk; "How Bobbi Brown Put a New Face on the Makeup Industry," *CBS News*, accessed January 20, 2014, www.cbsnews.com/news/how-bobbi-brown-put-a-new-face-on-the-makeup-industry; Bobbi Brown and Athena Schindelheim, "How I Did It," *Inc.*, accessed January 20, 2014, www.inc.com/magazine/20071101/how-i-did-it-bobbi-brown-founder-and-ceo-bobbi-brown_pagen_2.html.
28. Donna Fenn, "The Kid Behind a $170 Million Website," *Inc.*, accessed March 15, 2010, www.inc.com/articles/2009/09/mint-qa.html.
29. Amy S. Choi, "Entrepreneurs Who Thrive on Risky Business," *Businessweek*, December 4, 2009, www.bloomberg.com/bw/magazine/content/09_72/s0912056528669.htm.
30. Kasey Wehrum, "How I Did It: Ralph Braun of BraunAbility," *Inc.*, December 1, 2009, www.inc.com/magazine/20091201/how-i-did-it-ralph-braun-of-braunability.html.
31. "Entrepreneurial America: A Comprehensive Look at Today's Fastest-Growing Private Companies," *Inc.: The Handbook of the American Entrepreneur*, accessed April 9, 2010, www.inc.com.
32. Darren Dahl, "How to Read a Term Sheet," *Inc.*, accessed March 1, 2010, www.inc.com/magazine/20100301/how-to-read-a-term-sheet.html.
33. Alexandra Paul, "City's First Urban Reserve Open," *Winnipeg Free Press*, January 10, 2012, accessed on January 20, 2012, www.winnipegfreepress.com/breakingnews/136997393.html.
34. Michael Goldman Inc., accessed March 16, 2010, www.michaelgoldman.com.
35. 3M, "A Culture of Innovation," accessed March 16, 2010, www.3M.com; Michael Goldman Inc., www.michaelgoldman.com.
36. 3M, "A Culture of Innovation."

Part 2 Case Study Beau's All Natural Brewing Company: Getting Started: Choosing a Location, Building the Plant and Hiring Employees

Based on interviews with Steve Beauchesne at Beau's All Natural Brewery Company offices, Vankleek Hill, Ontario, on March 30, 2015; Beau's All Natural Brewery Company, accessed April 3, 2015, www.beaus.ca; Beau's Beer Blog, "How to Start a Brewery in 1 Million Easy Steps," January 9, 2007, accessed April 3, 2015, http://beausbeer.blogspot.ca/2007/01/brewery-measurements.html.

Part 2: Launching Your Entrepreneurial Career

1. Michael Ames, cited in "Is Entrepreneurship for You?" Small Business Administration, accessed April 9, 2010, www.sba.gov.
2. Business Development Bank of Canada, "A Quick Refresher on Patents and Trademarks for Business Services," accessed May 1, 2012, www.bdc.ca/EN/advice_centre/articles/Pages/a_quick_refresher_on_patents_trademarks_for_business_services.aspx.

Chapter 7

1. Based on information from BlackBerry, accessed April 10, 2015, http://ca.blackberry.com/company.html; "Research In Motion Names Thorsten Heins President and CEO," press release, January 22, 2012, accessed January 23, 2012, www.rim.com/investors/documents/pdf/financial/2012/Research_In_Motion_Names_Thorsten_Heins_President_and_CEO.pdf; RIM stock chart, *Globe and Mail*, accessed January 23, 2012, www.theglobeandmail.com/globe-mvestor/markets/stocks/chart/?q=RIM-T; Tim Kiladze and Iain Marlow, "RIM Shakeup Brings Muted Market Response," *Globe and Mail*, January 23, 2012, accessed January 23, 2012, www.theglobeandmail.com/globe-investor/rim-shakeup-brings-muted-market-response/article2311427.
2. Loblaw, accessed April 10, 2015, www.loblaw.ca.
3. TD Bank, "Meet Our President & CEO," accessed April 10, 2015, www.td.com/about-tdbfg/corporate-information/executive-profiles/president.jsp; John Greenwood, "Canada's Outstanding CEO of the Year," *Financial Post*, January 14, 2011, accessed April 5, 2011, www.financialpost.com/executive/ceo/Canadas+Outstanding+Year+Clark/4110716/story.html.
4. "*Businessweek* Names Customer Service Champs," Customers 1st Blogspot, February 23, 2010, www.customers1stblogspot.com.
5. Cold Stone Creamery, accessed March 28, 2010, www.coldstonecreamery.com.
6. "Zappos.com Power by Service," accessed March 28, 2010, http://about.zappos.com.
7. Helen Coster, "The State of the CEO in 2010," Forbes, January 21, 2010, www.forbes.com/2010/01/21/state-of-ceo-leadership-governance-boards.html.
8. John Shmuel and Scott Deveau, "Stronach Resigns as Chairman of Magna," *Financial Post*, March 31, 2011, accessed April 5, 2011, www.canada.com/business/Frank+Stronach+step+down+Magna+chair man/4536966/story.html.
9. Christopher Steiner, "Go Green and Stay in the Black," *Forbes*, March 8, 2010, www.forbes.com/2010/03/08/green-small-business-entrepreneurs-technology-small-biz-toolkit-green-tips.html.

10. Facebook, accessed April 5, 2011, www.facebook.com/facebook.
11. Coster, "The State of the CEO in 2010."
12. Mattel, "Mattel Named One of the World's Most Ethical Companies Again in 2010," press release, March 22, 2010, http://news.mattel.com/news/mattel-named-one-of-the-world-s-most-ethical-companies-again-in-2010.
13. Reid Hoffman, as told to Mark Lacter, "How I Did It: Reid Hoffman of LinkedIn," *Inc.*, May 1, 2009, www.inc.com/author/reid-hoffman,-as-told-to-mark-lacter.
14. Geoff Colvin, "Housing Is Back—and so Is Home Depot," *Fortune*, September 19, 2013, accessed January 22, 2014, http://fortune.com/2013/09/19/housing-is-back-and-so-is-home-depot.
15. Brent Robinson, "Omnichannel Retailing and the Mobile Solution to Showroom Shoppers," *Bazaar Voice*, accessed January 23, 2014, http://blog.bazaarvoice.com/2013/10/23/omnichannel-retailing-and-the-mobile-solution-to-showroom-shoppers.
16. Sylvia Hui, "British Airways Cabin Crews Strike for 2nd Day," *Businessweek*, March 21, 2010, www.businessweek.com/ap/financialnews/D9EJ49700.htm.
17. Starbucks, accessed January 25, 2014, www.starbucks.com; Candice Choi, "Starbucks Hit by Migration to Online Shopping," *Yahoo Finance*, accessed January 25, 2014, http://finance.yahoo.com/news/starbucks-hit-migration-online-shopping-180105714.html;_ylt=AwrBT83vi3dVhC8A.UtXNyoA;_ylu=X3oDMTEyYzc5ams3BGNvbG8DYmYxBHBvcwMxBHZ0aWQDQjAwMjd-fMQRzZWMDc3I-; Annie Gasparo, "Green Mountain to Change Name to Include Keurig Brand," *Wall Street Journal*, accessed January 20, 2014, www.wsj.com/articles/SB10001424052702303754404579312940698163828; Stephanie Strom, "Starbucks Aims to Move Beyond Beans," *New York Times*, accessed January 20, 2014, www.nytimes.com/2013/10/09/business/a-juice-and-croissant-with-that-starbucks-latte.html.
18. Ibid.
19. Brooks Barnes, "But It Doesn't Look Like a Marriott," *New York Times*, accessed January 25, 2014, www.nytimes.com/2014/01/05/business/marriott-international-aims-to-draw-a-younger-crowd.html.
20. Becel, accessed April 5, 2011, www.loveyourheart.ca/en_ca/about_becel/default.aspx.
21. "How Companies Manage the Front Line Today," McKinsey & Company, pp. 1–2.
22. Jena McGregor, Alli McConnon, and David Kiley, "Customer Service in a Shrinking Economy," *Businessweek*, March 9, 2010, www.bloomberg.com/bw/stories/2009-02-18/customer-service-in-a-shrinking-economy.
23. Apple, accessed April 1, 2010, www.apple.com.
24. "Best 50 Corporate Citizens 2014," *Corporate Knights Magazine*, accessed April 10, 2015, www.corporateknights.com/reports/2014-best-50/2014-best-50-results-14020615/; "CR's 100 Best Corporate Citizens 2013," *Corporate Responsibility Magazine*, accessed January 25, 2014, www.thecro.org.
25. Bruce Horovitz, "CEO Profile: Campbell Exec Nears 'Extraordinary' Goal," *USA Today*, January 26, 2009, http://usatoday30.usatoday.com/money/companies/management/profile/2009-01-25-campbell-ceo-conant-profile_N.htm.
26. Scott D. Anthony, "Google's Management Style Grows Up," *Businessweek*, March 9, 2010, www.businessweek.com/managing/content/jun2009/ca20090623_918721.htm.
27. Dean Foust, "US Airways: After the 'Miracle on the Hudson,'" *Businessweek*, March 9, 2010, www.bloomberg.com/bw/stories/2009-02-18/us-airways-after-the-miracle-on-the-hudson.
28. Google, "Corporate Information," accessed March 30, 2010, www.google.com/corporate/culture.html.
29. Walt Disney Company, "Culture," accessed March 30, 2010, http://corporate.disney.go.com/careers/culture.html.
30. Ben Fritz, "Company Town," *Los Angeles Times*, March 30, 2010, http://latimesblogs.latimes.com.
31. Enterprise Rent-A-Car, "Enterprise Facts," accessed March 30, 2010, www.erac.com.
32. 3M, "Products and Services," accessed April 5, 2010, www.3M.com.
33. Brandon Gutman, "Zappos' Marketing Chief: 'Customer Service Is the New Marketing!'" *Fast Company*, March 15, 2010, www.fastcompany.com/1583321/zappos-marketing-chief-customer-service-new-marketing.
34. Mike Gordon, Chris Musso, Eric Rebentisch, and Nisheeth Gupta, "The Path to Successful New Products," *Forbes*, January 7, 2010, www.forbes.com/2010/01/07/new-products-innovation-leadership-managing-mckinsey.html.
35. Jason Del Rey, "How I Did It: Omniture's Josh James," *Inc.*, March 1, 2010, www.inc.com/magazine/20100301/how-i-did-it-omnitures-josh-james.html.

Chapter 8

1. Charles Duhigg and Keith Bradsher, "Iron Law of Economics," *New York Times*, published in *National Post*, January 23, 2012, p. FP3; Allan Swift, "Stretching with the Times," *Montreal Gazette*, November 20, 2006, pp. B1–B2; Industry Canada, "Canadian Apparel Profile," accessed January 29, 2012, www.ic.gc.ca/eic/site/026.nsf/eng/h_00070.html#statistical; Industry Canada, "Clothing Manufacturing," accessed January 29, 2012, www.ic.gc.ca/cis-sic/cis-sic.nsf/IDE/cis-sic315empe.html; Apparel Human Resources Council, "Pressing Ahead: Canada's Transforming Apparel Industry, 2011 Labour Market Information Study," March 31, 2011, accessed January 29, 2012, www.apparelconnexion.com/apparel/tools/files/b891ecaf-4376-7b1f.pdf; The Conference Board of Canada, "Canada's Textiles and Apparel Industry," Spring 2011.
2. Brandresume.com, "Predicting the Top 5 In Demand Skills for 2014," accessed January 25, 2014, https://brandredresume.com/2013/12/24/top-5-in-demand-skills-for-2014-prediction/.
3. Jobs in Pods, accessed January 25, 2014, www.jobsinpods.com.
4. Peter M. LaSorsa, "UPS Settles EEOC Lawsuit for $46,000," *Illinois Sexual Harassment Attorney Blog*, February 20, 2010, http://eeoc.gov/eeoc/newsroom/release/2-17-10.cfm.
5. "Executive Recruiting Advice—Don't Underestimate the Cost of a Mis-Hire," *Fortune 100 Best Companies to Work For*, accessed April 13, 2010, www.focussearchpartners.com/articles.html?item=executive-recruiting-advice-dont-underestimate-the-cost-of-a-mis-hire.

6. "McDonald's Puts Apprenticeships on the Menu," accessed April 15, 2010, https://people1st.wordpress.com/2009/01/08/mcdonalds-put-apprenticeships-on-the-menu/; McDonald's UK, "Apprentice," accessed April 11, 2015, www.mcdonalds.co.uk/ukhome/People/Join-the-team/Pick-your-role/Apprentice.html.

7. "Welcome to EYU," accessed January 25, 2015, www.ey.com.

8. "Systems Integration Consulting Training," accessed April 13, 2010, https://microsite.accenture.com.

9. The Conference Board of Canada, "Education and Learning," accessed April 11, 2015, www.conferenceboard.ca/topics/education/default.aspx.

10. Samuel A. Culbert, "Yes, Everyone Really Does Hate Performance Reviews," *Wall Street Journal*, April 19, 2010, http://finance.yahoo.com.

11. "Turn Your Performance Review System into One That Works," *Quality Digest Magazine*, accessed January 29, 2014, www.qualitydigest.com/inside/twitter-ed/turn-your-performance-review-system-one-works.html.

12. "Gather and Analyze 360 Degree Feedback More Quickly and Easily," Halogen Software, accessed April 11, 2015, www.halogensoftware.com/uploads/pdf/product-sheet/360-degree-feedback-datasheet.pdf.

13. Bureau of Labor Statistics, "Employer Costs for Employee Compensation, September 2013" press release, accessed January 25, 2014, www.bls.gov/news.release/archives/ecec_12112013.pdf.

14. Qualcomm, accessed January 25, 2014, www.qualcomm.com; "100 Best Companies to Work For 2013: Best Benefits," *Fortune*, accessed January 26, 2014, http://money.cnn.com/search/index.html?sortBy=date&primaryType=mixed&search=Search&query=100+Best+Companies+to+Work+For+2013%3A+Best+Benefits&symb=BEYSQ%20BBY%20FTEG%20ANNO%20BEST%20XSJDX%20XSCOX%20MUAB%20KRFDX%20BSJD.

15. "Advantages and Disadvantages of Paid Time Off," *The Thriving Small Business*, March 19, 2010, www.thethrivingsmallbusiness.com.

16. Eugene Eteris, "European Social Market Economy: Flexibility Issues," *The Baltic Course*, March 16, 2010, www.baltic-course.com.

17. "Things You Should Know about BidShift" San Angelo Community Medical Center, accessed April 14, 2010, www.sacmc.com.

18. Dan Schawbel, "Why a Flexible Workplace Makes Sense," accessed January 26, 2014, http://ehotelier.com; Richard Eisenberg, "It's High Time for a Four-Day Workweek," *Next Avenue*, accessed January 26, 2014, www.nextavenue.org.

19. Curt Finch, "The Rise of Telecommuting and What It Means for Your Business," *Small Business Trends*, accessed January 26, 2014, http://smallbiztrends.com/2013/05/telecommuting-business-benefits.html.

20. Millennial Branding, "The GenY Workplace Expectations Study," *Millennial Branding*, accessed January 28, 2014, http://millennialbranding.com.

21. Marshall Goldsmith, "How to Keep Good Employees in a Bad Economy," February 26, 2010, https://hbr.org/2010/02/how-to-keep-good-employees-in.

22. Dustin Ensinger, "Why Layoffs Are Not Beneficial to Companies," *Economy in Crisis*, February 8, 2010, http://economyincrisis.org/content/why-layoffs-are-not-beneficial-companies; Laura Hemphill, "Amid Layoffs—A Financial Analyst's Survivor Guilt," *Bloomberg Businessweek*, accessed January 27, 2014, www.businessweek.com; Ken Eisold, "The American Way of Unemployment," *Psychology Today*, accessed January 28, 2014, www.psychologytoday.com/blog/hidden-motives/201108/the-american-way-unemployment.

23. Ibid.

24. Christopher D. Zatzik, Mitchell L. Marks, Roderick D. Iverson, "Downsizing Case Studies," *MIT Sloan Management Review*, January 7, 2010, www.nationalpost.com.

25. "Maslow's Hierarchy of Needs," Accel-Team.com, accessed April 14, 2010, www.accel-team.com.

26. Mediacorp Canada Inc., "Canada's Top Employers for Young People," accessed January 30, 2012, www.canadastop100.com/young_people/.

27. Canadian Labour Congress, accessed April 11, 2015, www.canadianlabour.ca/home; Human Resources and Skills Development Canada, "Union Membership in Canada 2010," accessed January 30, 2012, www.hrsdc.gc.ca/eng/labour/labour_relations/info_analysis/union_membership/2010/unionmembership2010.shtml#results.

28. Jim Balsillie, *An Investigation into the Collective Bargaining Relationship between the NHL and the NHLPA 1994–2005* (Kingston, ON: Queens University Industrial Relations Centre, 2005), accessed January 30, 2012, http://irc.queensu.ca/gallery/1/dps-nhl-lockout.pdf.

29. Jamie Doward, "BA Strike: Airline and Union Swap Barbs on Second Weekend of Walkouts," *Guardian*, March 27, 2010, www.theguardian.com/business/2010/mar/27/british-airways-strike-heathrow-gatwick.

30. Ibid.

31. Human Resources and Skills Development Canada, "Union Membership in Canada 2010."

Chapter 9

1. Interview with Pam Cooley, March 16, 2012; Pam Cooley, accessed April 11, 2015, www.pamcooley.ca; CarShareHFX, accessed April 11, 2015, http://carsharehfx.ca; "CarShareHFX Welcomes a New Mobility Option at Dalhousie University," *CNW CanadaWire*, March 11, 2011, accessed online March 16, 2012, www.newswire.ca/en/story/753625/carsharehfx-welcomes-a-new-mobility-option-at-dalhousie-university.

2. Anderson & Associates, accessed April 11, 2015, www.andassoc.com.

3. Chris Atchison, "Pride of Ownership," *Globe and Mail*, October 7, 2011, accessed February 1, 2012, www.theglobeandmail.com/report-on-business/careers/top-employers/top-employers-2012/pride-of-ownership-works-both-ways/article2193177.

4. The ESOP Association Canada (Employee Share Ownership Plan), accessed April 11, 2015, www.esop-canada.com; ESOP Association, "Corporate Performance," accessed February 1, 2014, www.esopassociation.org.

5. National Center for Employee Ownership, "Employee Ownership as a Retirement Plan," accessed February 1, 2014, www.nceo.org.
6. "Employee Stock Options Fact Sheet," The National Center for Employee Ownership, accessed February 1, 2014, www.nceo.org/articles/employee-stock-options-factsheet.
7. Ibid.
8. Toyota, accessed May 10, 2010, www.toyota.com/recall.
9. "Whole Foods Market's Core Values," accessed February 1, 2014, www.wholefoodsmarket.com/site_search/Whole%20Foods%20Market%E2%80%99s%20Core%20Values.
10. "Harley-Davidson: The Sound of a Legend," accessed April 19, 2010, www.lmsintl.com.
11. BBC, accessed May 10, 2010, www.bbc.co.uk; Lynda Gratton, Andreas Voigt, and Tamara Erickson, "Bridging Faultlines in Diverse Teams," *MIT Sloan Management Review*, summer 2007, pp. 22–29.
12. Kate Rogers, "Commitment to Standards, Mission, Clients and Fun," *Nonprofit Times*, April 1, 2010, www.thenonprofittimes.com/news-articles/commitment-to-standards-mission-clients-and-fun.
13. Robert Grice, "How to Build a Unified Team," *Helium*, accessed April 19, 2010, www.helium.com.
14. Nick Grabbe, "Experts: Don't Fear Workplace Conflict," *Gazettenet.com*, March 1, 2010, www.gazettenet.com.
15. Ken Thomas and Larry Margasak, "Toyota Waited Months to Tell U.S. about Sticking Accelerator Fixes It Gave to Dealers in Europe," *Associated Press*, April 6, 2010, www.cleveland.com/business/index.ssf/2010/04/toyota_waited_months_to_tell_u.html.
16. Ibid.
17. David Woods, "i-level Redesigns Its Employee Reward Communication Strategy," *HR Magazine*, March 8, 2010, www.hrmagazine.co.uk/hro/news/1017558/-level-redesigns-employee-reward-communication-strategy-reflect-innovative-image.
18. Norma Chew, "Are You a Good Listener?" Associated Content, accessed April 19, 2010, www.associatedcontent.com.
19. Open Text Corporation, accessed February 1, 2012, www.opentext.com/2/global.htm.
20. "Expand Trust in Your Organization," *Peter Stark.com*, accessed April 19, 2010, www.peterstark.com.
21. Joni F. Johnston, "How to Deal with Office Gossip," *Ezine Articles*, accessed April 19, 2010, http://ezinearticles.com.
22. John Boe, "How to Read Your Prospect Like a Book!" *John Boe International*, accessed April 19, 2010, http://johnboe.com.
23. Amar Toor, "Nestlé's Palm Oil PR Crisis Pervades Facebook," *Switched*, March 22, 2010, www.switched.com.
24. "Nestlé's Social Media PR Crisis: How Would You Handle It?" *Pierce Mattie Public Relations*, accessed April 19, 2010, www.piercemattiepublicrelations.com.
25. Emily Steel, "Nestlé Takes a Beating on Social-Media Sites," *Wall Street Journal*, March 29, 2010, www.wsj.com/articles/SB10001424052702304434404575149883850508158.

Chapter 10

1. GE, "Additive Manufacturing Is Reinventing the Way We Work," accessed February 22, 2014, www.ge.com/stories/advanced-manufacturing; Tim Catts, "GE Printing Engine Fuel Nozzles Propels $6 Billion Market," *Bloomberg News*, accessed February 22, 2014, www.bloomberg.com/news/articles/2013-11-12/ge-printing-engine-fuel-nozzles-propels-6-billion-market; Chelsey Levingston, "3-D Manufacturing Next Industrial Revolution?" *Dayton Daily News*, accessed February 22, 2014, www.daytondailynews.com/news/news/3-d-manufacturing-seen-to-be-next-industrial-revol/nbdcb; Rich Benvin, "3D Printing—The Future of Manufacturing," Association of 3D Printing, accessed February 22, 2014, http://associationof3dprinting.com.
2. Honda, "Operations Facilities," accessed February 5, 2014, http://corporate.honda.com; "Honda Builds Record 84% of 2009 U.S. Auto Sales in North America," *Auto Channel*, accessed April 26, 2010, www.theautochannel.com/news/2010/01/08/461055.html.
3. Shibui Designs, accessed February 5, 2014, www.custommade.com; Lydia Dishman, "Retire? Forget about It," *Entrepreneur*, January 11, 2010, www.entrepreneur.com/article/204568.
4. Barbara Quinn, "Carving a Roadway to Sustainability," *Pollution Engineering*, May 2010, p. 17.
5. Canada Green Building Council (CaGBC), accessed April 14, 2011, www.cagbc.org; "LEED," U.S. Green Building Council, accessed May 27, 2010, www.usgbc.org.
6. Consolidated Technologies, accessed April 14, 2011, http://consolidatedtechnologies.ca.
7. Clara Maria Cabrera, "CAD/CAM Dental Technology," Associated Content, accessed April 26, 2010, www.associatedcontent.com.
8. Roger Schreffler, "Nissan's Flexible Manufacturing Moves to India, Other JVs," Wards Auto.com, February 3, 2010, http://wardsauto.com/ar/nissan_flexible_manufacturing_100203.
9. Vince Lapinski, "We Are Print," Manroland, www.manroland.us.com.
10. Anupam Govil, "Shifting of the Global Sourcing Axis," *Near Shore Americas*, April 6, 2010, www.nearshoreamericas.com/nearshoring-shift-of-the-global-sourcing-axis.
11. Mike Pare, "VW Prototypes on Local Horizon," *Chattanooga Times Free Press*, January 11, 2010, www.gaccsouth.com/en/news/single-view/artikel/vw-prototypes-on-local-horizon/?cHash=03a5e0fcfa650ffc17108a0241002afb.
12. "Holland Car's Assembly Line to Evolve," *Fortune*, April 18, 2010, www.addisfortune.com/Vol%2010%20No%20507%20Archive/Holland%20Car%E2%80%99s%20Assembly%20Line%20to%20Evolve.htm.
13. "Advantages and Disadvantages of Outsourcing," The Thriving Small Business, February 8, 2010, www.thethrivingsmallbusiness.com.
14. "Supplier Management," Ariba, accessed April 26, 2010, www.ariba.com/solutions/buy/supplier-management.
15. Shruti Date Singh, "Deere Shortage Prompts Kansas Farmer to Buy Dragotec," *Bloomberg Businessweek*, April 26, 2010,

www.bloomberg.com/news/articles/2010-04-09/deere-shortage-pushes-kansas-farmer-to-dragotec-risking-sales-at-dealers.

16. SAP, "Loblaw Selects SAP to Strengthen Its Business Processes in Canada," November 10, 2008, accessed April 14, 2011, www.sap.com/press.epx?pressid=10365.

17. "Seattle Children's Hospital Saves $2.5 Million in First Year with Streamlined Inventory Distribution," accessed April 26, 2010, www.seattlechildrens.org/news/2010/seattle-children%E2%80%99s-hospital-saves-_2-5-million-in-first-year-with-streamlined-inventory-distribution.

18. "Allan Candy Company," *Microsoft Case Studies*, April 19, 2010, www.microsoft.com.

19. Judy Miller, "Still Made in America: The Super Bowl Footballs from Ada, Ohio," *Encyclopedia Britannica Blog*, February 1, 2010, http://blogs.britannica.com/2010/02/still-made-in-america-the-super-bowl-footballs-from-ada-ohio.

20. "Success Stories: Sleepmaster, LTD," *Usersolutions.com*, accessed April 26, 2010, www.usersolutions.com.

21. "Contrite Facebook CEO Promises new Privacy Controls," *Yahoo! News*, May 24, 2010, http://news.yahoo.com.

22. Jamie Liddell, "Top Ten Tips for Better Benchmarking," *SSON Network*, accessed April 26, 2010, www.ssonetwork.com/articleiframe.cfm?id=10707.

23. Six Sigma Inc. Canada, accessed February 3, 2012, www.sixsigmacanada.net/; Vic Nanda, "Preempting Problems," *Six Sigma Forum Magazine*, February 2010, pp. 9–18.

24. "Maintaining the Benefits and Continual Improvement," International Organization for Standardization, accessed April 26, 2010, www.iso.org.

Part 3 Case Study Beau's All Natural Brewing Company: Managing the Pains of Early Growth

Based on interviews with Steve Beauchesne at Beau's All Natural Brewery Company offices, Vankleek Hill, Ontario, on March 30, 2015; Beau's All Natural Brewery Company, accessed April 3, 2015, www.beaus.ca; Beau's Beer Blog, "How to Start a Brewery in 1 Million Easy Steps," January 9, 2007, accessed April 3, 2015, http://beausbeer.blogspot.ca/2007/01/brewery-measurements.html.

Part 3: Launching Your Management Career

1. Living in Canada, "Canadian Salary Survey," accessed May 1, 2012, www.livingin-canada.com/wages-for-management-jobs-canada.html.

Chapter 11

1. Etsy for Lisa Lutz, accessed April 17, 2015, www.etsy.com/shop/beadcrazed; Etsy, accessed April 17, 2015, www.etsy.com; Hiroko Tabuchi, "Etsy I.P.O. Tests Pledge to Balance Social Mission and Profit," *New York Times*, April 16, 2015, accessed April 17, 2015, www.nytimes.com/2015/04/17/business/dealbook/etsy-ipo-tests-pledge-to-emphasize-social-mission-over-profit.html?_r=0; Artfire, accessed April 17, 2015, www.artfire.com; 1000 Markets, accessed April 17, 2015, www.1000markets.com; Janell Mooney, accessed April 17, 2015, www.etsy.com/shop/dancingmooney; Janell Mooney, "What You Should Know about Etsy.com," Associated Content, accessed March 25, 2010, http://associatedcontent.com; Cyndia Zwahlen, "Independent Artisans Are Crowding onto the Web," *Los Angeles Times*, March 1, 2010, http://articles.latimes.com/2010/mar/01/business/la-fi-smallbiz-crafts1-2010mar01; Alex Williams, "That Hobby Looks Like a Lot of Work," *New York Times*, December 17, 2009, www.nytimes.com/2009/12/17/fashion/17etsy.html?_r=0.

2. American Marketing Association, "AMA Adopts New Definition of Marketing," *Marketing-Power*, accessed February 24, 2014, www.danavan.net.

3. Target, accessed February 10, 2014, www.target.com; Brad Gilligan, "Target Starts Mobile Coupon Program," *All Tech Considered*, accessed February 10, 2014, www.npr.org/sections/alltechconsidered/2010/03/target_starts_mobile_coupon_pr.html; "Target Launches First-Ever Scannable Mobile Coupon Program," *Business Wire*, accessed February 10, 2014, www.businesswire.com/news/home/20100310005092/en/Target-Launches-First-Ever-Scannable-Mobile-Coupon-Program#.VZvoORtViko; Marguerite Reardon, "Attention Shoppers: Target Offers Mobile Coupons," *CNET News*, accessed February 10, 2014, www.cnet.com/news/attention-shoppers-target-offers-mobile-coupons.

4. Apple, www.apple.com, accessed April 17, 2015; "Apple IPAD: Get to Know the Apple iPad," *NY Breaking News*, n.d., www.nybreakingnews.com; Arik Hesseldahl, "Apple's Hard iPad Sell," *Businessweek*, February 5, 2010, www.bloomberg.com/bw/technology/content/feb2010/tc2010024_830227.htm; Erica Ogg, "Who Will Buy the iPad?" *CNET News*, January 28, 2010, www.cnet.com/news/who-will-buy-the-ipad.

5. Michael Hall, David Lasby, Steven Ayer, and William David Gibbons, *Caring Canadians, Involved Canadians: Highlights from the Canada Survey of Giving, Volunteering and Participating*, Catalogue no. 71-542-XWE, Chapter 2, Volunteering (Ottawa: Statistics Canada, 2007), accessed May 8, 2012, www.statcan.gc.ca/pub/71-542-x/2009001/chap/ch2-eng.htm; *Summary of the Findings of the National Survey of Nonprofit and Voluntary Organizations* (NSNVO), Statistics Canada, accessed January 23, 2011, www.statcan.gc.ca/pub/61-533-s/61-533-s2005001-eng.htm#5; "Facts and Figures about Charitable Organizations," *Independent Sector*, October 30, 2009, www.independentsector.org.

6. Lester M. Salamon, Megan A. Haddock, S. Wojciech Sokolowski, and Helen S. Tice, *Measuring Civil Society and Volunteering: Initial Findings from Implementation of the UN Handbook on Nonprofit Institutions*, Working Paper No. 23 (Baltimore: Johns Hopkins Center for Civil Society Studies, 2007), www.jhu.edu.

7. Scotiabank Rat Race for United Way, accessed October 28, 2015, www.unitedwaytyr.com/ratrace.
8. Avon Foundation, accessed April 25, 2015, www.avoncompany.com; "Avon Foundation for Woman Grants $500,000 to the U.S. Department of State Secretary's Fund for Global Women's Leadership," press release, April 25, 2015, www.newswire.ca/en/story/570469/avon-foundation-for-women-grants-500-000-to-the-u-s-department-of-state-secretary-s-fund-for-global-women-s-leadership.
9. "The Adventures of Quatchi, Miga, and Sumi Begin in Earnest," Vancouver 2010, accessed April 25, 2015, www.vancouver2010.com.
10. The Canadian Diabetes Association, accessed April 25, 2015, www.diabetes.ca.
11. The University of Western Ontario's Alternative Spring Break, accessed April 25, 2015, www.asb.uwo.ca.
12. Seventh Generation, accessed April 25, 2015, www.seventhgeneration.com.
13. Oprah's Angel Network, accessed April 2015, http://oprahsangelnetwork.org and www.oprah.com/pressroom/About-Oprahs-Angel-Network.
14. McDonald's, "Our Story," accessed February 11, 2014, www.mcdonalds.com/us/en/our_story.html; SUBWAY, "Restaurant Locator," accessed February 11, 2014, http://world.subway.com; SUBWAY Restaurants International, accessed February 11, 2014, http://world.subway.com; Marco Lui, "Subway Plans to Open 500 Stores across China in Next Five Years," *Bloomberg News*, accessed February 11, 2014, www.bloomberg.com/apps/news?pid=newsarchive&sid=acUIqNJjyUPQ; Farah Master, "Subway Eyes Matching McDonalds in China in 10 Years," *Reuters*, accessed February 11, 2014, www.reuters.com/article/2010/03/08/us-subway-china-idUSTRE62723220100308; Ben Yue, "Subway Eyes Further China Expansion," *China Daily USA*, accessed February 11, 2014, www.chinadaily.com.cn/business/2011-07/04/content_12827599.htm.
15. Blank Label, accessed April 25, 2015, www.blanklabel.com; Spreadshirt, accessed April 25, 2015, www.spreadshirt.com.
16. "Procter & Gamble Readies Online Market-Research Push," *InformationWeek*, accessed February 10, 2014, www.informationweek.com/procter-and-gamble-readies-online-market-research-push/d/d-id/1012232?; Hal Gregerson, "A.G. Lafley's Innovation Skills Will Weather P&G's Storm," *Knowledge.com*, accessed February 10, 2014, http://knowledge.insead.edu.
17. TRU-Insight, accessed April 25, 2015, www.tru-insight.com.
18. Stephanie Rosenbloom, "In Bid to Sway Sales, Cameras Track Shoppers," *New York Times*, March 20, 2010, www.nytimes.com/2010/03/20/business/20surveillance.html?_r=0.
19. Mark Clothier, "P&G's McDonald Pins Growth on Closer Shave than Mumbai Barber," *Bloomberg*, accessed February 11, 2014, www.bloomberg.com/apps/news?pid=newsarchive&sid=aK6vXFvwPUXA.
20. Andrew McMains, "CEO Pushes Soup Giant to Move Faster, 'Think Outside the Can,'" *AdWeek*, accessed February 11, 2014, www.adweek.com.
21. Unilever, "Challenges and Wants," accessed February 10, 2014, www.unilever.com/about/innovation/open-innovation/challenges-and-wants/; "5 Examples of Companies Innovating with Crowdsourcing," *Innocentive.com*, accessed February 10, 2014, www.innocentive.com/blog/2013/10/18/5-examples-of-companies-innovating-with-crowdsourcing.
22. Leah Betancourt, "How Companies Are Using Your Social Media Data," *Mashable*, accessed February 12, 2014, http://mashable.com/2010/03/02/data-mining-social-media; Jim Cooper, "Yahoo's Carol Bartz Touts Data," *Mediaweek*, accessed February 12, 2014, www.mediaweek.com; Jared Newman, "Google Buzz Bites the Dust," *PCWorld*, accessed February 12, 2014, www.pcworld.com/article/241965/google_buzz_bites_the_dust.html; Declan McCullagh, "Why No One Cares about Privacy Anymore," *CNETNews*, accessed February 12, 2014, www.cnet.com/news/why-no-one-cares-about-privacy-anymore.
23. Playnomics, accessed February 12, 2014, www.playnomics.com; "Playnomics Releases a Free Player Scoring Dashboard for Game Platforms and Publishers," PR Newswire, accessed February 12, 2014, www.prnewswire.com/news-releases/playnomics-releases-a-free-player-scoring-dashboard-for-game-platforms-and-publishers-141580613.html.
24. Pew Research Center, "Social Media User Demographics," accessed February 12, 2014, www.pewinternet.org/data-trend/social-media/social-media-user-demographics.
25. Craig Smith, "21 Interesting Pandora Statistics," *Expanded Ramblings*, accessed July 13, 2014, http://expandedramblings.com; Pandora, accessed February 12, 2014, www.pandora.com; Marcello Ballve, "Silicon Valley and Detroit Are Battling Over the Future of the Internet-Connected Car," *Business Insider*, accessed February 12, 2014, www.businessinsider.com/the-future-of-internet-connected-cars-2013-10; Peter High, "Gartner: Top 10 Strategic Technology Trends for 2014," *Forbes*, accessed February 12, 2014, www.forbes.com/sites/peterhigh/2013/10/14/gartner-top-10-strategic-technology-trends-for-2014; Farhad Manjoo, "Smart Cars: Fill 'Er with Apps," *Fast Company*, accessed February 12, 2014, www.fastcompany.com/3012499/tech-edge/why-cars-should-be-more-like-smartphones.
26. Ford, "Now on Duty," accessed February 12, 2014, www.ford.com; "Ford e-News—July 24, 2013," *P R Newswire*, accessed February 12, 2014, www.prnewswire.com/news-releases/ford-enews---july-24-2013-216800001.html; Brandon Turkus, "Ford's Explorer-based Police Interceptor to Get 365-hp EcoBoost Option," *Auto Blog*, accessed February 12, 2014, www.autoblog.com/2013/08/20/fords-explorer-based-police-interceptor-365-hp-ecoboost/; Brent Snavely, "Ford to Unveil Police Interceptor," *Detroit Free Press*, accessed February 12, 2014, www.managemylife.com; Chris Woodyard, "Ford Unveils Next-Generation, V-6-Only Taurus Police Car," *USA Today*, accessed February 12, 2014, http://content.usatoday.com/communities/driveon/post/2010/03/ford-unveils-next-generation-v-6-only-taurus-police-car/1#.VZ6awF9Viko; Fran Spielman, "Chicago Police Department to Buy 500 Police Cars from South Side Ford Plant," *Chicago Sun Times*, accessed February 12, 2014, www.suntimes.com; Owen Ray, "San Francisco Police: Ford Police Interceptor to Replace Crown Victoria," *Examiner*, accessed February 12, 2014, www.examiner.com/article/san-francisco-police-ford-police-interceptor-to-replace-crown-victoria.
27. Joseph Yi, "Male Shopping Habits vs. Female Shopping Habits," *E-Commerce Rules*, accessed February 12, 2014, http://

ecommercerules.com/male-shopping-gabits-versus-female-shopping-habits.

28. Nielsen, "Women Control the Purse Strings," accessed February 12, 2014, www.nielsen.com/ca/en/insights/news/2013/u-s--women-control-the-purse-strings.html.

29. Amazon, "Join Amazon Mom and Enjoy," accessed February 12, 2014, http://join-amazon-mom-and-enjoy-today.blogspot.ca/2014/01/learn-more-about-amazon-mom.html.

30. U.S. Census Bureau, "2012 Statistical Abstract, Resident Population Projections by Sex and Age: 2010 to 2050," accessed February 10, 2014, www.census.gov.

31. Emily Brandon, "The Recession's Impact on Baby Boomer Retirement," *US News Money*, accessed February 13, 2014, http://money.usnews.com/money/retirement/articles/2011/10/31/the-recessions-impact-on-baby-boomer-retirement.

32. Jeanine Poggi, "Nickelodeon Targets 'Post-Millennials' in Upfront," *Advertising Age*, accessed February 13, 2014, http://adage.com/article/special-report-tv-upfront/nickelodeon-targets-post-millennials-upfront/240045/.

33. General Motors, "Social Hub," accessed April 17, 2015, www.gm.com/company/social_hub.html.

34. "Research Shows $15.39 Billion Spent on Video Game Content in US in 2013, a One Percent Increase over 2012," *NPD Group*, accessed February 25, 2014, www.npd.com/wps/portal/npd/us/news/press-releases/research-shows-15.39-billion-dollars-spent-on-video-game-content-in-the-us-in-2013-a-1-percent-increase-over-2012/; Toy Industry Association, "Annual Sales Data for Traditional Toy Categories," accessed February 25, 2014, www.toyassociation.org/tia/industry_facts/salesdata/industryfacts/sales_data/sales_data.aspx?hkey=6381a73a-ce46-4caf-8bc1-72b99567df1e#.VZ6ejl9Viko.

35. Crate & Barrel, accessed April 17, 2015, www.crateandbarrel.com.

36. Sodexo, accessed February 10, 2014, www.sodexousa.com; "Sodexo Introduces Food Truck at Assumption College," *Food Service Director*, January 30, 2014, www.foodservicedirector.com/industry-news-opinion/news/articles/sodexo-introduces-food-truck-assumption-college.

37. McDonald's, "About Us," accessed April 25, 2015, www.aboutmcdonalds.com/mcd.html; Katherine Glover, "More Bad News for Starbucks as McCafé Moves in for the Kill," *CBS Money Watch*, April 20, 2009, www.cbsnews.com/news/more-bad-news-for-starbucks-as-mccafe-moves-in-for-the-kill.

38. Resources for Entrepreneurs staff, "Consumer Habits Could Be Permanently Changed by Recession," *Resources for Entrepreneurs*, accessed February 13, 2014, www.gaebler.com/News/Small-Business-Marketing/Consumer-habits-could-be-permanently-changed-by-recession-19690314.htm; Joshua Brustein, "Walgreen's Beth Stiller on Customer Behavior and the Recession," *Bloomberg Businessweek*, accessed February 13, 2014, www.bloomberg.com/bw/articles/2013-10-03/walgreens-beth-stiller-on-retail-customer-behavior-since-the-recession.

39. Timberland, accessed April 17, 2015, www.timberland.com.

40. Marriott, accessed April 17, 2015, www.marriott.com.

41. Apple, accessed April 17, 2015, www.apple.com/ipod/nike.

42. Netcall, accessed April 17, 2015, www.netcall.com.

Chapter 12

1. Monster Gym, accessed April 24, 2015, www.monstergym.net; Cielo Studios, accessed April 24, 2015, www.cielostudios.ca; Grant Brothers Boxing & MMA Gym, accessed April 24 16, 2015, http://grantbrothersmma.com; interviews with Carmine Petrillo and Howard Grant.

2. "Research and Markets: Global Retail Touch Screen Display Market 2014–2018: One of the Main Drivers Contributing to Market's Growth Is the Use of Hi-Tech Touchscreen Display," Reuters, January 24, 2014, accessed February 16, 2014, www.reuters.com/article/2014/01/24/research-and-markets-idUSnBw245379a+100+BSW20140124.

3. "Pepsi to Sign Rock Star to Distribution Deal," *AdWeek*, February 19, 2009, accessed February 15, 2014, www.adweek.com/news/advertising-branding/pepsico-signs-rockstar-distribution-deal-105310.

4. Natalie Jarvey, "Tablet Company Fuhu Launches Original Animated Series on BabyFirst TV," *The Hollywood Reporter*, March 10, 2014, www.hollywoodreporter.com/news/tablet-company-fuhu-launches-original-687204; Nabi, accessed February 15, 2014, http://nabitablet.com; Burt Helm, "Kid You Not: The Very Serious Business of Building the Fastest Growing Company in America," *Inc.*, accessed February 15, 2014, www.inc.com/magazine/201309/burt-helm/inc.500-2013-number-one-company-fuhu.html.

5. "A Strong Holiday Quarter for the Worldwide Tablet Market, But Signs of Slower Growth Are Clear," *IDC*, January 29, 2014, accessed February 16, 2014, www.idc.com/getdoc.jsp?containerId=prUS24650614; Michael Endler, "iPad Dominates Enterprise Tablet Market," *InformationWeek*, February 12, 2014, accessed February 15, 2014, www.informationweek.com/mobile/mobile-devices/ipad-dominates-enterprise-tablet-market/d/d-id/1113813; "Kindle vs. Nook vs. iPad2 Video Comparison," *Deaf Tech News*, February 20, 2012, accessed February 15, 2014, www.deafhh.net/wp/2012/02/20/kindle-vs-nook-vs-ipad-2-video-comparison.

6. Raymond Soneira, "From Tablets to TVs: What's Next for Display Tech in 2014," *Gizmodo.com*, February 4, 2014, accessed February 15, 2014, http://gizmodo.com/from-tablets-to-tvs-whats-next-for-display-tech-in-20-1515670567; Ken Werner, "HDTV Expert—What Do You Do after You Realize LCD's Glory Days Are Gone?" *HDTV Magazine*, accessed February 15, 2014, www.hdtvmagazine.com/forum/viewtopic.php?t=16944; Alfred Poor, "HDTV Almanac—LED Backlight Prices Falling," *HDTV Magazine*, accessed February 15, 2014, www.hdtvmagazine.com/forum/viewtopic.php?t=13366.

7. "A Gadget's Life: From Gee-Whiz to Junk," *Washington Post*, accessed February 15, 2014, www.washingtonpost.com/wp-srv/special/business/a-gadgets-life; Adam Griff, "Retail after Disruption: DVD Rental," accessed February 15, 2014, www.adamgriff.com.

8. Adam Tschorn, "Old Spice Talks to the Ladies, Man," *Los Angeles Times*, March 6, 2010, http://articles.latimes.com/2010/mar/06/image/la-ig-oldspice-20100306; Drew Grant, "Old Spice's Spicy Ad Campaign," *Mediaite*, February 20, 2010, www.mediaite.com; Liz Shannon Miller, "The Viral Genius of Wieden+Kennedy's New Old Spice Campaign," *Gigaom*, February 19, 2010, https://

gigaom.com/2010/02/19/the-viral-genius-of-wiedenkennedys-new-old-spice-campaign.

9. Mattel, accessed April 26, 2015, www.mattel.com; Amy Graff, "Are Today's Girls Abandoning Their Dolls Too Soon?" *SF Gate*, April 6, 2010, http://blog.sfgate.com/sfmoms/2010/04/06/are-todays-girls-abandoning-their-dolls-too-soon; Andrea Chang, "Toy Fair 2010: After Strong Holiday Sales, Barbie Flaunts New Jobs and Fashions," *Los Angeles Times*, February 14, 2010, http://latimesblogs.latimes.com/money_co/2010/02/toy-fair-2010-mattel-strong-holiday-sales-barbie-flaunts-new-jobs-and-fashions.html; The White House Project, "Barbie Celebrates 125th Career with Global Initiative to Inspire Girls," press release, January 21, 2010, http://thewhitehouseproject.org.

10. Febreze, accessed April 26, 2015, www.febreze.com; PR Newswire, "P&G Leads 2010 Edison Best New Product Award Finalists with Five Nods," press release, February 11, 2010, http://ca.sys-con.com/node/1282608.

11. Electronic Arts, accessed April 26, 2015, www.ea.com; Ben Gilbert, "Report: EA Planning Premium, Pre-Launch DLC for Retail Games at $10-$15," *Engadget*, March 22, 2010, www.engadget.com/2010/03/22/report-ea-planning-premium-pre-launch-dlc-for-retail-games-at-10-15.

12. Tom Merritt, "Top 10 Worst Products," *CNET*, accessed April 30, 2010, www.cnet.com; John Biggs, "Ten Years: The Biggest Product Flops of the Decade," *TechCrunch*, December 31, 2009, http://techcrunch.com/2009/12/31/tenyears-the-biggest-product-flops-of-the-decade.

13. IKEA, accessed February 15, 2014, www.ikea.com.

14. Quiznos, accessed April 26, 2015, www.quiznos.com; Quiznos, "Quiznos Rolls Out Green Packaging," press release, February 23, 2010, www.chainleader.com.

15. Fedex, accessed April 26, 2015, www.fedex.com.

16. Industry Canada, "Canadian Industry Statistics: Wholesale Trade (NAICS 41): Establishments," accessed April 20, 2015; www.ic.gc.ca/app/scr/sbms/sbb/cis/establishments.html?code=41&lang=eng; Statistics Canada, "Annual Wholesale Trade Survey — 2009," March 29, 2011, accessed April 20, 2015, www.statcan.gc.ca/cgibin/imdb/p2SV.pl?Function=getSurvey&SDDS=2445&lang=en&db=imdb&adm=8&dis=2; Bureau of Labor Statistics, "Occupational Outlook Handbook, 2013– 2014 Edition," accessed February 15, 2014, www.bls.gov; U.S. Census Bureau, "County Business Patterns," accessed February 15, 2014, www.census.gov.

17. Federated Co-operatives Limited, accessed April 26, 2015, www.coopconnection.ca.

18. U.S. Census Bureau, "Quarterly Retail E-Commerce Sales, 3rd Quarter 2013," accessed February 16, 2014, www.census.gov.

19. Herb Weisbaum, "The Future of Banking: Putting Human Tellers in ATMs," *CNBC*, August 3, 2013, accessed February 15, 2014, www.cnbc.com/id/100925605.

20. Seventh Generation, accessed April 25, 2015, www.seventhgeneration.com; Romy Ribitzky, "Talking about an Ad Generation," *Upstart Business Journal*, February 11, 2010, http://upstart.bizjournals.com/companies/rebel-brands/2010/02/11/seventh-generation-embarks-on-first-ever-national-ad-campaign.html?page=all; Romy Ribitzky, "7 Facts about Seventh Generation," Upstart *Business Journal*, February 11, 2010, http://upstart.bizjournals.com/industry-news/advertising-marketing/2010/02/11/seven-facts-about-seventh-generation.html?page=all; Elaine Wong, "How Seventh Generation Is Going Mainstream," *Adweek*, January 26, 2010, www.adweek.com/news/advertising-branding/how-seventh-generation-going-mainstream-106986.

21. Under Armour, accessed February 16, 2014, www.underarmour.com.

22. Mondou, accessed April 25, 2015, www.mondou.com.

23. Starbucks Coffee Twitter feed, accessed June 16, 2014, http://twitter.com/starbucks; Starbucks Facebook page, accessed June 16, 2014, http://facebook.com/starbucks; Starbucks, accessed February 16, 2014, http://mystarbucksideas.com; Robert Gembarski, "How Starbucks Built an Engaging Brand on Social Media," *Branding Personality*, accessed February 16, 2014, www.brandingpersonality.com/how-starbucks-built-an-engagin-brand-on-social-media; "Happy Third Anniversary My Starbucks Idea," accessed February 16, 2014, http://blogs.starbucks.com/blogs/customer/archive/2011/03/18/happy-anniversary-my-starbucks-idea.aspx.

24. James Kanter, "Luxury Goods May Pick and Choose Venues for Sales," *New York Times*, April 20, 2010, www.nytimes.com/2010/04/21/technology/21goods.html?_r=0.

25. easyGroup, "About Us," accessed April 25, 2015, www.easy.com.

26. Samuel Axon, "How Small Businesses Are Using Social Media for Real Results," *Mashable*, March 22, 2010, http://mashable.com/2010/03/22/small-business-social-media-results.

27. Brooke Crothers, "iPad Sold Out at Best Buy Nationwide," *CNET News*, April 7, 2010, www.cnet.com/news/ipad-sold-out-at-best-buy-nationwide; Mary Ellen Lloyd, "Best Buy Shares Benefit from Apple iPad Launch," *Dow Jones Newswires*, April 5, 2010, www.advfn.com/nyse/StockNews.asp?stocknews=BBY&article=42253421; Michael Grothaus, "Best Buy to Carry iPad on April 3 at ASC-Stores Only," *Engadget*, March 26, 2010, www.engadget.com/2010/03/26/best-buy-to-carry-ipad-on-april-3-at-asc-stores-only.

28. Beyond the Rack, accessed April 25, 2015, www.beyondtherack.com.

29. "Nano-Based RFID Tags Could Replace Bar Codes," *Science Daily*, March 19, 2010, www.sciencedaily.com/releases/2010/03/100318113300.htm; "Verayo Launches Next Generation of Unclonable RFID Chips," *BusinessWire*, March 2, 2010, www.businesswire.com/news/home/20100302005719/en/Verayo-Launches-Generation-Unclonable-RFID-Chips#.Va1AgaRViko.

30. Gord Baldwin, "Too Many Trucks on the Road?" Statistics Canada, November 12, 2009, accessed April 20, 2015, www.statcan.gc.ca/pub/11-621-m/11-621-m2005028-eng.htm; American Trucking Associations, "Reports, Trends & Statistics," accessed March 12, 2014, www.trucking.org.

31. Association of American Railroads, "Class I Railroad Statistics," accessed March 12, 2014, www.aar.org.

Chapter 13

1. Wasserman & Partners Advertising Inc., interview with Alvin Wasserman, May 13, 2011; Wasserman & Partners Advertising Inc., accessed May 18, 2011, www.wasserman-partners.com; WorkSafeBC, accessed April 20, 2015, www.worksafebc.com; WorkSafeBC, "WorkSafeBC Statistics 2009 Report," accessed

May 19, 2011, www.worksafebc.com/publications/reports/statistics_reports/assets/pdf/stats2009.pdf.

2. "Monster.com Launches New Integrated Marketing Campaign to Help Job Seekers and Employers 'Get a Monster Advantage,'" press release, January 25, 2010, www.bloomberg.com/apps/news?pid=newsarchive&sid=asDGv_DSrOjA.

3. Alexandra Sifferlin "Why We're Spending $1 Trillion on Health Medications," *Time*, accessed February 21, 2014, http://healthland.time.com/2013/11/19/why-were-spending-1-trillion-on-health-medications; "Persuading the Prescribers: Pharmaceutical Industry Marketing and Its Influence on Physicians and Patients," *Pew Charitable Trusts*, accessed February 19, 2014, www.pewtrusts.org/en/research-and-analysis/fact-sheets/2013/11/11/persuading-the-prescribers-pharmaceutical-industry-marketing-and-its-influence-on-physicians-and-patients.

4. Michelle Krebs, "For Upcoming Chevrolet Cruze, GM Bets Safety Will (Up) Sell," *Edmunds Auto Observer*, April 19, 2010, www.edmunds.com/autoobserver-archive/2010/04/for-upcoming-chevrolet-cruze-gm-bets-safety-will-up-sell.html.

5. Edward Owen, "10 Incredibly Shameless Product Placements in Well-Loved TV Shows," *WhatCulture.com*, accessed February 20, 2014, http://whatculture.com/tv/10-incredibly-shameless-product-placements-well-loved-tv-shows.php; Anthony Crupi, "Ford, Coca-Cola Return for Season 13 of American Idol," *AdWeek*, accessed February 20, 2014, www.adweek.com/news/television/ford-coca-cola-return-season-13-american-idol-155001; Brad Tuttle, "Superman the Sellout? Man of Steel Has over 100 Promotional Partners," *Time*, accessed February 20, 2014, http://business.time.com/2013/06/04/superman-the-sell-out-man-of-steel-has-over-100-promotional-partners.

6. "Cathay Pacific Staff Surprise Travelers with Festive Flash Mob," *HR Grapevine*, accessed February 20, 2014, www.hrgrapevine.com/markets/hr/article/2013-12-12-cathay-pacific-staff-surprise-travellers-with-festive-flash-mob.

7. Lorraine Carter, "Guerrilla Marketing: Targeting One to Reach Many with Your Brand," *Persona Design*, accessed February 20, 2014, www.personadesign.ie/blog/guerrilla_marketing_targeting_one_to_reach_many_with_your_brand; Calum McGuigan, "Red Bull: Masterminds of New Age Marketing," *Creative Guerrilla Marketing*, accessed February 20, 2014, www.creativeguerrillamarketing.com/viral-marketing/red-bull-masterminds-of-new-age-marketing.

8. Jim Tierney, "Live from NEMOA: Why Your Brand Should Be Like Elvis," *Multichannel Merchant*, March 11, 2010, http://multichannelmerchant.com/news/live-from-nemoa-why-your-brand-should-be-like-elvis-11032010.

9. Bradley Johnson, "10 Things You Should Know About the Global Ad Market," *Advertising Age*, accessed February 22, 2014, http://adage.com/article/global-news/10-things-global-ad-market/245572.

10. Research and Management, "WSI Internet Marketing Trends Report, 2010 Executive Summary," accessed February 4, 2012, www.wsisme.com/files/Articles/TrendsReport10_Canada.pdf; Statistics Canada, "Advertising and Related Services—2012," accessed April 20, 2015, www.statcan.gc.ca/pub/63-257-x/63-257-x2014001-eng.htm.

11. "Kantar Media Reports U.S. Advertising Expenditures Increased 3.5% in the Second Quarter of 2013," *Kantar Media*, accessed February 21, 2014, www.kantarmedia.com; "Top 10 Advertisers January–September 2013," *Kantar Media*, accessed February 21, 2014, http://content.kantarmedia.com.

12. Avon company, "Corporate Responsibility," accessed June 14, 2010, http://responsibility.avoncompany.com.

13. Johnson, "10 Things You Should Know About the Global Ad Market."

14. James Bradshaw, "More Canadians Cutting the Cord? TV Subscriber Numbers Fall for First Time," *Globe and Mail*, May 15, 2014, accessed April 20, 2015, www.theglobeandmail.com/report-on-business/more-canadians-cutting-the-cord-tv-subscriber-numbers-fall-for-first-time/article18685129; CRTC, "How Many Canadians Subscribe to Cable TV or Satellite TV?" August 2006, accessed May 11, 2011, www.crtc.gc.ca/eng/publications/reports/radio/cmri.htm; Erick Schonfeld, "Estimate: 800,000 U.S. Households Abandoned Their TVs for the Web," *TechCrunch*, April 13, 2010, http://techcrunch.com/2010/04/13/800000-households-abandoned-tvs-web; John Latchem, "More U.S. Homes Have Game Consoles than Cable Boxes," *Home Media Magazine*, March 3, 2010, www.homemediamagazine.com; Bill Carter, "DVR, Once TV's Mortal Enemy, Helps Ratings," *New York Times*, November 1, 2009, www.nytimes.com/2009/11/02/business/media/02ratings.html?pagewanted=all&_r=0; Jim Edwards, "TV Is Dying and Here Are the Stats That Prove It," *Business Insider*, accessed February 23, 2014, www.businessinsider.com/cord-cutters-and-the-death-of-tv-2013-11.

15. Small Business Big Game, accessed February 20, 2014, www.smallbusinessbiggame.com.

16. Jane Sasseen, Kenny Olmstead, and Amy Mitchell, "The State of the News Media 2013," *State of the Media*, accessed February 23, 2014, www.stateofthemedia.org/2013; "Most Digital Ad Growth Now Goes Mobile, Desktop Growth Falters," *eMarketer*, accessed February 23, 2014, www.emarketer.com/Article/Most-Digital-Ad-Growth-Now-Goes-Mobile-Desktop-Growth-Falters/1010458; Jane Sasseen, Kenny Olmstead, and Amy Mitchell, "Digital: As Mobile Grows Rapidly, the Pressure on News Intensifies," *State of the Media*, accessed February 23, 2014, www.stateofthemedia.org/2013/digital-as-mobile-grows-rapidly-the-pressures-on-news-intensify.

17. Laura Stampler, "How Dove's 'Real Beauty Sketches' Became the Most Viral Video Ad of All Time," *BusinessInsider*, accessed February 20, 2014, www.businessinsider.com/how-doves-real-beauty-sketches-became-the-most-viral-ad-video-of-all-time-2013-5; "Dove's Sketches of Real Women Hit 30 Million Views, Tops Viral Chart," *Advertising Age*, accessed February 20, 2014, http://adage.com/article/the-viral-video-chart/dove-s-sketches-real-women-top-viral-chart/241055.

18. "Newspapers: By the Numbers," *StateoftheMedia*, accessed February 23, 2014, http://stateofthemedia.org; Amy Mitchell, Mark Jurkowitz, and Emily Guskin, "The Newspaper Industry Overall," *Pew Research Journalism Project*, accessed February 23, 2014, www.journalism.org/2013/08/07/the-newspaper-industry-overall.

19. Levi Shapiro, "State of the Digital Music Industry 2014: An Insider's View," *The Jerusalem Post*, accessed February 21, 2014, www.jpost.com/Blogs/Unleavened-Media/State-of-the-Digital-Music-Industry-2014-An-Insiders-View-364175; "Online Radio

Consumption Growing," *Marketing Charts*, accessed February 19, 2014, www.marketingcharts.com/online/online-radio-consumption-growing-36978; "Despite Small Audience, Internet Radio Ads Have a Special Appeal to Marketers," *eMarketer*, accessed February 19, 2014, www.emarketer.com.

20. Outdoor Advertising Association of America, "Out of Home Advertising Second Quarter Revenue up 5%," accessed February 19, 2014, www.oaaa.org/NewsEvents/News/PressReleases/tabid/327/id/3915/Default.aspx.

21. E.J. Schultz, "Forecast: Sponsorship Spending Will Slow in 2014," *Advertising Age*, accessed February 20, 2014, http://adage.com/article/news/forecast-sponsorship-spending-slow-2014/290961.

22. Jennifer Wood, "10 Best Selling Infomercial Products," *Mental Floss*, accessed February 21, 2014, http://mentalfloss.com/article/50246/10-best-selling-infomercial-products.

23. "Local Biz Spending on Promotion Easily Trumps Ad Dollars," *Marketing Charts*, accessed February 21, 2014, www.marketingcharts.com/uncategorized/local-biz-spending-on-promotions-easily-trumps-ad-dollars-28011.

24. Motorola, "Motorola Trade Up," accessed February 21, 2014, www.motorolatradeup.com; "Inmar Releases Coupon Trends for 2013," *Inmar*, accessed February 21, 2014, www.inmar.com/Pages/InmarArticle/Press-Release-01152014.aspx.

25. Herb Weisbaum, "Fewer Rebates Offered, but Deals Are Getting Better," *Today News*, accessed February 21, 2014, www.today.com/news/fewer-rebates-offered-deals-are-getting-better-1C6749597; Wirespring, accessed February 21, 2014, www.wirespring.com; Josh Constine, "Facebook Reveals 78% of Its Users Are Mobile as It Starts Sharing User Counts by Country," *TechCrunch*, accessed February 21, 2014, http://techcrunch.com/2013/08/13/facebook-mobile-user-count.

26. Wirespring, accessed February 21, 2014, www.wirespring.com; Josh Constine, "Facebook Reveals 78% of Its Users Are Mobile as It Starts Sharing User Counts by Country," *TechCrunch*, accessed February 21, 2014, http://techcrunch.com/2013/08/13/facebook-mobile-user-count.

27. Steve Crowe, "CES 2014 Attendance Tops 150,000," *CEPro*, accessed February 21, 2014, www.cepro.com/article/ces_2014_attendance_tops_150000; "U.S. Trade Shows Certified by U.S. Department of Commerce," *International Trade Administration*, accessed February 21, 2014, http://export.gov.

28. U.S. Department of Labor, Economic News Release, "Table 5. Occupations with the Most Job Growth, 2012 and Projected 2022," Bureau of Labor Statistics, accessed February 21, 2014, www.bls.gov/news.release/ecopro.t05.htm.

29. Mark Huber, "Life of a Salesman," *Air & Space Magazine*, February-March 2007, www.airspacemag.com/flight-today/life-of-a-salesman-15987478/?no-ist.

30. Matthew Hathaway, "Recession-Weary Consumers Find Haggling Can Cut Costs," *Chicago Tribune*, March 14, 2010, http://articles.chicagotribune.com/2010-03-14/business/sc-ym-0314-haggling-20100311-2_1_lower-prices-consumers-hagglers; Michael S. Rosenwald, "In Tough Economic Times, Shoppers Take Haggling to New Heights," *Washington Post*, January 31, 2010, www.washingtonpost.com/wp-dyn/content/article/2010/01/28/AR2010012803512.html.

31. Lee Howard, "Pfizer Ups Its Commitment to E-Marketing," *The Day*, January 21, 2010, www.theday.com/article/20100121/BIZ02/301219500.

32. Canadian Radio-television and Telecommunications Commission, "Canadian Radio-television and Telecommunications Commission Unsolicited Telecommunication Rules," accessed May 21, 2012, www.crtc.gc.ca/eng/trules-reglest.htm.

33. Bruce Wilson, "Generating B2B Sales Leads Using Social Media," *Many Doors Marketing*, February 24, 2010, http://manydoors.net.

34. Nat Robinson, "SlideRocket Presentation Tip—4 Ways For Using MultiMedia Strategically," *SlideRocket*, April 1, 2010, www.sliderocket.com/blog/2010/04/sliderocket-presentation-tip-4-ways-for-using-multimedia-strategically.

35. David Parker Brown, "Spirit Airlines Installs 'Pre-Reclined' Seats on New Airbus A320's," *Airline Reporter*, April 21, 2010, www.airlinereporter.com/2010/04/spirit-airlines-installs-pre-reclined-seats-on-new-airbus-a320s.

36. Jennifer Campbell, "Social Notes," *Montreal Gazette*, May 14, 2011, accessed May 15, 2011, www.montrealgazette.com/sports/Social+Notes/4783511/story.html#ixzz1MRJHiWPy.

37. Elaine Wong, "Dove Super Bowl Spot Scores Initial Points with Men," *Adweek*, February 9, 2010, www.adweek.com/news/advertising-branding/dove-super-bowl-spot-scores-initial-points-men-107033; Jack Neff and Rupal Parekh, "Dove Takes Its New Men's Line to the Super Bowl," *Advertising Age*, January 5, 2010, http://adage.com/article/special-report-super-bowl-2010/dove-takes-men-s-line-super-bowl/141312.

38. Justin Scheck, "Windows 7 Fails to Boost Profits of PC Makers," *Wall Street Journal*, January 31, 2010, www.wsj.com/articles/SB10001424052748704343104575034233214601248.

39. Sean Poulter, "The High Price of Fashion: Sales of Luxury It Bags Soar by 60%," *Mail Online*, March 12, 2010, www.dailymail.co.uk/femail/article-1257208/The-high-price-fashion-Sales-luxury-It-bags-soar-60.html.

40. Meg Sullivan, "For California Vintners, It's Not Easy Being Green," *UCLA Newsroom*, March 4, 2010, http://newsroom.ucla.edu/releases/for-california-vintners-it-isn-154669.

Part 4 Case Study Beau's All Natural Brewing Company: Building Brand Awareness

Based on interviews with Steve Beauchesne at Beau's All Natural Brewery Company offices, Vankleek Hill, Ontario, on March 30, 2015; Beau's All Natural Brewery Company, accessed April 3, 2015, www.beaus.ca; Beau's Beer Blog, "How to Start a Brewery in 1 Million Easy Steps," January 9, 2007, accessed April 3, 2015, http://beausbeer.blogspot.ca/2007/01/brewery-measurements.html; Mojo Junction, "Beau's All Natural Brewing: Crafting Beer. Inspiring Community," accessed April 12, 2015, http://mojojunction.com/articles/beaus; Mirella Amato, "Who Really Came First . . ." Beerology.ca, Fall 2009, accessed February 1, 2015, http://beerology.ca/articles/who-really-came-first . . .; Howe Sound Brewing, accessed February 1, 2015, www.howesound.com/aboutus/history.aspx.

Chapter 14

1. Stock-Trak, "Academic Solutions," accessed April 23, 2015, www.stocktrak.com/public/products/Stock-Trak.aspx; Stock-Trak, "Stock-Trak Group Partners with Scottrade to Provide Stock and Option Simulation Training Tools," press release, October 29, 2008, accessed May 23, 2012, www.stocktrak.com/pdf/Scottrade_102908.pdf.

2. Ernest Von Simpson, "The New Role of the CIO," *Bloomberg Businessweek*, May 22, 2013, accessed February 24, 2014, www.bloomberg.com/bw/articles/2013-05-22/the-new-role-of-the-cio; David Moschella, Doug Neal, John Taylor, and Piet Opperman, "Consumerization of Information Technology," *Leading Edge Forum*, November 18, 2004, accessed February 24, 2014, https://leadingedgeforum.com/publication/the-consumerization-of-information-technology-1701.

3. Rhea Wessel, "Airbus Signs Contract for High-Memory RFID Tags," *RFID Journal*, January 19, 2010, www.rfidjournal.com/articles/view?7323.

4. TradeInsight, accessed April 24, 2015, www.tradeinsight.com.

5. IEEE Computer Society, "History of Computing Timeline," www.computer.org/cms/Computer.org/Publications/timeline.pdf; Computer History Museum, accessed May 24, 2010, www.computerhistory.org; Roy Schestowitz, "Computer History Development Timeline: Microsoft Perspective," *Techrights*, February 4, 2010, http://techrights.org/2010/02/04/microsoft-perspective.

6. Stephen Vaughan-Nichols, "A Third of American Adults Now Own Tablet Computers," *ZDNet*, June 16, 2013, accessed February 25, 2014, www.zdnet.com/article/a-third-of-american-adults-now-own-tablet-computers.

7. Nicole Kobie, "Tablet Sales to Overtake PCs This Quarter," *PC Pro*, September 12, 2013, accessed February 21, 2014, www.alphr.com/news/384172/tablet-sales-to-overtake-pcs-this-quarter.

8. "'Come Together'—Intranets Are Re-emerging as a Way to Connect Dislocated Employees," *HR Monthly*, April 12, 2010, www.intranetdashboard.com/blog/2010/latest-news/lesson-learned-jetstar-mr-monthly.

9. Elliott Drucker, "Tech Insights—The Future of Voice," *Wireless Week*, March 7, 2010, www.wirelessweek.com/articles/2010/03/tech-insights-future-voice; "Future of VoIP in 2010, a New Beginning?" *Cheapest VoIP Calls.net*, January 2010, http://cheapestvoipcalls.net.

10. Diane Bartz, "Apple Users Lose Some Immunity to Cybercrime," *Reuters*, April 20, 2010, www.reuters.com/article/2010/04/20/us-cybersecurity-symantec-idUSTRE63J0K420100420; Jeremy Kirk, "E-Crime Reporting Format Draws Closer to a Standard," *CIO*, March 23, 2010, www.cio.com/article/2419561/security0/e-crime-reporting-format-draws-closer-to-a-standard.html; Sue Marquette Poremba, "Report: Dangers of Cyber Crime on the Rise," *IT Business Edge*, January 27, 2010, www.itbusinessedge.com/cm/blogs/poremba/report-dangers-of-cyber-crime-on-the-rise/?cs=39029.

11. Gillian Mahoney, "Hackers Steal Credit Card Data from Neiman Marcus Customers," *ABC News*, January 11, 2014, accessed February 25, 2014, http://abcnews.go.com/Business/hackers-steal-credit-card-data-neiman-marcus-customers/story?id=21499430.

12. Abby Simmons, "Lawmakers Take on Smart Phone Theft," *Star Tribune*, January 5, 2014, accessed February 26, 2014, http://www.startribune.com/lawmakers-take-on-smartphone-theft/238736851.

13. Gautum Prabhu, "Protect Your iPhone Against Theft with Activation Lock in iOS 7," iPhone Hacks, September 27, 2013, accessed February 26, 2014, www.iphonehacks.com/2013/09/ios-7-protect-iphone-against-theft-with-activation-lock.html.

14. Dan Steiner, "Staggering Cost of Malware Is Now over $100 Billion a Year," Yahoo Small Business, accessed February 26, 2014, https://smallbusiness.yahoo.com/advisor/staggering-cost-malware-now-over-100-billion-023014986.html.

15. Elinor Mills, "Malware Delivered by Yahoo, Fox, Google Ads," *CNET News*, March 22, 2010, www.cnet.com/news/malware-delivered-by-yahoo-fox-google-ads; Joseph R. Perone, "Expect New, Evolving Computer Viruses in 2010," *Star-Ledger*, December 31, 2009, www.nj.com/business/index.ssf/2009/12/expect_new_evolving_computer_v.html.

16. Tony Bradley, "McAfee Debacle Shows Why Malware Defense Must Evolve," *PCWorld*, April 27, 2010, www.pcworld.com/article/195093/mcafee_debacle_shows_why_malware_defense_must_evolve.html.

17. Associated Press, "Mastermind of World's Worst Computer Virus Still at Large," *Fox News*, March 4, 2010, www.foxnews.com/tech/2010/03/04/mastermind-worlds-worst-virus-large/.

18. "New Security Threat Against 'Smart Phone' Users, Researchers Show," *Science Daily*, February 22, 2010, www.sciencedaily.com/releases/2010/02/100222121624.htm.

19. Joshua Levinson, "Watchout—There's a New Android Trojan Horse About," Cult of Android, June 10, 2013, accessed February 26, 2014, www.cultofandroid.com/29156/watch-out-theres-a-new-android-trojan-horse-in-the-wild.

20. "Data Loss Statistics," *Boston Computing Network*, accessed May 24, 2010, www.bostoncomputing.net/consultation/databackup/statistics.

21. Bureau of Labor Statistics, "Work-at-Home Patterns by Occupation," *Issues in Labor Statistics*, March 2009, www.bls.gov/opub/btn/archive/work-at-home-patterns-by-occupation-pdf.pdf.

22. Infosys, accessed February 27, 2014, www.infosys.com.

Part 5: Case Study: Beau's All Natural Brewing Company: Using Technology to Manage Communications and Information

Based on interviews with Steve Beauchesne at Beau's All Natural Brewery Company offices, Vankleek Hill, Ontario, on March 30, 2015; Beau's All Natural Brewery Company, accessed April 3, 2015, www.beaus.ca; Beau's Beer Blog, "How to Start a Brewery in 1 Million Easy Steps," January 9, 2007, accessed April 3, 2015, http://beausbeer.blogspot.ca/2007/01/brewery-measurements.html; Mojo Junction, "Beau's All Natural Brewing: Crafting Beer. Inspiring Community," accessed April 12, 2015, http://mojojunction.com/articles/beaus.

Part 5: Launching Your Information Technology Career

1. U.S. Department of Labor, "Tomorrow's Jobs," *Occupational Outlook Handbook, 2010–2011*, Bureau of Labor Statistics, accessed June 28, 2010, www.bls.gov.

Chapter 15

1. "SEC Charges Four More Former Nortel Execs with Fraud," *CBC News*, September 12, 2007, accessed June 2, 2011, www.cbc.ca/news/business/story/2007/09/12/sec-nortel.html; "Toronto's Longest-Running Musical Returns," Broadway World, accessed June 2, 2011, http://toronto.broadwayworld.com/article/TORONTOS_LONGESTRUNNING_MUSICAL_RETURNS_20061017; "Livent Co-founders Drabinsky, Gottlieb Convicted of Fraud and Forgery," *CBC News*, March 25, 2009, accessed June 2, 2011, www.cbc.ca/news/business/story/2009/03/25/livent-decision-fraud.html; Dave Itzkoff, "Convicted Producers Suggest Lecture Tour Instead of Prison," *Arts Beat* (*New York Times* blog), July 8, 2009, accessed June 2, 2011, http://artsbeat.blogs.nytimes.com/2009/07/08/convicted-producers-suggest-lecture-tour-instead-of-prison/; Allison Jones, "Drabinsky, Gottlieb, Found Guilty of Livent Fraud, Take Case to Appeal Court," *City News*, April 30, 2011, accessed June 2, 2011, http://www.citynews.ca/2011/04/30/drabinsky-gottlieb-found-guilty-of-livent-fraud-take-case-to-appeal-court/; Anders Ross, "22 Largest Bankruptcies in World History," Instant Shift, February 3, 2010, accessed June 2, 2011, www.instantshift.com/2010/02/03/22-largest-bankruptcies-in-world-history/; Ronald Fink, "Beyond Enron: The Fate of Andrew Fastow and Company Casts a Harsh Light on Off-Balance-Sheet Financing," *CFO Magazine*, February 1, 2002, accessed June 2, 2011, www.cfo.com/article.cfm/3003186/c_3036065; "How to Hide $3.8 Billion in Expenses," *Bloomberg Business*, July 7, 2002, accessed June 2, 2011, www.businessweek.com/magazine/content/02_27/b3790022.htm.

2. Statistics Canada, "2011 National Household Survey: Data Tables," accessed August 13, 2014, www12.statcan.gc.ca/nhs-enm/2011/dp-pd/dt-td/Rp-eng.cfm?LANG=E&APATH=3&DETAIL=0&DIM=0&FL=A&FREE=0&GC=0&GID=0&GK=0&GRP=0&PID=105897&PRID=0&PTYPE=105277&S=0&SHOWALL=1&SUB=0&Temporal=2013&THEME=96&VID=0&VNAMEE=&VNAMEF.

3. Robert Colapinto, "Yes, We'll Show You the Money," *CPA Magazine*, January 1, 2014, accessed August 13, 2014, http://cpacanada.ca/en/CPA-magazine/Articles/yes-well-show-you-the-money.

4. Imran Ahmed, "CEO Talk: Brian Hill, Chief Executive Officer, Aritzia," Business of Fashion, August 25, 2009, accessed June 3, 2011, www.businessoffashion.com/2009/08/ceo-talk-brian-hill-chief-executive-officer-aritzia.html#more-5968.

5. Bottom Line News, *Canada's Accounting Top 30*, accessed August 13, 2014, www.thebottomlinenews.ca/documents/Canadas_Accounting_Top_30.pdf.

6. "IFRS FAQs," IFRS.com, accessed May 27, 2011, www.ifrs.com/ifrs_faqs.html#q3.

7. Johnson & Johnson, *Annual Report 2013*, accessed August 13, 2014, http://files.shareholder.com/downloads/JNJ/3357129072x0x733042/DDD2ABD5-2CC6-41D2-8ACB-EC2A967727E4/ar2013_JNJ.pdf.

8. "Sage 300 ERP: Extending Enterprise Suite—Industry Examples," Business Solutions Inc., accessed May 27, 2011, www.caplus.com/articles.aspx?aid=150.

9. Quicken, accessed February 20, 2012, http://quicken.intuit.ca/personal-finance-software/index.jsp.

10. Air Canada, *Annual Report 2013*, accessed August 13, 2014, www.aircanada.com/en/about/investor/documents/2013_ar.pdf.

11. Thomas Black, "Weak Dollar Is 'Welcome Change' for McDonald's, PPG Profits," Bloomberg.com, October 29, 2009.

Chapter 16

1. *CTV News*, "U.S.-Style Meltdown Won't Happen Here: Harper," September 24, 2008, accessed May 25, 2012, www.ctv.ca/CTVNews/TopStories/20080924/mortgage_meltdown_080924; Keith B. Richburg, "Worldwide Financial Crisis Largely Bypasses Canada," *Washington Post*, October 16, 2008, accessed July 14, 2011, www.washingtonpost.com/wp-dyn/content/article/2008/10/15/AR2008101503321.html; Anthony Haddad, "Ever-Growing Yields from Post-Crisis Winners," Street Authority, October 13, 2009, accessed July 14, 2011, www.streetauthority.com/a/ever-growing-yields-post-crisis-winners-909; Anup Shah, "Global Financial Crisis," Global Issues, December 11, 2010, accessed July 14, 2011, www.globalissues.org/article/768/global-financial-crisis.

2. Gaurav Raghuvanshi, Jason Ng, and P.R. Venkat, "Government Fund with Majority Malaysia Airlines Stake Considers Taking It

Private—Sources," *Wall Street Journal*, July 20, 2014, www.wsj.com/articles/government-fund-with-major-stake-in-malaysia-airlines-considers-taking-company-private-1405869189#.

3. Yahoo Finance, accessed August 13, 2014, https://ca.finance.yahoo.com.

4. Catarina Saraiva, William Selway, and Brendan A. McGrail, "California Markets Second-Biggest Taxable Bond Sale of 2010," Bloomberg.com, March 25, 2010, www.bloomberg.com; Katrina Nicholas, "Russian Nanotechnology Corporation Considers $1.7 Billion Bond Sale," *Nanowerk*, March 11, 2010, www.nanowerk.com.

5. "Strong Global IPO Market in Q1 Sets Tone for 2010," Ernst & Young, news release, April 8, 2010, www.ey.com; Eric Fox, "The Worst IPOs of 2009," *Investopedia*, December 16, 2009.

6. "NYSE Euronext Announces First Quarter 2010 Financial Results," news release, May 4, 2010, www.nyse.com; "New York Stock Exchange," *Money-Zine*, accessed June 21, 2010, www.money-zine.com.

7. Savvis, "Financial Services: Toronto Stock Exchange Connectivity," accessed July 6, 2011, www.savvis.com/en-US/Info_Center/Documents/FIN-US-TorontoStockExchangeConnectivity.pdf.

8. Office of the Superintendent of Financial Institutions, "Federally Regulated Financial Institutions," accessed August 13, 2014, www.osfi-bsif.gc.ca/Eng/wt-ow/Pages/wwr-er.aspx?sc=1&gc=1#WWRLink11; Relbanks, "Top Banks in Canada," accessed August 13, 2014, www.relbanks.com/rankings/top-banks-in-canada.

9. Federal Deposit Insurance Corporation, "Statistics on Depository Institutions Report," accessed June 21, 2010, www2.fdic.gov.

10. Allan Crawford, "The Residential Mortgage Market in Canada: A Primer," Bank of Canada, accessed August 18, 2014, www.bankofcanada.ca/wp-content/uploads/2013/12/fsr-december13-crawford.pdf; Canadian Bankers Association, "Bank Lending to Businesses," accessed August 21, 2014, www.cba.ca/en/media-room/50-backgrounders-on-banking-issues/128-business-credit-availability.

11. Interac, "Research and Statistics: Interac Debit Transactions," accessed April 22, 2015, www.interac.ca/en/total-transactions.

12. Department of Finance Canada, "Canada's Banks," accessed July 6, 2011, www.fin.gc.ca/toc/2002/bank_eng.asp.

13. Credit Union Central of Canada, "Facts & Figures," accessed August 14, 2014, www.cucentral.ca/SitePages/Publications/FactsAndFigures.aspx.

14. Credit Union Central of Canada, accessed June 14, 2011, www.cucentral.com/ Q1Results14JUN11.

15. Dave Cooper, "Credit Union Connect Launches across Alberta," *Edmonton Journal*, May 2, 2011, accessed July 6, 2011, www.edmontonjournal.com/business/Credit+Unions+Connect+launches+across+Alberta/4710413/story.html?cid=megadrop_story.

16. Canadian Life and Health Insurance Association, "About the Canadian Life and Health Insurance Industry," accessed August 14, 2014, www.clhia.ca/domino/html/clhia/clhia_lp4w_lnd_webstation.nsf/page/CBCBAF89BB17D8488525793B0063A1C9.

17. CPP Investment Board, accessed August 14, 2014, www.cppib.com/en/home.html.

18. The Investment Funds Institute of Canada, "Our Industry," accessed August 14, 2014, www.ific.ca/en/articles/who-we-are-our-industry/, LuAnn LaSalle, "Two-thirds Canada Contributed to RRSPs with 49% Choosing Mutual Funds, 12% ETFs," *Financial Post*, accessed August 8, 2014, http://business.financialpost.com/personal-finance/retirement/rrsp/two-thirds-canada-contributed-to-rrsps-with-49-choosing-mutual-funds-12-etfs.

19. Investment Company Institute, "Money Market Fund Assets: August 14, 2014," accessed August 14, 2014, www.ici.org/research/stats/mmf.

20. Bank of Canada, "Regulation of the Canadian Financial System," accessed May 18, 2012, www.bankofcanada.ca/wp-content/uploads/2010/11/regulation_canadian_financial.pdf.

21. Investment Industry Regulator Organization of Canada, accessed July 28, 2011, www.iiroc.ca/English/Pages/home.aspx.

22. Accuity, "Bank Rankings—Top Banks in the World," accessed August 14, 2014, www.accuity.com/useful-links/bank-rankings.

23. Emily Mathieu, "No-Interest MasterCard Aims at Devout Muslims," *Toronto Star*, April 12, 2010, accessed July 12, 2011, www.thestar.com/business/article/794124--operating-financies-in-good-faith?bn=1; Toronto Financial Services Alliance, "Islamic Financial Working Group," accessed August 21, 2014, www.tfsa.ca/resources/pdf/TFSA_IFWG_Prelim_Report_May14_2010_final_2.pdf.

Chapter 17

1. Ratiopharm GmbH, accessed June 24, 2010, www1.ratiopharm.com; Pfizer Inc., accessed June 24, 2010, www.pfizer.com; Teva Pharmaceutical Industries Ltd., accessed June 24, 2010, www.tevapharm.com; Actavis, accessed June 24, 2010, www.actavis.com; Yoram Gabison, "Teva Snubs Israelis: Ratiopharm Purchase Being Financed Abroad," *Haaretz*, May 14, 2010, www.haaretz.com; Robert Daniel and Polya Lesova, "Teva to Acquire Ratiopharm in Deal Valued Near $5 Billion," *MarketWatch*, March 18, 2010, www.marketwatch.com; Frank Siebelt, Ludwig Burger, and Lewis Krauskopf, "Pfizer to Make Bid for Ratiopharm: Source," Reuters, March 16, 2010, www.reuters.com; Andrew Ross Sorkin, ed., "Bidding War Pits Pfizer against Teva," *New York Times DealBook*, March 9, 2010, http://dealbook.blogs.nytimes.com; Frank Siebelt, "Pfizer Woos Ratiopharm with Ramp-Up Pledge—Sources," Reuters, March 7, 2010, www.reuters.com; Aaron Kirchfeld, "Pfizer Chief Said to Make Case for Ratiopharm Deal (Update 2)," Bloomberg.com, March 5, 2010, www.bloomberg.com; Cyrus Sanati, "Pfizer Said to Set Sights on German Drug Maker," *New York Times DealBook*, March 2, 2010, http://dealbook.blogs.nytimes.com; Ludwig Burger, "Pfizer, Teva Set to Tussle for Ratiopharm: Report," Reuters, January 18, 2010, www.reuters.com; Apotex Inc., "About Apotex," accessed August 1, 2011, www.apotex.com/global/about/default.asp, Industry Canada, "Canadian Pharmaceutical Industry Profile," accessed August 14, 2014, www.ic.gc.ca/eic/site/lsg-pdsv.nsf/eng/h_hn01703.html.

2. Equilar, "2010 CEO Pay Analysis & Strategies for Mid-Caps," May 2010, www.equilar.com.

3. Josh Funk, "Warren Buffet Still Gets $100K Salary at Berkshire Hathaway, but Security Costs Grow to $345K," *Business News*, March 10, 2010, http://blog.taragana.com.

4. Aude Lagorce, "Emirates in Record Airbus A380 Order," *MarketWatch*, June 8, 2010, www.marketwatch.com; Andrea Rothman, "Airbus A380 Order Dearth Risks Double-Decker-Dud Fate (Update 1)," *Bloomberg Businessweek*, May 13, 2010, www.businessweek.com; David Kaminski-Morrow, "A380 to Remain a Financial Burden for Years: Airbus Chief," *Flightglobal*, January 12, 2010, www.flightglobal.com.

5. Sarah Johnson, "CFO: Stop Treating Your Inventories Like Fine Wine," CFO.com, September 10, 2009, http://cfo.com.

6. Lauren Coleman-Lochner, "Target Sets Canada for First Expansion Outside U.S.," *Businessweek*, January 13, 2011, accessed August 8, 2011, www.businessweek.com/news/2011-01-13/target-sets-canada-for-first-expansion-outside-u-s-.html; Target, press release, accessed August 15, 2014, http://pressroom.target.ca/news/target-confirms-store-locations-236413.

7. Stefania Moretti, "Walmart Canada to Open 40 Supercenters," *CNews*, accessed August 2, 2011, http://cnews.canoe.ca/CNEWS/Canada/2011/01/26/17039171.html; *CBC News*, "Wal-Mart Planning $500M Expansion in Canada," accessed August 15, 2014, www.cbc.ca/news/business/wal-mart-planning-500m-expansion-in-canada-1.2522424.

8. Lochner, "Target Sets Canada for First Expansion Outside U.S."; Bloomberg, "Target Replaces Canada President after Troubled Expansion," accessed August 15, 2014, www.bloomberg.com/news/2014-05-20/target-replaces-canadian-president-after-troubled-expansion.html; Marina Straus, "How Target Botched a $7-Billion Rollout," *Globe and Mail*, January 15, 2015, accessed August 20, 2015, www.theglobeandmail.com/report-on-business/international-business/us-business/target-killing-canadian-operations/article22458161.

9. Air Canada, *Annual Report 2013*, accessed August 13, 2014, www.aircanada.com/en/about/investor/documents/2013_ar.pdf.

10. Historical Exchange Rates, OANDA website, accessed September 21, 2015, www.oanda.com/currency/historical-rates.

11. Yahoo Finance, accessed August 28, 2014, https://finance.yahoo.com.

12. Barchart, "Commercial Paper Interest Rates," accessed August 15, 2014, www.barchart.com/economy/commercialpaper.php.

13. "BP Suspends Dividend after Deepwater Horizon Spill," *MarketWatch*, June 16, 2010, www.marketwatch.com; "The Case for (and against) BP Cutting Its Dividend," *U.S. News & World Report*, June 14, 2010, www.usnews.com; Jeff Plungis and Christopher Condon, "U.S. Lawmakers Say BP Should Suspend Dividends, Ads (Update 2)," *Bloomberg Businessweek*, June 9, 2010, www.businessweek.com; Whitney Kisling, "Dividend Slump Ending as Record Profits Lift Payouts for S&P 500," *China Post*, April 29, 2010, www.chinapost.com.tw.

14. Canadian Tire, *2013 Annual Report*, accessed August 15, 2014, http://corp.canadiantire.ca/EN/Investors/Documents/2013%20Annual%20Report.pdf.

15. Federal Reserve Board, "Commercial Paper Outstanding," Federal Reserve Release, May 12, 2010, http://federalreserve.gov.

16. Jonathan Ratner, "Bondholders Find Safety in Canada," *Financial Post*, October 10, 2012, accessed August 15, 2014, http://business.financialpost.com/2012/10/10/bondholders-find-safety-in-canada-2/.

17. Board of Governors of the Federal Reserve System, "Federal Reserve Statistical Release, Z.1, Flow of Funds Accounts of the United States," March 12, 2009, www.federalreserve.gov.

18. Covington, accessed August 3, 2011, www.covingtonfunds.com.

19. *CBC News*, "Onex Buys Boeing Parts Plant for $1.5 Billion," February 22, 2005, accessed August 2, 2011, www.cbc.ca/news/business/story/2005/02/22/onex-050222.html.

20. Andy Hoffman and Tara Perkins, "China's Sovereign Wealth Fund Sets up Shop in Toronto," *Globe and Mail*, January 17, 2011, accessed August 3, 2011, www.theglobeandmail.com/report-on-business/chinas-sovereign-wealth-fund-sets-up-shop-in-toronto/article1867917/; Jeremy van Loon and Jim Polson, "Albert to Win Chinese Oil-Sands Investment, Minister Says." *Bloomberg*, May 17, 2011, accessed August 3, 2011, www.bloomberg.com/news/2011-05-17/alberta-to-win-chinese-oil-sands-investment-minister-says-1-.html.

21. Alastair Sharp, "Canadian Hedge Funds' Growth Dreams Face Tough Reality," *Globe and Mail*, January 31, 2013, accessed August 18, 2014, www.theglobeandmail.com/globe-investor/canadian-hedge-funds-growth-dreams-face-tough-reality/article8058888/.

22. Hedge Fund Association, "About Us," accessed August 18, 2014, http://thehfa.org/aboutus.

23. Cecilia Kang, "AT&T, DirecTV Announce $49 Billion Merger," *Washington Post*, May 18, 2014, accessed August 18, 2014, www.washingtonpost.com/business/technology/atandt-directv-announce-48-billion-merger/2014/05/18/62ffc980-dec1-11e3-810f-764fe508b82d_story.html; Alex Sherman and Scott Moritz, "AT&T Joins U.S. TV Revamp with $48.5 Billion DirecTV Deal," Bloomberg, accessed August 21, 2014, www.bloomberg.com/news/2014-05-18/at-t-agrees-to-buy-directv-for-48-5-billion-to-add-video-users.html.

24. Emre Peker, "Cerberus Taps Banks for LBO as Leveraged Loan Rally Spurs M&As," *Bloomberg Businessweek*, May 14, 2010, www.businessweek.com; David Russell, "LBOs Loom as Credit Market Recovers," NASDAQ, March 19, 2010, www.nasdaq.com.

25. Oilweek, accessed August 5, 2011, www.oilweek.com/news.asp?ID=34515; "Canadian Company Sells Natural Gas Assets in T&T," Caribbean 360, March 4, 2010, accessed August 5, 2011, www.caribbean360.com/business/canadian_company_sells_natural_gas_assets_in_t_t.rss#axzz1Tzqz6XRf.

Launching Your Career

1. Human Resources and Skills Development Canada, "Looking Ahead: A 10-Year Outlook for the Canadian Labour Market" (2006–2015), accessed May 20, 2012, www.hrsdc.gc.ca/eng/publications_resources/research/categories/labour_market_e/sp_615_10_06/supply.shtml.

2. Payscale, "Bachelor's Degree, Finance Average Salary," accessed August 28, 2014, www.payscale.com/research/CA/Degree=Bachelor's_Degree,_Finance/Salary.
3. U.S. Department of Labor, "Financial Managers," *Occupational Outlook Handbook 2010–2014*, Bureau of Labor Statistics, accessed July 8, 2010, www.bls.gov.

Appendix B

1. Arik Hesseldahl, "Apple's Smartphone Battle Plan," *Bloomberg Business*, March 2, 2010, www.bloomberg.com/bw/technology/content/mar2010/tc2010032_755256.htm; Philip Elmer-DeWitt, "Apple Talks Tough to Handset Makers," *Fortune*, March 9, 2010, http://fortune.com/2010/03/09/apple-talks-tough-to-handset-makers; "Will Apple's Patents Banish HTC Phones?" *TechHive*, March 3, 2010, www.techhive.com/article/190746/will_apples_patents_banish_htc_phones.html; Marguerite Reardon, "Apple Sues HTC Over iPhone Patents," *CNET News*, March 2, 2010, www.cnet.com/news/apple-sues-htc-over-iphone-patents; Brad Stone, "Apple Sues Nexus One Maker HTC," *New York Times*, March 2, 2010, www.nytimes.com/2010/03/03/technology/03patent.html?_r=0; Ted Livingston, "A Sad Day in Waterloo," Kik Interactive Blog, December 1, 2010, accessed March 30, 2011, www.kik.com/blog/2010/12/a-sad-day-inwaterloo.
2. "Frivolous Lawsuits," *NFIB*, accessed May 7, 2010, www.nfib.com.
3. Peter J. Brown, "US Lawsuit May Flood China Drywalls," *Asia Times*, April 10, 2010, www.atimes.com/atimes/Global_Economy/LD10Dj01.html.
4. Mark Sweney, "Google Wins Louis Vuitton Trademark Case," *The Guardian*, March 23, 2010, www.theguardian.com/media/2010/mar/23/google-louis-vuitton-search-ads.
5. B. Smith, "Google Digital Library Faces Major Public Outcry at NYC Hearing," *Daily News*, February 18, 2010, www.nydailynews.com/news/money/google-digital-library-faces-major-public-outcry-nyc-hearing-article-1.197867.

Appendix C

1. Joey Garrison, "Private Flood Damage Estimate Climbs to $1.9 Billion," *The City Paper*, May 19, 2010, http://nashvillecitypaper.com/content/city-news/private-flood-damage-estimate-climbs-19-billion; Tom Weir, "In Nashville, a Way of Life Washed Away," *USA Today*, May 7, 2010, http://usatoday30.usatoday.com/weather/floods/2010-05-06-nashville-flood_N.htm; Melinda Hudgins, "Few Take Advantage of Flood Insurance," *DNJ.com*, May 9, 2010, www.dnj.com; "Stories of Tragedy, Survival Surface as Tennessee Flood Waters Recede," CNN.com, May 5, 2010, www.cnn.com/2010/US/weather/05/05/tennessee.flooding; Emily Holbrook, "Few in Tennessee Covered by Flood Insurance," *Risk Management Monitor*, May 6, 2010, www.riskmanagementmonitor.com/few-in-tennessee-covered-by-flood-insurance; Geert de Lombaerde, "Less Than 4,000 Davidson Homes Insured against Floods," *The City Paper*, May 4, 2010, http://nashvillecitypaper.com/content/2010-flood/less-4000-davidson-homes-insured-against-floods.
2. *ACLI Life Insurers Fact Book 2009*, accessed May 9, 2010, www.acli.com/Tools/Industry%20Facts/Life%20Insurers%20Fact%20Book/Pages/GR09-%20215.aspx.
3. "Lightning Sparks Concern for Insurance Industry; Homeowners Claims Rise Sharply over Last Five Years," Insurance Information Institute, March 31, 2010, www.iii.org/press-release/lightning-sparks-concern-for-insurance-industry-homeowners-claims-rise-sharply-over-last-five-years-033110.
4. Walmart, "Insurance Requirements," accessed May 9, 2010, http://walmartstores.com.

Appendix D

1. Patrick Lohmann, "Campus Debtors," *Alibi*, May 6–12, 2010, http://alibi.com/news/32025/Campus-Debtors.html; David Ellis, "Credit Card Relief Is Here, But Watch Out for New Traps," *CNN Money.com*, February 22, 2010, http://money.cnn.com/2010/02/17/news/companies/credit_card_rules; Jennifer Liberto, "Under 21? Getting a Credit Card Just Got Tougher," CNN Money.com, February 22, 2010, http://money.cnn.com/2010/02/19/news/economy/student_credit_cards; George Gombossy, "New Credit Card Rules Go into Effect Monday," *Connecticut Watchdog*, February 20, 2010, http://ctwatchdog.com; David K. Randall, "New Credit Card Choices for College Students," *Forbes*, February 4, 2010, www.forbes.com/2010/02/04/college-credit-cards-personal-finance-credit-card-rules.html.
2. "Employee Tenure, 2008, and Retiree Health Benefit Trends among the Medicare-Eligible Population," *Employee Benefit Research Institute*, 31, no. 1 (January 2010), www.ebri.org/publications/notes/index.cfm?fa=notesDisp&content_id=4447.

Appendix E

1. Next, accessed May 9, 2010, http://nextrestaurant.com; Pete Wells, "In Chicago, the Chef Grant Achatz Is Selling Tickets to His New Restaurant," *New York Times*, May 4, 2010, www.nytimes.com/2010/05/05/dining/05achatz.html; "'US' Next Hot Restaurant Will Require Prepaid Tickets," *AOL News*, May 5, 2010, www.aolnews.com; Chuck Sudo, "Achatz's Next Two Projects: Time Travel, Cocktails," *Chicagoist*, May 4, 2010, http://chicagoist.com/2010/05/04/achatzs_next_two_projects_cocktails.php; Paul Frumkin, "Grant Achatz to Open New Restaurant and Bar," *Nation's Restaurant News*, May 4, 2010, http://nrn.com/archive/grant-achatz-open-new-restaurant-and-bar-0.

NAME INDEX

A
A Bis Gourmet, 377
Abercrombie & Fitch, 361
Aboriginal Pipeline Group, 489
About.com, 163
Accenture, 212, 214
Actavis, 471
Activision Blizzard Inc., 198
Adidas, 339t
ADP, 35
Advertising Age, 361
African Barrick Gold, 7
Agency3, 161
Agilent Technologies, 404
Agropur, 338
AHA, 520
AIG, 460
Airbnb, 153, 154
Air Canada, 37–38, 70, 140, 278, 437, 478
Airbus, 393, 474, 478
Alberta Health Services, 417
Alberta Securities Commission, 53
Alberta Society for the Prevention of Cruelty to Animals, 198, 296
Aliant, 489
Alibaba Group, 17
Allan Candy Company, 275
Amazon, 15, 17, 127, 182, 315, 326, 338, 344, 373, 395
Amazon.ca, 340, 361
American Express, 330, 361
American Federation of Labour and Congress of Industrial Organizations (AFL-CIO), 226
American Management Association, 403
American Marketing Association, 292
American National Standards Institute, 279
Angel Network, 299
Anheuser-Busch InBev, 117
AOL, 218, 219, 360, 489
AOL Time Warner, Inc., 489
Apotex Inc., 471
Apple Computer, Inc., 11, 23, 68, 111, 125, 163, 179, 190, 191, 202, 295, 305, 314, 324, 326, 344, 358, 360, 374, 395, 396, 401, 454, 489, 510, 511, 533–534
Apptio, 473
Aritzia, 417
Arizona Diamondbacks, 123
Arm & Hammer, 327, 330
Army & Navy, 339t
Art Gallery of Ontario, 417
Art Meets Commerce, 344
ArtFire, 291
Associated Press, 81
Association of Collegiate Entrepreneurs, 160
AT&T, 18, 193, 488
Avon Foundation for Women, 296, 359
Avon Products, 50, 296, 359
Ayurvedic, 160

B
Bank of Montreal (BMO), 30, 292, 485
Bank of Nova Scotia. *See* ScotiaBank
Barnes & Noble, 326, 373
Barrick Gold Corporation, 6
Barron's, 181
Bass Pro Shops, 339t
The Bay, 522
   see also Hudson's Bay Company
BC Hydro, 417
BCE Inc. *See* Bell Canada Enterprises
Beau's All Natural Brewing Company, 117, 174, 284–285, 383, 410–411
Becel, 190
Bed Bath & Beyond, 477
Beedie School of Business, 160
Bell Aliant, 10, 489
Bell Canada Enterprises, 4, 124, 292, 530
Bell Canada Inc., 10, 12, 62, 392, 398, 400, 489, 494
Berkshire Hathaway, 192
Berkshire Partners, 417
Best Buy, 44, 326, 338, 344
Better Business Bureau, 138
Beyond the Rack, 7, 345
Biodegradable Products Institute, 333
BlackBerry Ltd., 4, 50, 179, 202, 330, 358, 534
Blank Label, 302
Bloomberg, 108t
BMO. *See* Bank of Montreal (BMO)
BMW, 44, 268, 345
BNP Paribas, 473
Bobbi Brown, 163
The Body Shop, 159
Boeing, 404
Bombardier Inc., 90, 109, 193, 451, 485
Bon Appetit, 301
Boni Soir, 339t
Boston Bruins, 514
Bottleworks, 410
BraunAbility, 165
Brisco, 95
Bristol-Myers Squibb, 193
British Airways, 187, 228
British Broadcasting Corporation (BBC), 241
Budweiser, 360
Burberry, 344, 524
Burberry Group PLC, 519
Burger King, 110, 135, 138, 364
Business Development Bank of Canada, 174, 569, 570
Business for Social Responsibility (BSR), 29
BusinessWeek, 569
Buy.ca, 340

C
Cable and Wireless, 473
Cal Pacific Specialty Foods, 532
Campbell Soup Company, 193–194, 303, 336
Canada Business, 154f

Canada Deposit Insurance Corporation (CDIC), 448, 457–458, 462
Canada Green Building Council (CaGBC), 264
Canada Industrial Relations Board, 226
Canada Life, 459
Canada Mortgage and Housing Corporation (CMHC), 445, 449
Canada Post, 7, 362, 392
Canada Revenue Agency (CRA), 139, 417, 419
Canada's Gateways, 108*t*
Canada's Top 100 Employers, 50
Canadian Airlines International, 70
Canadian Apparel Federation, 209
Canadian Armature Works, 503
Canadian Association of Business Incubation (CABI), 133
Canadian Breast Cancer Foundation, 47, 146, 363
Canadian Business, 529
Canadian Business for Social Responsibility (CBSR), 41
Canadian Cancer Society, 292, 299
Canadian Centre for Occupational Health and Safety (CCOHS), 49
Canadian Chamber of Commerce, 154*f*
Canadian Diabetes Association, 292, 298
Canadian Federation of Independent Businesses (CFIB), 154, 457
Canadian Franchise Association (CFA), 138
Canadian Human Rights Commission, 52, 53
Canadian Intellectual Property Office (CIPO), 166
Canadian Labour Congress (CLC), 226
Canadian Marketing Association, 362
Canadian Medical Association, 296
Canadian National Railway Company, 527
Canadian Olympic Committee, 296
Canadian Olympic Team, 523
Canadian Pacific, 45, 526–528
Canadian Pacific Hotels, 529
Canadian Radio-television and Telecommunications Commission (CRTC), 10, 69, 529, 535
Canadian Red Cross, 5, 47
Canadian Securities Administrators (CSA), 462, 485
Canadian Security Intelligence Service (CSIS), 419–420
Canadian Society for the Prevention of Cruelty to Animals, 5
Canadian Society of Immigration Consultants, 76
Canadian Tire Corporation, 326, 327, 483, 494
Canadian Trade Commissioner Service, 108, 108*t*
Canadian Trade Data Online, 108*t*
Canadian Treasury, 448
Canadian Union of Public Employees (CUPE), 228
Canadian Venture Capital & Private Equity Association, 569
Canarm Ltd., 502–504
Canon, 263
Canon Canada, 297
Canopco, 530
Canpar, 146
Capital and Private Equity Association, 134
Capital One, 358
CARE, 312
Carling, 383
CarShare Atlantic Limited, 235
CarShareHFX, 235, 253
Cartier, 35
Cathay Pacific, 357
CBC, 134, 160, 167, 169
Cenovus Energy, 193
Centrica Plc, 489
China Investment Corporation, 487
China Petrochemical Corporation, 487
Choices Markets, 339*t*
Chouinard Equipment Ltd., 501
Chrysler, 268
CIBC, 30, 47, 50, 146, 455, 457, 463
Cielos Studios, 321
Cirque du Soleil, 29
Cisco Systems, 331, 405, 406, 477
Citigroup, 452, 464
City of St. John's, 420
City of Toronto, 450
City Year, 312
Citytv.com, 62
Clean Air–Cool Planet, 312
Clean Nova Scotia, 235
Clearasil, 361
Clinique, 364
Clorox, 251, 252
Co-operative Retailing System (CRS), 338
The Co-operators, 548
Co-operators Group, 193
Coca-Cola Company, 18, 46, 69, 325, 330, 345, 357, 360, 539
Coca-Cola Enterprises, 193
Coca-Cola Foundation, 42
Cold Stone Creamery, 182
Columbia University, 389
Competition Bureau, 45, 48
Conference Board of Canada, 214, 481
Consolidated Technologies Inc., 264
Consumer Reports, 194, 518
Consumers' Association of Canada (CAC), 48
Cooper–Hewitt Smithsonian Design Museum, 98
Corporate Knights, 485, 497
Corporate Knights Magazine, 193
Costco Wholesale, 50, 63, 72, 190, 339, 339*t*, 340, 343
COSTI Immigrant Services, 46
Covington Funds, 486
CPS, 424
Crate & Barrel, 309

D

Danor Manufacturing Co. Ltd., 502
Datamonitor, 479
Dell Computer, 182, 273
Deloitte, 418, 424–425
Dennison's Brewing, 174
Department of Finance, 462
Designer Depot/Style Depot, 522
Deutsche Bank, 161
DigiScent, 329
Direct Marketing Association, 362
DirectBuy, 339*t*
DirecTV, 488
Doctors Without Borders, 5
Dollar Store, 340
Dominion Bond Rating Service (DBRS), 449
Dove, 360, 372
Dow Chemical, 202, 481
DP Image Consulting, 82
Dragons' Den, 134, 160, 167, 169
Dropbox, 391
Dunkin' Donuts, 135, 331
DuPont, 475

E

East Side Mario's, 146
easyGroup, 344
Eat Local, 64
Eaton, 193
eBay, 17, 49, 291, 338, 344, 367, 374
Economic Development Corporation, 363
Ecosphere, 163
Ecosphere Technologies Inc., 163, 264
Edition, 190
Edward Jones, 455
Egg Farmers of Ontario, 354
Egyptian Orascom Telecom Holding, 529
Electronic Arts (EA), 329, 510–512
Elle, 356
Empire Life, 548
Employment and Social Development Canada, 494
Enbridge, 412
Encana Corporation, 6, 487
Endura Energy, 15
Enron Corporation, 415
Enterprise Rent-A-Car, 198
Entrepreneur, 154, 569
Environmental Defense Fund, 146
Environmental Technologies Ltd., 264
ePolicy Institute, 403

Equifax, 300
Ernst & Young, 18, 213, 241, 418
Estée Lauder, 163
Etelesolv, 392
Ethisphere Institute, 184
Etsy.com, 291, 292
Europages, 108t
European Alliance, 344
Evernote, 391
ExoPC, 10
Expedia, 367, 473
Experian, 300

F
Facebook, 15, 68, 127, 129, 156, 161, 183, 245, 252, 278, 295, 303, 304, 333, 342, 343, 344, 353, 355, 360, 366, 403
Fast Company, 154, 355
Federal Emergency Management Agency (FEMA), 544
Federal Reserve Board, 463, 481
Federal Reserve System, 78
Federated Co-operatives Limited (FCL), 338
FedEx, 335, 396
FIFA, 100, 241
Financial Post, 452
Financial Times, 17
Fitch, 449
Fitness City, 321, 322
Five Guys and a Burger, 66
FlightCar, 153
Forbes, 154, 361, 507
Ford Credit, 459
Ford Motor Company, 15, 98, 106, 145, 261, 268, 305, 306
Foreign Affairs, Trade and Development Canada, 108, 108t
Forest Stewardship Council, 30
Fortune, 23, 31, 189, 215, 361
Forzani Group, 327
Fox, 62
Frito-Lay, 332, 333
Front Row Marketing Services, 363
Fruits & Passion, 158, 159
Fuhu, 325–326
Fujitsu, 368
Fund for Global Women's Leadership, 296
Future Shop, 522

G
G Adventures Canada, 508–509
The Gap, 193, 520
GazMet, 392
GENCO Marketplace, 475–476
General Electric, 17, 118, 145, 259, 279, 426
General Mills, 50
General Motors, 44, 49, 91, 193, 194, 268, 306, 308, 356
Giant Tiger, 339t

Globalive Carrier Services, 530
Globalive Communications Corp., 529–531
Globe and Mail, 308, 452
GNC, 376
GoldieBlox, 360
Golf Town, 339t, 486
Goodwill Industries, 260
Goodyear, 362
Google, 62, 68, 127, 179, 184–185, 195, 196, 219, 238, 330, 360, 395, 397, 400, 402, 534, 539
Gourmet Chips and Sauces, 334, 335
Grant Brothers Boxing, 321
Grant Thornton, 418
Green Grid, 397
Green Mama, 128
Green Mountain Roasters, 190
GreenLawn, 263
Greenpeace, 251–252, 397
Gucci, 344
Guidance Financial, 464

H
Haagen-Dazs, 296, 297
Habitat for Humanity, 47, 296, 299
Hachette Book Group, 373
Hakim Wealth Management, 464
Hallmark, 473
Halogen Software, 214
Hamilton Tire & Garage Ltd., 327
Hanns R. Neumann Stiftung Foundation, 46
Harley-Davidson, 38, 239, 272
Harvard Business School, 39
Harvest Partners, 486
Hasbro, 193
Hay Group, 23
HBSC, 464
Health Canada, 48
Heinz, 279, 394
Hewlett-Packard, 44, 330, 454
H&M, 34–35, 520, 521
Holland Car PLC, 271
Holt Renfrew, 63, 340, 343
Holy Crap, 167
Home Depot, 13, 125, 182, 186, 238, 361, 483
Home Outfitters, 522
Honda, 262, 268, 479
Hospital for Sick Children (SickKids), 5–6, 260
H&R Block, 263
HR Executive, 355
HTC, 533–534
Hudson's Bay Company, 339t, 522–524
Hulu.com, 62, 326, 360
Human Resources and Skills Development Canada, 494
Humane Society, 47
Husky Energy, 193

I
Iberdrola Renewables, 72
IBM, 18, 50, 101, 102, 211, 331, 394, 412
IESE, 521
IHOP, 357
Ijara Canada, 464
IKEA, 91, 331
iLEVEL, 245
Inc., 154, 161, 569
Indiana Pacers, 363
Indigo, 125
Inditex Group, 519, 520, 521
Industry Canada, 30, 138, 166
Instagram, 15
Intel, 193, 211, 331
International Business School, 158
International Consumer Electronics Show, 366
International Franchise Association, 135
International Organization for Standardization, 279
Internet and American Life Project, 395
Internet Engineering Task Force (IETF), 401
Intuit, 164, 360, 436
Investment Industry Regulatory Organization of Canada (IIROC), 462
Islamic Credit Union of Canada, 464

J
J.D. Power, 196
JetBlue, 404
Jewish General Hospital, 371
Jiffy Lube, 357
Jim Pattison Group, 154
John Deere Capital Corporation, 459
Johnson & Johnson, 18, 31, 32f, 188, 330, 422, 481, 488
JP Morgan Chase, 363
Junior Achievement, 508
Juvenile Diabetes Research Foundation, 359

K
Kauffman Center for Entrepreneurial Leadership, 160
Kauffman Foundation, 154f
Kellogg, 91, 394
Kelly Services, 324
Keurig, 190
Keystone XL Pipeline, 99
KFC, 504, 505
Kik Interactive Inc., 161–162, 534
Killam Properties, 235
King Diesel, 45
King's Wharf, 235
KitchenAid, 330
KitchenAid Canada, 47
Kleinfeld Bridal, 523

The Knot, 156
KPMG, 418
Kraft, 96, 330, 332
Krispy Kreme, 130
Kwantlen Polytechnic University, 507

L
La Boulange Café and Bakery, 189
Labatt, 383
Lance Armstrong Foundation, 6
LCBO, 174, 410
Le Bistro Fit, 321
Lijjat Papad, 156
LinkedIn, 15, 129, 161, 185, 295, 343
LinkExchange, 182
Live Nation Entertainment, 8, 9
Livent Inc., 54, 415
Livestrong Foundation, 6
Lloyds Bank, 464
Loblaw, 68, 180, 273, 330, 339t, 341, 365
London Business School, 521
London Stock Exchange, 454
Long Plain First Nation, 169
Lord & Taylor, 522
L'Oréal, 331, 358, 394
Lotus Development, 50
Lotus Software, 50
Louis Vuitton Moët Hennessey (LVMH), 344, 519, 539
Lululemon Athletica Inc., 90, 308, 330, 506–508

M
Maclean's, 30
Mac's, 339t
Magna International, 182–183, 436
Make-a-Wish Foundation, 292
Malaysian Airlines, 451
Mall of America, 341
Manitoba Hydro, 50, 140
Manitoba Securities Commission, 462
Manroland, 266
Manulife Financial, 455, 459, 495, 548
Maple Leaf Foods, 48
Marie Claire, 356
MarketWatch, 389
Mark's Work Wearhouse, 327
Marriott Corporation, 190, 314
Marriott International, 18
Marvel Entertainment, 307
Matsushita, 111
Mattel, 50, 184, 193
Mazda, 268
MBNA Canada Bank, 314
McAfee, 402
McAuslan Brewing, 174
McCain Foods Limited, 504–505

McDonald's, 66, 69, 110, 135, 136, 138, 146, 213, 263, 292, 302, 311, 330, 364, 479, 504, 505, 508, 539
McGill University, 249, 250, 371, 389
MCI, 39
Médecins Sans Frontières (MSF), 5
Mediacorp Canada Inc., 497
MEI Computer Technology Group, 394
Merck, 68
Metro Group, 346
MGM Studios, 62
Miami Heat, 363
Microsoft, 10, 145, 162, 182, 202, 238, 308, 329, 356, 360, 391, 396, 402, 405, 472, 534
Millennium Development Corporation, 59
Minnesota Twins, 123
Mint.com, 164
Mitnick Security Company, 165
MMA Gyms, 321
Molson Coors, 117, 383
Mondou, 341
Monster.com, 354–355
Monster Gym, 156, 321
Moody's, 449
Morinaga, 110
MOSAIC, 76
Motor Trend Magazine, 194
Motorola, 489
Motorola Enterprise Mobility and Networks, 489
Motorola Mobile Devices and Home, 489
Mount Polley Mining Corporation, 43
Mountain Equipment Co-op, 193
Mouvement des caisses Desjardins (The Desjardins Group), 193
Mr. Lube, 263
MTP Energy Management, 486
Mulberry, 374
Multilateral Investment Fund, 509
MyStarbucksIdea.com, 342

N
Nabisco, 359
NASDAQ Stock Market, 453
National Collegiate Athletic Association (NCAA), 123
National Franchise Association, 138
National Hockey League, 227
National Hockey League Players' Association, 227
National Union of Public and General Employees (NUPGE), 228
National Venture Capital Association, 134, 569
Natura Foods Inc., 124
Natural Products Group, 486
Natural Resources Canada, 45, 79
Naturalizer, 356

NBA, 362
NBC, 62
NCR Corporation, 338
Neiman Marcus, 401
Nestlé, 251–252, 253, 437, 478
Netflix, 7, 326, 360
New Balance, 146
New Brunswick Power, 140
New Locomotion, 52
New York City Clothing Bank, 34
New York Knicks, 363
New York Stock Exchange (NYSE), 453
New York Times, 34
New York University, 389
New York University's School of Business, 525
Next, 563
Nickelodeon, 326
Nielsen Company, 360
Nike, 111, 314, 315, 330, 426
Nipissing University, 389
Nissan Motor Company, 266, 268
Nokia, 118, 489, 533
Nordstrom Inc., 523
Nortel Networks, 419
Norton, 402
NPD Group, 500
NRDC Equity Partners, 522
Nuance Spa, 321

O
Odeo, 16
Office Depot, 340
Office of Energy Efficiency, 79
Office of Financial Stability, 449
Office of the Superintendent of Financial Institutions (OSFI), 462
Offshore Odysseys, 117f
Oil & Gas Journal, 361
O'Keefe, 383
Old Navy, 522
Olympic Games, 241, 297
One Connect, 530
1000 Markets, 291
Onex Corporation, 486
Ontario Craft Brewers Association, 174
Ontario Energy Board, 68
Ontario Hospital Association, 513
Ontario Human Rights Commission, 52
Ontario Lottery and Gaming Corporation, 279
Ontario Securities Commission, 53, 462
Ontario Teachers' Pension Plan, 455
OpenText Corporation, 248
Operation Come Home, 410
Operative Plasterers' and Cement Masons' International Association (OPCMIA), 228, 229
Opryland, 543

Oracle, 368, 424
Orascom Telecom Holding, 529
Orbitz, 367
Origin, 511
Osgoode Hall, 36
The Ottawa Hospital, 512–514
OvernightPetTags.com, 161
Overstock, 15, 367

P
Pacific Biodiesel, 45
PacSun, 361
Pampered Chef, 339
Panasonic Automotive Systems Asia Pacific, 111
Pandora Internet Radio, 305
Paralympic Winter Games, 297
Patagonia, 499–502
Patent Office, 166
PayPal, 17, 68, 155
Peabody Energy, 451
PepsiAmericas, 325
Pepsi Bottling Group, 325
Pepsi Bottling Ventures, 325
PepsiCo, 325, 329, 473
Pershing Square Capital Management, 527
PetroChina Company, 487
PetSmart, 340, 341
Pew Research Center, 395, 524
Pfizer, 68, 368, 471
Pharmaprix, 327
Pi Athlete Management Inc., 123, 124, 147
Pillsbury, 95
Pinkerton, 324
Piper Cub, 367
Pizza Hut, 136
Planeterra Foundation, 509
Play It Again, 162
Playnomics, 304
Popular Science, 301
Population Reference Bureau, 307
PotashCorp, 89, 113
Pottery Barn, 339t
Priceline, 367
PricewaterhouseCoopers (PwC), 418, 437
PricewaterhouseCoopers Canada, 41
Primerica Inc., 452
Prince Edward Island Credit Union Deposit Insurance Corporation, 458
Procter & Gamble, 202, 303, 328, 330, 332, 358
Province of Manitoba, 420
Public Service Alliance (PSA), 228

Q
Qualcomm, 217
QueueBuster, 315
Quiznos, 175, 332

R
Ralph Lauren, 339t
Rapleaf Inc., 304
Ratiopharm, 471
RBC Financial Group, 392, 436, 455, 457, 463, 464, 494
RE/MAX, 337
Reader's Digest, 361
Real Canadian Superstore, 339t
Red Bull, 358
Red Cross. *See* Canadian Red Cross
Red Cross/Red Crescent, 296
Regency Energy Partners, 486
Research In Motion Ltd., 179
 see also BlackBerry Ltd.
Restaurant Brands International Inc., 135
Revlon, 146
Rexall, 49
Rockstar Energy Drink, 325
Rogers Communications Inc., 4, 48, 62, 124, 279, 392, 398, 436, 530
RONA, 392
Rotman School of Management, 445
Royal Bank of Canada, 4, 118, 124, 298, 529
Royal Dutch Shell, 481
Running Room, 125, 146
RUSNANO, 451

S
Safeway, 339t
SAI Global, 38
Saint Luke's Health System, 473
Salesforce.com, 391
Salvation Army, 198
Samsung, 363, 395, 489
SAP, 273, 424
Scotiabank, 292, 337, 447, 455, 463, 464
Scotia Capital, 494
ScotiaMcLeod, 337
Scottrade Inc., 389
Seagate, 278
Sears, 279, 330, 357
Selfridges, 374
ServiceMaster, 324, 331
Services Canada, 212
Servus Credit Union, 458
7-Eleven, 339t, 340, 357
Seventh Generation, 263, 299, 340
Shell Canada, 489
Shibui Designs, 262
Shoppers Drug Mart, 49, 327
Sierra Club, 163, 252
Silpada, 339
Simon Fraser University, 5, 160
The Skald Group, 38
Skype, 276, 400
Sleeman Breweries, 174
Sleepmaster, 276
Small Business Administration (SBA), 133, 154f

Small Business Investor Alliance, 569
Society for Human Resource Management (SHRM), 212, 221
Sodexho Marriott Services, 310
Solar City, 155
Sony, 62, 395
Southwest Properties, 235
SpaceX, 155
Sports Illustrated, 361
Spreadshirt, 302
Spud.ca, 64
Square, 16
STA, 315
Standard & Poor's (S&P), 449, 464, 488
Standards Council of Canada (SCC), 279
Stanford University, 219
Staples, 44
Starbucks, 40, 189, 331, 342, 404, 426, 473, 479
STAT-USA, 108t
Statistics Canada, 10, 44, 77, 127, 131, 133, 209, 306, 336, 358, 392
Stella & Dot, 156
Stock-Trak Global Portfolio Simulations, 389, 406
Stouffer, 311
SUBWAY, 136, 137, 302
Success, 154
Suncor Energy, 489
Sunlife Financial, 392, 495
Sun Microsystems, 45, 404
SunOpta, 531–532
SunOpta Distribution Group (SDG), 531
SunOpta Food Group, 531
Sun Youth Organization, 140
Super 8, 136
Sustainalytics, 30
Symantec, 402
Syncrude Canada Ltd., 487
Sysco, 336

T
T-Mobile, 360
Take Our Daughters and Sons to Work Foundation, 327
Target Corporation, 33, 111, 294, 326, 340, 346, 478, 520
Tata Motors, 97, 98, 145
TD Ameritrade, 90
TD Bank, 4, 90, 181, 193, 447, 464
TD Canada Trust, 354, 447, 455
TD Friends of the Environment Foundation, 447
TD Securities, 452
TD Waterhouse, 455
Team Canada 1972, 514–516
Teavana, 189
Technomic, 66
Teck Resources Limited, 193, 485

Teen Vogue, 361
Teenage Research Unlimited, 303
Telfer School of Management, 31, 32*f*
Telsey Advisory Group LLC, 520
TELUS Corp., 30, 48, 392, 398, 400, 448, 472, 530
Tesla Motors, 44, 155
Teva Pharmaceutical Industries, 471
Texas Instruments, 39
3G Capital, 136
3M, 169, 170, 198, 279
Ticketmaster Entertainment, 9
Tiffany & Co., 35
Tim Horton Children's Foundation, 41
Tim Hortons Coffee Partnership, 46
Tim Hortons Inc., 30, 110, 135, 136, 175, 238, 293, 331, 472, 485
Timberland, 299, 312, 313
Time, 361
Time Warner, 219, 489
Tommy Hilfiger, 339*t*
TOMS Shoes, 131, 132
Topshop, 520, 523
Toronto Raptors, 363
Toronto Stock Exchange (TSX), 238, 419, 438, 453, 462
Toronto Transit Commission, 141
Toyota, 118, 239, 244, 262, 479, 516–518
Toyota Financial Services, 459
TradeInsight, 394
TransCanada Corporation, 99, 451
Transparency International, 100
TransUnion, 300
TronSports.ca, 155, 159
TRU-Insight, 303
The Trunk Club, 128
Tumblr, 15
Twitter, 15, 16, 129, 161, 245, 295, 303, 304, 342, 343, 344, 353, 360
Tylenol, 359

U
Uber, 153, 154
Under Armour, 341
UNFI Canada Inc., 531
Unilever, 303, 358, 478
United Nations, 509

United Natural Foods Inc., 531
University of British Columbia, 76
University of Idaho, 45
University of Ottawa, 31
University of Saskatchewan, 36
University of Toronto, 5, 50, 52, 314, 389, 445, 529
University of Waterloo, 162
University of Western Ontario, 298
Unsynced, 162
UnusualThreads.com, 161
Upper Canada Brewing, 174
UPS, 396
UPS Freight, 211–212
U.S. Census Bureau, 306, 394
U.S. Chamber of Commerce, 154*f*
U.S. Department of Commerce, 108
U.S. Department of Justice, 539
U.S. Federal Trade Commission, 138
U.S. International Trade Commission, 533
U.S. Patent and Trademark Office, 166
U.S. Securities and Exchange Commission (SEC), 22, 183
U.S. Small Business Administration, 570
U.S. Treasury, 449
US Airways, 21, 195

V
Vancity. *See* Vancouver City Savings Credit Union
Vancouver 2010 Olympic Games, 59
Vancouver City Savings Credit Union, 76, 193, 497–499
VeloCity, 162
VIA Rail Canada, 141
Vice, 9
Videotron, 400
Vistakon, 488
Volkswagen, 43, 145, 268

W
Wall Street Journal, 154*f,* 355
Wall Street Survivor, 389
Walmart, 63, 72, 92, 111, 190, 263, 326, 327, 338, 339*t,* 341, 346, 365, 376, 499, 520, 522, 534, 550
Walmart Canada, 31, 32, 478

Walmart International, 92
Walt Disney Company, 16, 50, 62, 195, 307, 326
Walt Disney World, 267
Wasserman & Partners Advertising Inc., 353
WeddingChannel.com, 155
Wendy's, 66
West Edmonton Mall, 341
WestJet Airlines, 50, 190, 196
Westpac Banking Corporation, 485
The Westwood, 235
White House Project, 327
Whole Foods Market, 127, 239, 292, 339*t*
Wildeboer Dellelce, LLP, 36
Williams-Sonoma, 339*t*
Wilson Sporting Goods Company, 275
WIND Mobile, 529–530
Wired, 355
Workers' Compensation Board of Alberta, 49
Workers' Compensation Board of Nova Scotia, 49
Workplace Safety and Insurance Board (Ontario), 49
WorkSafeBC, 353, 379
World Economic Forum, 445

X
Xerox, 331
Xilinx Inc., 219

Y
Yahoo, 360, 402
Yak Communications, 530
Yale University, 389
Yellow Pages, 364
Yellowquill College, 169
YMCA, 180
YouTube, 7, 15, 62, 344, 353, 358, 360

Z
Zappos, 182, 199, 307
Zara International, 519–521
Zellers Inc., 111, 522, 523
Zhena's Gypsy Tea, 50, 158
Zipcar, 525–526

SUBJECT INDEX

A

absolute advantage, 92–93
accessory equipment, 324
accountants, 415, 418–420, 494
accounting, 415
    accounting cycle, 422–424, 422f
    accounting equation, 422–424
    accounting professionals, 418–420
    accounting software programs, 424
    accrual accounting, 430
    business activities involving accounting, 417
    career, 494–495
    computers, impact of, 424
    cooking the books, 415, 438
    financial statements, 425–431
    foundation of the accounting system, 420–421
    generally accepted accounting principles (GAAP), 420
    international accounting, 437–438
    Internet, impact of, 424
    users of accounting information, 416–417, 416f
accounting cycle, 422–424, 422f
accounting equation, 422–424, 479
accounting identity, 423
accounting professionals, 418–420
accounting standards, 420
Accounting Standards Board (AcSB), 420
Accounting Standards for Private Enterprises (ASPE), 420, 421
accounts receivable, 477
accrual accounting, 430
acid-test ratio, 432t, 433
acquisition, 111, 145, 488
active listening, 247
activity ratios, 432t, 433–434
actuarial tables, 547
adaptation strategy, 112–113, 301–302

adapting strategic plans, 190–191
Addison, John, 452
address lists, 361–362
adjourning stage, 242
administrative agencies, 535
administrative barriers, 102, 104
administrative services managers, 286
admired companies, 22–23
advertising, 355t, 358
    advertising media, 359–364, 359f
    advocacy advertising, 359
    cause advertising, 359
    comparative advertising, 359
    cooperative advertising, 371
    deceptive advertising and packaging, 10
    floor ads, 363
    informative advertising, 359
    institutional advertising, 358–359
    outdoor advertising, 362
    persuasive advertising, 359
    point-of-purchase (POP) advertising, 366
    product advertising, 358
    and product life cycle, 359
    reminder-oriented advertising, 359
    specialty advertising, 366
    truthfulness in, 48
    types of advertising, 358–359
    viral advertising, 360
advertising media, 359–364, 359f
    direct mail, 361–362
    Internet advertising, 360
    magazines, 361
    newspapers, 361
    other media options, 363–364
    outdoor advertising, 362
    radio, 361
    sponsorship, 363
    television, 359–360
advertising specialties, 366
advocacy advertising, 359

affective conflict, 243
affinity programs, 314
after-tax profits, 9
age, 307
age discrimination, 52
age of industrial entrepreneurs, 12
agency, 537
agents, 337
aggressive competitive practices, 10
aging population, 18, 81t
agriculture, 45, 64
AIO statements, 308
alliances, 314
alternative energy development, 72
ambiguity, 165
analysts, 332
analytic production system, 263
angel investors, 169
angry customers, 313
Anti-Bribery Convention, 100
apparel manufacturing, 209
Appleton, Frank, 383
application service provider (ASP), 405
application software, 396
approach, 369
arbitration, 226
Armstrong, Tim, 219
articles of incorporation, 142f
ASEAN, 105
asking for a raise, 215
assembly line, 261, 271
assessment of competitive position, 188–190
asset, 422, 476–477
asset management, 476–479
Association of Southeast Asian Nations (ASEAN), 105
audience feedback, 245
Australia, 105
auto insurance, 550
auto manufacturing, 268

autocratic leadership, 194
automated teller machines (ATMs), 338–339, 364, 447, 457, 457
automatic merchandising, 338

B
baby boomers, 199, 304, 524–525
backup, 404
bailment, 538
balance of payments, 93
balance-of-payments deficit, 93
balance-of-payments surplus, 93
balance of trade, 93
balance sheet, 426–427, 428f
balanced budget, 80, 105
Balsillie, Jim, 179
Bank Act, 461–462
bank loan, 168, 483–484
Bank of Canada (the Bank), 78, 175, 460–461, 462, 465
Bank of England, 464
Bank of Japan, 464
bank regulation, 461–462
bankruptcy, 430, 540
banks, 168, 436, 455–458
Barberini, Marco, 161
Barra, Mary, 194, 194f
barriers to international trade, 96–103
    administrative barriers, 102, 103
    cultural differences, 96–97
    economic differences, 97–99
    legal differences, 99–101
    nontariff barriers, 102, 103
    political differences, 99–101
    reducing barriers to international trade, 104–107
    religious attitudes, 97
    social differences, 96–97
    tariffs, 102
    trade restrictions, 102–103
    values, 97
Beatty, Douglas, 419
Beauchesne, Steve and Tim, 117, 174, 284–285, 383, 410–411
being your own boss, 156–157
belongingness needs, 222
benchmarking, 278
benefits sought, 309
Bernanke, Ben, 481
"The Best Corporate Citizens," 193
Beyoncé, 294
Bieber, Justin, 3, 4, 10, 23
Bill 198, 33, 54, 421, 426
Billes, John W. and Alfred J., 327
Bindman, Marty, 123
biodiesel fuel, 45
blogs, 308
board of directors, 144
bond rating, 449–450, 450t

bonds, 448–450, 449t, 485
botnet, 402
Bourgeois, Marc, 123
boycott, 228
boycott in restraint of trade, 536
brand, 13, 329, 332f
brand awareness, 331
brand categories, 330
brand equity, 331–332
branding, 13
brand insistence, 331
brand loyalty, 310, 331
brand manager, 331
brand name, 330
brand preference, 331
brand recognition, 331
Braun, Scooter, 3
breach of contract, 537
breakeven analysis, 375–376, 375f
breakeven point, 375–376
bribes, 100
brokers, 337
Brooke, Beth, 241
Brookshire, Mark, 389
Brown, Bobbi, 163f
Brunei, 105
budget, 79–80, 435–437, 558
budget deficit, 80
budget surplus, 80
Buffett, Warren, 192
business, 4
business analysis, 328
business buying behaviour, 311
business cycle, 71–73
Business Development Bank of Canada (BDC), 133, 154f, 175
business ethics, 23, 30
    see also ethical controversies
    avoiding ethical dilemmas at work, 34
    Bill 198, 33
    concern for ethical and societal issues, 30–31
    conflict of interest, 35
    contemporary ethical environment, 31–37
    creating a good ethical foundation, 34
    development of individual ethics, 34
    ethical action, 39
    ethical awareness, 37–38
    ethical education, 38–39
    ethical leadership, 39–40
    ethical tone of business, 184
    ethics compliance officers, 33
    ethics training programs, 38–39
    honesty, 35–36
    individuals making a difference, 33
    information system, 403
    integrity, 35–36
    loyalty vs. truth, 36
    on-the-job ethical dilemmas, 34–37

    Sarbanes-Oxley Act of 2002, 33
    shaping ethical conduct, 37–40
    whistle-blowing, 36–37
business goods, 323–324
business history eras, 12–14
business incubator, 133
business intelligence, 303
business intelligence software, 392
business interruption insurance, 550
business law, 536
    bailment, 538
    bankruptcy, 540
    contract law, 536–538
    core of, 536
    law of agency, 537
    legal system and administrative agencies, 535
    negotiable instruments, 538
    product liability, 540
    property law, 538
    regulatory environment, 536
    tax law, 540
    torts, 539–540
    trademarks, patents, and copyrights, 539
    types of law, 535–536
    warranties, 537
business markets, 310
business meetings, 273
business ownership. See forms of business ownership
business plan, 131–132, 167, 167t, 564–570
    executive summary, 565–566
    financing section, 568
    introduction, 566–567
    marketing strategy, 567–568
    outline, 567
    resources, 569–570
    résumés of principals, 568
business products, 323
business-to-business (B2B), 301, 305
business-to-consumer (B2C), 299–301, 305
buyer's market, 295
buying an existing business, 166
buying offices, 337–338

C
C-SOX. See Bill 198
cable television, 360
cafeteria plans, 217
CAFTA-DR. See Central America-Dominican Republic Free Trade Agreement
callable bonds, 450
call provision, 450
calming the angry customer, 313
Cameron, James, 20f
Canada, 97
    Anti-Bribery Convention, 100
    balance of trade, 93

and credit crisis, 445
financial institutions, 456f
GDP per capita, 74, 91t
hedge funds, 488
and IFRS, 420
low-context culture, 245
major exports and imports, 93–94, 94t
NAFTA, 105, 310
national debt, 80
political stability, 99
population, 80, 91t
railroads, 347
tariffs, 102
top trading partners, 92
trade with U.S., 92
Trans-Pacific Partnership (TPP), 105
treaties, 100–101
unions in, 228
vacation time, 97
venture capital, 134
Canada Pension Plan (CPP), 459
Canada Savings Bonds, 448
Canada Small Business Financing Program (CSBFP), 133
Canadian apparel manufacturing, 209
Canadian Census of Population, 392–393
Canadian Charter of Rights and Freedoms, 51
Canadian Disability Vocational Rehabilitation Program, 51t
Canadian Human Rights Act (CHRA), 51t, 52, 53
Cantin, Murielle, 29
capital, 7
capital investment analysis, 478
capitalism, 8, 67–69, 70–71t
capital structure, 479–483
Carbone, Michael, 123
career choice, 558
careers
  accounting or finance career, 494–495
  entrepreneurial careers, 175–176
  global business and economics career, 118–119
  information technology career, 412
  management career, 286–287
case study, 117, 174, 284–285, 410
cases, 497–532
cash, 476–477
cash budget, 436–437, 436f, 484
cash flow, 430
cash flow statement, 429–430, 431f
category advisor, 332
category manager, 332
cause advertising, 359
cause marketing, 298–299
cause-related marketing, 47
Central America-Dominican Republic Free Trade Agreement (CAFTA-DR), 106–107

central banks, 103
centralization, 200
CEO compensation, 144, 481
certificate of deposit (CD), 448
Certified Fraud Examiner (CFE), 418, 419
Certified Internal Auditor (CIA), 418
chain of command, 200
Chan, Sherman, 76
change. *See* organizational change
Chartered Professional Accountants (CPAs), 418
Chelios, Chris, 123
Chen, John S., 179, 202
chief executive officer (CEO), 30, 43, 144, 145, 180, 183, 286, 421, 472, 473
chief financial officer (CFO), 144, 145, 180, 183, 286, 421, 472
chief information officer (CIO), 144, 286, 390
chief operating officer (COO), 144, 286, 472
Chile, 105
China, 17, 19, 69, 72, 73, 74, 81, 81t, 89, 91t, 93, 96, 97, 100, 101, 104, 110, 111, 112, 160, 184–185, 244, 278, 279, 437, 487
choice, 49
Choquette, Éric, 29
CHRA. *See* Canadian Human Rights Act (CHRA)
CIA *World Factbook*, 108, 108t
classic entrepreneurs, 155
classification of goods and services, 322–324
  business goods, 323–324
  consumer goods and services, 322–323, 323f
  marketing strategy implications, 324–325
  services, 324
classroom training, 213–214
"clean capitalism" report, 485
closed corporation, 143
closely held corporation, 143
closing, 370
cloud computing, 397f, 405, 406
co-branding, 314
code of conduct, 37–38
cognitive conflict, 243
cohesive groups, 242–243
collaboration, 19
collective bargaining, 226
collective ownership of business, 140–142
colonial period, 12
colony collapse disorder (CCD), 297
co-marketing, 314–315
commerce treaties, 100–101
commercial and business insurance, 550
commercial banks, 455–458
commercial paper, 484
committee organizations, 201
commodity prices, 81t

common law, 535
common market, 105
common shares, 144, 450
communication, 244
  communication process, 244–245, 244f
  context, 245
  crisis management, 251–253
  downward communication, 248
  external communication, 251–253
  formal communication channels, 246t, 248, 249f
  forms of, 246–251, 246t
  informal communication channels, 246t, 249, 249f
  integrated marketing communications. *See* integrated marketing communications (IMC)
  noise, 245
  nonverbal communication, 246t, 249–251
  open communication, 248
  oral communication, 246–247, 246t
  sender, 244–245
  upward communication, 248
  via mobile devices, 396
  written communication, 246t, 247–248
communication barriers, 96–97
communication process, 244–245, 244f
communism, 69, 70–71t
company responsibilities
  to consumers, 47–49
  to employees, 49–53
  to investors and financial community, 53–54
comparability, 420
comparative advantage, 93
comparative advertising, 359
compensation, 215–218
  employee benefits, 216–217
  executive compensation, 144, 481
  flexible benefit plans, 217
  flexible work plans, 217–218
  incentive compensation, 216, 216f, 236–238
competition, 8, 67–69
  see also market structures
Competition Act, 48, 68, 536
Competition Bureau, 46t, 48
competitive differentiation, 8, 190
competitiveness, 67
competitive performance, 344
competitive pricing, 377–378
competitive tactics of unions and management, 227–228
complaints, 347
component parts and materials, 324
compressed workweek, 217
computer-aided design (CAD), 259, 265
computer-aided manufacturing (CAM), 265

253

computer-based information system, 391
computer-based training, 213–214
computer hardware, 391, 394–396
computer-integrated manufacturing (CIM), 266
computer networks, 398–400
computer security specialists, 412
computer software, 396, 397t, 424
computerized trading, 454
Conant, Doug, 193f
concept development, 328
concept testing, 328
conceptual skills, 182
confidentiality, 304
conflict, 243–244, 248
conflict of interest, 35
conglomerate merger, 145
Connor, Michael, 164
consistency, 420
construction industry, 228
construction managers, 286
consumer behaviour, 311–312, 312f
Consumer Bill of Rights, 48
consumer complaints, 347
consumer desire, 354
consumer goods and services, 322–323, 323f
consumerism, 47–49
consumer markets, 305–310
consumer orientation, 13
consumer-oriented promotions, 364–366, 364f
consumer perceptions of price, 378
Consumer Price Index (CPI), 75
consumer's rights, 47–49
contests, 366
context, 245
contingency planning, 186–187
continuous production process, 263
contract, 536
contract-based agreements, 109–110
contract law, 536–538
contract requirements, 536–537
controller, 472
controlling, 183
convenience products, 322
convenience store, 339t
convertible securities, 451
Cook, Gary, 397
cooking the books, 415, 437, 438
Cool, Tracy, 192
Cooley, Pam, 235, 253
Cool IT Challenge, 397
cooperative advertising, 371
cooperatives, 140–142, 337–338
copyrights, 539
core inflation rate, 74
corporate charter, 142–143
corporate culture, 195–196
corporate insiders, 462

corporate management, 143–145, 143f
corporate philanthropy, 42, 46–47
corporate social responsibility (CSR), 30, 425
corporation, 140
  articles of incorporation, 142f
  board of directors, 144
  closed corporation, 143
  closely held corporation, 143
  corporate charter, 142–143
  corporate officers and managers, 144–145
  how to incorporate, 142–143
  incorporation, 142–143
  management, 143–145, 143f
  open corporation, 144
  organizing a corporation, 142–145
  publicly held corporation, 144
  shareholder rights, 143–144
  stock ownership, 143–144
  where to incorporate, 142
corruption, 100, 101f
Corruption of Foreign Public Officials Act (CFPOA), 100, 421
Corruption Perceptions Index, 100
cost-based pricing, 374
cost-push inflation, 74
costs, 375
countertrade, 109
coupons, 365
CPI market basket, 75, 76f
creative leadership, 21
creative selling, 368
creativity, 21, 164, 169
credit, 559
The Credit CARD Act, 553
credit cards, 130, 401, 457, 553–554
credit crisis, 445, 449, 454, 460, 465
credit management, 559–560
Credit Reporting Act, 300
credit reports, 300
credit unions, 458
crisis management, 251–253
critical path, 276
critical thinking, 20–21
Crosby, Sidney, 123
cross-functional team, 239
cultural differences, 96–97
currency blocs, 95
currency conversion and shifts, 98–99
currency devaluation, 95
current assets, 476
current ratio, 432t, 433
customer-based segmentation, 310
customer departmentalization, 198
customer-driven production, 262
customer-oriented layout, 270f, 271
customer relationship management (CRM), 315
customer service standards, 347
customer service strategy, 341

customs union, 105
cyberattacks, 402
cybercrime, 400–401
cyclical unemployment, 77
cynical listening, 247

D
damages, 537
data, 390
database, 392–393
database programs, 397f
data mining, 304
data warehouse, 304
Davis, Jeffrey T., 137
debenture, 448
debt capital, 479, 480
debt financing, 168
debt forgiveness, 79
debt ratio, 432t, 435
decentralization, 200, 249
deceptive advertising and packaging, 10
deceptive marketing, 48
decision making, 191
  how managers make decisions, 192
  make, buy, or lease decision, 271
  nonprogrammed decision, 191
  programmed decision, 191
decision-making authority, 236
decision support system (DSS), 393–394
decline stage, 326
defensive listening, 247
deflation, 75
DeFlorio, Michael, 486
delegation, 198–199
demand, 61
  changes in quantity demanded, 62–63
  factors driving demand, 61–63
  interaction of demand and supply, 64–66
  primary demand, 354
  selective demand, 354
demand curve, 62–63, 63f, 63t
demand-pull inflation, 74
democratic leadership, 194–195
demographics, 567
demographic segmentation, 306–307, 306f, 310
demographic trends, and the entrepreneur, 161–162
demonstration, 369
Denham, Robert E., 481
department store, 339t
departmentalization, 198, 199f
deposit insurance, 457–458
depository institutions, 455
deregulation, 68–69
desktop publishing, 397f
detailers, 368
devaluation, 95, 99
developing countries, 92, 105
development banks, 104–105

diabetes, 42
Dickinson, Arlene, 134f
digital ad market, 360
direct distribution channel, 334, 335–336
direct exporting, 109
directing, 183
direct mail, 361–362
direct reports, 200
direct-response retailing, 338
direct-response television (DRTV), 364
direct selling, 339
disability income insurance, 550
disaster recovery planning, 404
discount pricing, 376
discount rate, 460
discount store, 339t
discrimination, 51, 52
dispatching, 277
distributed workforce, 404–405
distribution channel decisions, 343–345
distribution channels, 334–336, 334f, 344
distribution intensity, 345
distribution strategy, 301, 334
    logistics, 345–346
    physical distribution, 334, 345–346, 346f
    retailing, 338–343
    wholesaling, 336–338
diverse workforce, 18–19
diversity, 18–19, 240–241
divestiture, 489
dividend policy, 482–483
dividends, 450–451, 482
Dorsey, Jack, 16
double-entry bookkeeping, 423
downsizing, 127, 218–220, 219
downward communication, 248
Drabinsky, Garth, 415
Drake, *See* Graham, Aubrey Drake
drop shipper, 337
Drucker, Peter, 224
drug testing, 212
dumping, 103
Dungan, Peter, 445
Dunn, Frank, 419

E
ebusiness, 15
economic differences, 97–99
economic performance, 71–77
    employment levels, 77
    flattening the business cycle, 71–73
    gross domestic product (GDP), 73–74, 74f
    inflation, 74
    management of economy's performance, 78–80
    price level changes, 74–77
    productivity, 73–74, 75
economics, 60
    budget, 79–80
    evaluation of economic performance, 71–77
    fiscal policy, 78–79
    global business and economics career, 118–119
    global economic challenges, 80–82, 81t
    macroeconomics, 60, 66–71
    market structures, 67–71
    microeconomics, 60–66
    monetary policy, 78, 460–461
economic systems, 60
    capitalism, 8, 67–69, 70–71t
    communism, 69, 70–71t
    comparison of alternative economic systems, 70–71t
    mixed market economy, 70–71t
    planned economy, 69
    socialism, 69, 70–71t
economic trends, and the entrepreneur, 161–162
economic union, 105
education, 46, 160
Edwards, Mickey, 185
EEA. *See* Employment Equities Act (EEA)
80/20 principle, 310, 314
electronic banking, 456–457
electronic communications, 157
electronic communications networks (ECNs), 455
electronic funds transfer systems (EFTSs), 456–457
email, 157, 248
embargo, 103
employee benefits, 216–217
employee motivation, 220–225
    equity theory, 223
    expectancy theory, 223, 223f
    goal-setting theory, 224, 224f
    Herzberg's two-factor model of motivation, 222–223
    job design, 224–225
    management by objectives (MBO), 224
    managers' attitudes, 225
    Maslow's hierarchy of needs, 221–222
    process of motivation, 220f
    Theory X, 225
    Theory Y, 225
    Theory Z, 225
employee separation, 218–220
employee stock ownership plans (ESOPs), 236–238, 237t
employee theft, 36
employees
    age discrimination, 52
    drug testing, 212
    empowerment. *See* empowerment
    equal opportunity, 51–52
    flexible work schedules, 50
    high employee morale, 220
    input of, 248
    Internet use, 403
    intrapreneurship, 169–170
    monitoring employees' social media activities, 221
    overseas assignments, 118
    quality-of-life issues, 50–51
    recruitment and selection, 211–213, 211f
    responsibilities to, 49–53
    sexism, 53
    sexual harassment, 53
    workplace safety, 49
employer businesses by firm size, 126t
Employment Equity Act (EEA), 52
employment levels, 77
Employment Standards Act, 97
empowerment, 195, 236
    decision-making authority, 236
    ethical controversies, 237
    information sharing, 236
    linking rewards to company performance, 236–238
end-use segmentation, 310
EnerGuide, 79
Energy Efficiency Act, 79
energy level, 163
ENERGY STAR symbol, 79
English, 96
enterprise resource planning, 397f
enterprise zones, 169
entrepreneur, 10, 154–156
    categories of, 155–156
    characteristics of, 162–165
    classic entrepreneurs, 155
    creativity, 164
    demographic trends, 161–162
    economic trends, 161–162
    education, 160
    environment for, 159–162
    and ethics, 164
    and globalization, 159–160
    high energy level, 163
    homepreneurs, 161
    information technology (IT), 160–161
    internal locus of control, 165
    need to achieve, 163
    optimism, 163
    self-confidence, 163
    serial entrepreneurs, 155
    social entrepreneur, 156
    starting a new venture, 165–169
    tolerance for ambiguity, 165
    tolerance for failure, 163–164
    vision, 162
entrepreneurship, 7, 10–11
    being your own boss, 156–157
    financial success, 158
    job security, 158
    lifestyle entrepreneurship, 158
    quality of life, 158
    reasons for choosing, 156–159, 156f

environmental concerns, 15
environmental impact study, 267
environmentally friendly packages, 332
environmental protection, 43–46
equal opportunity, 51–52, 51*t*
equal pay for equal work, 51*t*
equal rights, 51*t*
equilibrium price, 65
equity capital, 479, 480
equity financing, 168–169
equity theory, 223
esteem needs, 222
e-readers, 395
ethical action, 39
ethical awareness, 37–38
ethical controversies
    alternative energy development, 72
    CEO compensation, 144
    CEO responsibility, 43
    China, and quality controls, 279
    employee empowerment, 237
    entrepreneurs and ethics, 164
    executive compensation, 481
    free credit reports, 300
    free e-books, 373
    Google, and Chinese market, 184–185
    Keystone XL Pipeline, 99
    monitoring employees' Internet use, 403
    monitoring employees' social media activities, 221
    securities fraud, 22
    securities market self-regulation, 462
    teens at the mall, 342
    whistle-blowers, 426
ethical education, 38–39
ethical leadership, 39–40
ethics. *See* business ethics
ethics compliance officers, 33
ethics training programs, 38–39
EU. *See* European Union (EU)
euro, 95, 107, 454
European Central Bank, 464
European Commission, 344
European Union (EU), 95, 97, 104, 107, 107*f*, 228, 420, 445, 454
evaluation, 214
event marketing, 298
everyday low pricing (EDLP), 376
exchange control, 103
exchange process, 293
exchange rates, 95–96, 438
exclusive distribution, 345
executive compensation, 144, 481
executive summary, 131
executive support system (ESS), 394
executive vice-president, 180, 286
expansionary monetary policy, 78
expectancy theory, 223, 223*f*
expert system, 394

exporters, 109
export management company, 109
exports, 90, 93–94
external communication, 251–253
external data, 303

F
facility layout, 269–271, 270*f*
factor, 484
factoring, 484
factor payments, 6*t*
factors of production, 6–7, 6*t*, 64, 90–91
factory outlet, 339*t*
failed products, 329*t*
failure, 163–164
Fair Credit Reporting Act (FCRA), 300
fair trade, 50
False Claims Act, 426
family brand, 330
family medical leave, 51*t*
fast-food chains, 66
federal budget, 79–80
Feed-in Tariff Program, 15, 16
feedback, 214, 224, 245, 248
Ferrari, Michael and Mary, 161
field robots, 265
field selling, 367
finance, 472
    asset management, 476–479
    capital structure, 479–483
    career, 494–495
    dividend policy, 482–483
    finance organization of typical firm, 472*f*
    long-term financing, 484–488
    mixing short-term and long-term funds, 481–482
    short-term funding options, 483–484
    sources of funds, 479–483
finance charge, 559
finance companies, 459, 484
Financial Accounting Standards Board, 421
financial assistance, 133
financial community, 53–54
financial crisis, 445, 449, 454, 460, 465
financial institutions, 455–459
    in Canada, 456*f*
    commercial banks, 455–458
    credit unions, 458
    depository institutions, 455
    finance companies, 459
    as financial market experts, 453
    insurance companies, 459
    mutual funds, 459
    nondepository institutions, 455, 459
    pension funds, 459
    and small business, 133
financial manager, 472–474, 495
financial markets, 451–453, 462
financial plan, 474–476

financial planning, 474–476
financial ratio analysis, 432–435, 432*t*
financial records, 302
financial section, 131
financial software, 397*f*
financial statements, 425–431
financial success, 158
financial system, 98, 446
    Bank of Canada, 460–461
    bank regulation, 461–462
    financial institutions, 455–459
    financial markets, 451–453, 462
    global perspective, 463–465
    overview, 446*f*
    regulation, 461–463
    securities, 448–451
    stock markets, 453–455
    understanding the financial system, 446–447
financing
    debt financing, 168
    equity financing, 168–169
    finding financing, 168–169
    inadequate financing, and small businesses, 130–131
    seed capital, 168
    for small businesses, 132–134
financing activities, 417
firewall, 399
fiscal policy, 78–79
fishing, 67*f*
fixed costs, 375
fixed-position layout, 270*f*, 271
flag colours, 333
flattening the business cycle, 71–73
flexibility, 19
flexible benefit plans, 217
flexible manufacturing system (FMS), 265–266
flexible production, 262
flexible work plans, 217–218
flexible work schedules, 50
flextime, 217
floating exchange rates, 95
floor ads, 363
focus group, 303, 328
follow-up, 277, 370
Food and Drugs Act, 48
food service managers, 286
Ford, Henry, 13, 261
Foreign Corrupt Practices Act, 100, 426
foreign exchange rates, 95–96, 438
foreign licensing agreement, 110
foreign stock markets, 453–454
forensic accountants, 418, 419
form utility, 293
formal communication channels, 246*t*, 248, 249*f*
forming stage, 242

forms of business ownership
   corporation, 140
   partnership, 139
   sole proprietorship, 138–139
fourth market, 455
franchise, 109–110
franchisee, 136
franchising, 135
   benefits of, 136–138
   buying a franchise, 166
   franchise fee, 135
   franchising agreements, 136
   franchising sector, 135–136
   problems of, 136–138
franchisor, 136
Frankel, Stuart, 137
fraud, 10, 22, 415, 419, 426
free credit reports, 300
free e-books, 373
free-rein leadership, 195
free trade, 106
free-trade area, 105
freedom of choice, 9–10
frequency marketing, 314
frequency of use, 326
frictional unemployment, 77
friendship treaties, 100–101
full-function merchant wholesalers, 337
functional departmentalization, 198
Furman, Don, 72

G
G7 countries, 105
gain sharing, 216
games, 366
Gantt chart, 276, 277f
gasoline prices, 62, 63f, 64f
GATT. *See* General Agreement on Tariffs and Trade (GATT)
GDP. *See* gross domestic product (GDP)
GDP per capita, 74
Gelinas, Johanne, 425
gender, 306, 307–308
General Agreement on Tariffs and Trade (GATT), 104
general public, responsibilities to, 42–47
generally accepted accounting principles (GAAP), 420
Generation X, 18, 199, 524
Generation Y, 18, 199, 218, 307, 524–525
geographical departmentalization, 198
geographical segmentation, 305–306, 310
gift-giving traditions, 97
Gillespie, Manda Aufochs, 128
Gillis, Derek, 235
global business. *See* international business
global business and economics career, 118–119
global business strategy, 112

global economic challenges, 80–82, 81t
global economy, 80–82, 93
global financial system, 463–465
global information economy, 81t
globalization, 73, 159–160, 464
goal acceptance, 224
goal difficulty, 224
goal-setting theory, 224, 224f
goal specificity, 224
going global. *See* international business
gold, 65, 65f
Gollogly, Michael, 419
Goodman, Jodi, 9
Gorsky, Alex, 188
gossip, 249
Gottlieb, Myron, 415
government accountants, 419–420
government agencies, 124–125
government bonds, 448
government regulation, 131, 462
government support for new ventures, 169
Graham, Aubrey Drake, 3, 23
Grant brothers, 321
grapevine, 249
Graziano, Fred, 447
Great Depression, 73, 454
green initiatives, 17
green manufacturing processes, 263–264
green marketing, 45, 46t
green packaging, 332–333
Greenspan, Alan, 462, 463
grid computing, 405
grievance, 226–227, 227f
gross domestic product (GDP), 73–74, 74f, 92
gross profit margin, 432t, 434–435
growth stage, 326
guerilla marketing, 357–358
Gupta, Rajiv, 481

H
hackers, 401
hand-held devices, 395, 401
handling objections, 369–370
hard currencies, 95–96
hardware, 394–396
health insurance, 550
heart disease, 42
hedge funds, 488
Heins, Thorsten, 179
Herzberg, Frederick, 222
Herzberg's two-factor model of motivation, 222–223
hierarchy of needs, 221–222
high-context cultures, 245
home-based businesses, 125, 161
home-based work programs, 218
homeowners' insurance, 550
homepreneurs, 161
honesty, 35–36

honey bee research, 297
Hong Kong, 437
horizontal merger, 145
hosts, 402
households, 446
Howe, Gordie, 123
human factors, and location decision, 266t, 267
human resource management, 210
   compensation, 215–218
   downsizing, 218–220
   drug testing, 212
   employee separation, 218–220
   evaluation, 214
   finding qualified candidates, 211
   hiring restrictions, 212
   human resource plans, 211
   laws, understanding of, 212
   management development, 214
   orientation, 213–214
   outsourcing, 220
   performance appraisal, 214
   recruitment and selection, 211–213, 211f
   responsibilities, 210f
   selecting and hiring employees, 211–213
   training programs, 213–214
   turnover, 218
human resource managers, 286
human resource plans, 211
human resources, 7
human skills, 182
Hurteau, Guy and Jean, 159
hydraulic fracturing, 264
hygiene factors, 222
hyperinflation, 74

I
illegal payoffs, 100
IMC. *See* integrated marketing communications (IMC)
immigration, 18, 18f
implementation of strategy, 190
importers, 109
imports, 90, 93–94
inbound telemarketing, 368
incentive compensation, 216, 216f, 236–238
income, changes in, 63
income statement, 427, 429f
incorporation, 142–143
independent wholesaling intermediaries, 337
India, 73, 81t, 91t, 93, 97, 98, 110, 112, 160, 244, 245, 420
indirect exporting, 109
individual branding, 330
individuals, and ethics, 33–34
Industrial Revolution, 12, 14
industry creation, 127–128
industry self-regulation, 462
inflation, 74
infomercials, 363–364

informal communication channels, 246t, 249, 249f
information, 356, 390
information overload, 392
information sharing, 236
information system, 390
   administration, 401
   application service provider (ASP), 405
   backup, 404
   cloud computing, 405
   components of, 391–394
   computer-based information system, 391
   computer hardware, 394–396
   computer software, 396, 397t
   cybercrime, 400–401
   database, 392–393
   decision support system (DSS), 393–394
   design of, 391
   disaster recovery planning, 404
   distributed workforce, 404–405
   and ethics, 403
   executive support system (ESS), 394
   expert system, 394
   grid computing, 405
   malware, 401–402
   management information system (MIS), 393
   management support systems, 393–394
   on-demand computing, 405
   operational support systems, 393
   process control systems, 393
   security issues, 400–402
   transaction processing systems, 393
   trends, 404–406
   types of, 393–394
information technology (IT), 160–161, 220, 404, 473
information technology career, 412
informative advertising, 359
infrastructure, 98
initial public offering (IPO), 452
innovation, 19, 128–129
insider trading, 462
installations, 324
institutional advertising, 358–359
insurable interest, 546
insurable risk, 547
insurance, 545–552, 560–561
insurance companies, 459
intangible assets, 422
intangible property, 538
integrated marketing communications (IMC), 354
   objectives of promotional strategy, 356–357, 356f
   promotional mix, 355, 355t
   promotional planning, 357–358
integrity, 35–36
intellectual property, 539

intensive distribution, 345
interconnection, 80
intermittent production process, 263
internal locus of control, 165
international accounting, 437–438
International Accounting Standards Board (IASB), 420
international assets, 478–479
international barter, 109
international business
   see also international trade
   adaptation strategy, 112–113
   contract-based agreements, 109–110
   countertrade, 109
   expanding into overseas market, 107–111
   exporters, 109
   foreign licensing agreement, 110
   franchise, 109–110
   global business and economics career, 118–119
   global business strategy, 112
   importers, 109
   international direct investment, 110–111
   levels of involvement, 108–111
   multidomestic business strategy, 112–113
   multinational corporation (MNC), 111
   offshoring, 110
   packaging, 332–333
   reshoring, 111
   standardization strategy, 112
   strategy development, 112–113
   subcontracting, 110
international direct investment, 110–111
international economic communities, 105–107
International Financial Reporting Standards (IFRS), 420, 426, 427
international fiscal policy, 79
international law, 535
International Monetary Fund (IMF), 105
International Organization for Standardization, 279
international regulations, 100–101
international terrorism, 81t
international trade
   see also international business
   absolute advantage, 92–93
   balance of payments, 93
   balance of trade, 93
   barriers to international trade, 96–103
   comparative advantage, 93
   exchange rates, 95–96
   exports, 90, 93–94
   importance of, 90
   imports, 90, 93–94
   international economic communities, 105–107
   international sources of factors of production, 90–91

Internet research resources, 108
   major Canadian exports and imports, 93–94, 94t
   measurement of, 93–96
   organizations promoting international trade, 104–105
   reasons for trade, 90–93
   reducing barriers to international trade, 104–107
   risks of, 81
   size of international marketplace, 91–92
   trade restrictions, 102–103
international travel, 82
international union, 226
Internet
   accounting, impact on, 424
   advertising, 360
   China, and censorship, 184–185
   cultural sensitivity, 97
   and globalization, 73
   international trade research resources, 108
   monitoring employees' Internet use, 403
   and music industry, 3
   online banking, 457, 458f
   social networking, 14
   supplier selection, 272–273
Internet retailing, 338
interpersonal skills, 182
intimate zone, 250–251, 251t
intranets, 399
intrapreneurship, 169–170
introduction (business plan), 131
introduction stage, 325–326
inventors, 12, 166
inventory control, 273, 346
inventory management, 477–478
inventory turnover, 432t, 433
investing activities, 417
investment-grade bonds, 449
investment planning, 561
investors, 53–54, 133–134, 169, 455
invisible hand, 8
involuntary turnover, 218
Islam, 97, 464
ISO standards, 279–280

J

Japan, 105
Japanese management style, 225
job applications, 35–36
job creation, 127
job design, 224–225
job enlargement, 224
job enrichment, 225
job rotation, 225
job search, 129
job security, 158
job sharing program, 217–218
Jobs, Steve, 163, 179

joint venture, 111, 145–146
judiciary, 535
junk bonds, 449
junk mail, 362
just-in-time (JIT) system, 274

K
Kelsay, Will, 167
King, Robert, 45

L
labels, 332–333
labour-management relations
    arbitration, 227
    collective bargaining, 226
    grievance, 226–227, 227f
    labour relations board, 226
    labour unions, 225–226, 228–229
    management tactics, 228
    mediation, 226–227
    settling labour-management disputes, 226–227
    union tactics, 227–228
labour market, 555
labour productivity, 73
labour relations board, 226
labour unions, 104, 225–226, 228–229
Labuda, Stephen, 161
Laliberté, Guy, 29
language differences, 96
Latin America, 97, 106–107, 112, 245, 251
law, 535–536
law of agency, 537
law of large numbers, 547–548
layoffs, 219
Lazaridis, Mike, 179
leadership, 193
    autocratic leadership, 194
    creative leadership, 21
    democratic leadership, 194–195
    ethical leadership, 39–40
    free-rein leadership, 195
    leadership styles, 194–195
    managers as leaders, 193–195
leadership styles, 194–195
LEED (Leadership in Energy and Environmental Design), 188, 235, 264, 425, 447
legal differences, 99–101
legal environment, 100
legal system, 535
leverage, 479–480, 480f
leverage ratios, 432t, 435
leveraged buyout (LBOs), 488–489
liability, 423
liability insurance, 550
life insurance, 551–552
lifestyle centres, 342
lifestyle entrepreneurship, 158

lifetime value of a customer, 313
lights out facilities, 263
limit order, 455
limited-function merchant wholesalers, 337
line-and-staff organizations, 200–201, 200f
line managers, 200
line of credit, 168
line organizations, 200
liquidity ratios, 432t, 433
listening, 246–247
loan officers, 495
local area networks (LANs), 398, 398f
local union, 226
location decision, 266–268, 266t, 341–342
lockout, 228
locus of control, 165
lodging managers, 287
logistics, 345–346
long-term debt to equity ratio, 432t, 435
long-term financing, 484–488
long-term funds, 481–482
low-context cultures, 245
loyalty, 36
Lui, Tim, 437
lump-sum bonuses, 216
Lutz, Lisa, 291
luxury taxes, 540

M
M1, 460
M2, 460
Ma, Jack, 17
MacDonald, Chris, 164
macroeconomics, 60, 66–71
Madoff, Bernard, 22
magazines, 361
major purchases, 560
make, buy, or lease decision, 271
Malaysia, 105
Mallette, Patricia, 3
malware, 401–402
management, 180
    see also managers
    career, 286–287
    conceptual skills, 182
    controlling, 183
    corporate management, 143–145, 143f
    directing, 183
    human skills, 182
    interpersonal skills, 182
    Japanese management style, 225
    management hierarchy, 180–181, 180f
    managerial functions, 182–183
    middle management, 181, 187t
    organizing, 183
    planning, 182–183, 185–187
    production and operations management. See production and operations management

    shortcomings, in small business, 129–130
    skills needed for managerial success, 182
    supervisory management, 181, 187t
    tactics, in labour-management relations, 228
    technical skills, 182
    top management, 180–181, 184, 187t
management accountant, 418–419
management by objectives (MBO), 224
management development program, 214
management information system (MIS), 393
management support systems, 393–394
managerial functions, 182–183
managers, 144–145
    see also management
    ability to lead change, 21
    administrative services managers, 286
    attitudes of, and motivation, 225
    brand manager, 331
    category manager, 332
    construction managers, 286
    creativity, 21
    critical thinking, 20–21
    as decision makers, 191–193
    employee motivation, 220–225
    financial manager, 472–474, 495
    food service managers, 286
    human resource managers, 286
    as leaders, 193–195
    line managers, 200
    lodging managers, 287
    marketing managers, 354
    medical and health services managers, 287
    multigenerational workforce, 199
    product manager, 331
    production and operations managers, 269–275
    production managers, 287
    purchasing managers, 287
    staff managers, 200
    team conflict, management of, 243–244
    twenty-first-century manager, 20–21
    vision, importance of, 20
Mandarin Chinese, 96
manufacturer-owned wholesaling intermediaries, 337
manufacturers' agents, 337
manufacturer's brand, 330
manufacturers' reps, 337
manufacturing, 260
market allocation, 536
market basket, 75, 76f
market economy, 67–69
market interest rate, 450
market order, 455
market penetration, 568

market segmentation, 304–310, 305f
  by benefits sought, 309
  by brand loyalty, 310
  business markets, 310
  consumer markets, 305–310
  criteria, 304t
  customer-based segmentation, 310
  demographic segmentation, 306–307, 306f, 310
  end-use segmentation, 310
  geographical segmentation, 305–306, 310
  how it works, 305
  product-related segmentation, 308–310
  by product usage rate, 310
  psychographic segmentation, 308
market structures
  monopolistic competition, 67–68, 67t
  monopoly, 67t, 68–69
  oligopoly, 67t, 68
  pure competition, 67, 67t
market surveillance, 462
marketable securities, 476–477
marketing, 292
  affinity programs, 314
  cause marketing, 298–299
  cause-related marketing, 47
  co-marketing, 314–315
  consumer behaviour, 311–312, 312f
  deceptive marketing, 48
  event marketing, 298
  evolution of the marketing concept, 294–295, 295f
  frequency marketing, 314
  green marketing, 45, 46t
  guerilla marketing, 357–358
  marketing research, 302–304
  marketing strategy, 299–302
  market segmentation, 304–310
  nontraditional marketing, 296–299, 296f
  not-for-profit marketing, 296
  one-on-one marketing, 315
  organization marketing, 299
  person marketing, 297
  place marketing, 297
  relationship marketing, 312–315
  utility, creation of, 293–294, 336
marketing concept, 294–295
marketing era, 13–14, 294
marketing intermediary, 334, 336, 336f
marketing managers, 354
marketing mix, 301–302, 323
marketing research, 302–304
  application of data, 303
  data mining, 304
  obtaining marketing research data, 302–303
marketing section, 131
marketing strategy, 299–302
  classification of goods and services, 324–325

marketing mix for international markets, 301–302
  product life cycle, 326–327
  target market, 299–301
Markopolos, Harry, 22
Marx, Karl, 69
Maslow, Abraham H., 221–222, 225
Maslow's hierarchy of needs, 221–222
mass customization, 302
mass production, 261–262
material inputs, 275
materials handling, 346
materials requirement planning (MRP), 274–275
matrix structure, 201–202, 201f
maturity stage, 326
McClung, Gavin, 168f
McElroy, Mark W., 425
McGregor, Douglas, 225
McMillon, Doug, 435f
mechanization, 261
mediation, 226–227
medical and health services managers, 287
Menard, France, 159
mental disabilities, 51t
merchant wholesalers, 337
Mercosur, 105
merger, 145, 488
Mexico, 97, 105, 106, 110, 244, 245, 268, 310, 347
Meyer, Stephanie, 373
microeconomics, 60–66
  demand, 61
  demand curve, 62, 63f, 63t
  factors driving demand, 61–63
  factors driving supply, 63–64
  interaction of demand and supply, 64–66
  supply, 61
  supply curve, 63–64, 64f, 64t
Middle East, 100, 112
middle management, 181, 187t
middleman, 334
millennials. See Generation Y
Mintzberg, Henry, 249, 250
misleading representations, 48
mission, 131
missionary selling, 368
mission statement, 188
Mitchell, John, 383
mixed market economy, 70–71t
mobile devices, 395, 396, 401
mobility, 19
modified breakeven analysis, 376
monetary policy, 78, 460–461
money management, 558–559
money market instruments, 448, 477
money supply, 460
monitoring
  employees' Internet use, 403

employees' social media activities, 221
  strategic plans, 190–191
monopolistic competition, 67–68, 67t
monopoly, 67t, 68–69, 69
Moody, Jeff, 137
mortgage-backed securities (MBSs), 449
mortgages, 445
motivation. See employee motivation
motivator factors, 222
MRO (maintenance, repair, and operating supplies), 324
Mullins, Corin and Brian, 166f, 167
multidomestic business strategy, 112–113
multigenerational workforce, 199
multinational corporation (MNC), 111
multivitamins, 279
municipal bonds, 448
Murrell, Jerry, 66
Muslim. See Islam
mutual funds, 459
Muzyka, Zhena, 50

N
NAFTA. See North American Free Trade Agreement (NAFTA)
national brand, 330
national debt, 80
National Do Not Call List, 339
national union, 226
national unity, 97
natural gas, 264
natural resources, 6–7
navigation treaties, 100–101
nearshoring, 19
need to achieve, 163
negative balance of payments, 93
negotiable instruments, 538
net profit margin, 432t, 434–435
net savers, 446–447
net users, 446
net worth, 447, 558
network administrators, 412
new industries, 127–128
new-product development, 328–329, 328f
newspapers, 361
new ventures. See starting a new venture
New Zealand, 105
noise, 245
nondepository institutions, 455, 459
nonpersonal selling, 355
nonprogrammed decision, 191
nonstore retailers, 338–339, 338f
nontariff barriers, 103
nontraditional marketing, 296–299, 296f
nonverbal communication, 246t, 249–251
Nooyi, Indra, 473f
norming stage, 242
North America, 97, 251

North American Free Trade Agreement (NAFTA), 105–106, 310, 420, 535
North American Industry Classification System (NAICS), 310
not-for-profit accountants, 419–420
not-for-profit corporations, 140
not-for-profit marketing, 296
not-for-profit organizations, 5–6, 76, 296

O
obesity, 42
objections, 369–370
objectives, 190
observational studies, 303
odd pricing, 378
offensive listening, 247
officers, 144–145
offset agreement, 109
offshoring, 19, 110
O'Hara, Matthew, 174, 285
oligopoly, 67t, 68
on-demand computing, 405
one-on-one marketing, 315
on-the-job ethical dilemmas, 34–37
    conflict of interest, 35
    honesty, 35–36
    integrity, 35–36
    loyalty *vs.* truth, 36
    whistle-blowing, 36–37
on-the-job training, 213
online banking, 457, 458f
open communication, 248
open corporation, 144
open market operations, 460
operating activities, 417
operating plans, 474
operating system, 396
operational planning, 186
operational support systems, 393
optimism, 163
oral communication, 246–247, 246t
order processing, 368
Organisation for Economic Co-operation and Development, 100
organization, 196
organizational change, 21
organizational structures, 196–202
    centralization, 200
    committee organizations, 201
    decentralization, 200
    delegation, 198–199
    departmentalization, 198, 199f
    line-and-staff organizations, 200–201, 200f
    line organizations, 200
    matrix structure, 201–202, 201f
    span of management, 200
    types of, 200–202
organization chart, 197, 197f
organizing, 183, 197f

organization marketing, 299
orientation, 213–214
Ouchi, William, 225
outbound telemarketing, 368
outdoor advertising, 362
output per labour-hour, 73
outsourcing, 19, 220
over-the-counter selling, 367
overnight rate, 460
overseas business. *See* international business
overseas division, 111
owners' equity, 423
ownership utility, 293

P
pacing programs, 170
packages, 332–333
paid time off (PTO), 217
Pandit, Vikram, 452
Papandreou, George, 454
parental leave, 51t
partnership, 139
passwords, 401
patent, 533–534, 539
Pattison, Jim, 155f
Pavlovsky, Kathryn, 424
pay for knowledge, 216
penetration pricing, 376
pension funds, 459
People's Republic of China. *See* China
performance appraisal, 214
performance feedback, 224
performing stage, 242
perpetual inventory, 273
Persia, Dana, 82
personal finance, 554–562
personal financial goals, 557–558
personal financial management, 554
personal financial management model, 556
personal financial plan, 556–557
personal financial planners, 495
personal information managers, 397f
Personal Information Protection Act (PIPA), 300
Personal information Protection and Electronic Document Act (PIPEDA), 300
personal selling, 355, 355t, 367–371
    approach, 369
    closing, 370
    creative selling, 368
    demonstration, 369
    field selling, 367
    follow-up, 370
    handling objections, 369–370
    missionary selling, 368
    order processing, 368
    over-the-counter selling, 367
    presentation, 369
    prospecting, 369

    qualifying, 369
    sales process, 369–370
    sales tasks, 368–369
    telemarketing, 367, 368–369
personal space, 250–251, 251f
personal zone, 250–251, 251t
person marketing, 297
persuasive advertising, 359
PERT (program evaluation and review technique), 276, 277f
Peru, 105
Petrillo, Carmine, 268f
Pfeffer, Jeffrey, 219
pharmaceutical industry, 471
physical disabilities, 51t
physical distribution, 334, 345–346, 346f
physical factors, and location decision, 266t, 267
physiological needs, 222
picketing, 227–228
P&L statement, 427
place marketing, 297
place utility, 293
planned economy, 69
planned shopping centre, 341
planning, 182–183, 187t
    contingency planning, 186–187
    at different organizational levels, 187
    importance of, 185–187
    operational planning, 186
    production planning, 275
    promotional planning, 357–358
    strategic planning, 186
    strategic planning process, 187–191, 187f
    tactical planning, 186
    types of, 185–187
plastic shopping bags, 365
point-of-purchase (POP) advertising, 366
polite listening, 247
political climate, 99–100
political differences, 99–101
Poloz, Stephen S., 78
Ponzi scheme, 22
Pope, Carl, 252
population projections, 18f
portfolio managers, 495
positioning, 356
positive balance of payments, 93
potential sales revenue, 568
The Practice of Management (Drucker), 224
preferred shares, 144, 451
pregnancy leave, 51t
premiums, 364–365, 459, 545
presentation, 369
presentation software, 397f
prestige objectives, 373–374
price, 372
price discrimination, 10
price-fixing, 536

price level changes, 74–77
price-quality relationships, 378
price war, 373
pricing objectives, 372–374
pricing strategy, 301
   alternative pricing strategies, 376–378
   breakeven analysis, 375–376, 375f
   competitive pricing, 377–378
   consumer perceptions of price, 378
   cost-based pricing, 374
   discount pricing, 376
   everyday low pricing (EDLP), 376
   odd pricing, 378
   penetration pricing, 376
   price determination in practice, 374–375
   price-quality relationships, 378
   in retailing, 341
   skimming pricing, 376
primary data, 303
primary demand, 354
primary markets, 451
privacy norms, 304
private brand, 330
private enterprise system, 7, 8–11, 67–69
   basic rights, 8–10, 8f
   entrepreneurship alternative, 10–11
private equity funds, 486–487
private insurance company, 548–549
private placements, 485
private property, 9
private sector employees, 11f
privatization, 70
problem-solving team, 239
process control systems, 393
process departmentalization, 198
process layout, 270f, 271
product, 322
product advertising, 358
product departmentalization, 198
product differentiation, 356
product identification, 329–333
product layout, 270f, 271
product liability, 48, 540
product life cycle, 325–327
   and advertising, 359
   decline stage, 326
   growth stage, 326
   introduction stage, 325–326
   marketing strategy implications, 326–327
   maturity stage, 326
   stages of, 325–326
product lines, 324–325
product manager, 331
product mix, 324–325
product placement, 357
product-related segmentation, 308–310
product strategy, 301, 322–325
   labels, 332–333
   packages, 332–333

product identification, 329–333
   in retailing, 341
product usage rate, 310
product value, 357
production, 260
   see also production and operations management
   analytic production system, 263
   continuous production process, 263
   customer-driven production, 262
   flexible production, 262
   intermittent production process, 263
   mass production, 261–262
   production process, 260, 260f, 262–263
   strategic importance of, 260–262
   synthetic production system, 263
   technology, 263–266
   typical production systems, 261f
   vs. manufacturing, 260
production and operations management, 260
   dispatching, 277
   follow-up, 277
   inventory control, 273
   just-in-time (JIT) system, 274
   location decision, 266–268, 266t
   make, buy, or lease decision, 271
   materials requirement planning (MRP), 274–275
   planning the production process, 269
   production. See production
   production and operations managers, 269–275
   production control, 275–277
   production management tasks, 269f
   production plan, 271–275
   production planning, 275
   quality, 278–280
   routing, 276
   scheduling, 276, 277f
   selection of facility layout, 269–271, 270f
   suppliers, selection of, 272–273
production and operations managers, 269–275
production control, 275–277
   dispatching, 277
   follow-up, 277
   production planning, 275
   routing, 276
   scheduling, 276, 277f
production era, 13, 294
production managers, 287
production plan, 271–275
production planning, 275
production process, 260, 260f, 262–263
productivity, 73–74, 75
productivity ratios, 73
profit-and-loss statement, 427
profit sharing, 216
profitability objectives, 372, 372f

profitability ratios, 432t, 434–435
profits, 4–5
   after-tax profits, 9
   quest for profits, 5
programmed decision, 191
promotion, 354
promotional mix, 355, 355t
   advertising. See advertising
   personal selling, 367–371
   public relations, 370–371
   sales promotion. See sales promotion
promotional planning, 357–358
promotional strategy, 301, 356–357, 356f
   pulling strategy, 372
   pushing strategy, 371
   in retailing, 342
property, 538
property and liability insurance, 549–550
property law, 538
prospecting, 369
protectionist policies, 95
protective tariffs, 102
provincial court, 535
provincial employment standards acts, 51t
provincial human rights codes, 51t
provincial labour ministries, 51t
provincial vocational rehabilitation acts, 51t
psychographic segmentation, 308
public accountant, 418, 494
Public Company Accounting Oversight Board, 421
public health issues, 42
public insurance agency, 548
public ownership of business, 140–142
public relations, 355t, 370–371
public relations crisis, 251–253
public sales of securities, 485
Public Sector Accounting Board (PSAB), 420
Public Servants Disclosure Protection Act, 426
public zone, 250–251, 251t
publicity, 371
publicly held corporation, 144
pulling strategy, 372
purchasing managers, 287
purchasing power, 306–307
purchasing power parity (PPP), 73–74
pure competition, 67, 67t
pure risk, 544
pushing strategy, 371

Q
qualifying, 369
quality, 278
   benchmarking, 278
   importance of, 278–280
   ISO standards, 279–280
   price-quality relationships, 378
   quality control, 278–279

quality control, 278–279
quality of life, 158
quality-of-life issues, 50–51
quick ratio, 432t, 433
quotas, 103

R

rack jobber, 337
radio, 361
radio-frequency identification (RFID) technology, 333, 346
raises, 215
Rapino, Michael, 9
ratio analysis, 432–435, 432t
raw materials, 324
real property, 538
rebates, 365
receivables turnover, 432t, 434
recession, 72, 454
recovery, 73
recruitment, 211–213, 211f
recycling, 44
Reece, Daryl, 45
regional differences, 97
regional malls, 341–342
registered retirement savings plans (RRSPs), 459
regular dividend, 482
regulated monopoly, 68
relationship era, 14–15, 294
relationship management, 15
relationship marketing, 312–315
relevance, 420
religious attitudes, 97
reminder-oriented advertising, 359
renewable electricity standard (RES), 72
representational faithfulness, 420
reserve requirement, 461
reservists, 51t
reshoring, 111
responsibilities of companies. *See* company responsibilities
restaurants, 563–564
restrictive monetary policy, 78
résumés, 35–36
résumés of principals, 131
retailer-owned cooperatives or buying offices, 337–338
retailers, 336, 338
retailing, 338–343
　automatic merchandising, 338
　competition, 340–343
　customer service strategy, 341
　direct-response retailing, 338
　direct selling, 339
　Internet retailing, 338
　"last three feet," 338
　location, 341–342
　nonstore retailers, 338–339, 338f
　pricing strategy, 341
　product strategy, 341
　promotional strategy, 342
　store retailers, 339, 339t
　target market, 340
　wheel of retailing, 340, 340f
Reti, Tom, 389
return, 473
return on equity, 432t, 434
revenue tariffs, 102
right to be heard, 49
right to be informed, 48
right to be safe, 48
right to choose, 49
rights
　of consumers, 47–49
　equal rights, 51t
　in private enterprise system, 8–10, 8f
　shareholder rights, 143–144
risk, 473, 544–546
risk management insurance, 545
risk-return tradeoff, 474
robots, 264–265
Rosen, Al, 419
Ross, Rich, 308
routing, 276
Rubinfeld, Arthur, 40
rule of indemnity, 547
runs, 458

S

safety issues, 48
safety needs, 222
saffron, 92f
salary, 215, 287, 423
sales branches, 337
sales era, 294
sales increase, 356
sales law, 537
sales office, 337
sales process, 369–370
sales promotion, 355t, 364
　consumer-oriented promotions, 364–366, 364f
　trade-oriented promotions, 366–367
sales stabilization, 356–357
sales tasks, 368–369
samples, 365–366
sandwich generation, 50
Sarbanes-Oxley Act of 2002, 33, 54, 183, 415, 421, 426
savers, 446–447
Sawhney, Robert, 437
scarcity, 374
scheduling, 276, 277f
seasonal unemployment, 77
secondary data, 303
secondary market, 453
secured bond, 448

securities, 448–451, 476–477
securities fraud, 22
security analysts, 495
seed capital, 168
selection, 211–213, 211f
selective demand, 354
selective distribution, 345
self-actualization needs, 222
self-confidence, 163
self-managed team, 239
self-regulation, 462
seller's market, 295
selloff, 489
sender, 244–245
serial entrepreneurs, 155
server, 395
services, 324
sexism, 53
sexual harassment, 53
shaping ethical conduct, 37–40
share offering, 451–452
shareholder rights, 143–144
shareholders, 143–144
shares, 144, 450–451, 485
shopping malls, 341
shopping products, 323
short-term assets, 476
short-term funding options, 483–484
short-term funds, 481–482
short-term loans, 483–484
shrinking labour pool, 18
Singapore, 105
Silver, Adam, 363
Six Sigma, 279
skimming pricing, 376
skunkworks, 170
Smajovits, Daniel, 123, 147
small business, 124
　assistance for, 132–135
　business plan, 131–132
　contributions to economy, 127–129
　failure, 129–131
　government regulation, 131
　inadequate financing, 130–131
　industry creation, 127–128
　innovation, 128–129
　job creation, 127
　management shortcomings, 129–130
　social media, 343
　typical small-business ventures, 125
　women and, 134–135
smartphones, 395, 396
Smith, Adam, 8
social audits, 41
social differences, 96–97
social entrepreneur, 156
social era, 15–17, 294–295
social media, 3, 15, 221, 343
social needs, 222

263

social networking, 14, 129, 157, 161, 304
social responsibility, 23, 40-47, 41*f*
   corporate philanthropy, 46-47
   environmental protection, 43-46
   general public, responsibilities to, 42-47
   public health issues, 42
   social audits, 41
social zone, 250-251, 251*t*
socialism, 69, 70-71*t*
software, 396, 397*t*, 424
software as a service (SaaS), 405, 406, 473
sole proprietorship, 138-139
sovereign wealth funds, 487, 487*f*
S&P/TSX 60 Shariah Index, 464
spam, 362
span of control, 200
span of management, 200
specialized skills, 261
specialty advertising, 366
specialty products, 323
specialty store, 339*t*
speculative bonds, 449
speculative risk, 544
Spierkel, Yannick, 29
"spinning" bad news, 248
spinoff, 489
sponsorship, 355*t*, 363
spreadsheets, 397*f*
spyware, 402
staff managers, 200
stakeholders, 39-40
standard of living, 554
standardization, 261
standardization strategy, 112, 301
Stanton, John, 125*f*
starting a new venture, 165-169
   business plan, 167, 167*t*
   buying an existing business, 166
   finding financing, 168-169
   government support, 169
   selecting a business idea, 165-166
statement of cash flows, 429-430, 431*f*
statement of changes in equity, 429, 430*f*
statement of comprehensive position, 427
statement of financial position, 426
statistics, 307
statutory law, 535
stock. *See* shares
stock exchanges, 453-455
stock markets, 453-455
stock options, 216, 237*t*, 238
stock ownership, 143-144
store brand, 330
store retailers, 339, 339*t*
storming stage, 242
strategic alliance, 15
strategic planning, 186
strategic planning process, 187-191, 187*f*
   assessment of competitive position, 188-190
   defining the organization's mission, 188
   implementation of strategy, 190
   monitoring and adapting strategic plans, 190-191
   objectives, 190
   strategies for competitive differentiation, 190
strategic plans, 474
strategy
   adaptation strategy, 112-113, 301-302
   customer service strategy, 341
   distribution strategy. *See* distribution strategy
   implementation of strategy, 190
   marketing strategy. *See* marketing strategy
   pricing strategy. *See* pricing strategy
   product strategy, 301, 322-325
   promotional strategy, 301, 342, 356-357
   pulling strategy, 372
   pushing strategy, 371
   standardization strategy, 112, 301
   strategies for competitive differentiation, 190
strengths, weaknesses, opportunities, and threats. *See* SWOT analysis
strike, 227
structural unemployment, 77
subcontracting, 110
subprime mortgages, 445, 449
substance abuse, 42
supercentre, 339*t*
supercomputers, 395
superior court, 535
supermarket, 339*t*
supervisory management, 181, 187*t*
suppliers, 272-273
supplies, 324
supply, 61
   factors driving supply, 63-64
   interaction of demand and supply, 64-66
   money supply, 460
supply chain, 345
supply curve, 63-64, 64*f*, 64*t*
Supreme Court of Canada, 535
sustainability, 424-425
sustainable, 45
sustainable agriculture, 45
sweepstakes, 366
SWOT analysis, 188-190, 189*f*
symbolism, 97
synthetic production system, 263

T
tablets, 395
tactical planning, 186
tangible assets, 422
tangible property, 538
target market, 299-301, 340
tariffs, 101, 102
tax, 540
tax court, 535
taxes, 80, 131
tax planning, 560
team, 238
   characteristics of, 240-241
   conflict, 243-244
   cross-functional team, 239
   problem-solving team, 239
   self-managed team, 239
   stages of team development, 242, 242*f*
   team cohesiveness, 242-243
   team diversity, 240-241
   team level, 240
   team norm, 243
   team size, 240
   types of, 239, 239*f*
   virtual team, 239
   work teams, 239
team cohesiveness, 242-243
team development stages, 242, 242*f*
team diversity, 240-241
team level, 240
team norm, 243
technical skills, 182
technical support specialists, 412
technology, 7, 18
   computer-aided design (CAD), 265
   computer-aided manufacturing (CAM), 265
   computer-integrated manufacturing (CIM), 266
   flexible manufacturing system (FMS), 265-266
   green manufacturing processes, 263-264
   information technology (IT), 160-161, 220, 404
   and production process, 263-266
   radio-frequency identification (RFID) technology, 333
   robots, 264-265
teen market, 307
telecommuters, 218
telemarketing, 367, 368-369
television, 359-360
tender offer, 488
terrorism, 81*t*
test marketing, 328
texting, 157
Theory X, 225
Theory Y, 225
Theory Z, 225
Thierry, Christopher, 392
360-degree performance review, 214
time utility, 293
timeliness, 420
tolerance for ambiguity, 165

tolerance for failure, 163–164
tombstone, 452
top management, 180–181, 184, 187t
torts, 539–540
total asset turnover, 432t, 434
total cost, 375
total productivity, 73
total revenue, 375
trade. *See* international trade
trade credit, 483
trade deficit, 93
trademark, 330, 539
trade promotion, 366–367
trade restrictions, 102–103
trade shows, 366
trade surplus, 93
trade unions. *See* labour unions
training programs, 213–214
transaction management, 14
transaction processing systems, 393
Trans-Pacific Partnership (TPP), 105
transportation, 266t, 346, 346f
travel etiquette, 82
treasurer, 472
Treasury bills, 80, 448
Treaty of Lisbon, 107
Trojan horse, 402
Trottier, Marie, 29
trust, 248
truth, 36
Tsouflidou, Cora, 158f
Turley, James S., 241
turnover, 218
twenty-first-century manager, 20–21
two-factor model of motivation, 222–223

U

understandability, 420
underwriting, 453, 485
underwriting discount, 485
unemployment, 73, 77
unemployment rate, 77
union tactics, 227–228
unions. *See* labour unions
United States, 33, 54, 72, 74, 78, 80, 91t, 92, 93, 94, 97, 100, 101, 105, 106, 134, 183, 228, 245, 300, 310, 347, 415, 421, 426, 445, 449, 454, 460, 488
Universal Market Integrity Rules (UMIR), 462
universal product code (UPC), 333
upset customers, 313
upward communication, 248
urban reserve, 169
U.S. Federal Reserve, 65, 454, 460, 462, 464
usage-based billing, 10
users, 446–447
users of accounting information, 416–417, 416f
Usher, 3
utility, 260, 293–294, 336, 372
utility computing, 405

V

vacation time, 97
values, 97
variable costs, 375
vendor-managed inventory, 273, 346
venture capital, 133–134
venture capitalists, 168–169, 486
verifiability, 420
vertical merger, 145
vice-president of financial management, 472
Vietnam, 105
viral advertising, 360
virtual offices, 404
virtual private networks (VPNs), 400
virtual team, 239
viruses, 402
vision, 20, 131, 162, 183–184
VoIP, 400
volume objectives, 372
voluntary turnover, 218
volunteerism, 47
Vroom, Victor, 223

W

wage, 215, 423
warehouse club, 339t
warehousing, 346
warranties, 347, 537
The Wealth of Nations (Smith), 8
wheel of retailing, 340, 340f
whistle-blowing, 36–37, 426
wholesalers, 336
wholesaling, 336–338
wide area networks (WANs), 398
Wi-Fi, 398
Williams, Rick, 452
Wi-Max, 398
Winfrey, Oprah, 163, 299
Winterkorn, Martin, 43
wireless fidelity, 398
wireless local networks, 398
women
    as entrepreneurs, 160
    GM's first female CEO, 194
    purchasing power, 306
    and small business, 134–135
Woods, Tiger, 123
word processing software, 397f
work teams, 239
workers' compensation, 49
workforce
    changes in, 18–19
    and changing nature of work, 19
    distributed workforce, 404–405
    diverse workforce, 18–19
    enhancement of competitiveness of, 81t
    multigenerational workforce, 199
    quality of the workforce, 46
    today's business workforce, 17–19
workplace safety, 49
World Bank, 79, 104–105
world's top 10 nations, 91t
World Trade Organization (WTO), 104, 108t, 209, 535
World War II, 13
worm, 402
written communication, 246t, 247–248

Y

Yakadawela, Dharmasena, 76
Yamashita, Asafumi, 130f
Yani, Shlomo, 471
Yellen, Janet, 78
Young, David, 373

Z

Zuckerberg, Mark, 184f

NOTES

NOTES

NOTES

NOTES

NOTES